THE PRADOS OF SÃO PAULO, BRAZIL

AN ELITE FAMILY AND SOCIAL CHANGE, 1840–1930

THE

PRADOS

OF SÃO PAULO

BRAZIL

AN ELITE FAMILY AND

SOCIAL CHANGE, 1840–1930

DARRELL E. LEVI

The University of Georgia Press

Athens & London

© 1987 by the University of Georgia Press
Athens, Georgia 30602

Set in Linotron 202 Trump Mediaeval
with Trump Mediaeval Black and
Letraset Glaser Stencil display.

The paper in this book meets the guidelines for
permanence and durability of the Committee on
Production Guidelines for Book Longevity of the
Council on Library Resources.

Printed in the United States of America

91 90 89 88 87   5 4 3 2 1

Library of Congress Cataloging in Publication Data
Levi, Darrell E.
The Prados of São Paulo, Brazil.
Revision of thesis (Ph.D.—Yale University,
1974), originally presented under title: The Prados
of São Paulo. Thesis also published in Portuguese,
1977, under title: A família Prado.
Bibliography: p.
Includes index.
1. São Paulo (Brazil: State)—History.
2. Prado family. I. Title.
F2631.L44 1987   981'.61   86-30826
ISBN 0-8203-0944-3 (alk. paper)

British Library Cataloging in Publication Data available.

The illustrations in this volume are family portraits,
reproduced from the books
In Memoriam: Martinho Prado Junior, 1843–1943
(São Paulo: Elvino Pocai, 1944) and
*Primeiro Centenário do Conselheiro António
da Silva Prado* (São Paulo: Revista dos Tribunaes, 1946).

FOR CHRIS, MARC, AND TOD

Numa terra radiosa vive um povo triste.

PAULO PRADO

➔ CONTENTS ⋲

List of Tables / ix

List of Appendixes / x

Preface / xi

Acknowledgments / xii

Preliminary Notes / xiii

Introduction: The Family in Brazilian History
1

CHAPTER I
Origins, 1700–1840
17

CHAPTER II
Family Life in the Second Empire, 1840–1889
33

CHAPTER III
Europe Discovered
53

CHAPTER IV
Coffee Capitalists
67

CHAPTER V
The Politics of Family, 1868–1889
88

CHAPTER VI
Family Life in the First Republic, 1889–1930
104

Contents

CHAPTER VII
Eduardo and Paulo Rediscover Brazil
123

CHAPTER VIII
Entrepreneurs and Fazendeiros
138

CHAPTER IX
At the Margins of Politics
159

Conclusion / 184

Appendixes / 193

Notes / 205

Glossary / 249

Bibliography / 251

Index / 275

⋑ TABLES ⋐

1. Genealogical Relationships of
Principal Prados
3

2. Population of São Paulo, 1765–1816
20

3. São Paulo's Coffee Production and
Exports from Santos, 1849–89
68

4. Marriage Patterns in the Prado Family
105

⇒ APPENDIXES ⇐

A. Principal Kin of the Prado Family
193

B. Accounts of Martinho Prado, 1856–64
196

C. Immigrants' Earnings at Two
Prado Fazendas, 1888
197

D. Agricultural Properties of the
Prado Family and of the Prado-Chaves
Export Company
198

E. Contract for the Planting of
200,000 Coffee Trees
200

F. *Partido Democrático:*
Class Composition (1926)
203

⋙ PREFACE ⋘

This book originated as a Ph.D. dissertation at Yale University in 1974 with the title "The Prados of São Paulo: An Elite Brazilian Family in a Changing Society, 1840–1930." In 1977, with minor changes, it was published in Portuguese in São Paulo as *A família Prado*. Several colleagues urged the preparation of an English book version, which turned out to be a project pursued intermittently over many years, vying with other research interests and university teaching.

This revision incorporates literature published after 1974 on the Prados, on the family institution in Brazil, and on family history generally. It also includes a new introduction and conclusion, and heavy revisions of the first, fourth, eighth, and ninth chapters. My original factual findings have not changed, but they are augmented with new information. What has changed is my perspective on Brazilian history, which has become much more critical, in large part because of the catastrophic events during the military dictatorship of 1964–85. I hope my concern for Brazil and for all of Latin America and the Caribbean is evident in the pages that follow.

➔ ACKNOWLEDGMENTS ↢

My greatest debt of gratitude is to the members of the Prado family who were my gracious, generous hosts in São Paulo: Luíz Prado, Antônio Augusto Monteiro de Barros Neto, Ana Candida Ferraz Sampaio, and Caio Prado Júnior. By granting me access to family papers and by sharing their recollections of family life, they made this study possible.

Olinto Moura provided original documents in his collection, and Pericles Pinheiro let me use his excellent private library. Several Brazilian scholars and friends helped in various ways: my thanks to the late Sérgio Buarque de Hollanda, João and Ana Mae Barbosa, Celso and Betty Lafer, Antônio and Angela Dimas de Morais, and Edson and Vilma Mustafá.

Special thanks are due to Richard M. Morse, my faculty advisor at Yale, who suggested the subject and oversaw its completion in dissertation form. The writings of E. Bradford Burns have profoundly influenced my views of Brazilian and Latin American history. Several teachers have contributed in important ways to my development: Dauril Alden, C. R. Boxer, Joseph Illick, Rollie Poppino, and C. Vann Woodward. Three colleagues in the Florida State University's Department of History deserve special recognition: Rodney Anderson, my colleague in Latin American history and a true friend of the region and its peoples; James P. Jones, for constant encouragement; and C. Peter Ripley, without whom this book would not have appeared. The map was prepared by Mr. Peter Krafft of the Florida State University Cartography Laboratory. Gerri Frost, Wanda Mitchell, and Bobbi Christie assisted in preparing the manuscript. Ellen Harris, a free-lance copyeditor, made many valuable suggestions that are incorporated herein.

Financial support from the Ford Foundation's Foreign Area Fellowship Program, the Yale University Graduate School, and Florida State University's Professional Development Grant program made this work possible and is gratefully acknowledged.

The responsibility for any errors or other shortcomings is mine alone.

⋛ PRELIMINARY NOTES ⋚

Brazilian Money

For the period studied, the basic nominal unit was the *real* (plural, *réis*). One thousand réis equaled one *milréis*, written 1$000, the common unit for small transactions. One thousand milréis equalled one *conto* (*conto de réis*), written 1:000$000, a term common in larger transactions. Dollar equivalents are given in the text where appropriate. These are taken from a conversion table covering the years 1821 to 1930 in Julian Smith Duncan, *The Public and Private Operation of Railways in Brazil* (New York, 1932), 183. Duncan's table contains one major and three minor errors (correct values in parentheses): 1910, value of milréis given as $.33 ($.32); 1918, $.65 ($.25); 1919, $.26 ($.27); and 1920, $.21 ($.23).

Orthography and Brazilian Words Used in Text

The spelling of Portuguese words and of most proper names used in the text has been modernized in accord with current usage. However, the spelling of some proper names of living individuals who prefer traditional forms has been retained, where such preferences were known to me. In the footnotes and bibliography, spelling and the use of diacritical marks appear as in the original sources, accounting for the variations that appear (e.g., Antônio, António, Antonio). Portuguese words used in the text are underlined on first usage only, when equivalents or translations are given in the text or in the footnotes.

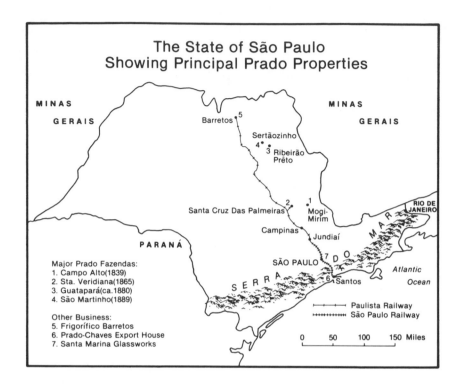

The State of São Paulo
Showing Principal Prado Properties

MINAS
GERAIS

MINAS
GERAIS

Barretos •5

Sertãozinho
4 • •
3 Ribeirão
Prêto

RIO DE
JANEIRO

Santa Cruz Das Palmeiras
2 • •1
Mogi-
Mirim

Campinas
Jundiaí

PARANÁ

SÃO PAULO

SERRA DO MAR

Atlantic
Ocean

Major Prado Fazendas:
1. Campo Alto(1839)
2. Sta. Veridiana(1865)
3. Guatapará(ca.1880)
4. São Martinho(1889)

6 Santos

Other Business:
5. Frigorífico Barretos
6. Prado-Chaves Export House
7. Santa Marina Glassworks

Paulista Railway
São Paulo Railway

0   50   100   150 Miles

ᣝ INTRODUCTION ᣞ

THE FAMILY IN

BRAZILIAN HISTORY

Many poor and few rich: this
is the prime reality of Brazilian history since the European conquest.
This basic fact implies other realities: a dominant culture and a sub-
ordinate one;[1] economic dependency and exploitation; inequality of
political power under dictatorship and "democracy" alike; and, most
important, society's failure to meet the basic needs of most people.[2]

The sixteenth-century European invaders who began to take Brazil from its original Amerindian residents—a theft that is in its final
stages today—brought with them superior technology and a Judeo-
Christian world view emphasizing the possibility, the God-pleasing
desirability, of change and of dominance over nature and over other
humans. The Portuguese conquerors were also agents of an emerging capitalist world system[3] that would fix on Brazil its colonial,
export-oriented economy with boom-and-bust cycles of dyewoods,
sugar, gold, rubber, and coffee. That economic order in turn required
the plantation, slavery, latifundia, and elite dominance over the vast
majority of Amerindians, blacks, mixed-race *mestiços,* and poor
whites. In areas such as São Paulo, integrated relatively late into the
export economy, even the transition from subsistence agriculture
to a commercialized market economy—long before industrialization—caused severe socioeconomic distress for the majority.[4]

The prime reality—many poor and few rich—has persisted in the
neocolonial era of Brazilian history since formal independence from
Portugal in 1822. The Brazilian Empire (1822–89) added innovations
such as the misnamed "free trade" and elitist constitutional parlia-
mentarism to the durable bases of monarchy, latifundia, and slavery.
The situation of the Brazilian folk probably deteriorated after independence.[5] In 1889 new military and civilian elites abolished the
monarchy, introducing a century of fitful political experiment: elit-

ist republic (1889–1930); provisional, military-backed government (1930–34); constitutional republic (1934–37); dictatorial corporate state (1937–45); democratizing republic (1945–64); military dictatorship–civilian technocracy (1964–85), and, after 1985, a new attempt at democracy. Immigration, urbanization, industrialization, and "associated-dependent development"[6] have introduced new social and economic complexity and sophistication into urban Brazil, especially in the southeastern triangle of São Paulo, Rio de Janeiro, and Minas Gerais, and in Rio Grande do Sul, while the historic patterns of inequality and deprivation intensify, as a recent survey of the 1970s shows.[7]

What accounts for this distressing half-millennium of elite dominance and majority deprivation? First, Brazil's disadvantageous position in the world economy, at least as compared with the capitalist powers of Western Europe and North America, has limited the possibilities for authentic "development"[8] and therefore for a fairer distribution of wealth, well-being, and power. Second, the imitation of European and North American political, economic, and social models has produced inappropriate, ineffective "solutions" to problems rooted in a physical environment and socioeconomic milieu vastly different from Europe or the United States, despite the efforts of generations of Brazil's best minds to break the bonds of intellectual dependency. A third cause of continuity has been the rise of the military since 1870. Deeply suspicious of civilian politics, communism, socialism, populism, mass mobilization, real democracy, and redistributive economics, the military is largely indifferent to most Brazilians' welfare.[9] A fourth cause of continuity, of stability paid for in mass poverty, is the dominance of Brazilian elites, largely family-based. The present study explores this dimension of the prime reality of Brazil by examining the history of one elite family from São Paulo. The Prado story is a case study of the complex and sometimes contradictory actions and reactions of the Brazilian elite during nearly a century of profound change between 1840 and 1930.

The Prado Family

The Prado family[10] rose slowly from obscurity in the early eighteenth century to great wealth, power, and prestige in the nineteenth century, only to suffer a relative eclipse in the twentieth century. The first Brazilian-born generation, that of Martinho Prado (d. 1770), remained small and undistinguished. The economic environment of São Paulo in the 1770s forced family members to engage in a variety of interrelated pursuits: livestock trading, slave trading, sugar growing, urban commerce, and local politics. Dynastic marriages, such as Ana Vicência Rodriguez de Almeida's second marriage, to her brother-in-law Eleutério Prado, prevented fragmentation of scarce family resources. Her first husband, Antônio Prado (d. 1793), represented an "urban" tendency in the family, while Eleutério typified a "rural" strain. This combining of urban and rural interests via marriage was an important key to family strength.

The pattern of urban and rural specialization continued in the

TABLE I

Genealogical Relationships of Principal Prados

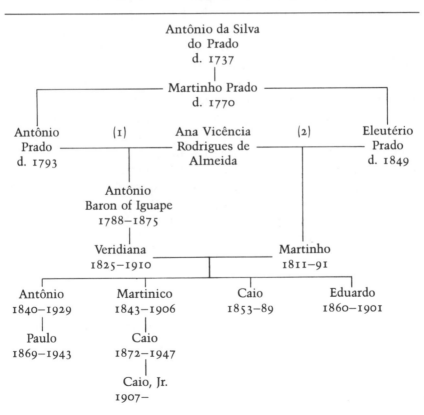

third and fourth generations, and in the early nineteenth century the family became economically and politically influential at the provincial and national levels. Antônio Prado (1788–1875), the baron of Iguape, was an urban capitalist and entrepreneur of extraordinary importance in legitimizing the family's leadership role in São Paulo. His brother Martinho (1811–91) was primarily a *fazendeiro* (planter), first in sugar and then in coffee, as Brazil entered the economic cycle dominated by that crop. The dynastic marriage of Martinho to his niece Veridiana (1825–1910), the baron of Iguape's daughter, again joined the rural and urban tendencies within the family. In her own right, Veridiana evolved from a sad-eyed thirteen-year-old bride into an iron-willed, iconoclastic matriarch, a leader of São Paulo's soirée society who explicitly challenged some traditional assumptions about the role of elite women in Brazilian society, while confirming others.

The core of this study is an analysis of the lives of Veridiana's and Martinho's sons, exemplars of the generation that matured after 1860 and brought the family to its peak of power and prestige. Antônio Prado (1840–1929) and Martinico Prado (1843–1906) were pioneering coffee planters, but also men of considerable urban and European experience. Antônio wielded great influence as one of Brazil's principal men of affairs during the crucial 1880s, when both slavery and monarchy—pillars of the Prados' rise—were ended. Martinico, as a Republican opponent of the regime his brother served, helped speed the demise of the monarchy, only to experience rapid disillusionment thereafter. The younger brothers, Caio (1853–89) and especially Eduardo (1860–1901), were more clearly urban in their tastes, despite Eduardo's eventual doubts about the cosmopolitan life. Eduardo marked the full development within the Prado family of European cultural influence, a process that helped mold his brother Antônio; his mother, Veridiana; and many other Prados. The family's reaction to foreign influence was multifaceted, reflecting the internal tensions in the re-Europeanization of nineteenth-century Brazil and, in the 1890s, the strengthening of United States influence in Brazil.

The preoccupation of nineteenth-century Prados with foreign influence carried over to family members who matured in the twentieth century. Paulo Prado (1869–1943) and the Marxist historian Caio Prado Júnior (b. 1907) both criticized external influence in their land. These concerns perhaps reflect the Prados' gradual corporate economic decline and political marginalization during the First Republic (1889–1930). Toward the end of his long life, Antônio Prado, who died in 1929 at the end of the era of planter domination of Brazil, called for "revolution" to save Brazil from its errant ways.

The rich, complex Prado family experience adds nuance and specificity to the generalizations about families, oligarchies, and ruling classes that abound in the literature. To appreciate the Prado story fully, however, it is necessary to place it in the context of older and newer views of the role of the family in Brazilian history.

Family and History in Brazil: The Old Patriarchal Model

Scholars of diverse political outlook, academic discipline, and nationality have agreed that the patriarchal elite family has been a pivotal institution in Brazilian history and that its legacy is still felt today. Their portrayal of the patriarchal family has been widely accepted.[11] From their studies and other sources, a model of the patriarchal family can be outlined as a conceptual frame or "ideal type."

Structurally, the patriarchal "family" was a vast kinship network extended vertically through miscegenation and horizontally by marriage and ritual kinship among the white and near-white elite. *Minha família* ("my family") has long signified to elite Brazilians a social structure that includes not only the nuclear family and the extended family, but the even larger *parentela*. During the colonial period and most of the nineteenth century, the prototypical elite parentela consisted of the patriarch, his wife and concubines, all recognized blood relatives on the paternal and maternal sides, godparents and godchildren, ritually adopted friends and retainers, and even slaves. It was maintained by blood ties, godparenthood (*compadrío*), and a complex system of duties and loyalties. This patriarchal parentela is probably the source of most generalizations in the traditional literature about the "family" in Brazilian history. Scholars have differed about its nature. Francisco José de Oliveira Vianna, who called the parentela a "kinship clan," diminished its importance by characterizing it as "indecisive, fluctuating, imprecise, without legal organization, nor its own patrimony, nor a common religious life, nor predetermined collective duties."[12] Charles Wagley, in contrast, sees the parentela as the "most important institution in traditional Brazil," the powerful engine of economic and political control, far more important than the nuclear or even the extended family.[13] Perhaps these opposing views can be reconciled; while the parentela was loose and fluctuating, it was also a vast reservoir of *potential* influence and support available to the individual.

At the parentela's apex was the patriarch, whose authority had its origins in Luso-Roman family law and customs transmitted to colonial Brazil. A salient feature of this tradition was the father's "right to direct the person and fortune of the son, whatever the latter's age might be."[14] During the Empire the legal supports of the Brazilian family were left untouched, with one exception. The law of 31 October 1831 fixed the age of twenty-one for a son to gain full civil rights. The traditional *poder pátrio*, or customary right of the father to control the lives and the property of his wife and children, was not otherwise altered during the Empire.[15] Moreover, custom was stronger than law in family matters. The jurist Lafayette Rodrigues Pereira wrote in 1869 that sons over twenty-one were still obliged to obtain their fathers' consent to celebrate the marriage contract (*esponsal*), if only "because of the duty of obedience and filial respect."[16] Customs such as the parental arrangement of marriage are said to have continued throughout the nineteenth century as parents "decided marriage without the intervention nor the audience of those most interested, their children."[17]

In nineteenth-century Brazil, according to the older literature, patriarchal domination remained very strong, extending to the power of life and death. Though rarely exercised (and then notably in cases of sexual transgression), this ultimate power still revealed the authority enjoyed by the family head.[18] Older children, especially first sons, by custom had great authority over younger siblings, since the former were heirs to parental authority. Antônio Candido cites a late-nineteenth-century sexagenarian who wrote to his older brother as follows: "Your Excellency the Barão [Baron] de C. and my dear Brother: I write this to your excellency . . ."[19]

Although the submission of women in the traditional Brazilian elite may have been exaggerated, it nonetheless appeared to many to have been exceptional even by nineteenth-century Western standards. A French resident in Brazil in the 1860s, Charles Expilly, summed up the elite woman's status by citing a traditional proverb: "A woman is sufficiently educated when she reads her prayers correctly and knows how to write the recipe for *goiabada*. More than this would be a danger for the home."[20] To Expilly, the Brazilian woman was little more than "the chief slave of her home." Other foreigners made the analogy between slavery and family life in Brazil, arguing with sometimes puritanical fervor that slavery had a corrupting influence on the elite family.[21] Joaquim Nabuco, a prominent Brazilian abolitionist, looked to the United States as an example of what Brazil evidently lacked, respect for the woman.[22]

As trustees, many widows preserved the family patrimony, and, of course, women exercised an important influence over family life: one observer reckoned that the Empire's leading men were products of their mother's "domestic schools," which "molded their souls before their intellects were educated."[23] Beyond such functions, and with the exception of a few notable women, according to traditional views, the elite female's role was restricted. As late as 1916, an avant-garde journal advocated female education on the basis that it would produce more efficient domestic administrators.[24] The double standard in sexual behavior survives today in Brazil as one of the strongest inheritances from the patriarchal past.[25]

Children in the patriarchal family were trained in a dependency which carried over into their adult years. Until about the age of six or seven, they were idealized as *anjinhos* (little angels). Thereafter, they were viewed as subject to satanic influence and were encouraged to imitate adult behavior to stifle this threat.[26] Expilly described frock-coated lads of twelve who seldom smiled and who strutted about self-importantly, posing as miniature men of the world.[27] A similar observation of the adolescent Brazilian boy was made by the North American missionaries James Fletcher and D. P. Kidder: "He is made a 'little old man' before he is twelve years of age, having his stiff black silk hat, standing collar, and cane; and in the city he walks along as if everybody were looking at him, and as if he were encased in corsets. He does not run, or jump, or trundle hoop, or throw stones, as boys in Europe and North America [do]."[28] Elite children addressed their parents as "*Senhor pai*" and "*Senhora mãe*" (Candido renders these as "father, my lord" and "mother, my lady") or as *"Vossa Mercê"* ("Your Worship"). With bowed heads and folded hands, they asked the blessings of the parents and were forbidden the physical touch of the patriarch.[29] The marked social distance between children and parents was increased by the delegation of most aspects of child-rearing to black servants, foreign governesses, priests, and boarding schools. According to Fletcher and Kidder, though an elite boy might reside in the same city as his parents, "he boards in the *collegio*, and only on certain occasions does he see his father and mother." While elite boys' formal education frequently prepared them for a career, the few years of schooling elite girls received, if they got any at all, was primarily designed to enhance their marital value.[30] Gilberto Freyre has written that it was a "great shame" to be a child in the nineteenth century, and thus the tendency was to shorten childhood as much as possible.[31]

The hierarchical interior structure of the patriarchal family was supplemented by its monolithic exterior image. At least in popular perception individual families were often stereotyped: "There is not a Wanderly who does not drink, an Albuquerque who does not lie, a Cavalcanti who does not owe, nor a Sousa Leão nor Carneiro da Cunha who does not like black women."[32] The novelist Graciliano Ramos wrote of a schoolmaster in the Brazilian northeast who "commanded because he had power: he was an Albuquerque and a priest."[33] Wagley notes that certain unspecified families have reputations for "love of luxury," "ability as scientists," and "astuteness in politics." Families like the Feitosas of Ceará in northeastern Brazil controlled backlands politics for generations and have contributed to the view of the patriarchal family as a monolithic institution pursuing common goals.[34]

According to the patriarchal model, the family has been more influential than church and state throughout most of Brazilian history. Nestor Duarte has listed the following effects of Brazilian familism: the retardation of urbanization; the exacerbation of factionalism and disunity; the enfeeblement of the church; the deformation and privatization of nominally public organs such as municipal councils; and the development of an enduring class structure based on the degradation and dependency of blacks, lower-class whites and mestiços, and women. As late as 1954, Emílio Willems wrote that "there is probably not a single major institution in Brazil which is not to a considerable extent controlled or deflected by family interests."[35]

In broad and necessarily oversimplified form, then, this is the patriarchal model: a vast, hierarchical, monolithic kinship network, presided over by the authoritarian patriarch, characterized by the submission of women and the young, a "private order" impervious to public forms of organization and control. However, new findings have raised many questions about this long-accepted model.

The "New Family History" and Brazil

Since 1960 a "new family history" has rapidly developed to the point where even a selective international bibliography included over 6,000 entries, 547 of them on Latin America.[36] This new field is most advanced in the United States and Western Europe; in 1978 it was still considered to be in the pioneer stage in Latin America. In the United States and Western Europe, research has centered on three subjects: household structure, the family cycle of domestic groups, and kinship. More recent research focuses on the entire life course as it "relates to family transitions and to the timing of demographic and family events."[37] Most research has been synchronic rather than diachronic; change has been studied only over short periods.

Perhaps the principal finding of the new family history in the United States and Western Europe is the continuity in household structure (the predominance of the nuclear family) over the last three centuries. This fact has cast significant doubt on earlier assumptions about the impact of the Industrial Revolution on the family; industrialization did not cause the limitation of the family's size, the separation of the family of procreation from the family of orientation, the predominance of nuclear households, or the destruction of traditional kinship structures. Scholars in family history have also shown that the family is not merely the passive recipient of social and economic change, but to a limited extent it can initiate and influence change; that old patterns of behavior are not replaced by new ones, but persist and are modified by circumstances; and that change varies by class, region, and cultural or ethnic group.[38]

The state of knowledge precludes a statement as to whether findings about family history in the United States and Western Europe apply to Latin America. Some Latin Americanists hypothesize that "industrialization has effects on 'the family' in Latin America that differ from its impact in Europe and North America because of the historical circumstances in which Latin American nations have experienced industrialization—that is, because of the colonial or dependent capitalistic nature of Latin American economies."[39] Similarly, Elizabeth Anne Kuznesof, who discovered tremendous changes in household composition caused by changes in mode of production before industrialization in São Paulo, notes that

> the differences between the Latin American experience of modernization and those of England or Europe include population density, the uses of slavery, the frontier context, the importance of agricultural export crops and mining development, the predominance of foreign capital in the development process, the structure of imports and exports, the slow extension of factories, and the significance of basically non-monetary subsistence economies in Latin America as late as the end of the 19th century.[40]

Non–Latin Americanists, on the other hand, seem more inclined to see universal patterns of family history. Edward Shorter argues that "the changes in intimate life that modernization fosters are essentially the same everywhere" and that "the New World was for the most part 'born Modern.'" Tamara Hareven sees parallels between the United States/Western European experience and the Latin American one in the family's ability to guide change, in the persistence and modification of traditional behavior, and in regional, class, and cultural variations in family behavior.[41] More research is needed to clarify whether Latin American history exhibits regional specificity or is a minor variant of patterns in Europe and its settlement colonies.

Recent research in Brazilian family history has followed two approaches, one largely quantitative, demographic, and structural, and the other, focusing on elite families, largely qualitative and functional. An outstanding example of the demographic approach is Kuznesof's work on São Paulo between 1765 and 1836, when its economy changed from subsistence agriculture to a local market economy and still later to an export economy. Kuznesof found many surprises: the predominance of small nuclear families in 1765, with families tending to become larger and more complex later only among the elite; female-headed households as the most common type of headship, followed by single, never-married men, with, in third place, only 29 percent of family heads as "married" couples;[42] a tremendous increase in household residents unrelated to the head of household; evidence of the breakdown of the nuclear family, child abandonment, and the migration of young, single, and unattached women from rural to urban areas, where they worked in textile production, food stores, street vending, and prostitution. Only elite families, which controlled the means of production, were able to sustain the nuclear, biological family. Employment opportunities for the lower class were restricted by elite dominance and the competition of foreign goods. The absence of a factory system in Brazil during that era intensified the economic suffering of the lower class, even as compared to its European and United States counterparts. Women in particular were "relegated to an insecure and unprotected outer margin of the Brave New World."[43]

Donald Ramos's excellent research on urban and rural society in Minas Gerais between 1804 and 1838 led to many similar findings. Ramos found that the extended or multiple-family household existed for only a handful; the nuclear family was much more common. In urban Vila Rica (Ouro Prêto) very large numbers of people also lived alone, a fact that points to "a life of alienation for many," the antithesis of the "myth" of the Mineiro traditional family. Families headed by women were also common, even among the extended elite families, suggesting that "the typical extended family, formerly thought to have been patriarchal, was often really headed by a matriarch."[44] Marriage, practiced significantly less frequently than in Western Europe, served mainly to differentiate the white upper caste from the mulatto and black lower castes. Women, particularly lower-caste women, played a larger role in the economy and society than has generally been recognized but were exploited through prostitution, concubinage, and false promises of marriage. As in São Paulo, child abandonment was a serious problem. Brazil's racial hierarchy affected family structure: black households were more likely than white households to be female-headed and tended to be smaller (reflecting lower socioeconomic status); the fertility rates of mulatto and black women were also lower than those of white women. As compared to Western Europe, Ramos found average household size to be similar, Brazilian women to be younger at childbirth, and age differential of spouses to be greater in Brazil.[45]

Studies such as Kuznesof's and Ramos's have challenged the older "patriarchal school," by showing the patriarchal or extended family to be a minority type; indeed, the Brazilian demographic histories have raised fundamental questions about the nature of traditional Brazilian society. Such analyses are not without limitations, however. According to a leading authority, similar research on nineteenth-century United States family structures based on census manuscript schedules has resulted in an "emerging pattern [that] contributes little to the understanding of the complexity of family life." Hareven sees the family "as a process over time rather than a static unit within certain time periods." To reveal the complexity and fluidity of family structures and processes, longitudinal analysis of the family cycle is needed. "The life-cycle approach provides a meaningful framework for the correlation between general demographic trends . . . [and] the analysis of individual family and household structure."[46]

The qualitative track in the new family history of Brazil aims to analyze the fluid dynamics of social change itself, left inaccessible to the quantitative, demographic approach. It has focused thus far on the elite few, evidently because of the availability of source materials such as genealogies, letters, and wills and testaments. Thus there are disadvantages of class bias and unrepresentativeness in this approach.[47] Though these disadvantages must be kept in mind, they must be weighed against the fact that in Brazil, particularly before 1945, social and political mobilization was low and the power of the elite to guide change was high. Moreover, going beyond the immediate concerns of family history into the realm of elite studies, analysis of elite family behavior has great bearing on the persistent reality of the few rich and the many poor.

Kuznesof's work covers family elites as well as the demographic dimension of family history. She has described how, between 1750 and 1850 in São Paulo, elite family clans based in the *bairro* (neighborhood) and controlling the militia, the real executive power, were the crucial engines of political and economic change. These clans expanded the role of the militia far beyond defense of colony and community into such areas as public works construction. In addition, the development of commerce and trade and the rise of a merchant class, largely of immigrant origins, were mediated through the elite parentela, which was able to command the labor of its constituents.[48]

Alida Metcalf's research on eighteenth-century Santana de Parnaíba, São Paulo, reveals that elite families followed definite, almost
calculated strategies to accumulate and defend capital. These complex plans included six major elements: (1) the evasion of the intent
of inheritance law; (2) markedly unequal distribution of wealth,
even within elite families; (3) manipulation of women as objects, in
this case dowry-pawns; (4) highly controlled, restricted recruitment
of family leaders; (5) creation of "surplus" family members and their
forced migration; and (6) power relationships of authoritarianism,
dependency, and avoidance of conflict.[49] Intriguingly, these patterns
are those by which the few maintain their wealth and power over the
many in the larger society down to the present day. In excavating the
family strategies of eighteenth-century Parnaíba, Metcalf may have
found the socioeconomic bedrock that must be blasted if real change
is to occur in Brazil.

The painstaking research of Linda Lewin extends the new family
history chronologically to the late nineteenth and early twentieth
centuries and geographically to the poor northeastern pro-
vince/state of Parnaíba. Regarding the existence of traditional, colo-
nial-era patriarchalism as "an open question," Lewin depicts the decline of the paterfamilias in the nineteenth century as the result, in
part, of the liberating aspects of new law and medical schools. These
allowed elite sons to resist such pillars of patriarchy as forced marriage, while they added new skills to elite parentelas. The decline of
patriarchy, however, was not the twilight of the parentela. Clans reorganized along more collective lines with "the fundamental bond-
ing at the level of male siblings," including "male cousins who were
inscribed as brothers-in-law."[50] Lewin wonders whether such patterns might have existed earlier as alternatives to the hierarchical,
patriarchal tradition. Her research, like that of others, describes a
flexibility and adaptability that explains the survival and persistence
of the elite parentela.

The new Brazilian family history shares an indistinct boundary
with the new Brazilian women's history, which also has largely
focused on the elite. The research previously mentioned calls for a
re-evaluation of women's roles in Brazilian history. A. J. R. Russell-
Wood notes that Brazilian women of all races have been stereotyped
in previous historical writing. Focusing on the white women in the
colonial era, Russell-Wood argues that "the female played a signifi-

cantly more important role in the social, economic and ideological development of the colony than has been appreciated." Women were venerated and protected, he says, and, except for politics, enjoyed many legal rights. In addition to heading households, "women managed estates and properties, involving themselves in the day-to-day workings of gold mines, cattle ranches, and sugar plantations."[51]

Susan Soeiro's study of the Destêrro convent in Bahia, Brazil's only nunnery from 1677 to 1733, pictures it as "a social mechanism permitting the elite to restrict marriages ultimately with the aim of maintaining itself as a self-perpetuating and exclusive body." Within the convent itself, there was a wide gap between the theory of how life should be led—renunciation of the secular world, self-abnegation, strict discipline, and dedication to the service of God—and the facts: "the life of a nun could foster individual initiative, independence, and self-fulfillment in non-religious spheres." Illicit romances; reading, writing, and arithmetic; leadership of the convent itself; selling, purchasing, and renting property; money lending; and the employment of slaves as street vendors: these were among the many activities of the not very cloistered upper-class women of the Destêrro.[52]

Between the mid-nineteenth century and the 1920s—the period studied in this book—Brazilian women of all classes were deeply affected by socioeconomic change.[53] Elite widows took over urban businesses as they had earlier run plantations. They also entered the professions: teaching (at lower salaries than men), and (against great male resistance) medicine, law, and the bureaucracy. Female typists and salesclerks swelled the ranks of the burgeoning middle sectors. Working-class women were employed by the tens of thousands in industry. Class differences among the few elite and bourgeois women, on the one hand, and the many working-class, poor females, on the other, prevented feminist solidarity. In São Paulo, privileged women attacked the injustice of the supposed "traditional family," and the "hypocrisy, . . . egoism, cruelty, and machiavellianism of men."[54] They proposed changing the terms of marriage: later nuptials, fewer children, release from the home, dignifying the role of housewife and mother. These plans were limited to the privileged few and required the labor of proletarian domestics.[55] The "attack on the family" evidently failed to embrace the family's roots in the class structure and economic regime.

The new Brazilian family history is in the pioneer stage. It does not yet offer a coherent comprehensive view replacing the old patriarchal model, parts of which appear viable. The new research has, however, made some things clearer and has raised questions about significant aspects of the older historical tradition. It seems clear that the extended family was a minority type, limited mainly to the few rich, and hence scarcely a "national" type. Even among the elite it appears that alternatives to patriarchalism existed in the forms of matriarchalism or male-sibling corporative management. There is general agreement, moreover, that the roles of women have been misrepresented. There is also increasing recognition—even while there is ample evidence of continuity and cultural persistence—of change, flexibility, and dynamism in the history of Brazilian family life.

Purpose, Scope, and Limits of This Study

This study falls within the qualitative, elite family approach of the "new Brazilian family history." It has two interrelated objectives. The first is to narrate the history of a family whose deeds have long been of great interest to foreigners and Brazilians. The main characters—the baron of Iguape; his daughter, Veridiana; her sons, Antônio, "Martinico," and Eduardo; and Antônio's son, Paulo—have been studied often, but usually in pursuit of relatively limited themes and with little attention to interaction in the family network. Second, I attempt an interpretation of the Prado family experience in light of existing knowledge of the family institution in Brazil.

This study's chronological scope, 1840 to 1930, imposes certain limits. I attempted no major research on the Prados in the colonial era; nor did I attempt to study the family after 1930, a period of apparent relative decline for the Prados and also one in which the family institution generally attracted increased attention from the state. The sheer size and nature of an elite Brazilian family also imposes limits on what a single researcher can do. An elite Brazilian family, traced over several generations, may consist of hundreds of members, the majority of whom it is highly impractical or even impossible to study in detail. Thus, in what follows there is an unintended emphasis on those few Prados whose prominence, whose notable successes and failures, and whose articulateness resulted in a documentary and published record susceptible of analysis.

The nature of the elite Brazilian family creates the practical necessity of defining the varieties of the word *family*. Most students have indicated three primary levels of meaning for the word: the nuclear or conjugal family, the extended family (extended biologically or by ritual kinship), and, in the Brazilian case, the parentela.[56] One weakness of the descriptive literature is the failure to keep these distinctions clear. I use the following terminology: in reference to a nuclear or conjugal group, phrasing such as "the (nuclear) family of Martinho and Veridiana"; for the extended family, which for working purposes I have defined as those persons born with the da Silva Prado family name and those who acquired it by marriage, "the Prado-surname extended family"; for the larger group of interrelated families including the Prados and allied familial groups, the "Prado parentela." Under this scheme, the children born to Prado women who married non-Prados are considered to be part of the Prado parentela, not of the "Prado-surname extended family." Such distinctions, necessary for analysis, are admittedly somewhat artificial, since a Prado would probably recognize members of nuclear, extended, and parentela groups as all part of the "family," at least in an ideal sense. In reality, the circle of meaningful family relationships was much smaller than the ideal, and I attempt to show, throughout the study, which of these were functionally important. Finally, since the work focuses primarily on the principal Prado family branches, the phrase "the Prados," unless otherwise modified, should be understood as denoting primarily the principal branches.

A final limitation is inherent in the type of data I was able to collect from family papers, public manuscript collections, and published works. In particular, the data precluded an analysis of Prado family wealth and its fluctuations, transmission, and dispersal. I also found little correspondence dealing with the Prados' politics. Hence, the treatment of these subjects is based largely on more accessible published documents. On the other hand, the family papers did allow a fairly rich and intimate treatment of two subjects: family life and the effect of the cultural re-Europeanization of Brazil on it. Despite the uneven distribution of original evidence, I have been guided by the conviction that family life is lived as a whole and, within the linearity of the written word, the historian should try to recapture its kaleidoscopic and multifaceted nature.

ᴥ CHAPTER I ᴥ

ORIGINS, 1700–1840

When Sergeant-major Antônio da Silva do Prado, founder of the da Silva Prado family, arrived in Brazil in the early 1700s, he took up residence in the captaincy of São Paulo, one of Brazil's most distinctive regions. When Europeans of that era thought of Brazil, they may have pictured its lush sugar plantations, its tropical coasts and exotic jungles, and perhaps its enslaved Afro-Brazilian labor force. Perhaps they thought of the principal cities—Recife, Salvador da Bahia, and Rio de Janeiro—whose commerce in sugar and gold and whose accessibility to Portugal's maritime lifelines made them the most important centers of colonial Brazilian economy, society, and imperial administration.

By contrast, the São Paulo in which the Prado family tree took root and slowly matured occupied a generally marginal place in colonial Brazilian life. Although São Paulo lies astride the Tropic of Capricorn, its climate is mostly temperate because the bulk of its territory consists of a plateau of rolling hill-country two to three thousand feet above sea level. Except for its narrow tropical coastal belt, São Paulo was not well suited to the production of the tropical goods demanded by the European consumer of the eighteenth century. Along with climatic differences between São Paulo and the more northerly coastal cities went variations in social patterns: São Paulo society showed less fixity, more nomadism; less African influence, more Indian. These differences were reinforced—at a time when most long-distance travel in Brazil was by coastal vessel—by São Paulo's physical isolation from the rest of Brazil. The precipitous Serra do Mar, the coastal escarpment, sundered the Paulista plateau from its own coast, from the rest of Brazil, and to some extent from the querulous demands of Portuguese monarchs.[1]

Earlier, in the sixteenth and seventeenth centuries, the prototypical Paulista figure had been the *bandeirante*, a wandering half-Indian frontiersman who sought the remedy for São Paulo's endemic poverty in epic, wide-ranging searches for Indian slaves and mineral riches.[2] Ironically, the bandeirante's success in finally discovering gold in the late seventeenth and early eighteenth centuries may have led to his demise. His gold fields were soon taken by others more successful in getting the crown's support (or more willing to accept it), and the bandeirantes were defeated in the War of the Emboabas (1708–9).[3] The bandeirantes went on to discover other mines, but for São Paulo itself the net effect of the feverish search for quick wealth was probably negative: the region's population declined because of migration to the mines, and most of the mineral wealth found its way into other hands.[4]

Thus begun, São Paulo's eighteenth century traditionally has been regarded as a decadent era sandwiched between the supposed glories of the bandeirante epoch and the coffee boom of the late nineteenth century.[5] More recently some historians have argued that the 1700s in São Paulo were years of preparation for later developments that were to make São Paulo the most dynamic, prosperous region of Brazil. While São Paulo gained little direct economic benefit from Brazil's gold rush, the Portuguese crown did invest new political importance in the formerly neglected region. In 1709 the captaincy of São Paulo and the Mines of Gold was created, encompassing the territory from the south of present-day Minas Gerais to the La Plata estuary. Two years later, the town (vila) of São Paulo de Piratininga on the interior plateau was raised in legal status to a city (cidade) and replaced coastal São Vicente as the captaincy's capital. São Paulo's status was further enhanced when it became a bishopric in 1745. A humiliating lapse in São Paulo's improving status occurred when the captaincy was annexed to Rio de Janeiro in 1748, although the proud plateau regained local administrative autonomy in 1765.[6]

The administration of the royal governor Dom Luíz Antônio de Souza Botelho Mourão coincided with significant, fateful changes in São Paulo. New economic types—the itinerant trader and the cash-crop sugar planter—began to replace the opportunistic bandeirante and the subsistence farmer.[7] Buttressed by control of the colonial militia, elite families began to concentrate wealth by dominating land and labor, creating great hardship for the majority of poor subsistence farmers and their families, which often fell apart under the forces generated by changing patterns of economic activity.[8] Poor farmers could no longer support families and left them; children were abandoned in shocking numbers; single women migrated from rural to urban areas, and some of them were forced into prostitution and concubinage by limited economic opportunities. Aware of this social pathology but unaware of its causes—blaming sin and immorality instead of change in economic activity—royal officials supported the economic changes as likely to increase imperial revenues. They encouraged the growth of São Paulo city, which steadily increased its dominance of its hinterland. Annual fairs were started in order to stimulate commerce. A municipal market was organized in 1773 to regularize food supply. In 1798 postal service was started down a treacherous path to Santos on the coast and thence to Rio de Janeiro, the colonial capital.[9] São Paulo's isolation was slowly yielding by 1800, although another half-century of poor communications yet lay in front of it.

These changes occurred in what was still a small, colonial, frontier society, a distant margin of the Portuguese Empire even after well over two hundred years of European settlement. Governor Dom Luíz Antônio de Souza Botelho Mourão's reports to the crown in the 1760s and 1770s provide a colorful view of the Paulistas and their customs, though the view was biased by imperial assumptions. According to Dom Luíz Antônio, one of the Paulistas' chief characteristics was distrust, which the governor attributed to the colonists' supposed impotence in the face of nature; more likely it reflected the conflict of material interest between settler and crown over taxes. The governor reckoned that the Paulista plateau quickly corrupted recent arrivals from Portugal who "fill themselves with vices because of the ease of the land and become willful."[10] Adding to the social flux, Dom Luíz Antônio said, was the fact that the Paulistas did not know "the utility which comes from permanent property, which fathers can leave to their children."[11] Quite to the contrary, however, elite families pursued elaborate strategies to evade the intent of royal inheritance law and concentrate their wealth in a few heirs, usually daughters, whose marriages expanded parentelas.[12] More accurate was Dom Luíz Antônio's observation that marriage was uncommon in late eighteenth-century São Paulo. The number of bastards was very high. Such facts reflected the predominantly rural pattern of settlement, the costs and inconvenience of marriage, and the relative backwardness of the region. The remedy for these problems, wrote the governor, lay in a kind of forced urbanization. Paulistas would be compelled to congregate in villages and towns where they could be turned from sin and made productive subjects of the crown.[13]

The striking growth of population in São Paulo in the late eighteenth and early nineteenth centuries (table 2) was less the result of imperial design than of changed economic activity. Generally, free whites made up two-thirds of the population. There was a consistent surplus of free white females for over a century after 1765. Economic patterns required geographic mobility of elite and poor males alike.[14] Generally speaking, social and economic conditions in late colonial São Paulo were not propitious for legal marriage and family life, especially for the poor.

Among the elite the patriarchal *ideal* may have been strong. There is no doubt that family ties were important. But given the relative isolation and poverty of São Paulo, its economic and social backwardness (just beginning to change in the late eighteenth century), there is little reason to believe that Paulista patriarchalism could rival that of the more established regions centered at Recife, Salvador da Bahia, and Rio de Janeiro. The weaker Paulista patriarchalism facilitated the partial adoption of "modern" ways.

TABLE 2
Population of São Paulo, 1765–1816

Year	São Paulo City	São Paulo Captaincy
1765	(20,873)	(80,000)
1772	21,272	100,537
1798	21,304	(158,450)
1803	24,311	188,379
1816	25,486	219,867

Source: Maria-Luiza Marcílio, *La ville de São Paulo*, 119.
Note: Figures in parentheses are estimates.

The Prados in the Eighteenth Century

The founder of the da Silva Prado family, the sergeant-major Antônio da Silva do Prado, arrived in São Paulo between 1700 and 1710.[15] He was born in Prado, Portugal, but almost nothing is known of his origins, though one writer traced these back to the thirteenth-century nobility.[16] Such a remote connection to Portugal's aristocracy carried little weight in eighteenth-century São Paulo.[17] Thus, one of Antônio da Silva do Prado's first acts was to establish family connections in the new land. Sometime before 1710 he married Felippa do Prado, a member of a family which had lived in São Paulo since the sixteenth century and which included many bandeirante notables in its ranks.[18]

Antônio da Silva do Prado's first wife died, probably before 1720, and he subsequently married Francisca de Siqueira Morais, also of an old and upper-class Paulista family.[19] In light of the class values that governed marriage, it seems likely that Antônio had prospered somewhat from his early endeavors in Parnaíba, a small town some eighteen miles northwest of São Paulo city on the Tietê River. In 1730 the first Antônio Prado mortgaged his property in Parnaíba to finance a gold-hunting expedition to Goiás. The mortgage shows that he owned a farm (*sítio*) "with its houses constructed of pounded earth and tile roofs, a mill and two copper stills and other processing equipment [for sugar?]" as well as a multiple-structure residence on Parnaíba's central plaza. Also mortgaged were ten slaves. The transaction netted Antônio four other African slaves valued at 679 *oitavas* in gold and 610 in liquid capital.[20] Accompanying the mortgage was a power of attorney to protect Antônio's wife, Francisca, from civil, criminal, and ecclesiastical suits during her husband's absence. This authorized fifteen persons in Parnaíba, São Paulo city, Santos, Jundiaí, and the mines in Goiás, as well as the Jesuit fathers in Rio de Janeiro, to act on behalf of Francisca in such suits.[21] There is no evidence that Antônio da Silva do Prado struck it rich in Goiás, but it seems that when he died in 1737, the Prado family founder left his heirs a modest fortune. More important, he left a network of friends and associates, without which no family in traditional Brazil could prosper.

The most important member of the first Brazilian-born generation of Prados was the first Martinho Prado (1722/23–70), one of six children of Antônio da Silva do Prado and Francisca de Siqueira Morais.[22] Born in Parnaíba, Martinho later moved to the larger town of Jundiaí, where he was a lower court judge (juiz ordinário) and alderman from 1745 to 1750 and also served as orphan's judge in the early 1750s. In 1758 he requested a land grant measuring one by one-half league in Jundiaí-Mirim. In December 1766 Martinho was named captain-major (capitão-mór) of Jundiaí.[23] He was married to Maria Leme Ferreira, member of another prestigious Paulista family. Of their eight surviving children, one daughter, Ana Joaquina, married three times and established ties with the Morais Leme, the Queirós Teles, and the Pereira de Queirós families, which were to be important in Paulista history (see Appendix A).

In the second Brazilian generation, the Prados intensified their political activities and expanded their network of kin. This generation's key members were Martinho Prado's sons, the second Antônio Prado (d. 1793) and his younger brother Eleutério (d. 1849). In 1786 Antônio married Ana Vicência Rodrigues de Almeida (1768/69–1854), the seventh child of the Portuguese-born lieutenant and later brigadier, Manuel Rodrigues Jordão. Rodrigues Jordão had made a substantial fortune as a trader in Goiás and Mato Grosso. When he died, he left five houses on Rua São Bento and Rua do Carmo in São Paulo city; this property, evidently left to Ana Vicência, was the start of the permanent presence in the city of what was to become the most successful Prado family branch. Other, ultimately less successful, Prados remained in secondary towns such as Jundiaí.[24]

In 1787, the second Antônio Prado was elected to the town council of São Paulo.[25] His economic activities were more significant, and they illustrate the expanded opportunities in late-eighteenth-century São Paulo. The second Antônio Prado's economic endeavors also foreshadow a development that has sometimes been overlooked in writings about the Prados, their role as urban-based merchant entrepreneurs. Following his father-in-law's example and perhaps using his connections, Antônio entered into trading and lending. His business activities were plagued by a shortage of money in the colony, by the difficulty of finding reliable business partners, and by trouble in collecting debts. Nonetheless, the entrepreneurial spirit burned hot, and a year before his death Antônio's appetite for new business had not dulled. In 1792 he informed an associate that he had six hundred animals in Curitiba ready for sale in Goiás. When Antônio died in

1793, Ana Vicência petitioned Queen Maria I of Portugal, asking to be appointed legal guardian of their children. With the help of her brothers-in-law Eleutério, Raimundo, and Joaquim Prado, Ana Vicência attempted for years to collect the debts by then owed to the family. Surviving records attest both to the difficulty of this and to the family's creditor status.[26]

In 1800 Ana Vicência married her brother-in-law Eleutério, probably to keep the Prado fortunes in family hands. Like several Prados, Eleutério was a capitão-mór in the militia and as such was a participant in an early type of *coronelismo,* or local rule by planters and other members of the elite who were granted militia offices in return for supporting the crown.[27] Upon the nomination of other officers, Eleutério submitted oaths that the nominees' public duties would not be compromised by family interests, a reminder of the uneasy relationship between the public and private spheres in Brazilian life. In addition to his militia activities, Eleutério became a relatively prosperous sugar planter in Jundiaí. An 1817 census showed him the master of fifty slaves, the third highest total in the locale. Most of the sugar he produced after 1816 was sent to his nephew-stepson, the third Antônio Prado, for marketing. After Brazil gained its independence in 1822, Eleutério held important local political posts, as did his brother Joaquim, a lieutenant colonel of the First National Guard Battalion in São Paulo, and his nephew-stepson Antônio.[28]

The Economic and Political Career of the Third Antônio Prado

Despite the advances that had occurred in São Paulo in the late eighteenth century, the captaincy was still a relatively impoverished, isolated, backward region in the early 1800s. In 1808—the year the Portuguese court, fleeing Napoleon's invasion of the Iberian peninsula, arrived in Brazil—the Englishman John Mawe noted the contrasting sentiments that his arrival in São Paulo produced among the local populace:

> Our appearance at S. Paulo excited considerable curiosity among all descriptions of people, who seemed by their manner

never to have seen Englishmen before. The very children testi-
fied their astonishment, some by running away, others by
counting our fingers, and exclaiming that we had the same
number as they. . . . It was gratifying to us to perceive that this
general wonder subsided into a more social feeling; we met with
civil treatment every where, and were frequently invited to dine
with the inhabitants. At the public parties and balls of the governor we found both novelty and pleasure; novelty at being
much more liberally received than we were in the Spanish set-
tlements, and pleasure at being in much more refined and polished company.

Mawe went on to comment on some aspects of Paulista family and
social mores. He noted that elite women "trouble themselves very
little with domestic concerns, confiding whatever relates to the in-
ferior departments of the household to the negro or negra cooks, and
leaving all other matters to the management of servants"; upper-
class women's main activities were sewing, embroidery, and lace-
making. The children of white masters and of black slaves were
brought up together as playmates, establishing "a familiar equality . . . between them which has to be forcibly abolished when they
arrive at that age, at which one must command and live at his ease,
while the other must labour and obey."[29]

Some years later, in 1819, the French naturalist Auguste de Saint-
Hilaire observed that São Paulo suffered from a high degree of violence, which he felt was typical of a young, relatively poor society.
Saint-Hilaire noted that the inhabitants of rural areas feared the
"evil eye," and he came to expect that a run-down farm would be
owned by a Paulista rather than by (as he depicted them) the more
industrious folk of neighboring Minas Gerais. Fazendeiros in remote
regions of the captaincy were unused to seeing outsiders and were
untouched by their influence. These planters dominated their slaves
"by force or by intelligence," beat their dogs without restraint, and
kept their women hidden away. The rural woman, the French naturalist remarked, "is many times the first slave of the house, as the
dog is the last."[30]

Saint-Hilaire's comments on women in São Paulo city indicate
that social relations and family life among its elite were still essentially patriarchal. During his stay in the city, many prominent cit-

izens received him warmly, but, like the country folk, they kept their women out of sight. Upper-class females spent their days embroidering, arranging flowers, and playing music. The number of poor women driven to prostitution shocked the urbane Saint-Hilaire as much as did the city's high incidence of venereal disease; he observed, however, that Paulistana prostitutes behaved with a discretion that far exceeded that of their cynical Parisian sisters.[31]

In other ways the city presented a strong contrast with its hinterland. Whereas Saint-Hilaire generally thought Minas Gerais more highly developed than São Paulo captaincy, he believed that the Paulista capital had a more orderly, active life than the Mineiro capital, Ouro Prêto. São Paulo's many functionaries and workers, its large merchant class, its resident fazendeiros, and its many vendors of fruits and vegetables all attested to its emerging importance as a commercial center. There were a good many attractive but simple large houses, though Saint-Hilaire reckoned that there were few wealthy persons in the city, in part because of inheritance patterns that divided a father's property. Nonetheless, Saint-Hilaire, sensing a certain economic dynamism in the city, predicted its eventual emergence as a manufacturing center.[32]

The career of the third Antônio Prado (1788–1875, named baron of Iguape in 1848) was intimately associated with the growth of São Paulo city as a commercial center. In 1801 he was one of only twenty-four first-year students attending the city's Latin grammar school. In 1805 at the age of seventeen, Antônio was driven by the slimness of local prospects to begin conducting troops of mules from São Paulo to Goiás and Bahia; thus he followed both the geographical and the career paths of the family elders. This was no easy route to success since the young mule trader was often forced to accept years-old notes of credit in lieu of cash in return for his labor. His travels provided opportunity to check on the Prados' far-flung debtors. He was sustained in these efforts by his mother, Ana Vicência, who urged him on in the family name. In 1815, styling herself as "your longing mother and loving friend," Ana Vicência extolled Antônio's constant efforts on the Prados' behalf and gave him a detailed account of the complicated family finances.[33] Ana Vicência's active role in the Prados' financial life provides an exception to patriarchal norms.

After his initial migrations, Antônio fixed his residence in the small Bahian town of Caiteté, where he engaged in profitable though small-scale trading. When he returned to São Paulo in 1816, he left in Caiteté a brother with whose help he maintained his business ties in the northeast. Unlike most of his ancestors, his brothers, and many of his descendants, the third Antônio eschewed the rural life. His purchase of a *fazenda* (plantation) in Jundiaí seems to have been inspired more by traditional class values than by the business possibilities.[34]

The third Antônio Prado's real interests and talents were those of a capitalist-speculator. From 1817 until at least 1829, he was a sugar and livestock trader and a tax collector. These occupations were closely related because sugar was then the main source of wealth in São Paulo, mules were in demand as beasts of burden for, among other things, sugar, and taxes were often paid in kind. At the height of Antônio's sugar-merchant business (1818–21), he may have sold from 6 to 10 percent of São Paulo's sugar. His investment in the trade in 1819–20 was some forty *contos* (forty thousand dollars), and in good times he made a profit of as much as 12 percent.[35]

Another enterprise chosen by Antônio was the slave trade. Acting for himself and as middleman for Prado family members and other planters, he ordered sixty slaves from Rio de Janeiro in 1819 and another twenty or thirty in 1820. More ambitious and speculative was his partnership with other Paulista merchants to finance two shiploads of sugar to be traded in Mozambique for blacks. By May of 1820, however, the chronic instability of the sugar trade and the difficulty of selling the low-quality Paulista product led Antônio to write a brother that he wished to quit the troublesome business: "I think I will succeed in the future, since I already have deposited 8:000$000 in the bank. As soon as I have more funds there, I will have solid returns, without work."[36]

To Antônio "work" apparently meant physical labor, not the mental effort of financial transactions, for his second major activity, the collection of public taxes on a contract basis, soon became his most profitable endeavor. Tax collecting was more stable than sugar trading, and Antônio had the power of the crown behind him. With some ruthlessness he wrote to one of his agents in 1820 that the royal treasury demanded a certain payment "with speed" and that as a representative of the crown he cared little whether the harvest necessary to pay the tax had been sold or not.[37] The developing Prado entrepreneurial mentality was not without its unrelenting side.

It was natural that Antônio, as tax collector, would become more directly involved in politics. In 1819 he was appointed militia captain in São Paulo city and was elected alderman, a post he held until 1822. At one point he was placed on a royal proscription list because of his friendship with the Andrada family of Santos, which furnished leaders to Brazil's independence movement and royal advisers to Dom Pedro I after independence was achieved. The third Antônio Prado's political emergence came as events moved Brazil along a collision course with Portugal. Since 1808 the Portuguese court had resided in Brazil. In December 1815 Prince-Regent João raised Brazil to the status of a kingdom coequal with Portugal, at least in theory. In 1816 the prince-regent became Emperor João VI of the United Kingdom of Portugal, Brazil, and the Algarves. During the next few years the parliament in Portugal grew increasingly restive about the exotic situation of a European monarch's residing on the jungle shores of tropical South America—and about the Brazilian claim to equality with the mother country—and in 1821 that body demanded that the emperor return to Portugal. Dom João complied. His son, Pedro, stayed on as prince-regent of Brazil. In October the Portuguese parliament ordered Pedro home as well, a move seen by native Brazilians as designed to return Brazil to its former colonial status. Brazilians in São Paulo strongly suspected that intermediary royal officials were sponsoring plans to "enslave" Brazil. On 31 December 1821 Antônio Prado, his brother Francisco, his half-brother Eleutério, and their father and stepfather, also named Eleutério, were among Paulistas who appealed to Dom Pedro to defy the order to return home. This appeal was partly responsible for Pedro's decision to remain in Brazil, a key step toward independence.[38]

In São Paulo, meanwhile, several groups—apparently united more by ambition and family alliances than by ideology—competed for power during the uneasy twilight of the old regime. On 23 May 1822 the legal government was deposed in a coup known as the *Bernarda*.[39] Although in June Pedro succeeded in re-establishing royal control, his subsequent attempt to send in troops provoked local resistance. In August many leading Paulistas, including Antônio Prado and his brother, Francisco, asked Pedro to visit São Paulo and reconcile the competing factions.[40] Pedro agreed and sent word that he wished to be received by those aldermen who had been serving legally before the coup of 23 May; that group included Antônio

Prado. In São Paulo, Dom Pedro lodged with Antônio and his uncle, the brigadier Manuel Rodrigues Jordão. On 5 September the prince-regent left to inspect fortifications in Santos. Returning to São Paulo city two days later, he was informed of new demands from Portugal that he return; this development precipitated Pedro's declaration of Brazilian independence, a decision he communicated personally to Antônio Prado.[41] For his loyalty to the new regime, Antônio was soon named a knight (cavalheiro) in the Royal Order of Christ and in 1826 became capitão-mór of São Paulo city.[42] His friendship with the Andradas, his support for independence, and his personal loyalty to the new emperor, Dom Pedro I, made the third Antônio Prado a welcome guest at court and established the Prados' close ties with the Brazilian royal house, ties that lasted until the monarchy fell in 1889.

Family Alliances, 1820–40

As husband and father, the third Antônio Prado brought the same awareness of opportunity, forcefulness, and even cunning to arranging family alliances that he had brought to business and politics. With his economic and political position well established by the early 1820s, Antônio turned his attention to family concerns. An attractive descendant of a distinguished Paulista family, Maria Cândida de Moura Vaz, caught his eye. She had been abandoned by her first husband, by whom she had had three daughters, and formal marriage to Antônio was impossible under such circumstances. Nonetheless, Antônio and Maria Cândida established together a household that lasted over forty years, until Maria Cândida's death in 1868. It is perhaps a measure of both Antônio's position and his strong will that they were able to do so without evident censure in the small city of São Paulo. The couple had two children: Veríssimo, who later enjoyed moderate success as a militia officer and planter; and Veridiana (1825–1910), who became one of the most influential women in Paulista history.

Until the third Antônio's era, the Prado-surname extended family had remained small as a result of outmigration from São Paulo and a shortage of married male heirs. Antônio's generation consisted of nine brothers and sisters, a substantial base from which to expand the Prado parentela.[43] As the family's chief marriage broker, Antônio presided over its rise to prominence. One example of his marital diplomacy, the marriage of his half-sister Maria Marcolina (1805?–1887) and Rodrigo Antônio Monteiro de Barros (1804/5–44), is particularly illustrative. Rodrigo received a law degree at the University of Coimbra in Portugal and was named magistrate (*juiz de fóra*) in São Paulo in 1827. His father, Lucas Antônio Monteiro de Barros, viscount of Congonhas do Campo, was São Paulo's first post-independence provincial president (1824–27) and organized the provincial administration on a solid footing.[44] The viscount gave his son a letter of introduction to Antônio Prado, by then one of the most prominent residents of São Paulo city, asking Antônio to introduce Rodrigo to the most important Paulistano families. Antônio, however, was in no hurry to do so. He opened his own home to the young stranger—"a rare thing among the families of that time, proverbially withdrawn and reserved toward strangers, impermeable toward newcomers"—but kept him secluded, virtually a hostage. Rodrigo pined away for the pleasures of Coimbra and Rio. At a presumably crucial psychological point, Antônio introduced Rodrigo to his young half-sister, the "pretty, educated, intelligent, and informed" Maria Marcolina. The result of this carefully staged encounter was the marriage of the young couple on 3 July 1828, "amidst the special pleasure of all the family and its enormous parentela, and amidst noisy festivities."[45]

It was a classic match, uniting the destinies of the Prado and Monteiro de Barros families. The Monteiro de Barroses benefited by association with what has been called, with a bit of exaggeration, the "enormous prestige of the Silva Prado family, allied with the Jordão family, the Pachecos of Itú, the Pereira Mendes and Fonseca families and others representing fortunes acquired in agriculture and commerce."[46] The Prados, in turn, were now linked to one of the Empire's most important families, one that profited from the early coffee boom in Rio de Janeiro, had an influential branch in Minas Gerais, and later boasted important capitalists and industrialists. More immediately, in Rodrigo Monteiro de Barros the Prados gained a voice in national politics. He was elected deputy to the second, third, and fourth national legislatures, named commander (*comendador*) in the Order of Christ, and made an officer of the imperial household.[47] The Prados had their man in Rio.

With the cooperation of his uncle-stepfather, Eleutério, Antônio Prado arranged other marriages for his siblings. His brother Francisco married Maria Benedita Pacheco e Jordão, reinforcing the Prados' ties to the Jordãos, important planters in Itú. Ana Brandina, Antônio's sister, was married to Dr. José Manuel da Fonseca (1803–71), holder of a Coimbra law degree, a lawyer in Itú, alderman in Jundiaí, provincial and national deputy, national senator in 1854, and also a journalist and planter. Another important tie was established with the family of João da Silva Machado, later baron of Antonina, whose career as livestock trader, vice-president of São Paulo (1837–38), and loyalist defender of the crown in São Paulo's Liberal revolt of 1842 was remarkably similar to that of the third Antônio Prado. In 1830 both men served as witnesses to the marriage of Antônia Emília de Moura Vaz, Antônio's stepdaughter, who married into Machado's family. Machado's second daughter married Antônio's half-brother, Joaquim, in 1835. Much later, in 1856, Antônio Prado and Machado served as witnesses for the fifth of Machado's daughters.[48]

It cannot be assumed that all relationships in the burgeoning Prado parentela were arranged and conducted smoothly; one incident in particular demonstrates that family ties sometimes were strained by internal struggles. Antônio Prado's uncle and political ally, Manuel Rodrigues Jordão, died in 1827, leaving a large fortune. Rodrigues Jordão had married under a contract providing for absolute separation of property; thus his wife, Gertrudes Galvão de Moura Lacerda, was not a legal heir. Moreover, Rodrigues Jordão had named his legally recognized illegitimate son, Antônio Rodrigues de Almeida Jordão, as guardian for his and Gertrudes's minor children. When his father died, Antônio Rodrigues was studying law at Coimbra. In May 1827 Antônio Prado wrote advising him to "come take charge of what is yours, which will render more than any good place in letters, and without responsibility." Prado also warned that Gertrudes, whose brother was managing the Rodrigues Jordão affairs, might cut off Antônio Rodrigues's funds. Antônio Rodrigues accepted Prado's advice and returned to São Paulo. Meanwhile, Antônio Prado's intrusion had angered Gertrudes, who sent him an offensive letter. Prado responded that "such expressions are strange indeed for any man even of very low status, and especially for a lady. I could respond to you in the same way, for which I have vast material, but I will not do it, because what would people who saw it say? The same as those to whom I have shown your most insulting letter."[49] It is possible that Antônio Prado's actions were designed only to enforce the last wishes of his uncle, Jordão, but he may have guessed also that he would be able to exert more influence over the young Antônio Rodrigues than over the recalcitrant Gertrudes and her kin.

Conflicts such as this could be, and sometimes were, seriously disruptive in their impact on family fortunes. The third Antônio Prado arranged the most important marriage of the family's history—that of his daughter Veridiana and his brother and cousin Martinho (1811–91)—within the network of his immediate kin, probably at least partly to avoid such a conflict.

By 1840 the Prados had been established in São Paulo for over 130 years; but unlike the Paulista *quinhentista* families, which traced their origins in São Paulo to the 1500s, the Prados could claim no stirring role in the founding of São Paulo nor in the "heroic" episodes of seventeenth-century bandeirismo. Indeed, in the eighteenth century the Prado surname signified to most Paulistas the do Prado family, which met the historical criteria for elite status as the Silva Prados did not.[50] Throughout that century the family name found its way before royal authorities only on the relatively routine occasions of confirming a land grant or a militia post, or appointing of a guardian for orphaned children. Among the eighteenth-century elite of São Paulo, the Prados were relative newcomers. In later years they could afford to view the quinhentistas' pride in "heroic" origins with the cynical amusement that became known as a Prado family trait.

But while the Prados were scarcely more than an anonymous element of the Paulista colonial elite before independence, they worked diligently at acquiring several bases of power. As local militia and political officials, first in Jundiaí and later in São Paulo city, they first exercised some limited authority. In business the Prados' very lack of bandeirante traditions may have made them more alert to the new economic opportunities of the late colonial era; their willingness to engage in the vulgar work of muleteering, of trading to Goiás and far-off Bahia, and of urban commerce led to modest success within the limited pre–coffee boom economy of São Paulo. Although the plantation figured large in Prado history, it is evident that an emerging capitalist mentality was equally important, even during the 1700s. The Prados came to embody both urban and rural economic interests, a pattern evident in the careers of the second Antônio as urban-based merchant and his brother, Eleutério, as rural fazendeiro. Although siblings specialized in urban or rural business, town and country interests merged within the family itself, a pattern that continued in future generations.

Between 1800 and 1840, a heightened Prado family self-consciousness developed. The marriage in 1800 of Ana Vicência Rodrigues de Almeida to her brother-in-law, Eleutério Prado, is evidence of this and of a desire to avoid fragmenting the family's fortune. This self-awareness reached new heights in the person of the third Antônio Prado. His successful commercial and tax-collecting career enriched the family, and his support of Dom Pedro I during the independence crisis magnified its political stature. It was largely the third Antônio who controlled the marital diplomacy that added necessary social dimension to the family's economic and political emergence on the provincial level. As the most successful and influential Prado of the first half of the nineteenth century—the closest approximation to a classic patriarch the family ever knew—the third Antônio Prado, future baron of Iguape, provided the living and later the ancestral figure that inspired future generations. His direct influence on the Prado family continued to be one of its principal assets until his death in 1875.

ᙞ CHAPTER II ᙟ

FAMILY LIFE IN THE

SECOND EMPIRE,

1840–1889

In Gilberto Freyre's synthesis of Brazilian social history, the nineteenth century is a watershed between colonial patriarchalism and the "disintegration" of patriarchal and scmipatriarchal forms in the early twentieth century. According to Freyre, the period witnessed the decline of rural patriarchy and the emergence of urban "semi-patriarchy." Freyre leaves the latter term undefined but apparently means it to describe the dominant social ethic resulting from the erosion of the traditional patriarch's powers by the church, the academy, the foreigner, and the urban milieu itself. Freyre sees the nineteenth century as an epoch of conflicts: the plantation versus the city plaza, the home versus the street, father versus son, man versus woman, Brazilian versus European, East versus West, and the mansion versus the shanty. Yet these conflicts, apparent dialectical confrontations, seem in Freyre's account to lack focus and resolution. Sons, while sometimes rebelling against fathers, also strove to imitate them; women, says Freyre, remained "orientalized," as much prisoners in the nineteenth-century urban *sobrado* (town house) as they had been in the colonial *casa grande.*[1] Perhaps the breadth of Freyre's perspective—that of all Brazilian history, of all Brazilian regions, and, presumably, of all Brazilian families—is partly responsible for this lack of resolution, this conflict without anguish.

Focusing on one elite family during the Second Empire can supply some specificity to the general, ideal pattern painted by Freyre. The structure and dynamics of Prado family life in the period emerge with sufficient detail that they can be tested against the patriarchal model. Prado family life was also an important factor underlying the cultural, economic, and political experiences and contributions of family members.

After a brief characterization of the Prado parentela and extended family, we narrow our focus to relationships within the nuclear family. For while the parentela and extended family may have been the most important economic and political units, it was in the nuclear family that personalities were formed, socialization occurred, and rebellions burst forth.

Parentela and Extended Family

The Prado parentela's precise dimensions are difficult to define. The genealogist Frederico de Barros Brotero estimated that three-quarters of the thousands of persons listed in his nearly seven-hundred-page study of the Jordão "family" descended from the Prado progenitor, Antônio da Silva do Prado.[2] Directly and collaterally, the Prados were thus related to a host of elite families, including, but not limited to, the Camargos, the Pereira Mendeses, the Morais Lemes, the Queiros Teleses, the Pereira de Queiroses, the Pachecos, the Fonsecas, the Pacheco e Silvas, and the Pacheco Jordãos. Each of these was related to other families, so that in theory the Prado parentela extended almost without limit within the province of São Paulo and beyond. To the Brazilian saying "God is a Brazilian" should be added the corollary "Adam and Eve were Brazilians too."

In practice, however, the "effective" parentela was much smaller. Some of its families, such as the Camargos and the Morais Lemes, served to link the parentela to the supposed glories of the colonial past, but they were in evident decline in the nineteenth century. The pragmatic, future-oriented Prados showed little interest in such historical claims.[3] More significant, and constituting the "effective" parentela, were those families who joined the Prados in common economic and political tasks, who enjoyed status based on contemporary achievement, and who accorded each other the resulting recognition: the Monteiro de Barroses, the Jordãos, the Chaveses, the Pachecos, the Queiros Teleses, the Sousa Queiroses, the Costa Pintos, and the Costa Carvalhos. The parentela was not monolithic: only some of its families and only a few individuals in those families played important roles in Prado family history.

The same was true of the Prado-surname extended family.[4] The fourth generation of the extended family consisted of thirty members in five nuclear groups. All were direct descendants of Ana Vicência Rodrigues de Almeida and her two husbands, the brothers Antônio Prado (d. 1793) and Eleutério Prado (d. 1849). Common descent was, of course, the primary condition of family identity, a situation neatly resolved by the endogamous second marriage of Ana Vicência, which prevented the development of two potentially rival branches.

Marriage was the second condition of family identity. Prado elders, who continued to control marriage throughout the Second Empire, had three choices in deciding such alliances: marriage within the existing parentela, marriage within the extended family, or marriage to nonrelatives. Of twenty-two fourth-generation nuptials that occurred roughly in the middle third of the nineteenth century, six were between Prados and non-Prado cousins (that is, within the existing parentela), five were with cousins in the Prado-surname extended family (both parties bearing the Prado name), and eleven were with nonrelatives. Half the unions, then, were with close relatives, which indicates the importance still placed on maintaining already-established family bonds. The most important of the intrafamily marriages was that of Martinho Prado and his niece Veridiana, which gave rise to the most successful of fourth- and fifth-generation Prados. Broadly speaking, in the fourth generation the Prados harbored their resources by relying on endogamous marriage half the time; many, perhaps almost all, of the marriages were rationally arranged with economic and political considerations taking precedence over romantic love.

While endogamous marriage provided for continuity, exogamous marriage revitalized and restructured the extended family. In the fourth Prado generation, eleven exogamous alliances were arranged. One of these was of special importance, the marriage of the fourth Antônio Prado (1840–1929) to Maria Catarina da Costa Pinto, the oldest daughter of Antônio da Costa Pinto e Silva, an important imperial politician.[5] The Prados' political position was further buttressed by the marriage of Ana Blandina Prado to Antônio Pereira Pinto Júnior, son of another prominent politician.[6] The other exogamous marriages of the fourth generation had little broad impact on the family's fortunes.

In addition to common descent and marriage, the godparent (*compadrío*) system reinforced and extended family ties. *Compadres* could be chosen at birth, baptism, and marriage and were more important for the bonds formed between the participating adults than for those between godparent and godchild. From partial evidence, it appears that in the mid-nineteenth century the Prados used the compadrío system much as they did marriage: first to consolidate existing bonds and only secondarily to create new ties and mutual obligations. Of sixteen godparents (*padrinhos*) chosen for the children of Martinho and Veridiana Prado, thirteen were selected from the extended family, one was a religious entity, and only two were from outside the family.[7] One of the two "outside" godparents, however, was the highly influential viscount (later marquis) of Monte Alegre, José da Costa Carvalho, who had been one of Brazil's three regents from 1831 to 1835 during the minority of Dom Pedro II.[8] In another case, padrinhos were chosen to link the Paulista Prados to an obscure family branch from Rio Grande do Sul, Brazil's southernmost province.[9]

The Prado parentela and extended family fluctuated with the rhythms of birth, baptism, marriage, and death, and they were internally differentiated human groups. Several of the many family branches either never emerged from obscurity or lapsed back into it during the nineteenth century. They were ignored for marriage by the clan's more successful branches. In one extended family there were many nuclear families of unequal status, and the bonds of family often proved weaker than the ties of wealth, talent, class, and even race. Of all the Prados, one branch—the baron of Iguape to Martinho and Veridiana Prado to Antônio Prado and Martinico Prado progression—emerged as spectacularly successful on the regional scene and to a lesser, but still significant, extent on the national stage. It is in this branch that the complex nature of a nuclear component of an elite Brazilian family can be examined.

The Nuclear Family of Martinho and Veridiana Prado, 1840–68

The rise to prominence of the main branch of the Prado family during the Second Empire reflected developments in Brazilian society at large. During the years 1840 to 1868, when the Brazilian Empire was itself consolidated, the children of Martinho and Veridiana were born and the oldest of them matured. Later, during the years 1869 to 1889, significant fractures appeared in the family's life, divisions which were in part causally related to the schisms which overtook the Empire itself after 1870.

In July 1838 the third Antônio Prado and future baron of Iguape wrote to his brother-in-law, José Manuel da Fonseca, concerning what was to be the most important marriage in the family's history. In rather imperious style he informed Fonseca that "on the 24th day of June I made Veridiana marry Martinho and they are very happy and this ought to extend to all our people."[10] The nuptials of uncle and niece took place at the bishop of Cuiabá's residence on the Rua da Cadeia in Rio de Janeiro, with the bishop himself presiding.[11]

As a youth, Martinho Prado (1811–91) lived in the shadow of his older half-brother and cousin, Antônio. When Martinho was five, Antônio had made his first fortune in far-off Bahia; by the time Martinho was eight, his half-brother was mixing in pre-independence politics and holding important posts in São Paulo city's government; and when Martinho was eleven, his brother-cousin—who probably seemed more like an uncle—was playing host to the Emperor Dom Pedro I during the early days of Brazilian independence. A family story suggests the nature of the brothers' relationship. While Martinho was still a young man he would help prepare Antônio's house for the older brother's parties. Although Martinho enjoyed parties himself, he would withdraw before the guests arrived, because he lacked the money for proper clothes and apparently would not ask his successful brother for a handout.[12] The Prado values of pride and self-reliance were evidently ingrained at an early age. One wonders, however, how Martinho felt about the fact that after he married his brother's daughter, he was kept financially solvent for some years by her large dowry, the fruit of Antônio's labors.

Veridiana was born in 1825 at her father's house on the Praça do Patriarca in São Paulo city. Little is known of her childhood. At a tender age she was received at court in Rio de Janeiro by Dom Pedro I's mistress, the marquise of Santos. With her brother, Veríssimo, she received lessons from the engineer Daniel Pedro Müller, an educational experience surpassing that of most elite girls of the era.[13] When Veridiana married her uncle Martinho she was thirteen, not an unusual age or marital affiliation for the time. Fourteen years younger than her husband, she was only fifteen years older than her eldest son. Veridiana thus stood between two generations. Her youth and limited experience would lead her to attend her children's classes, ostensibly to "inspect" them but really to remedy the deficiencies of her own education.[14]

Martinho Prado, following the paternal example, chose the life of a fazendeiro, just as his half-brother Antônio had followed his father in pursuing a career as urban merchant-financier. Martinho and Veridiana spent the first decade of their married life at the fazenda Campo Alto in Mogi-Mirim, some 150 miles northwest of the provincial capital. They traveled to the city by oxcart and horse only when Veridiana was to give birth. The first such trip was in early 1840, when their first son, the fourth Antônio Prado, was born "exactly at noon" on 25 February, as Martinho noted with characteristic precision in his diary. In 1842 a daughter named Veridiana was born, but she survived only six weeks. In 1843 a second son, Martinho Prado Júnior (1843–1906; hereafter referred to as "Martinico" to distinguish him from his father) arrived. Ana Blandina, the couple's third surviving offspring, was born in November 1844, "during the trip with the family from the plantation to the city in a place known as the Ribeirão do [Ruim?] in a cabin belonging to José Barboza two leagues distant from the plantation." Veridiana's fifth child in six years, a daughter also named Veridiana, was born in 1846. In March of 1847 Veridiana suffered a premature birth while traveling again to São Paulo, and in that same unhappy year, young Veridiana died at the age of eighteen months.[15]

A photograph of Veridiana at this time showed her to be a "girl of tired, melancholy, and perhaps a little romantic aspect. She was not pretty, but had finely-traced features, delicate hands, a fair complexion, and black hair."[16] If she appeared tired and melancholy, no wonder, for by 1847, at the age of twenty-two, she had borne five children, had suffered one miscarriage, and had seen two of her daughters, both her namesakes, die in infancy. In 1848 Martinho bought a house in São Paulo city, where the last three children were born: Anézia (1850–1917), Antônio Caio (1853–89, hereafter referred to as "Caio"), and Eduardo (1860–1901). A full twenty years lay between the oldest and youngest children. When Eduardo was a baby, his oldest siblings were beginning their adult lives.

Martinho's and Veridiana's early relationship and their treatment of their children evidently differed little from the norm of such family patterns in mid-nineteenth-century São Paulo. Martinho, fourteen years older than his bride and a graduate (*bacharel*) of the São Paulo Law School, had the age and experience to dominate the marriage for many years. He was the main source of parental discipline, which, if it followed the usual patterns for the Prados' time, place, and class, took the form of stern example, moralizing, and, when necessary, scolding, shaming, and humiliation, rather than harsh corporal punishment.[17] The first decade at Campo Alto was economically difficult for Martinho, and the habits of independence, hard physical labor, and financial economy he learned then were passed on to his older sons, Antônio and Martinico. Martinho was the boys' earliest model, and he introduced them gradually to the duties of coffee-fazenda management, later acting as their senior partner. To Veridiana was left the religious and moral training of the children and the daughters' domestic training. The younger sons, Caio and Eduardo, were reared more in an urban setting than their older brothers, and their lives were shaped much more by urban and maternal influences than by rural, paternal forces.

The Prado children were also influenced by members of the extended family: grandparents, aunts and uncles, godparents, and cousins. Of these, the most important was their uncle-grandfather, the third Antônio Prado, who maintained a continuing influence on the family. From 1840 to his death in 1875, the third Antônio kept his active role in São Paulo's growth. Before and after Pedro II's elevation to the Brazilian throne in 1840, separatist revolts broke out throughout the country. In 1842 such a rebellion occurred in São Paulo. Antônio, who had been appointed provincial vice-president the previous year, became an important loyalist leader, selecting military chiefs who took command in rebellious areas.[18] As in the independence crisis, Antônio had chosen the victorious side, since Dom Pedro II and his military chieftain, the duke of Caxias, defeated separatist rebellions and reconfirmed centralized monarchy in Brazil. For his support of Dom Pedro, the third Antônio Prado received his title, baron of Iguape, in 1848; he was the only Prado ever to be so honored. In 1850 the baron became head of the new Bank of Brazil branch opened in São Paulo. He served as well for twenty-nine years as trustee of the Santa Casa de Misericórdia in São Paulo and in other charitable posts.[19] In the late 1860s the baron provided money for a theater company in São Paulo directed by the northern "poet of the slaves," Antônio de Castro Alves, demonstrating the concern for the city's cultural tone that marked the lives of many of his descendants.[20]

What sort of man was the baron of Iguape? A family anecdote reveals touches of aggressiveness, pride, irony, and eccentricity, traits not unknown in other Prados:

> The Baron was a curious man. Once a rumor was going around in São Paulo that the Baron was "broke." Finding out about it, he became extremely angry and as fast as possible ordered all his tremendous fortune in cash to be piled up on the sidewalk in front of his house on the Praça do Patriarca. Everyone who walked by asked the black man standing there fanning that fabulous quantity of money there in the street, "What's going on?" And the black responded, "The Baron wants his money to take a little air because it's getting all stuck together."[21]

While this vignette suggests the image of a whimsical, money-driven capitalist, another bit of evidence shows that the baron of Iguape could be moved deeply; the sight of a woman and her children deserted by their husband and father prompted him to write, "I have much pain for the little ones who will suffer a good deal." Like most Brazilians, the baron regarded his home as the ultimate sanctuary; he complained bitterly when a certain Dr. Balduino, accompanied by three sons and five slaves, arrived in São Paulo and "without my offering it to him, mixed himself into my house."[22] After his wife died in 1868, the baron withdrew from active social life but developed the habit of waiting for friends to pass by so that he could invite them to dinner. When he died at the age of eighty-seven in 1875, he left not only the fruits of a productive lifetime of economic and political endeavor, but an example of Christian humility for the family: his will specified a simple ceremony at night, with his casket to be borne by six poor men.[23]

The baron's family role illustrates the dominance of older brothers in traditional Brazil. At least in the surviving documents, it is the baron and not Martinho Prado who appears as the chief male influence in the lives of Veridiana and her children. The older brother provided the titled "lineage" so necessary in legitimizing the status of elite families. The baron was godfather to three of Martinho's and Veridiana's children and took an active interest in all of them, especially in the oldest, his namesake, Antônio. In 1851, for example, he recommended that eleven-year-old Antônio "take some medicine since I notice that he seems all stirred up."[24] The same letter shows that—far from being the fearsome, remote patriarch of Brazilian tradition—the baron was a tolerant grandfather: he admitted to missing eight-year-old Martinico's tricks "and even the noise he makes when he comes home from school." In 1852, when Veridiana had taken Antônio away to preparatory school at the Colégio Dom Pedro II in Rio de Janeiro, the baron wrote her of the remaining children left in his care: the baroness was overseeing their lessons, two-year-old "Nezinha" (Anézia) was "more and more elegant," eight-year-old "Chuchuta" (Ana Blandina) no longer cried at school, and rambunctious, fun-loving Martinico had settled down to his studies.[25] While Veridiana was away in Rio and Martinho was busy at the remote Campo Alto fazenda, the baron, with young Martinico at his side, saw to the redecoration of their city house. Meanwhile, Veridiana had taken sick—throughout her life she was chided by the family for neglecting her health—and the baron appealed to her on the basis of maternal responsibility to take better care of herself: "You ought to be careful, life is valuable, even more so for one who has 4 children of tender age. If those who are already grown need a father and a mother, your own need them even more. You should have a good diet and regular habits, because, while young, with this little sacrifice, you should regain your health."[26] Accompanying this advice was a further report on the children. The baron admitted to scolding Ana Blandina "more than is necessary"; Anézia was "a little fat, a little naughty," and "inseparable" from the baroness. The close relationship of the Prado offspring with their grandparents continued throughout their childhood.[27]

The Prado sons' entry into the São Paulo Law School was the first major challenge to the dominance of family tradition in their lives. The law students lived in boarding houses called republics, at a time when the word *republic* challenged the very political and social ethos of imperial Brazil. Inside the "republics" conversations questioning customary morality occurred, such as this one between a modernist and a traditionalist:

—To love, at the age of twenty, is to commit an act of wisdom.

—Yes, I don't doubt it, as long as it is done out of good motives.

—And what are these good motives?

—Not to change the old moral code, which is the constitution of a family, marriage.

—Well, now! You're very bourgeois. I am for the modern code and only would accept marriage Japanese-style.[28]

Most of the Prados, it should be added, would have voiced the traditionalist position in such dialogues, but the mere exposure to such points of view, combined with the normal rebelliousness of young adulthood then as now, helped separate Prado young men from their elders' traditional views.

More fundamental was the psychic trauma and generational friction resulting from prolonged absence from home. When Antônio Prado made his post–law school European tour in the early 1860s, he suffered enormous anxiety at the sudden loss of family contact. In his first letter home, he asked his mother for news of "all my brothers and sisters, of each one of them, how Martinico is doing with politics, Chuchuta with the piano, Nezinha with singing, Niquinho [Antônio Caio] with his teacher, and if Eduardo has grown and still speaks of me."[29] Six weeks with no news of home left Antônio "desperate with uncertainty," and worse yet, when Veridiana did write, she questioned both his alleged lack of patriotism and his personal behavior. Antônio wrote an impassioned reply attempting to restore the strained relations resulting from the first major separation of mother and son: "Ah!, my mother, how your words have wounded me! And with what injustice were they spoken. Insistently I ask you to write me in detail about this, so that I may know what I ought to answer: I can hardly see through such mystery."[30]

With Martinico Prado, generational conflict was more pronounced and prolonged. Upon entering the law school in his late teens, he began to advocate "revolutionary" causes. In 1865, when many of his peers were desperately seeking to avoid military service, Martinico went on a hunger strike to force his parents to allow him to volunteer for the Paraguayan War. His rebellion, however, did not aim at disrupting family ties. On his way to an ultimately disillusioning experience in Paraguay, Martinico wrote a curiously romantic letter explaining that what he really wanted to conquer was not so much the Paraguayans but "the pleasure of the family."[31]

By the late 1860s Martinho's and Veridiana's older children were approaching marital age. In 1866 Martinho received an intermediary's marriage proposal on behalf of Elias Pacheco e Chaves, asking sixteen-year-old Anézia's hand in marriage. Martinho's reply illustrates well the considerations involved:

> I am convinced of the excellent qualities of kinsman Elias, not only from my personal knowledge of him, but from hearing much talk of him, *principally from my children.* . . . However, as [Anézia] is still very young and since I do not wish that my daughter marry without completing her little education, I must first say no, with thanks, but will later say yes. Therefore, only with some more time, and *in accordance with her wishes*, can what you propose to me be realized.[32]

No patriarchal writ this. The children's participation in the decision, the concern for Anézia's personal well-being, and the emphasis on her consent to the match all illustrate the extent to which patriarchal prerogatives had declined and "modern" ideas about marriage had grown in the Prado family. Martinho was exercising the traditional paternal role, but not in the traditional absolute style.

The letters of Anézia's younger brother, Caio, provide further glimpses of the family's life in the late 1860s. Caio—more the product of the city than of the fazenda that molded his older brothers, Antônio and Martinico—revealed his preference for city life in a letter written in December 1867. Commenting on the two-month stay of his father and his brother Antônio at the family's fazendas, Caio wrote that for "the happier spirit" the time spent "in those backlands, in the greatest monotony possible," should be more than enough. Caio reported as well that Martinico—back from Paraguay before the conclusion of the war—was avidly courting fourteen-year-old Albertina Morais Pinto, a girl of Caio's own age: "He goes to Dona Francisca's [Albertina's mother's] house at 4 in the afternoon and returns at eleven. Jesus! . . . How does D. Francisca stomach the boredom of Martinico for *seven hours!*"[33] Quite obviously, romantic love *did* have something to do with this particular Prado liaison, and, equally as plainly, young Caio felt little awe for his older brother; both situations indicate further the erosion of patriarchalism in the Prado family. At any rate, Dona Francisca's ordeal of Martinico's seven-hour visits soon ended. On 22 January 1868 Martinico and Albertina were wed in a house overlooking the Anhangabaú ravine in São Paulo city.[34]

Five weeks later, the family pundit, Caio, had more important news, the impending marriage of his oldest brother, Antônio, to Maria Catarina, eldest daughter of the imperial political chieftain Antônio da Costa Pinto e Silva. During his studies in Rio de Janeiro, young Antônio Prado had resided with Costa Pinto, who later became his political mentor. Writing of the upcoming marriage, Caio suggested that Martinho and Veridiana sometimes disagreed over such matters; he emphasized that the wedding had been arranged "with the approval of my mother *as well as* my father." Noting that Antônio was going off to the interior for another twenty days before the wedding, Caio advised his older brother to take along *Don Quixote* "because that book will make him remember his Dulcinea and . . . will make his melancholy hours more sweet." As he had with Martinico and Albertina, Caio amused himself pitilessly at the expense of Antônio and Maria Catarina and left this frank portrait of the bride-to-be: "not pretty, but pleasant and nice."[35] The marriage took place later the same year. Shortly thereafter, Anézia Prado and Elias Chaves were also wed. In Elias the Prados gained a good friend, a political ally, and an energetic business partner.

The Family Divides, 1868–89

With the changing rhythms of the life cycle, families alter slowly but constantly in structure and function, and occasionally experience sharper permutations. The marriages of Martinho and Veridiana Prado's children, Antônio, Martinico, and Anézia, began changes in the most significant family branch. Though close relations continued to be the rule, the young Prados' establishment of separate households sometimes caused a loss of contact and even conflict between them and their parents. Anézia Prado Chaves was by 1871 the mother of two daughters: "Eponina talks a lot and is very mischievous [and] Anezita is already weaned from the breast, very fat, strong, and happy." When Anézia wrote to her mother, however, it was not primarily to report on the children. She had not had news of Veridiana for a long time and wrote "to find out how you are and if you are mad at us."[36]

More fundamental problems were in the offing. In 1875 the baron of Iguape died, and though his memory continued to provide a measure of family unity, the family also suffered the loss of some of the coherence that the baron had provided during five decades of carefully nurturing the family's destiny. Shortly after his death a significant fracture appeared in the edifice he had so carefully constructed. The occasion was the marriage of Ana Blandina, who after her thirtieth year was still without a husband, very likely because Martinho and Veridiana could not agree on a suitable match. In 1877, perhaps in some desperation (even in their late teens, unmarried women were pitied as old maids[37]), Veridiana urged that her eldest daughter marry Antônio Pereira Pinto Júnior, son of a notable politician.[38] Martinho Prado was unalterably opposed to this match for now-unknown reasons, a situation complicated by a fight that had occurred the previous year between his son Antônio and young Pereira Pinto in the São José Theater.[39] Significantly, and as an indication that male dominance was no absolute in the Prado family, the marriage was completed in accord with Veridiana's wishes. On the pretext of this disagreement (one suspects more fundamental discord), Martinho and Veridiana separated, never to live together again. At the time, the separation of husband and wife in an elite family was a most unusual event, strongly reproved by social custom, a public confession of intense, irreconcilable differences.

At this point the family entered a quasi-matriarchal phase. Freed of the most stringent of marital bonds, Veridiana was reborn in the sixth decade of her life. For the next thirty years she exercised a strong, independent, and sometimes unwanted influence on her children and their families. She and not Martinho retained the family residence in São Paulo, and in 1878 she purchased land in her own name on the Rua Santa Cecília (now Rua Dona Veridiana) in São Paulo city.[40] On this plot in 1884 she built a magnificent palace which was the material expression of her new-found independence and which became a primary focal point of both Prado family life and Paulista soirée society.

Veridiana's primary family preoccupation after her separation from Martinho was to safeguard the future of her unmarried sons, Caio and Eduardo. When Eduardo was still a law student in São Paulo in the late 1870s, Veridiana made him promise to marry a young cousin, Carolina Prado, who had become Veridiana's protégé. Eduardo agreed reluctantly on the condition that he be allowed first to see the world. For the next decade he traveled widely, resisting maternal authority, while Carolina bided her time in a convent. A letter written by Veridiana to Eduardo during his globetrotting days is worth quoting at length for the light it casts on the nuances of the mother-son relationship:

My Dear Son,

I received your letter of August 1 [1882]. What I experienced on receiving it, I could not say and you would little understand. I had the letter in my hand for more than a quarter of an hour with neither the spirit nor the courage to open it. Praise be to God that I touched your heart enough that you would write to me after 5 months of inexplicable silence. Complaints and re-criminations would be useless, and I do not want to make them. Like the prodigal son, whose touching parable I just finished reading at this moment, come back repentant, and like him you will be received with open arms. . . .

Time and, even more, displeasures have spent my life, and I ask God to preserve my life since it would be very sad for me to die without seeing and embracing you. There is *someone* [Carolina] whom, even more than me, you have offended and who has generously been my devoted daughter during your cruel absence. If it were not for the correspondence that she and I maintain constantly, writing to each other almost every day, I believe that we could not stand such displeasures. Happily, our religious beliefs and our faith in God being the same, we find in our religion the force and the courage that you lost since you were carried away by companies of impious folk, forgetting shamelessly what you owe to God, to your sad mother, and to yourself.

I will await news of you anxiously, placing, as until now, all my hope in God, Our Lord, and the Holy Virgin, who never fails those who trust in Him [*sic*]. May this letter carry to your heart the peace and tranquility that you so need.

Receive, my much loved son, the blessing of her who is, with devotion and tenderness,

Your mother who much loves you,

Viridiana [*sic*][41]

With its implications of long-distance matricide and cruel irresponsibility toward the godly, this letter was enough to inspire guilt and resentment in any son, especially in an age of more absolute filial duty. Moreover, far from being the sickly, about-to-expire mother she represented herself as here, Veridiana was a vigorous, powerful woman who lived on until 1910, leading a life notable for its cultural, civic, and economic accomplishments.

José Lins do Rego wrote that Eduardo Prado's life was governed by his oedipal relationship to a revolutionary mother.[42] This psychohistorical speculation cannot be proven, but it is clear that Veridiana wanted Eduardo at home and safely married, free from the corrupting influence of "impious folk." These were the traditional goals of the upper-class Brazilian mother, and Veridiana invoked traditional symbols—the prodigal son theme,[43] God, and mother—to attempt to enforce her will on footloose Eduardo, who managed to resist for a decade more.

With Eduardo inaccessible during his travels, Veridiana turned her attention to the brother closest to him in age and temperament, Caio. She arranged his marriage to Maria Sophia Rudge, the Brazilian-born descendant of sturdy English merchant-family stock.[44] To withdraw Caio from the "dispersive and bohemian life he carried on in São Paulo," Veridiana next arranged his appointments as president of the far-off provinces of Alagôas and Ceará, a course made possible through the influence of Veridiana's oldest son, Antônio, who by the mid-1880s was imperial minister of agriculture, commerce, and public works.[45] Eduardo's wanderlust was harder to tame, though Veridiana did succeed in 1892 in steering him into the long-delayed marriage with Carolina.

In the meantime, Veridiana's older sons, Antônio and Martinico, were presiding over their own families. Antônio and his wife, Maria Catarina, had eight children, born between the years 1869 and 1887.[46] During these years the fourth Antônio Prado became a leading coffee planter and Conservative party leader with a national and international reputation. He tried to implant the moral traits that had contributed to his success—hard work, love of the land, up-rightness, and steadfastness—in his children. One of his younger sons, Luíz, remembered his father as a hard, severe father, a man of strong principles.[47] Maria Catarina was a loving wife and mother, but evidently a rather dependent, conventional, and anxiety-prone woman as her letters to her oldest son, Paulo, from the imperial court in the mid-1880s attest.

Maria Catarina was no stranger to life at Rio de Janeiro and Petrópolis; her father, Antônio Costa Pinto e Silva, had long enjoyed great prestige in imperial circles. Nonetheless, she seems to have felt strangely alienated returning to the court as the wife of a young but powerful Paulista political leader. Once, while walking with her children in Petrópolis, the summer residence of the court, she met the sixty-year-old Emperor Dom Pedro II, who spoke pleasantly to her, asked after her husband, and played with the children. Perhaps because of some political feud between Antônio and the emperor, [48] Maria was "very annoyed" with the encounter and waited for the moment when she could "flee" from the apparently well-meaning monarch. Soon thereafter, when she went to pay her respects to the Empress Teresa Cristina, Maria Catarina was filled "with fear of committing some yokelism [*caipirada*]," though she acquitted herself well enough. Her behavior also reflected dependency on her husband. During his absences she felt herself to be in "complete isolation," despite the availability of family, friends, and servants. Maria Catarina was often "very bored" but refused to join the Rio de Janeiro elite's night life, though friends urged her to do so, and would go out, as she wrote her son, only "when your father can." The children, meanwhile, enjoyed themselves in Rio and Petrópolis at costume parties, dances, and recitals. When a governess was arranged for them, Maria Catarina was much relieved: "The girls will start their lessons today and I am peaceful, without having to scold them."[49]

When Antônio was able to take time out from business and politics during the hectic 1880s—when the end of slavery and the monarchy itself were inexorably approaching—he made a handsome sight strolling with his daughters in the bright sunlight of Petrópolis. A young student of the era described Antônio as "a tall gentleman, dressed elegantly but with notable simplicity, [who] wore a full, very black beard cut in the King of Spades style like the emperor and almost all the men of the time." Antônio's daughters had striking rosy-tan complexions, a reflection of their father's belief that a suntanned skin, the product of outdoor life, was something to be proud of.[50] In such small but important details, the Prados managed to distinguish themselves by flouting the prevalent mores, which held that a woman's pallor reflected her proper isolation from the outside world. Elitist seclusion of women was slowly coming to an end in late-nineteenth-century Brazil, and the Prados were in the vanguard of this movement, as of many others.

Martinico and Albertina Prado raised their twelve children[51] without contact with the lofty circles of the court. Like Antônio's offspring, Martinico's dozen grew up in an atmosphere shaped by their father's dynamic career. The difference was that by the 1880s, when Antônio, the first son, was a Conservative party minister of state, Martinico, the second son, was a Republican, devoted to ending the Brazilian monarchy and, in some respects, to reforming social and cultural traditions.

Though Martinico has been uncritically romanticized as "the perfect figure of the old Paulista patriarch,"[52] this image was far from the truth. From the memoirs of Ina von Binzer, the German governess who for a short while tutored his children, it is clear that Martinico presided over a wild, woolly, and willful clan that bore little resemblance to the disciplined, docile families supposedly typical of traditional, patriarchal Brazil. In 1882 Martinico personally came all the way from São Paulo to Rio to hire the governess. Ina later found out why he was willing to go to such lengths: because Martinico's children were reputed to be the "worst brought up" in all São Paulo, their father was unable to arrange a governess there.[53]

Ina was soon aware that her new charges were "perfect examples of rebellion"; only the oldest, Lavínia, showed the "adorable docility" dear to Ina's Germanic heart. The classroom in Martinico's home was a battlefield for ten-year-old Caio (not to be confused with his uncle, Antônio Caio) and his brother, nine-year-old Plínio: "If one of them gives a wrong answer, the other butts in, energetically correcting him, upon which the first reacts faster than lightning with blows from his ruler, and thus a serious fight starts, and not simply a quarrel which would be easy to pacify if the discord were not constant between the two brothers."[54]

Caio and Plínio inherited their combativeness from their father, an emotional man in public and private whose own childhood and adolescence were marked by a truculent, rebellious spirit. Even the names of Martinico's children had been carefully chosen as part of his "profession of political faith," as Ina von Binzer noted: "The oldest boy is called Caius Gracchus, [and his brother] Plinius, according to what Lavinia told me, would have been called Tiberius, but he did not receive that name because it is very common among the blacks."[55] Presumably because of Martinico's commitment to republicanism, in his house the older forms of addressing family elders, such as *Vossa Mercê* ("Your Worship") had been replaced by the modern, but not yet commonly accepted, forms, *o Senhor* and *a Senhora* (the formal "you"). On occasion even the informal *papai* and *mamãe*—in the 1880s the ultramodern "daddy" and "mommy"— were used.[56]

To Ina there seemed at first to be no limits to Martinico's and Albertina's permissiveness. Albertina, according to the governess, spent most of her time primping; she engaged in no other obvious activity and was oblivious to the children's tumult. Caio and Plínio rode their imported bicycles through the house with gay abandon and even took their meals at the family table astride them, all to their parents' apparent unconcern. The limit of republican permissiveness in child-rearing was reached, however, when the boys threw São João's Day firecrackers under a mule-drawn city trolley on São Paulo's main street, causing one creature to fall and break its leg. In anger over this public display of indiscipline, Martinico delivered his sons to the Catholic padres, forcing Ina von Binzer to seek employment elsewhere.[57]

As in their political loyalties, in short, Antônio and Martinico Prado, brothers separated by only three years in age, presented sharp contrasts in their child-rearing practices. This was one dimension of the emergent schism of the leading Prado line into rival "orthodox" and "radical" branches. Even Dona Veridiana was unable to check this trend. In 1887, during the Emperor Dom Pedro II's last visit to São Paulo, she assembled her grandchildren at Vila Maria, her palatial residence, to welcome the monarch. As the emperor strolled through this youthful review, six-year-old Martinho Prado Neto hit him in the face with a ball of rose petals. Dom Pedro stopped, placed his hand on the boy's head, and asked, "This one, who is he?" "Martinico's son," Veridiana replied. Smiling (so one version of the story goes), the emperor intoned, "So little and already with revolutionary instincts like his father."[58]

As her older children grew up during the 1880s (Eduardo being a bit of unfinished business), Veridiana left them more and more on their own, transferring her motherly concern to other relatives and to servants. One of the latter was a Botucudo Indian, Joaquim, "of somber disposition and very sensitive to any observations about his perforated lip," who served Veridiana as a waiter until his death in 1894.[59] Another was Veridiana's living companion, Maria das Dôres, a woman of apparently humble origins who occupied a special place in her affections. Veridiana named her palace, Vila Maria, after her, arranged a good marriage for her with a relative, Antônio Pacheco, and provided for her richly in her final testament.

That document, written in 1888, is an excellent guide to Veridiana's character and to those who stood high in her esteem. Under Brazilian law, two-thirds of the estate was assigned to her estranged husband and to her children; she was free to dispose of the remaining third (the legal *terça*) as she wished. In the terça were bequests of seventy-eight *contos* ($39,780) to religious groups and charities; seventy-eight and a half contos to various female relatives, including thirty contos to Eduardo's fiancée, Carolina Prado, who was still in the convent; and twenty-eight contos to servants and godchildren, including sixteen contos to her favorite, Maria das Dôres. Most of the bequests were in inalienable stocks and bonds that could not easily be squandered. The grants to female relatives were in several cases—including, significantly, that of Carolina Prado—made exempt from community property claims. Evidently Veridiana wanted to provide her female heirs with some financial independence. Though her death lay some twenty-two years off, she followed her father's example in ordering that her burial be made "without any pomp, [with] a carriage of the second class, and without any invitations." Veridiana added a final note which shows that her social relations were at times strained: "I humbly ask the pardon of all persons whom I may have offended or scandalized and I pardon with all my heart those who have offended or slandered me."[60]

The Second Empire was a classic period for the Prados. In its early decades, from 1840 to the 1860s, the baron of Iguape's political and economic influence was at its height. After 1870 the baron's descendants, particularly the fourth Antônio Prado, extended this power.

Yet the family was not monolithic, nor was there the overweening dominance of elders and of men. Instead, there were important currents of individual rebellion in the actions of Veridiana and of Martinico against traditional family patterns of male and of parental control. This is not so much evidence of an immediate, complete, irreversible shift from traditional to more modern behavior as it is an indication of conflicting, often unresolved forces that affected the family. Veridiana, rebelling against the ascriptive status of Paulista women, attempted also to control her sons' lives in a manner that would have done the classic patriarch proud. Martinico's permissiveness in child-rearing was carried out within certain limits, beyond which he resorted to traditional authority.

Nonetheless, and perhaps most significantly, as the Prado family gained in power and prestige during the Second Empire, it also clearly became less monolithic, less "patriarchal." To a degree, as this chapter shows, the modernization of the family during the Second Empire was reflected in its internal dynamics and sprang from individual desires for greater autonomy. Equally important to the Prado family's development during the Second Empire was the effect of outside cultural, economic, and political forces.

﹥ CHAPTER III ﴿

EUROPE DISCOVERED

The nineteenth century in Brazil was a period of "re-Europeanization," of cultural "reconquest," or of recolonization in which Portuguese domination, which had lasted for three centuries, was replaced by influences from other European nations, especially Great Britain and France.[1] In 1808 the Napoleonic invasion of Iberia forced the Portuguese court to migrate to Rio de Janeiro, an unprecedented event in the history of European colonialism and one that began a new era in Brazil's evolution. From the early 1820s until 1850, the disorders of the independence era and of early nationhood delayed the full manifestation of European cultural influence outside such centers as Rio de Janeiro, Salvador, and Recife. After 1850 European developments began to be felt as well in such then-secondary cities as São Paulo.

In the mid-nineteenth century, elite Brazilians steadily became aware of how much their country lagged behind Britain, France, and Germany.[2] They sought throughout the Second Empire to remedy supposed deficiencies by adopting European ideas, machines, and fashions. European culture—here broadly defined—represented social and political models for the reformer and rebel; capital, technology, and labor for the entrepreneur; advanced schooling for elite sons; Parisian fashion and classical music for their sisters; literary styles for the poet and novelist; and pleasure for the worldly. Pursuit of these and other desiderata implied that elite Brazilians felt a need to step into the modern world, a relatively easy feat for the gifted, favored individual but a difficult task for the nation as a whole, which lacked in 1850 (as for some time to come) the required conditions for modernization.

The role of European culture in the lives of Brazilian diplomats, politicians, entrepreneurs, and writers is an important theme of the period.[3] Single biographies and autobiographies are limited in chronological scope, however, and may represent extremely idiosyncratic experiences. A broader composite picture emerges from an examination of the experiences of a whole family whose members, however individualistic, shared a common social background, and whose collective exposure to Europe was intensive, multifaceted, prolonged, and indicative of the changing cultural relations between Brazil and Europe. The Prado family serves the case well.

The Cultural Discovery: Antônio Prado

Notwithstanding the optimistic appraisals of Saint-Hilaire some thirty years earlier, in 1850 São Paulo city remained considerably more parochial than such centers as Rio de Janeiro, Salvador da Bahia, and Recife.[4] Unlike them, São Paulo was isolated from the sea. Its population, still limited to twenty thousand, had little acquisitive power. Its more sophisticated residents, influenced by a fashionably romantic world view, saw the city as monotonous and boring. Antônio Prado later remembered the São Paulo of his youth as "completely backward; dark, ugly and sad." Some years later, his younger brother Caio wrote to a relative that the city was "very sad" and described the Paulistanos who had given a shabby welcome to a visiting Italian singer as "vinegary."[5]

The potential for a cultural awakening existed, however. A North American missionary, James C. Fletcher, visiting São Paulo in mid-century, felt "a more profound respect" for it than for other South American cities he had seen. Much of the small city's atmosphere came from its law school, established in 1827. It was one of only two such institutions in Brazil, and there were five hundred prelaw and law students at the time of Fletcher's visit. The missionary noted their anticlerical spirit and said that the students recalled those of "the Dane law-school of Harvard University and the students of Heidelberg."[6] Though the collegians were known more for love of mischief and of billiards than for scholarship, the serious of mind, such as Antônio and Martinico Prado, were exposed at the law school to such modern works as Alexis de Tocqueville's *Democracy in America* and Henri Baudrillart's treatises on political economy.[7]

The definitive date for the reawakening of European culture in São Paulo is 1860, in the middle of Antônio Prado's law-school days. In that year, the Casa Garraux, a French bookstore, printshop, and retail outlet for wines, art objects, and modern novelties such as umbrellas, opened its doors in the city.[8] Coffee provided the economic stimulus to the cultural reawakening. During the years 1856 to 1864, for example, Martinho Prado's profits from coffee rose greatly, his status changed from debtor to creditor, and he and Veridiana were able to provide their children with books, foreign tutors, governesses, and dancing masters, as well as an imported piano on which their daughters played classical music.[9]

In mid-1862 Antônio Prado embarked for the European "bath in civilization" which became standard for elite youths after law school.[10] Antônio brought a seriousness of purpose to his travels, as is evident in his criticism of compatriots who merely gave themselves up to Europe's pleasures. His original goal of studying political economy was soon broadened to "visiting the principal cities of Europe, studying . . . their customs, and trying to understand the institutions by which the various nations govern themselves."[11] Taken as a whole, Antônio's letters from Europe in the early 1860s show neither complete acceptance of European civilization nor rejection of all Brazilian values. As he wrote after four months abroad: "Civilized and enlightened Europe offers the foreigner everything that can enchant the imagination and that can clarify the mind, at the same time that it opens to him all the paths of pleasure which often lead to soundless depths."[12] The tension and ambiguity expressed here would deepen as Antônio's familiarity with the varieties of European culture grew.

Antônio's reaction to Europe was governed in the first instance by his family background. He was troubled greatly by his first prolonged absence from home and family and by his isolation as an outsider in Europe. Though joined by a cousin, Eleutério Prado, for part of his travels, Antônio's circle of friends was small and apparently included only one European. Reinforcing his anxiety was his mother's apparent concern that civilized Europe would seduce him away from backwater Brazil. Antônio tried to convince her that Lisbon's theater and actors were no better than Rio de Janeiro's, that Rio's commercial and banking houses were superior to Lisbon's, and that Lisbon's cafes and bookstores were "very ordinary"; that British ignorance of Brazil's independence day and of Brazil itself had not dampened his own patriotism; that Carnival in Versailles did not meet his expectations because he was used to the pre-Lenten festivities as celebrated in Mogi-Mirim in the Paulista interior; that the beauty of the Rhine had been greatly exaggerated by romantic poets; and even that the cathedrals of the Old World were not worth the little chapels of the New.[13] An epic effort, if not an entirely convincing one.

London, where Antônio Prado arrived on 21 August 1862, provided his first contact with the modern technological culture produced by the Industrial Revolution. He judged that the Englishman "is rude and antipathetic on the exterior, but when one cultivates relations with him, one appreciates his qualities and admires his character." By early September, Antônio had visited the London Exposition three or four times. He marveled at the Crystal Palace's beauty without understanding its construction and searched for two days for the Brazilian exhibit, lost in the maze of national displays. "A visit to the Exposition of 1862," he wrote, "is worth five years of study in books." Though his main interest was the "development of industry," a performance of the *William Tell* Overture by an eight-hundred-piece orchestra and the tightrope walking of Blondin ("the same who crossed Niagara Falls") contributed to his awe.[14] Weeks later, Antônio continued to visit the exposition "almost every day" and confessed himself more and more impressed with "its greatness and the greatness of the idea of the confraternization of industry which it represents, and with the varied and stupendous enterprise which only the English could put together." At the exposition, he continued, "one encounters the best and the most perfect in all the branches of industry perfected by men and all the marvels created by the human spirit."[15] Relating what he saw to Brazil, Antônio suggested to his father that Brazil ought to replace the United States, then in the midst of the Civil War, in producing cotton for English mills. Antônio reckoned that Brazil could expect the English government to support this, but direct contact with British manufacturers was also necessary, "because here in England all progress comes from private initiative."[16] The principle of laissez-faire was an important lesson of Antônio's stay in London, one that would deeply mark his future economic and political life.

Leaving the British industrial wonderland, Antônio entered the Parisian world in which he spent most of his two years in Europe. To his surprise, Paris seemed a new, uncompleted city, and he was dismayed at "the inconceivable mud that covers the principal streets."

The Versailles art collection was a welcome contrast: "It seems an incredible thing that one single country could produce so many magnificent things in painting in so short a time." On balance, there was no doubt in Antônio's mind that "this city is the first of the world."[17]

Soon, however, Antônio read a pamphlet on Italian politics by the French anarchist Pierre-Joseph Proudhon which incidentally ridiculed Dom Pedro II, including him in a list of incompetent Latin American leaders. Antônio's response showed the effect of his European surroundings. At first, his patriotism wounded, he intended to respond in the French press. Upon reflection, he decided that "what Proudhon says about our Emperor, when he calls him a figure of fantasy, is the pure truth." Antônio professed "the most complete ignorance" of Brazilian events; but from what he knew, he thought Brazil's politics the "most abject and ridiculous thing that can be imagined," and he bore it "the most complete indifference, if not aversion." A Brazilian friend's prophecy about the impact Europe would have on Antônio seemed to be coming true: "in the first place, the forgetting of our politics in São Paulo, as piddling and ridiculous as it is; second, the very modification of ideas to a more elevated and vaster sphere."[18]

In Paris Antônio attended classes in comparative law, political economy, and modern French literature. In January 1863 he frequented the lectures of St. Mar Girardin[19] on French literature. "Really," he wrote his mother, "one is carried away upon hearing him; for me it is difficult to believe there is a more eloquent man." At the great Parisian balls, held in the Tuileries, the Hôtel de Ville, and the government ministries, Antônio observed the "true world of Paris," the aristocratic world of Napoleon III. An outsider, he lamented that he could attend only the public balls, but even they were grand by Brazilian standards. Antônio missed the family ties required in Paris, because "it is in the society of [the best] families that good customs are learned, those which we ought to introduce into our country"; not to be transmitted were "the customs of the *demi-monde* of Paris, which are those generally carried by our countrymen."[20]

An Italian sojourn soon expanded Antônio Prado's familiarity with the varieties of European culture. Unlike London and Paris—the centers of material progress and high culture—Rome was not an inspiring place to the young Brazilian. To Antônio its meaning was clear: "Rome, which was one day the dominator of the world, . . . is today nothing more than the simple capital of the Roman States, whose existence is defined by vassalage to foreign domination."[21] He sent his parents a dutiful description of Rome's Holy Week. However, back in Paris two months later, when Ernest Renan's unorthodox *Life of Jesus* appeared in the French capital, Antônio confessed that in Rome, "in the midst of the most absurd superstition and fanaticism," he was surprised by his own disbelief and skepticism.[22] He thought of writing on the religious question and announced that "my banner will be 'liberty of conscience, religious liberty, a free Church in a free State, death to the temporal power of the Popes.' "[23]

On his way back from Rome to Paris, Antônio had passed through Switzerland, noting the "almost patriarchal life" of the rural Swiss, whose habits he contrasted with the supposed ways of the Brazilian lower class: "At night, when I passed through a village and saw in each house . . . [a] family which had spent the day at work seated so tranquil and satisfied at its front door, I remembered our *paysands* [*sic*] who spend the night dancing the fandango and the day sleeping, and I deplored our people's indolence compared to the active and at the same time happy life of the people I observed."[24] Like London's private enterprise and technology, Paris's aristocratic high culture, and Rome's religious fanaticism, this vision would haunt Antônio Prado for years as he wrestled with the Brazilian labor problem, eventually becoming a leading promoter of European immigration to Brazil.

The summer of 1863 was a trying time for Antônio. Being separated from family and assimilating his experiences were difficult enough. Moreover, he was greatly disturbed by his brief return to London during the Christie affair, an Anglo-Brazilian crisis which ended in severed diplomatic relations in June. Named for the British ambassador in Rio, the affair began with a cargo theft from a British shipwreck and with the alleged misconduct of British naval officers in Rio and soon escalated to such matters as slavery and the clandestine slave trade in Brazil, which Britain hoped to end.[25] A dramatic reminder of the gap between the two societies, the Christie affair troubled Antônio deeply, committed as he was both to British technological and institutional progress and to Brazilian sovereignty. He applauded Brazilian nationalistic resistance to the British but realistically doubted that the "mantle of patriotism" hastily donned by Brazilian politicians would result in their wearing "the simple uniform of the soldier" against mighty Britain.[26] The Russell-Palmerston ministry's handling of the dispute destroyed for a time Antônio's high regard for England. "I liked London, England, and the English," he wrote home, but "today, after our affair, I am antipathetic to everything English."[27]

Hurriedly leaving London, Antônio went to Scotland, which offered a startling, disturbing counterpart to Switzerland's contented peasantry:

> The traveler in Scotland . . . sees the misery of a large part of its inhabitants, represented by almost naked children and shoeless and disfigured women, in whose looks one sees the traces of hunger and cold. From this point of view there is perhaps no more miserable country in Europe. Meanwhile, alongside this pauperism, . . . colossal fortunes are raised which are based above all on large-property agriculture. It is in Scotland that agriculture has arrived at its highest state of perfection.[28]

The irony of this passage was unintentional, but Antônio Prado, himself a representative of large-property agriculture, had come to see the stark contrasts which "modern" Europe presented and the human suffering engendered by "progress."

The conflict Antônio felt between "civilization" and "backwardness" crystalized in Spain. Madrid's museums and theaters were almost the equal of Paris's, and the Spanish *beau monde* gave little away to that of "the first city of the world." Yet Spain's postal service was unreliable, Spanish railroads were poorly constructed and dangerous, and Spanish hotels were uncomfortable. These contrasts led to a lesson, perhaps the most basic of his travels, which Antônio quickly applied to Brazil:

> I do not want to say that I sympathize with the countries little advanced in civilization, or that I value the civilized ones less. However, I appreciate the countries [like Spain] that know how to conserve their original character in this great transfor-

mation of ideas and of customs which they receive from the more civilized. Unhappily, we [Brazilians] must be counted among those who easily deny their grandfathers' customs, to cover ourselves with the ridicule of a servile imitation of the caprices of Parisian style.[29]

The question thus posed, which would recur in the Prados' thoughts for many decades, was how to progress while preserving valuable Brazilian traditions, how to remain open to foreign influence without being dominated by it.

In his second year in Europe, Antônio turned his experiences inward. In October 1863 he wrote that he had been very ignorant, his mind filled with errors and preconceptions. He vowed to resume formal studies so as not to shame himself back in São Paulo. In November he recommenced his study of political economy, thought of attending a "school of bridges and pavements" in Paris, and considered taking courses in agriculture, "that branch of science so neglected among us." Advising his parents on European schooling for ten-year-old Caio, he recommended Belgium rather than Germany or Paris; the disadvantage of German schools was that they taught "entirely different customs from ours," while in Paris it was necessary that "a young boy have much judgment and much constancy not to lose himself in that city."[30]

By Christmas of 1863, Antônio had sunk into a pessimistic mood. In Europe, it seems, he felt trapped by his heritage:

> Life is like this, the mistake of one day, the illusion of another, deception almost always. Who is to blame? If it were not blasphemy I would say Nature; but no, we ought first to say the forgetting of it. The destiny of man reveals itself almost always from the first phase of his existence; it can be said that infancy is the mirror of the future in which we can see the entire picture of its existence unfolded.[31]

This deterministic fatalism had its roots in Brazilian pessimistic romanticism but was clearly aggravated by Antônio's European experiences. Close upon the ruminations above, he announced his intention to translate Brazilian poetry into French to show Europeans that Brazilians were not "ignorant persons or savages."[32]

The Political Discovery: Martinico Prado

Martinico Prado rebelled in many ways against his older brother's example. He refused Antônio's suggestion to study in Europe, and though he read Antônio's letters from Europe with interest, he chided him for their gallicisms.[33] Departing from the Prados' traditional conservatism, Martinico shocked São Paulo's elite during his law-school days by praising Europe's libertarian and democratic movements as models to be applied in Brazil.[34] In contrast with Antônio's European tour, Martinico chose to volunteer for the Paraguayan War, a significant difference in commitment, both geographical and ideological.

Martinico's first direct contact with Europe came only in 1886, when at forty-three he went to Italy to promote immigration. His early vision of Europe came from books rather than personal experience. His library included the works of the leading nineteenth-century economists, read avidly and annotated extensively.[35] Unfortunately, Martinico left no complex personal statement on European culture like Antônio's letters. What survives, in political speeches, is a morality-play vision of Europe in which, initially, republics were heroes and monarchies villains.

In the early 1870s Martinico used the pen name "Rossel," after a victim of the Paris Commune;[36] Antônio's "true world" of Louis Napoleon and the Parisian aristocracy was clearly not the "true world" of young Martinico. Elected as a Republican to the Provincial Assembly of São Paulo in 1878, Martinico used many European examples to dramatize the need for political reform in Brazil. To show the injustice of monarchies generally and the Brazilian monarchy's special spinelessness, he cited the French Empire's pressure on Brazil to recognize Maximilian's Mexican Empire in 1865.[37] He likened Brazilian politics to George III's unprincipled manipulation of Tories and Whigs in eighteenth-century England.[38] Noting in 1879 that Dom Pedro II had returned from Europe more conservative than ever, Martinico suggested that the emperor go to "uncivilized" China to bring back real reforms.[39] He said that the European republics, France and Switzerland, enjoyed "better conditions" than any of the monarchies, including Britain and Germany, an argument he used to urge adoption of the republican form in Brazil. At the same time, he recognized that Europe was predominantly monarchic, while America, except Brazil and colonial enclaves, was republican. In phrases suggesting his exposure to socialist thought, Martinico pictured Europe in a "constant struggle of capital with labor," in contrast to America "living in the peace, in this well-being, which its climate, the fruitfulness of its soil, and its customs and institutions give it." Adding generational conflict to his rhetoric, he urged America to say to Europe, "Old one, your forces are spent, your advanced age prostrates you, and you cannot fight against young warriors."[40]

In the 1880s, though Martinico continued to cite the French republicans Léon Gambetta and Louis Adolphe Thiers as his heroes, his faith in European political models declined. In 1888, after his first trip to Europe, he referred to it as a place with "principles always at the periphery, force played court to, [and] liberty besieged."[41] Prodded by a hostile fellow provincial deputy, Martinico admitted that even in France and Switzerland "anachronistic principles, incompatible with liberty, dominate," and he told of Swiss authorities ransacking travelers' suitcases to confiscate proscribed books and newspapers. By the late 1880s he saw the New World's inhabitants as the "only free peoples of the world," and urged America to break its ties with the Old World, with São Paulo leading the way in Brazil.[42] Martinico's belief in European republicanism had been eroded in part by developments in the continent's republics, in part by personal experience. Though he was a most effective recruiter of immigrant labor for São Paulo's coffee plantations, Martinico developed little liking for Europe itself. From Paris in 1897, his sister-in-law wrote that "Martinico is very impertinent and abuses the French in a horrible way."[43]

Europe Transplanted: Dona Veridiana's Salon

Gilberto Freyre has suggested that the re-Europeanization of Brazil affected men more strongly than women. While elite men began to look like "English missionaries with moustaches or North American doctors with beards," their women remained "more Oriental, more Asiatic, more rural."[44] Veridiana Prado was an exception to this observation. Her portrait in the Museu Paulista in São Paulo, painted by Carlo de Servi in 1899, shows a woman of self-confident, self-contained power, whose view is fixed directly on the viewer. Veridiana was, in her own way, a rebel who found her cause in transplanting European culture to São Paulo and who used that culture to achieve her own liberation.

Family tradition holds that Veridiana was the first in São Paulo to hire a foreign governess, "Mademoiselle Elizabeth," who came from France in 1854 to tutor her children.[45] As we have seen, until the 1860s Veridiana led the usual restricted life of an elite Paulista woman in a routine that alternated between the city and the family fazenda, Campo Alto in Mogi-Mirim. Antônio's European letters awakened her interest in the wider world and stimulated her restlessness with her own provincial situation; in this case, Europeanization flowed from son to mother. To make her own contact with Europe less vicarious, Veridiana had to free herself of the traditional, dependent role of the Paulista woman. The first step was her separation from her husband in 1877.

In 1884, at the age of fifty-nine, Veridiana made her first European trip. She stayed in Paris with her daughter Ana Blandina, whose diplomat husband had died a few years after their marriage, who continued to maintain a Parisian residence until her death in 1936, and who was named Countess Pereira Pinto by the Holy See for her pious services.[46] From Europe Veridiana brought back plans for a French Renaissance–style mansion, the material expression of her need to bring European culture to São Paulo and an important step symbolizing her newly acquired independence. The palace that she built was described by Princess Isabela, daughter of Pedro II, as having "an extremely beautiful exterior and interior . . . in very good taste" and "lawns worthy of England."[47]

"The *chácara* of Dona Veridiana," as the mansion soon became known, became a major focal point of social and intellectual life in São Paulo. It broke the traditional family-circle isolation of the city's cultural life, introducing salon society patterned on the French model.[48] Among a host of visitors to Veridiana's weekly soirées were the writer Afonso Arinos (who married one of Veridiana's granddaughters), the mulatto ethnologist-historian Teodoro Sampaio, the North American geologist Orville Derby, and the Portuguese writer and close friend of Eça de Queiroz, Ramalho Ortigão. Ortigão saw São Paulo in the 1880s as a center of progress, in contrast to a Rio de Janeiro still retarded by the evil of slavery. His view owed much to the impressions he had of Veridiana and her salon, as he wrote to Eduardo Prado:

> Your mother's house is a jewel, and without looking further you have a very singular type of intelligent woman at hand. What fine ability in the art of being pleasant! What natural perspicacity in the observation of men and of things! What a quantity of precise and just ideas let fall by chance in the most simple and unceremonious conversation! What subtle discernment of certain nuances, and finally, what perfect good taste in the selection of furniture, . . . and of words.[49]

No shy, retiring hostess, Veridiana took a spirited part in the wide-ranging discussions in her salon, adding comments that frequently had a biting edge of irony.[50] Her salon, in addition to encouraging intellectual exchange between Brazilians and foreigners, provided a stimulating milieu for the Prado family itself. Veridiana's son Eduardo and her grandson Paulo, who would achieve their greatest fame as writers who offered critiques of the re-Europeanization of Brazil, were constantly exposed in their youth to the heady intellectual fare at Veridiana's soirées.[51]

Well into her seventies, Veridiana continued to visit Europe with family members. In 1897 Eça de Queiroz wrote his wife that in Paris Veridiana practically commanded him to dine with her daily; the matron of Paulista society obviously was less than overawed by Portugal's leading novelist. "Dona Veridiana," he wrote, "is even more intelligent, pleasant, picturesque, and fine than we imagined, and it was too bad we did not cultivate her with intimacy." When the "immense pack train full of Prados"—as Eça called it—left Paris in September 1897, Eça noted that Veridiana was bathed in tears.[52]

In São Paulo, Veridiana's liberated behavior was viewed by the more staid members of polite society as scandalous. In addition to assuming many of her estranged husband Martinho's business activities after his death in 1891, she actively intervened in the publishing of a monarchist newspaper, *O Comércio de São Paulo*, which her son Eduardo had acquired; sold grapes on the street to benefit the poor; and refused the reclusive role tradition prescribed for widows. She received anonymous letters threatening bodily harm unless she stayed at home; her response was to sally forth on São Paulo's main streets unaccompanied except for her coachman.[53] Yet for all her unprecedented behavior, Veridiana maintained many traditional habits in her daily life. She generally dressed in black, liked to tend her rose garden personally, and favored the simple Luso-Brazilian title "Dona" to the more pretentious, French-inspired "Madame."[54] Like most of her family, Veridiana Prado thus strove to reconcile modern European cultural influence with valid aspects of Brazilian traditions.

The nineteenth-century re-Europeanization affected various regions of Brazil differently. São Paulo, as a young, upwardly mobile, developing society, was less fettered in responding to "modern" and "advanced" ideas and institutions than was Gilberto Freyre's tradition-bound northeast or even (if Ramalho Ortigão was right) the national capital. The "bandeirante myth" of pioneering greatness could be adapted to seeking cultural innovation and "modernity" abroad. In combination with economic and political trends, cultural bandeirismo contributed to a Paulista awareness that pictured its region as increasingly superior and separate from the rest of Brazil. The Prados' experiences of "discovering Europe" demonstrate the complexity and diversity of this process in one elite Paulista family, but those experiences also suggest broader patterns of history underlying the emergence of Brazil's foremost province.[55] At the same time, the Prados' windows on Europe sometimes introduced personal anxiety not easy to confine within traditional, supposedly patriarchal, norms of the submission of youth and of women.

From the beginning of the Prados' involvement in the re-Europeanization of Brazil, with Antônio Prado's two years in Europe in the 1860s, tension existed between their perceptions of European culture and Paulista traditions and realities. Coming from one of Brazil's poorer, more provincial regions, the family looked to Europe for models of progress. At the same time, in Antônio's reactions to the Christie affair, to Scotland's poor, and to Rome's religious "superstition," and in Martinico's disillusionment with European republicanism, it can be seen that Europe exerted not only an inspirational force in the family but a disquieting one as well.

Nor did the family react monolithically to the European experience. Antônio Prado's view of European culture was complex, ambiguous, and deeply personal, marked by an awareness of the contest between "advanced" and "backward" nations. His travels were an important stage in his own coming of age in an era of accelerated, often foreign-induced, and unpredictable social change. Martinico's vision was more stylized, more unequivocal, and, except for his interest in immigration, more narrowly political. The brothers' divergent politics added to their different perceptions of Europe. Yet in Antônio's and Martinico's economic interests they shared a large common ground, in which a certain orientation toward European technology and labor, transplanted in the Prados' interest, was very important. Veridiana's interest in European culture was turned to her special goal of transcending the limits imposed on women by traditional Paulista society.

During the Second Empire, Europe had exerted on the family an influence that was both stimulating and troubling. European cultural patterns were not an absolute "good" to be uncritically transferred whole to Brazil, but a "varied and stupendous enterprise" like the London Exposition, from which appropriate ideas, machines, and fashions could be selected. The mere involvement of the Prados in modern European trends gave them an aura of modernity that enhanced their stature as a leading Paulista family. Cultural prestige was an important base of family power.

⇒ CHAPTER IV ⇐

COFFEE CAPITALISTS

The coffee, sugarcane, bananas, and rice carried from the Old World to the New after 1492 had the inherent capacity to mold entire economies and social systems.[1] Seldom has a single product had greater impact on a region and its inhabitants than has coffee on São Paulo and its people. Coffee was introduced to Brazil in the northern captaincy of Pará in 1723 and by 1774 was being grown in the more suitable climate of Rio de Janeiro. In the 1830s it replaced sugar as Brazil's most important export, which it long remained. From Rio the crop spread southwestward through the Paraíba River valley to São Paulo province. Soil exhaustion eventually drove planters to seek new land to the northwest of São Paulo city, the region called the Paulista "west." There the green bushes found near-ideal growing conditions. Around the town of Campinas, for example, in 1835 nine fazendas produced 808 *arrobas* of coffee; a scant fifteen years later, eighty-nine plantations there yielded 200,000 arrobas.[2] In the period 1850 to 1889, the coffee frontier spread northward from Campinas to virgin purple soils in *municípios* (counties) such as Limeira, Rio Claro, Araraquara, and Ribeirão Prêto, the latter the "El Dorado" of coffee. The growth of the Paulista coffee economy during the Second Empire is summarized in table 3. The increasing proportion of coffee exported from Santos reflects the decline of coffee production in the Paraíba valley, with its main outlet in Rio de Janeiro, and the development of the Paulista west, which had Santos as its port.

Thus, between 1850 and 1889, coffee agriculture in São Paulo expanded greatly, creating the wealth that would transform the province into Brazil's economic dynamo and, through related changes such as immigration, greatly alter Paulista society. The Paulista coffee boom was a shift in the nation's economic center of gravity and a major sea-change in Brazil's economic history. The boom remains a

TABLE 3
São Paulo's Coffee Production and
Exports from Santos, 1849–89

Year	Production (Millions of *arrobas*)	Santos Exports (Millions of *arrobas*)	Santos Exports as Percentage of Total Production
1849–50	1.34	.15	11
1859–60	3.62	1.48	41
1869–70	4.17	n/a	n/a
1870–71	n/a	2.27	55
1879–80	6.59	4.22	64
1889–90	10.68	8.17	76

Sources: Paulo R. Pestana, "A expansão de lavoura cafeeira em São Paulo," 110–14;
São Paulo (Estado) Secretaria de Agricultura, Industria, e Commercio, *O café em São Paulo*, 17–19.

controversial subject. It was achieved at great cost: the destruction of magnificent virgin forests and sometimes lasting ecological calamity; the displacement of subsistence farmers and the usurpation of their lands; violence and slavery; and the initial concentration of land and wealth in few hands. Such problems represented more modern manifestations of deeply rooted Brazilian patterns, historical tendencies which the Prados could influence but not escape as they joined land, labor, and capital to become leading exemplars of the Paulista planter class enriched by the coffee boom.[3]

Land

The leading Prado of the mid-nineteenth century, the baron of Iguape, at first doubted the wisdom of investing heavily in coffee.[4] His sugar trading and tax collecting, however, created the capital necessary to finance family coffee ventures once they appeared less risky. In the meantime, the baron put aside a large dowry for his daughter Veridiana and used his wealth and imperial political ties to gain appointment in the early 1850s as first director and principal stockholder of the São Paulo branch of the Bank of Brazil. He and other Prados held 226 shares of the 1,000 initially issued by the bank; related families held an additional 256 shares, so that in 1858 nearly half of the bank's stock was held by the Prado parentela.[5] The bank initially served a severely limited clientele of "coffee barons," as a Prado family tradition illustrates: "When the directors would meet, one would say to another: 'You, Baron Such-and-so, do you need money?' And Baron Such-and-so would always respond: 'No.' The directors would close the meeting without deciding anything further, because they did not lend money to outsiders."[6] While this anecdote represents a more complacent, tradition-bound attitude than one might expect from the profit-minded Paulista capitalists, there is little question that the baron of Iguape, an insider, was well placed to provide the capital needed by the Prados, a crucial factor in their rise to economic power.

The actual task of pioneering the family's coffee fazendas fell to the baron's half-brother, Martinho Prado. Fortunately for Martinho, Veridiana brought a large dowry of sixteen contos ($9,120) to their marriage.[7] In 1839, using this dowry, the newly wed Martinho and Veridiana, in partnership with Joaquim Prado, purchased a 3,800-*alqueire* (22,800-acre) sugar fazenda, Campo Alto, in the district of Mogi-Mirim. The partnership contract specified that difficulties would be resolved by "whomever of our relatives on whom we shall agree." The extended family acted as guarantor for one of its nuclear components. In 1849 the partnership was dissolved, and Joaquim sold his share to Martinho and Veridiana for 41:500$00 ($21,580).[8]

Campo Alto was probably converted from sugar to coffee between the dissolution of the partnership in 1849 and the mid-1850s, when it began to show clear profits. The years 1856 to 1864 consolidated the transition to profitability. Income from the fazenda rose rapidly but irregularly from 1856 to 1859, declined and stabilized for four years, and then rebounded in 1864, a banner year when a second plantation acquired by Martinho, Santa Cruz, produced significant income. Throughout the years 1856 to 1864, Martinho's income from bank dividends and interest on loans rose steadily, reaching one-fourth of his total income in the years 1863 and 1864. Most of this non-fazenda income came from interest on loans granted to other fazendeiros. Martinho's income from such loans was 35 contos ($18,900) in 1864; since they were generally made at an annual rate of 12 to 18 percent, Martinho may have loaned out as much as 400 contos ($316,000). As tax collecting had done for the baron of Iguape, Martinho's steadily increasing income from loans shielded him from the vicissitudes of an export-crop economy. At any rate, the operating expenses of Campo Alto and Santa Cruz during the years 1856 to 1864 were never more than 20 percent of income and often closer to 10 percent. In this case, growing coffee with slave labor was a very profitable venture. As Martinho's profits from both coffee and moneylending rose, his payments of interest to others dropped drastically, ending completely in 1860. His general expenses—the costs of maintaining a city home, of educating his children, of trips to Rio, and of luxuries—increased as Martinho grew rich, but seldom exceeded 10 percent of gross receipts.[9] Martinho's fortune rose steadily throughout his life, reaching an estimated 22,000 contos ($6,600,000) in the depreciated currency of the early Republic at his death in 1891.[10]

In the late 1860s Martinho's older sons began to assume the duties of managing and extending the family's agricultural holdings. Martinho had acquired virgin land extending north from the Mogi-Guaçú River to the rolling hills of the Casa Branca region. Using slaves from Campo Alto, Martinho and his son Antônio supervised the planting of sixty thousand coffee seeds on the new land. Antônio returned a year later fearing the worst, but was surprised by the seedlings' good condition, Nature's ratification of the site, which traditional wisdom had held unsuitable for coffee.[11] For his wedding present in 1868, Antônio received the new fazenda, named Santa Veridiana after his mother.

By the 1880s Santa Veridiana was well on the road to becoming what has been called "one of the most famous fazendas in Brazil." While Antônio's claim that he realized twice the regional production average is difficult to prove, there is little question that Santa Veridiana was a model plantation.[12] Of forty-three fazendas in São Paulo and Rio de Janeiro studied by the Dutch coffee expert C. F. van Delden Laërne, in 1883, it had the seventh highest total production: of twelve Paulista plantations it was the third most productive. Average coffee yield from 1876 to 1883 was 275,400 kilograms, enough to give yearly minimum gross receipts of 100 contos ($46,000). The labor force consisted of sixty field slaves, fifty "factory" slaves, and forty-nine immigrant families who worked on a contract basis. Thus five years before the abolition of slavery, about one-third of Antônio Prado's labor force consisted of free whites.[13]

Meanwhile, in 1868 Antônio's brother Martinico, beginning a ten-year apprenticeship living in the interior, had been put in charge of Campo Alto and Santa Cruz. In the late 1870s Martinico moved to establish his own fortune, becoming one of the pioneer leaders who pushed the coffee frontier northward.[14] Leaving Casa Branca in 1877, Martinico explored the municípios of São Simão and Ribeirão Prêto, sending back reports praising their coffee potential. He noted that coffee planting begun by families such as the Pereira Barretos flourished in the area, but a major obstacle lay in the mentality of the more established residents. Martinico wrote that São Simão's inhabitants were "possessed by an extreme love of uncultivated lands; they own thousands of alqueires, do not wish to sell them, and, rather, would like to buy more." Further north, in Ribeirão Prêto, Martinico observed that the traditional residents, largely of Mineiro origins, preferred to continue a vegetative life, using their often enormous personal estates only for cattle and for hunting. To Martinico, land so used was "dead capital." The few large landholders who dominated Ribeirão Prêto, on the other hand, saw the capitalistic outsiders from the south as barbarians, bent on taking their lands and destroying their pastoral way of life.[15]

To modern eyes, the coming struggle for Ribeirão Prêto suggests a clash between traditional, almost-feudal land barons and the more modern capitalist class of coffee entrepreneurs. Martinico Prado, representative of the latter group but also a fervent Republican, saw the meaning of the area differently. Observing that in most of São Paulo extreme poverty existed alongside great wealth with no mediating middle sector, he hoped that Ribeirão Prêto could become a social experiment as well as an economic colossus. With the abolition of slavery, which Martinico predicted would happen in ten years (it occurred in eleven), planters and small farmers would need to cooperate, with the latter furnishing the seasonal labor needed on coffee fazendas.[16] This utopian vision was naive, perhaps, in view of Brazilian land-holding and social traditions, and immigration without real commitment to the creation of a middle class precluded the realization of the dream for a time, though Martinico and other Prados involved in promoting immigration continued to invoke it.[17]

Shortly after his survey of the northern municípios, Martinico purchased his first fazenda in Ribeirão Prêto, naming it Albertina after his wife. In 1885, most likely with money loaned by his father and with profits from Albertina, he bought a much larger fazenda, Guatapará, 6,000 alqueires (36,000 acres) in size, at a cost of 70 contos ($26,600). Hundreds of laborers from Bahia were employed—apparently as free, contract workers—to clear the land. Half a million trees were soon planted, and the number was gradually increased to nearly two million by World War I. Visiting Guatapará in 1889, only four years after its establishment, Martinho Prado observed that "Martinico is rich."[18]

In 1889, the last year of the monarchy, the Prados acquired their largest plantation, São Martinho, in the município of Ribeirão Prêto.[19] Describing the property in his customarily zealous way as a fascinating colossus like no other in the province, Martinico convinced Martinho to advance him his inheritance and to put up other money to buy it. Martinho, Martinico, and Antônio became partners in São Martinho, the second-largest coffee fazenda in Brazil, the largest on a single block of land. Measuring nearly 14,000 alqueires (84,000 acres), São Martinho was purchased for 600 contos ($324,000) and eventually sported 3,400,000 coffee trees laid out in straight lines over the undulating countryside.[20]

Around the globe, in capitalist and socialist economies alike, modern "development" has exacted a heavy price in the devastation of nature. In stark contrast to the rectilinear coffee rows at Guatapará, on another of his plantations, near Araras, Martinico preserved a few hectares of virgin forest, which was described by the historian Warren Dean in the 1970s: "It is an awesome sight. From a canopy of trees 150 feet tall—cabreúvas, perobas, jequitibás, smooth-trunked and dainty-leafed—the morning light filters down through the tangled strands of runners and lianas. The bulging trunks of the figueiras look like ruined battlements, hardly resisting the broaching waves of ferns and vines."[21] Was it, as Dean prefers, excessive pride, or was it awe and reverence that led Martinico to exempt a bit of natural forest from "development"?

The Prados' acquisition and development of land was only a part of a grand strategy involving European immigration, railroads, banks, a family export house with overseas subsidiaries, and industry. We will return to coffee and the Prado fazendas in chapter 8, when we discuss the family's economic role after 1889, but it is now necessary to turn to other aspects of the family's economic activities during the Second Empire.

Labor

The planters of the Paulista west during the coffee boom were the least committed of Brazil's fazendeiros to slavery. But other regions had slaves to sell, the Paulistas had money to buy them, and experiments with free labor in the 1850s, 1860s, and 1870s failed. Thus economics induced the Paulistas to invest heavily in a system to which they had little noneconomic commitment, so that their plantations "were at the same time the most progressive and most retrograde sector of Brazilian society." Slave labor in coffee, though menial and degrading, was less demanding than in most other plantation systems, and overseers (sometimes themselves slaves) usually disciplined with insults and threats, using the whip as last resort. Clearly, as in all economic systems, there were unscrupulous and even cruel masters. A Prado cousin, Dr. José Elias Pacheco Jordão, ran plantations where, according to a policeman's deposition, "the slaves are punished and mistreated badly"; Pacheco Jordão also was accused of abusing immigrant Portuguese minors who worked for him. Slavery was doomed by the end of the trans-Atlantic slave trade (since Brazilian slaves failed to reproduce themselves in sufficient numbers) and by the increasing rebelliousness of the slaves themselves. The inevitable transition to free labor was delayed, however, because planters "could not deal on a purely contractual basis with a real proletariat."[22] The transition from slave to free labor was certainly the major social drama of nineteenth-century Brazil, and the Prados played important roles in it.

While prospering as slaveowning fazendeiros, the Prados shared in the unjust, tragic events inherent in the master-slave relationship. These, combined with the increasingly evident demise of slavery after 1850 and pragmatic economic considerations, led them to play a leading role in promoting European immigration to São Paulo.

On 13 September 1851, at the Engenho do Arari, another fazenda that Martinho Prado had acquired in Mogi-Mirim, two slaves named David and Bernabé attacked and killed one of Martinho's overseers. After a five-hour trial in January 1852, David and Bernabé were hanged.[23] In the early 1860s Antônio Prado wrote of another tragedy that had overtaken the family's slaves, this time at Campo Alto: "I feel very strongly the fatal event that took place at Campo Alto: poor Negroes! True slaves of the most disgraceful condition one can imagine."[24]

Several years later, as a novice fazendeiro, Antônio heard that the slaves at Santa Veridiana had fled, alleging abuse by the resident administrator. Antônio immediately set out for the new plantation, induced the slaves to return, met with them on 8 December 1867, and heard their complaints:

> In the afternoon I met with the slaves. I made them see that from then on they were going to work for me, and that intending and desiring to be a good master, I wanted them to be good slaves; I would treat them well, giving them land to plant their food plots; if they wished to work on Sundays, they could work for me, since I did not agree with the custom of letting them work for neighbors.
> They were satisfied.[25]

The following week Antônio gave the slaves back pay for working on saints' days, took pains to see that they did not work too long in the rain despite the urgent need for planting, looked after their health as best he could, and considered firing the incompetent administrator. This episode shows that the slaves were not entirely powerless to affect their situation and tends to confirm Dean's observation that "the moral qualities of the slaves—grudgingly, condescendingly, incompletely recognized and rewarded—were, as everyone realized, essential to the survival of the slave system."[26]

Supervision of an often troublesome and sometimes rebellious slave labor force also occupied much of young Martinico Prado's time. This situation was complicated by his republicanism and his recognition of the basic injustice of slavery, which he once called a "horrible cancer" afflicting Brazilian society.[27] An 1876 letter reveals the conflict Martinico felt. In part of the letter he dwelt at length upon a violent typhus epidemic among the blacks at the Santa Cruz fazenda. His concern for these slaves, however, was matched by anger directed against a runaway female slave he had just bought; he asked that his brother-in-law have her placed immediately in São Paulo's House of Correction, should she be found in the city.[28] In April 1882, when Tibério, a young, strong house slave, escaped from Martinico's house in São Paulo city to a proabolitionist society, Martinico "screamed, got angry, called himself a burro for not having sent this slave to the fazenda a long time ago."[29] This from the Prado generally considered most radical in his time.

The Prados' attitude toward their slaves was probably accurately reflected in Antônio's pledge "to be a good master" to his bonded workers at Santa Veridiana. It is difficult to imagine them guilty of any of the horrible excesses typical of slave systems throughout the Americas. Yet Antônio's and Martinico's generation faced a difficult situation: slavery had been part and parcel of Brazilian life in all its aspects for nearly four hundred years. To avoid short-term economic loss and, no less important, to fulfill their parents' expectations and preserve the Prado patrimony, they had to maintain a long-established institution which they publicly admitted was tragic, disgraceful, unjust, and brutal. As Martinico's behavior shows, the Prados were not about to permit slaves to take a hand in their own liberation, but once São Paulo's slaves began to do so *en masse*, Antônio and Martinico did play a significant role in ending slavery in Brazil.

The Prado family's interest in alternate forms of labor dated from at least the early 1860s.[30] In 1863, it will be recalled, Antônio Prado contrasted the industrious, satisfied Swiss peasantry and Brazil's indolent *"paysands."*[31] In 1871 the newly created Association to Assist Colonization and Immigration (*Associação Auxiliadora de Colonização e Imigração*) was empowered by imperial decree to subsidize European immigration, and Antônio Prado became its vice-president.[32] His father, Martinho, soon arranged with the association to import ten German families for his fazendas.[33] This was a prelude to later immigration efforts, but in the 1870s the family did not wholly accept immigration as a solution to the growing crisis in Brazilian slave labor. In his reports on Ribeirão Prêto, for example, Martinico did not consider using immigrants in that underpopulated region. Later, in 1882, he argued for an easing of São Paulo's ban on the interprovincial slave trade (a measure he had sponsored in 1878), on the grounds that Ribeirão Prêto's development depended on the migration of slaveowners and their slaves from Minas Gerais and Rio de Janeiro.[34] The Prados' labor strategy, based on economics, was essentially pragmatic rather than ideological. They learned one thing from their early experiences with immigrant labor, as Antônio Prado later noted: it was more productive than slave labor.[35]

The two Prados primarily identified with the strategy of planter-sponsored immigration disagreed on tactics. Martinico, a Republican, represented the new, labor-starved, and relatively poor Ninth Assembly District in São Paulo's legislature, while his older brother Antônio, an imperial minister, represented the interests of São Paulo city in the Provincial Assembly and spoke for the already-prosperous, developed coffee regions. It was thus not surprising that differences occurred, that family loyalty was no absolute even in economic matters. In 1884, for example, Martinico introduced a bill in the Provincial Assembly to subsidize immigration. Many legislators, including his brother, Antônio, criticized a proviso in the bill which granted immigrants subsidies on arrival in Santos; they feared that immigrants would collect the money and abscond to other parts. The bill was amended to permit payment only after immigrants resided on fazendas for thirty days. Martinico, representing a region where such postponement was a hardship for fazendeiros to bear, protested against the amendment. As he predicted, the law was ineffective in producing the desired flow of immigrants.[36]

As this episode shows, although there was widespread agreement on the need for immigration by 1884, neither São Paulo's planters nor the Prados, both divided by regional interests, could agree on methods. Two years later, however, Martinico and other influential planters—many of them linked to the Prados by marriage—hit on the idea of creating a nonprofit immigration society to contract with the provincial government for subsidies. In April 1886 Martinico announced the creation of the Society to Promote Immigration (*Sociedade Promotora de Imigração*) and asked fazendeiros to send him requests for immigrant families along with statements about the "advantages offered to the *colonos* [immigrants] in the most detailed manner possible." He cautioned that "the colonos will not subject themselves [in advance] to contracts [specifying] the location of their service and will arrive free from all debt." On June 30 the Society to Promote Immigration met at the invitation of the baron (later count) of Parnaíba, Antônio Queirós Teles, the provincial vice-president and soon to be president, a Prado cousin deeply interested in immigration. Parnaíba proposed that the society become the sole contracting agent for immigration with the provincial government. Martinico Prado was elected the society's president.[37] On 3 July 1886 a contract was signed between the Society to Promote Immigration and the provincial government to import six thousand immigrants in the fiscal year 1886–87.[38] That relatively modest goal showed the society's desire to avoid past errors: seeking forty to sixty thousand immigrants at once had made it impossible to offer sufficient subsidies, had opened the way to abuses by unscrupulous recruiters, and had created problems in controlling labor contracts. Martinico himself went to Italy to oversee the recruitment of workers.[39]

As late as January 1888, four months before Brazilian slavery was abolished, immigration was still a hotly debated subject in São Paulo. Controversy focused on whether to abolish slavery at all, the number and type of immigrants that would be needed if slavery were abolished, the attitude of the Italian government toward immigration, and competition from Argentina and the United States. Back from Italy with more direct experience than any other planter-legislator, Martinico Prado became the chief local defender of immigration and set forth the principles of the Society to Promote Immigration in light of its initial experiences. He argued against an oversupply of immigrants and stated that only agricultural workers should be sought. Oversupply would drive down wages, which would be "a true disaster for our growing immigration, making useless all our efforts at advertising, [and] making the immigrant's ambition disappear." "In new countries that need immigration," Martinico added, "the best, only, and true advertising is that of secure profit."[40] The Society to Promote Immigration functioned until 1895, when its task was assumed by the state government, and imported 126,415 workers.[41] Its fazendeiro members were largely able to avoid the labor shortages other planters suffered after the abolition of slavery in May of 1888.

While Martinico and others took steps to ease the transition to free labor at the provincial level, Antônio Prado dealt with the problem as national minister of agriculture. Some studies have emphasized his long opposition to abolition and his eleventh-hour conversion to that cause in 1887, a conversion that broke the back of the Conservative opposition.[42] However, Antônio had consistently and for some years linked abolition and immigration together in the formula "gradual emancipation and intensive immigration." In 1884 he agreed to support the Liberal party's bill for emancipation of sexagenarian slaves but extracted as his price the concession that one-third of the emancipation fund be used to subsidize immigration. With the change from a Liberal to a Conservative ministry in 1885, Antônio became minister of agriculture, commerce, and public works and guided the amended bill to passage. One scholar has commented that "Prado designed and administered the [immigration] program in such a way that the fazendeiros of his native province would be the greatest beneficiaries of the new law." Antônio did not shy away from the charge. He maintained that because the immigration feature of the sexagenarian emancipation law was to "establish an element of progress which benefits one part of the Brazilian community, the Parliament should not refuse to approve it."[43] The parliamentary majority, for whatever combination of reasons, agreed. There is no doubt that on the issue of abolition Antônio Prado also pursued a cautious, conservative course, one that angered the more radical abolitionists. But it should be remembered that until 1887, São Paulo had no effective immigration program. Antônio's "miraculous" conversion to abolitionism was a response to both the rising tide of slave defections in São Paulo and to the initial success of the Society to Promote Immigration.

Perhaps more serious than charges of regional favoritism and excessive gradualism on the abolition issue were those alleging Antônio Prado's personal collusion in channeling government funds to his brother. In May of 1889 the Liberal journalist and future three-time presidential candidate Rui Barbosa accused Antônio of advancing three hundred contos ($162,000) in public funds to Martinico as president of the Society to Promote Immigration for the purpose of subsidizing immigrants; according to Barbosa, payment was made in violation of the law providing that such reimbursement could be made only after receipt of proof that immigrants had actually settled on fazendas. Barbosa attacked the "imprudencies and errors" of Antônio's practices and intimated that Antônio's resignation from the Ministry of Agriculture was linked to "administrative nepotism."[44] Antônio evidently did not reply to the charges, and no legal action resulted from them. Antônio had frequently complained that the government was slow to meet crucial problems, and it seems that he had little regard for the legal niceties involved. It is possible that in ordering payment to the president of the Society for the Promotion of Immigration, who happened to be his brother, Antônio felt that he was adhering to the law, since direct payment to fazendeiros was not made. At any rate, the incident shows a shadowy side of familism used to facilitate immigration in São Paulo. Having observed much earlier that in progressive Britain everything was done by private initiative, Antônio Prado evidently believed that when free enterprise needed a financial boost, government should be a ready partner.

The Prados' personal experience with immigrants reveals the mixed results achieved in the early years of the immigration program. In the early 1880s the Dutch expert Laërne noted that the immigrants at Antônio Prado's Santa Veridiana were "on the whole not particularly well satisfied." The crux of their discontent was a wage reduction of about 25 percent per liter of coffee beans harvested. Worse yet, Antônio announced this decision in 1883, while a previously established five-year contract was still in force and with but three months' notice, leaving the immigrants with "the alternative to comply with his terms or go." The Italian workers, who made up more than half of the total immigrant force, departed, while the Germans, "who shrank from removing with their families on such hasty notice," remained.[45]

The Italian exodus from Santa Veridiana attracted considerable notice in both São Paulo and Rio de Janeiro, since it involved a most prestigious Paulista politician-fazendeiro. In his defense Antônio noted that many of the Italians had gone to the Rio de Plata region and had returned, broke and unhappy, to work for him. He thought the basis of their discontent was not wages per se, but the obstacles immigrants faced in acquiring land that would yield rapid profits. Even the critical, objective Laërne acknowledged that workers on Paulista fazendas "had an excellent chance of making their way in the world," and he cited as proof the records of three immigrants at Santa Veridiana who made average yearly profits of £127, £86, and £59, after food and housing, in the years 1877 to 1883.[46] The French professor of "industrial biology" at Rio de Janeiro's Polytechnic School, Louis Couty, rightly recognized that the economic conditions that rendered the immigrant "a serf" for several years were only part of a larger conflict. Couty noted the need for a sociolegal basis of equality between fazendeiro and immigrant, not necessarily the homestead laws of the United States or Argentina, but at least "the legal equality of the immigrant and the fazendeiro, the social equality of the colono and the Brazilian."[47]

In late 1887 Martinico and other pro-immigration fazendeiros were accused, possibly by anti-immigration slavocrats who wished to prolong slavery, of mistreating colonos and denying them adequate medical care. On 31 January 1888 the provincial president, Francisco de Paula Rodrigues Alves (later president of Brazil, 1902–6) investigated and reported the findings of his investigation to the national minister of agriculture, commerce, and public works, Antônio Prado. The report noted that Martinico was the most energetic defender of immigration and that he had previously successfully defended himself in the press against similar charges. Martinico had 800 colonos in his "colony," probably at Guatapará, "who lived extremely contentedly." He had made available to 135 families free passage back to Italy, but only one family accepted because "it had relatives there who couldn't adapt" to Brazil. A vice-consul of Italy had interviewed "some" heads of family who had left Martinico's colony for Rio Grande do Sul; one had earned 1:700$000 ($782) after having worked for Martinico for only two years; the other continued on to Italy to bring his wife and children to São Paulo, "so content was he." The report went on to say that Martinico had zealously provided medical care to immigrants at his cost, and that two colonos were being treated in Martinico's home in São Paulo city at the very time the report was written. There were also about 50 persons in the Immigrants' Hostel who were bound for one of Martinico's fazendas, "called by relatives who are established there."[48]

Rodrigues Alves's report prompts several observations. First, it establishes that even rich, powerful, politically well-connected fazendeiros like Martinico Prado were subject to some publicity and control by forces such as the Italian vice-consul and the press, which could in turn provoke an investigation by state and national authorities; fazendas were no longer the exclusively private domains of all-powerful semifeudal lords. Second, it is clear that the public officials investigating the case shared the goals of promoting immigration in the interest of the planters and of São Paulo more generally.

Because coffee capitalists had tremendous political influence, the objectivity and completeness of the report are suspect. Third, notwithstanding the preceding observation, Rodrigues Alves's report cannot be taken as evidence that Martinico abused his colonists, as has been done in one scholarly account.[49] Fourth, there would be problems in any labor force of eight hundred, under any regime. And finally, as the report stated and the Prados repeatedly argued, "the ideal of the province is that the immigrant would be our primary propaganda agent, himself telling his relatives and friends that they will find sheltering hospitality and all the important factors of easy, remunerative labor here."

The work was not easy, and remuneration remained the exposed nerve of fazendeiro-colono relations. Remuneration is difficult to evaluate because it consisted of three sorts of money wages (for tending coffee trees through the year, for the harvest, and for occasional day labor in transport and in maintenance of the fazenda) and nonmonetary remuneration, consisting of free houses and use of land to raise livestock and grow subsistence and market crops. The nonmonetary income may have constituted 70 percent of family income and was thus more important to the colono families. The use of plantation land was the heart of the colono system, the positive incentive needed to maintain a free, mobile labor force in a competitive, labor-short market; it enabled colonos to save and to acquire their own land and hence to gain partial access to the means of production. So important was it that planters would sometimes expand their productive lands to offer land use to colonos, even if it went against the planters' own long-term interests.[50]

Although they are incomplete, data from the two Prado fazendas in 1888 add a quantitative dimension to our knowledge of the Prados' immigrant labor force. The data may be compared to estimates of a reasonable yearly cash wage in the 1880s, 200 milreis for an individual or 400 milreis minimum per family.[51] The value of nonmonetary remuneration (difficult to calculate) would have to be added to cash wages. Of 64 immigrants at Martinho Prado's Campo Alto, all of whom had arrived in January and May of 1888, only 4 had debts at year's end. However, 61 percent had net profits of less than 200 milreis and 84 percent earned profits of less than 400 milreis. At Martinico Prado's Albertina, where some immigrants had worked for several years, 95 of 113 immigrants had net profits for 1888, 16 owed debts, and 2 stood even. Most of the debtors had arrived late in the year. Overall, nearly half had profits of less than 200 milreis; two-thirds were below the 400 milreis figure.[52] Although crucial facts such as value of nonmonetary remuneration, actual length of employment, family size, and number of workers per family are missing, it may be said that most of the immigrants at Campo Alto and Albertina in 1888 were debt-free and earned a small, probably insufficient profit, in addition to the free house, pasture, and food plot provided them. They may have earned considerably more by selling surplus food in local markets.

The French journalist Max Leclerc visited Santa Veridiana in 1890. He had observed that in São Paulo generally, immigrants were tied to fazendas by debt peonage. Even at Santa Veridiana, "where things are run in complete fairness," only twenty-eight of eighty families were debt-free. One atypical family of seven workers had saved three contos ($1,380), which was lent out at interest, had a credit of 500 milreis at the fazenda, and owned five or six horses and thirty pigs. More normal was the account of a family of four: debt of 329 milreis in 1887, debt paid and profit of 90 milreis in 1888, profit of 103 milreis in 1889. According to Leclerc, the immigrants at Santa Veridiana were treated with "gentleness," were encouraged to maintain home and family, and lived in "clean and gay" houses. Once the first year or so of debts was overcome, the immigrant "lived happily for some years, but with his debts extinct and as master of some savings, he was taken with ambition." Eventually, Leclerc continued, most immigrants would leave, seeking to buy a small business or industry, or a small farm near the city. Leclerc recognized that the relatively good conditions he described at Antônio Prado's fazenda were not typical and that, in general, fazendeiros had not known how to treat immigrants. What they had done, therefore, was "to perpetuate the old colonial system, with small modifications."[53]

The Prados were a partial exception to Leclerc's generalization, as he himself pointed out. They realized that an unhappy free labor force, which could and did leave their fazendas, could never be a stable, productive one. They realized that in the final analysis they were heavily dependent on their colonos. While the Prados made mistakes, most notably in Antônio's arbitrary, highhanded wage reduction at Santa Veridiana in 1883, they seemed to learn from those errors, as a comparison of Laërne's 1883 account with Leclerc's of

1890 shows. In admitting several foreign observers to their fazendas, the Prados seemed anxious to show that the immigrant labor system could work, and most of the observers endorsed the Prados' efforts. As time went on, the Prados also delegated more responsibility to enterprising immigrants, as in an 1897 contract for the planting and care of 200,000 coffee trees at São Martinho.[54] By 1905 the Prado family employed over 2,800 immigrant farmworkers, who made up over 90 percent of their rural labor force,[55] and it seems unlikely that they could have attracted this number without some reputation for equitable labor relations. As leading promoters of immigration, the Prados recognized that the ultimate success of the program so important to them depended on the relationship of fazendeiro and colono. That the fazendeiro reaped much greater profit from that relationship and that labor relations remained paternalistic are un-deniable. Nonetheless, given the historical legacy of the slave re-gime, and the context within which the Prados worked, their role in the transition from slave to free labor was positive. It contributed to the modernization of labor relations in São Paulo, and to the even-tual emergence of a large body of immigrant landowners. It goes without saying that the Prados were motivated in all of this by eco-nomic self-interest, which they confused with the general good, a common enough error of liberal capitalism then and now.

Capital

Had the Prados viewed themselves only as coffee producers, their collective impact on São Paulo would have been relatively unimpor-tant. As we have already seen, they were also capitalists, as adept at tax farming as at sugar marketing, as eager to lend money as to de-velop coffee fazendas. The baron of Iguape's financial leadership gave special impetus to this family capitalism, and his leadership of the Paulista branch of the Bank of Brazil gave the family a distinct ad-vantage in the dynamic economic climate of the last half of the nineteenth century. Though much of the family's capital was gener-ated directly from coffee, the baron also used his position to expedite loans to relatives such as the future provincial president and immi-gration advocate Antônio Queiros Teles.[56] Shortly after the baron's death in 1875, his grandson, Antônio Prado, was named president of the fiscal council of an important charity in São Paulo, an appointment that signaled the transfer of economic leadership in the family. In the same year, 1876, young Antônio was awarded a contract to restore the São José Theater in São Paulo, a venture that, like many of the Prados' dealings, wedded the public interest to the possibility of large personal profit.[57]

During the Second Empire the Prados' most significant use of capital other than in plantation development was in railroads. As early as 1855, São Paulo's president had linked railroad development to free labor and immigration, central elements of the Prados' own eventual plans.[58] In 1867 the province's first railroad, the São Paulo Railway, was completed from Santos through São Paulo to Jundiaí; it was constructed by an English company sponsored by the Brazilian entrepreneur Irineu Evangelista de Sousa, viscount of Mauá.[59] The Prados and others soon organized to finance a railroad to tap the newer, more distant coffee areas.

Incorporated 30 January 1868, the Paulista Railway became an outstanding example of locally and privately controlled railway development in Latin America. Martinho Prado was one of its organizers, an important fundraiser, and one of its first directors. Although preliminary analysis of stock ownership in the Paulista does not reveal a high degree of family control, the Prados did hold a larger share of stock than their numbers alone would warrant. More important was the Prados' financial and leadership role. From Jundiaí the Paulista was completed to Campinas (1872) and to Rio Claro (1876). In 1877, when further construction to Piraçununga was threatened by lack of funds, Antônio Prado, whose fazenda still lay beyond the railhead, personally underwrote construction costs.[60]

Coffee made the Paulista Railway one of those rarities among Latin American railroads, an immediately and consistently profitable line. In the late 1870s and 1880s, however, the Paulista found itself checked on the west and east by zones of influence granted to the Rio Claro and Mogiana railroads. Complicating this was the imperial government's plan to construct a railroad westward to Mato Grosso, principally for strategic needs made painfully obvious during the Paraguayan War in the late 1860s. The Prado family, with holdings in the Mogi-Guaçú valley, one of the possible routes, argued for construction of the Mato Grosso line through the valley. The contract was instead awarded to the rival Rio Claro Railway interests, and the

Paulista, which controlled the Mogi-Guaçú route, was temporarily limited to developing transportation on the Mogi-Guaçú River.[61]

In the late 1880s the Paulista Railway was provoked into further expansion by the completion of the Mogiana Railroad's track to Lagé, bordering on Antônio Prado's personal domain at Santa Veridiana. Rather than ship his coffee by a rival road, Antônio saw to it that a branch of the Paulista was constructed from Piraçununga to his fazenda. In typical fashion, personal and corporate motives were intermixed. The Santa Veridiana branch was completed in 1892, the year in which Antônio began his long presidency of the Paulista Railway.[62]

Antônio's aggressive efforts on behalf of the Paulista were supplemented by those of his younger brother, Eduardo, who acted as European agent for public and private interests in São Paulo. In 1888 Eduardo negotiated the provincial government's first foreign loan, £787,500 at 5 percent, from the London firm of Louis Cohen and Sons. Displeased with the concern's handling of the loan, Eduardo recommended to the provincial president that "in better conditions for us, the Provincial Government should be represented in the London market by the Rothschilds' house itself, which would lend to this government the enormous and irresistible prestige of this very house."[63]

By the last years of the Second Empire, the Prado family had developed some irresistible prestige, and power, of its own. As the Prados' influence assumed international proportions, they came into conflict with established economic and political interests. In negotiating the 1888 São Paulo loan, Eduardo Prado had to overcome the strong resistance of the Brazilian minister in London, Francisco Inácio de Carvalho Moreira, baron of Penedo. Perhaps because of his own financial interests,[64] or because of the central government's opposition to upstart São Paulo, Penedo vigorously opposed the loan, despite a host of notes from Eduardo attempting to win him over. In early 1889 Penedo was demoted to France. He claimed that his transfer originated in 1888 with Antônio Prado (who became foreign minister briefly in that year), and that it was carried out by a cabal involved in the São Paulo loan, including Eduardo Prado and José Carlos Rodrigues. Rodrigues used his commission from the São Paulo loan to purchase a leading Rio de Janeiro newspaper, the *Jornal do Comércio*, a transaction witnessed by Eduardo Prado. Eduardo in turn became Rodrigues's partner and the European manager of the *Jornal*, which in their hands became a leading medium for the transmission of European business and cultural trends to Brazil. By the end of the Empire the Prados had reached a level of power far transcending the remote coffee plantations where their rise to wealth had been consolidated.

Economically, the Second Empire was a highly successful era for the Prados, who joined land, labor, and capital to achieve substantial wealth and power. The success of the baron of Iguape as a capitalist-entrepreneur, spanning the years 1816 to 1875, was the basis of the family fortune. With the baron's help, Martinho Prado added to that fortune by exploiting the opportunity presented by the Paulista coffee boom, thereby continuing the previously noted pattern of integrated urban and rural interests within the family. Urban-rural economic integration was also apparent in the complementary careers of Martinho's older sons, Antônio and Martinico, who extended the family's wealth and solidified its economic position by forging a successful, pragmatic, and self-interested approach to the transition from slave to free labor and by active capitalist endeavor, as in the Paulista Railway. The end of the Second Empire found Eduardo Prado negotiating in the London money market and on the verge of opening personal relations with the Rothschilds.

This chapter supports the Marxist hypothesis that the bourgeois family is an instrument for amassing and preserving capital.[66] It was in the economic sphere that the Prados showed their greatest unity. Political differences and serious family quarrels, important in other ways, rarely touched the family's economic destiny during the Second Empire. In later years, during the First Republic, the family expanded and diversified its economic interests but was faced with chronic problems in the coffee economy which threatened its economic position.

The Prado economic experience between 1840 and 1889 also suggests the need for more sophisticated understanding of such necessary (though stereotypical) terms as *planter* and *capitalist*. In the Prado case these terms were not mutually exclusive; plantation, urban, and international capitalism were linked in the same family and in the same individuals. Yet this was not universally so, as Martinico's 1877 observations about the traditional, precapitalist landholders of São Simão prove. Even within the Prado family, coffee capitalists like Antônio and Martinico (and later Eduardo) could have different interests depending on local economic variations. Class, and even family, behavior could be significantly tempered by individual economic needs and desires.

The Prados' economic success also requires a warning against confusing private profit with social progress. It has been argued that before the abolition of slavery the Paulista coffee regime was inefficient, wasteful, and ecologically destructive, with only railroads as "a surviving benefit of planter control," and that after abolition economic "development" derived from concessions that other social classes forced from the planters, who made them to avoid losing their estates.[67] The interplay of private and family economic motives with broader public and social concerns characterized Prado economic behavior. They adhered to the unchallenged wisdom— imported from Britain—of economic liberalism, a system that equated and equates private accumulation with social advancement, a system that has served most Brazilians poorly. All this was less clear then than now, but the Prados were certainly aware of the extreme inequalities of the system they mastered, and they hoped to remedy some of its injustices. British economic liberalism, however, exercised over them and their country an ideological hegemony that prevented them from so doing.

It is hard to imagine a more powerful or prestigious Brazilian family during the Second Empire than the Prados. But although they succeeded in creating and expanding their wealth, and influenced important adaptations to the world market economy, such as the coffee boom and the transition from slave to free labor, it is hard to see them and their allies as controlling the Brazilian economy. And if the Prados and their allies did not control it, which Brazilians could? The evidence suggests that—heroic myths of the planters' apologists and conspiracy theories of their critics notwithstanding— the Prados were themselves controlled: by nature (even as they "conquered" it), by Brazilian historical conditions (even as they sought to change some of them), and by a reflex economy that ultimately responded in knee-jerk fashion to foreign forces. This explains, in part, the alienation and skepticism to be found in various family members, most notably in their politics.

⇒ CHAPTER V ⇐

THE POLITICS OF FAMILY,

1868–1889

It is . . . unrewarding to search our history for any great lines of matured thought and great clashes of interest such as are present, for example in the United States."[1] This statement, written by a leading Brazilian historian, indicates the difficulty of analyzing Brazilian political history. Brazil's monarchy, which lasted from 1822 to 1889 and was unique in the history of the Western hemisphere, reflected a highly stratified social structure dominated by planter elites and their exporter allies. The very nature of the monarchy, which was designed to protect the status quo, was part of the reason for the lack of ideological thrust in Brazilian politics. The Constitution of 1824 provided the trappings of modern government, such as guaranteed freedoms and a bicameral parliament, in imitation of Western European and North American models.[2] To these imported features was added a uniquely Brazilian institution, the "moderating power" (*poder moderador*), giving the emperor the authority to name ministers of state and lifetime senators, to prorogue the parliament and call for new elections, to convoke extraordinary parliamentary sessions, to sanction and to veto laws, and to appoint provincial presidents (governors) and otherwise intervene in provincial government.[3] In practice, Brazil's monarchy was highly centralized. It was created when the state's chief problem was to preserve national allegiance and territorial integrity, a goal achieved in 1849 when the last regional revolt against the central government was forcibly quelled. After an "era of conciliation" in the 1850s, changing conditions—the most notable of which was perhaps São Paulo's economic emergence—placed strain on the centralized monarchy. This stress was felt within Brazil's political party system.

The coalescence of local political factions into national parties during the Second Empire was an important, if paradoxical, development: important, because the parties were institutions that extended political control from Rio de Janeiro to the provinces and rotated power among elite factions; paradoxical, because the Conservative and Liberal parties represented no clear ideological conflict. In the 1860s a foreigner observed simply but accurately that

> the parties are the *ins* and the *outs*, or Government and the opposition. . . .
> These parties contended for power and principle, and so warm were their struggles that at times they seemed to battle more for rule than for the success of principles.[4]

After 1868 there was an incipient, but never fully realized, crystallization of ideology, with the more committed liberals calling for such reforms as the extinction of the emperor's "moderating power," a temporary and elective senate, direct and generalized suffrage, and the substitution of free labor for slavery.[5] In 1870 many dissident liberals left the Liberal party to form the Republican party. The Republicans also attracted anti-emancipationist fazendeiros displeased with the government's passage of the Law of the Free Womb in 1871, which provided (in theory) freedom for slave children born after that date.[6] However, since large landholders, merchants, and bankers connected with the export economy continued to dominate both the Liberal and the Conservative parties and exercised veto power even in Republican party circles, certain subjects—most notably agrarian reform—remained taboo. The conflicts in Brazilian politics were primarily those of personality and of regional interest. These often focused on how the "ins" could retain their power or how the "outs" could become "ins." The Emperor Dom Pedro II, who styled himself the barometer of national political opinion, frequently resolved such issues himself. It became customary to say there was nothing so like a Conservative as a Liberal in power, and, on the other hand, several Liberal reforms were passed by Conservative parliaments.

There was, however, one genuine issue which dominated national politics after 1868 and which became a force tending to destroy the monarchy itself: slavery.[7] With the rise of the prosperous coffee economy in southern Brazil and especially in São Paulo, political regionalism developed and transcended party lines, largely because political reapportionment did not accompany the shift in economic power from north to south. Thus the south pictured itself as paying the national budget and receiving a minimum of services in return; it became the center of intense discontent expressed in movements for the federalization of the monarchy, the adoption of the republican form, and even separatism. After 1870, with the establishment of the Republican party, politics became more turbulent, and ideological questions were more widely debated. Yet even the Republicans were, figuratively and sometimes literally, the brothers of the monarchist Conservatives and Liberals they sought to dislodge.[8] On many truly important issues, such as the Law of the Free Womb, there was no consistent party sentiment; Conservatives, Liberals, and even Republicans were on both sides.[9]

It was in this context that the Prado family's growing economic power during the Second Empire was matched by significant political achievement. Antônio Prado enjoyed the most spectacular and important career. A Conservative, he was elected alderman in São Paulo city (1866), provincial deputy (1866–89), and national deputy (1869–75, 1885–89), and was appointed minister of agriculture (1885–88), senator (1887) and, for a brief period, minister of foreign affairs (1888).[10] As we have seen, Antônio played an important role in the abolition crisis of the 1880s, and he was regarded by many as an arbiter of national destiny. When João Alfredo Correia de Oliveira was asked to form the cabinet of 7 March 1888, which passed the "Golden Law" abolishing Brazilian slavery two months later, it was primarily to Antônio Prado that he turned for advice.[11] Antônio's brother Martinico became a leading Republican politician in São Paulo. First elected in 1878, he was the only Republican to serve continuously in the Provincial Assembly until 1889, when the monarchy was overthrown. A third brother, Caio, served as president of the northern provinces of Alagoas and Ceará from 1887 to 1889.

Some observers of nineteenth-century Brazilian politics have depicted the gradual emergence of regional family oligarchies as a response to the vacuum created by the decline of the centralized monarchy after 1870.[12] Case studies of this supposed process are few and are concerned primarily with the Brazilian northeast, where traditionally family power was stronger and socioeconomic change less marked than in the south.[13] It is in this context that the Prados' political behavior is important. Three aspects of this behavior are of particular interest: the Prados' relationship to the monarchy, the degree of family political solidarity, and the contrasting political styles of Antônio and Martinico Prado.[14]

The Politics of Skepticism

The Prados' rise to regional prominence in the nineteenth century was assisted by their ties to the monarchy. The baron of Iguape's hosting of Dom Pedro I at the time of Brazilian independence, his subsequent appointment to local offices, and his reception at the court in the late 1820s began this process. In 1842 the baron supported the imperial forces of royal conservatism against the Liberal revolt in São Paulo. In 1852 he was again called upon to ensure São Paulo's adherence to national control.[15] The Prados of the baron's generation regarded a strong monarchy as necessary to provide the political stability that seemed threatened during the First Empire, the Regency, and the early years of the Second Empire.

To the subsequent generation of Prados, this period of political turmoil was more remote, and after 1850 the dominant conservatism of the Prados was challenged by new socioeconomic conditions. Of the four sons of Martinho and Veridiana, only the second oldest, Martinico, formally repudiated conservatism and the monarchy itself. Antônio Prado and his younger brothers, Caio and Eduardo, continued to adhere to the Conservative party banner, but their loyalty lost its traditional *raison d'être* as São Paulo suffered from the monarchy's centralization. The dominant family tradition of conservatism was thus conditioned by a sharp skepticism engendered by the spectacle of Brazilian political practices, the example of European politics, and official neglect of the requirements of economic growth in São Paulo. However, their skepticism—directed at political systems—never became a cynicism directed at human nature.

In Europe in 1862, Antônio Prado drew a distinction between Brazilian Liberals and philosophical liberalism and stated that he had the worst possible impression of young men devoid of liberal principles. He continued that he was a Conservative because, in the 1860s, "there is no one in Brazil who is not a Liberal." In the same letter he blamed Brazil's "village politicians" for maintaining the status quo when the nation "could achieve a very prominent place" in the world.[16] In 1863 Antônio extended his criticism from the village to the court: "Unhappily our monarch has flattery galore at his disposition; from that, perhaps, come all our evils. Flattery that leads on to impotence and to nonchalance is worse than idolatry, because the latter at least, even if erroneously, supports itself in the cult of divinity."[17]

That it was not Conservative but Liberal ministers flattering Dom Pedro II had much to do with Antônio's feelings. Yet he was no friend of divine-right monarchy and was equally hostile to the regime of "social rights," or socialism. Instead, he placed his faith in the classic liberalism of the individual: "Today, at least in regimes based on sound theory, individual rights, which are born of liberty and which engender equality, dominate unique[ly] and exclusively."[18] Antônio's political philosophy was consistent with the economic orientation of unhampered private enterprise, which he had observed in its classic form, England of the Industrial Revolution.[19] His views also carried the germ of the egalitarianism and liberal democracy that marked his later political career.

Applying his views to contemporary Brazil induced grave misgivings in Antônio as he pondered the political career designed for him by family elders. As he wrote his father in 1864: "When one has real beliefs, the sacrifice of them to the petty exigencies of party interest becomes difficult if not impossible. To believe that the religion of ideas, or that honesty of convictions, can ever lead to the advancement of a young man among us is the simplest of all illusions. Transactions and more transactions, compromises and more compromises, these are the thorns on the road of politics."[20]

This was a prophetic personal statement. Despite making an uneasy peace with the political system and achieving considerable power within it, Antônio never lost his skepticism. In September 1887 he chided both fellow Conservatives and the Liberals for their ineffectiveness on the abolition issue and showed deep concern for the effects of partisanship on the political system:

> The time is already overdue to initiate a politics of vaster horizons and one which inspires itself in patriotism.
> . . . The struggle for power has spoiled all states of affairs, jumbling ideas, falsifying principles, weakening characters.

The parties no longer have banners; and, if they have them, they are banners without principles.[21]

This sentiment stemmed in part from Antônio Prado's own experience. To gain power he had modified principles himself, as when he lent support to the Liberals in promoting the 1885 law freeing slaves over the age of sixty despite his long-term opposition to emancipation. In the last years of the monarchy, he also began to repudiate one of the Empire's main features, centralization, and gingerly approached the federalist idea, a switch applauded by some as political realism and condemned by others as opportunism or betrayal of the Conservative party.[22]

Behind Antônio Prado's evolution from slavocrat and monarchist in 1871 to abolitionist and proto-federalist in 1888–89 were developments in São Paulo, where partisanship was usually put aside on matters of economic growth. Antônio lectured the national senate in 1886 that "one of the reasons, if not the principal reason, for the prosperity of my province is that the Paulista does not play politics when dealing with material improvements. There, there are railroads, navigation [companies] and other enterprises organized by the initiative of Conservatives, Liberals, and Republicans, who know how to forget disagreements when their cooperation is required for the province's good."[23] That the Brazilian monarchy did not operate in this manner, that it valued "village politics" over material improvement, was the root source of Antônio's skepticism toward national politics.

The other Prado brothers showed similar skepticism of Brazilian politics during the late Empire. As president of Alagoas and Ceará in the years 1887 to 1889, Caio Prado, also a Conservative, tried to bring the Paulista style of interparty cooperation north and to remain above the squabbling factionalism typical of the northeast. In Alagoas he was particularly successful, and he prided himself on having avoided "fomenting passions in the public mind, favoring partisan hatreds, [and] poisoning the sources of tranquillity of my fellow citizens," dangers he regarded as all too common in Brazilian politics. According to one historian, Caio's "democratic use" of his prerogatives was the major feature of his administration in Alagoas.[24] In Ceará, Caio faced a more difficult situation: the Conservative and Liberal parties were fragmented, and the drought of 1888 created a tumultuous situation unlike any he had ever seen in the prosperous south. Although he succeeded in gaining imperial relief for drought victims, Caio was accused of using the funds for partisan ends.[25] His political acts in Ceará, as he wrote his mother, provoked "the most infamous attacks on my person"; as a result, he was unable to maintain the aloof impartiality so successful in Alagoas and was drawn into partisanship, convinced he had on his side "the *healthy* part of the province."[26] Caio's brief career (he died in office in Fortaleza in 1889) can only have increased the Prados' political skepticism.

The youngest Prado brother, Eduardo, the only one never to occupy political office, was also the most devout monarchist, particularly after 1889. Nonetheless, he shared the family misgivings about Brazilian political life during the monarchy. In a remarkably objective essay published shortly before the collapse of the monarchy, Eduardo traced the malaise of Brazilian politics to that central, unique instrument, the moderating power:

> The parties are convinced of the uselessness of all their efforts for the conquest of power if they do not have the support of Imperial intervention. From that results the weakness of the opposition, the insolence of governments, and the false and demoralized situation of the political chieftains, dependent directly not on the electorate, but on the Emperor, the single axis of the State, about which gyrates all the machinery of the vast Brazilian monarchy.[27]

For a man who during the Republic made monarchism almost a religion, that was a strong statement. Like other Prados, Eduardo proposed decentralizing the monarchy, and he looked with favor on the federalist examples of Switzerland and the United States.

Martinico Prado was the only one of the brothers to reject completely the family's Conservative party traditions. Skepticism of the monarchy was the integrating theme of his politics. In Provincial Assembly speeches he gave long discourses on the bankruptcy of Brazilian political history and on the abandonment of principle by both Conservatives and Liberals. Typical was his satirical summary of Dom Pedro II's annual messages, a sly mixture of the emperor's personal life and his supposed abuses of power and neglect of Brazil's serious problems:

The first message from the throne, after the declaration of [Pedro's] majority in 1841, . . . said nothing more than that it was necessary to reform the electoral law.

In 1842 we had the dissolution [of the parliament] . . .

[In 1843] it was announced that the King had corrected his marriage contract [and] that he was heartsick over the rebellion in Sorocaba and Barbacena.

The royal message of May 3, 1843, announced the wedding of Princess Francisca with Sr. Joinville and there was hope for peace in Rio Grande do Sul.[28]

In other speeches Martinico sought to discredit the tradition that Dom Pedro had brought peace and stability to Brazil, and he emphasized the empire's dismal financial state.[29] As noted earlier, Martinico initially used models of European political experience to discredit the Brazilian monarchy.[30] Thus one of the factors tending to unite the Prados politically was the negative ground of profound skepticism directed at the monarchy.

The Politics of Family

Given the Prados' shared skepticism about the monarchy and their common concern for the growth of São Paulo, it is not surprising that their political behavior reflected a high degree of family cooperation. In some cases this phenomenon served to reinforce party loyalties, and in others it transcended them.

A striking example of family influence occurred in Antônio Prado's first national candidacy in 1868, when he stood for the seat representing São Paulo's Third District in the Chamber of Deputies. When proposed for the post by his father and grandfather, Antônio was in Portugal on his honeymoon. Adding to the controversy surrounding the election, one of his fellow aspirants on the three-man Conservative ticket was his political tutor and father-in-law, Antônio da Costa Pinto e Silva, then president of Rio Grande do Sul. A local judge, Vicente Ferreira da Silva Bueno, regarded the father-in-law and son-in-law tandem as "scandalous." To complete the family's involvement in this election, Martinico Prado, no philosophical ally of his brother (as he made clear), rose to Antônio's defense against Silva Bueno's "low and nauseating intrigue."[31] In his absentee appeal for voter support, meanwhile, Antônio Prado stressed that he had been a faithful Conservative soldier and with no little "sacrifices" had advocated "the cause of the persecuted [Conservatives], in spite of the menace of the government." His main promise to the electors was "the duty of loyalty."[32] Swept into national office with the Conservatives' return to power in 1869, Antônio joined his father-in-law in endorsing a Conservative slate for the Provincial Assembly, a slate on which his own name stood first.[33] Brazilian law allowed the simultaneous holding of national and provincial offices. This, together with property qualifications and other factors, severely restricted the political game to a small elite.

Further evidence of family solidarity lies in Conservative Antônio's and Republican Martinico's identification of common enemies. The first political ventures of both—Antônio in an election for the Provincial Assembly in 1865 and Martinico as district attorney in São Paulo in 1867—ended unsuccessfully as the result of partisan opposition from the Liberals.[34] In the 1870s Antônio and Martinico both fought the Paulista Conservative leader, João Mendes de Almeida. In 1872, after the passage of the Law of the Free Womb, which both Antônio and Martinico opposed,[35] two rival Conservative factions emerged in São Paulo. The anti-emancipationist *Pradistas*, led by Antônio Prado, soon emerged victorious over the pro-emancipationist *Mendistas*, led by João Mendes.[36]

The feud continued, however, and in 1876, despite attacks on Conservatives in his own município of Araras, where he had become an alderman, Martinico inserted himself into it. The Paulista Republicans, organized into a party at the Convention of Itú in 1873, were three years later considering election to provincial office. Martinico lacked the immediate family support that had started Antônio on his political career and looked for allies in the established parties. José Alves dos Santos, a Conservative and Eduardo Prado's godfather, asked Martinico for the Republicans' support in Araras, because the Republicans had only one candidate in the upcoming provincial elections, Américo Brasiliense. After conferring with other Republicans, Martinico made the deal: Republican votes for dos Santos, Conservative votes for Brasiliense. Criticized by the Liberals for this transaction, Martinico defended himself with a reply that is a succinct comment on the era's politics: "I obtained these votes exclusively through my personal relations, without the least hint of a deal." Martinico further wondered at the Liberals' moral outrage, because they themselves had made such trades, first vilifying Antônio Prado's rival, João Mendes de Almeida, then delivering votes to him. Martinico then revealed that Mendes's aides had sought his support as well and that he had refused.[37]

It seems apparent that behind the rather Byzantine partisan politics of São Paulo in the 1870s, the real loyalties were in significant measure those of family, such as the friendship between the Prado and Alves dos Santos clans.[38] Despite their different party loyalties, Antônio and Martinico Prado had selected as their chief enemy the ultramontane Catholic Conservative João Mendes de Almeida; ironically, Mendes and Eduardo Prado would become close allies in the monarchist movement in São Paulo in the 1890s.

In the 1880s family considerations continued as part of the Prados' politics. In 1885, when Antônio Prado was minister of agriculture, he exchanged notes with Rodrigo Augusto da Silva concerning the post of provincial engineer in São Paulo. Although Antônio could not name Francisco Jordão to the post as Rodrigo Silva urged, family and party interests were intermixed in the negotiations.[39] A more important example of family influence was the appointment of Caio Prado as president of Alagoas in 1887. The appointment originated in Veridiana's desire to remove her son from the supposed bohemianism of São Paulo and was implemented through Antônio Prado's influence.[40] A fellow parliamentarian attributed Antônio's power partly to his "numerous and important family."[41] Similarly, what prestige and influence Caio enjoyed as provincial president was due to the fact that he had "a brother in the government, considered an arbiter of the situation" and that he came from "a family of millionaires."[42]

Most significant of all factors uniting the Prados politically was their promotion of railroads, immigration, and, eventually, abolition, elements of nineteenth-century Brazilian liberalism which, especially in São Paulo, transcended formal party affiliation. In the 1880s, as fazendeiros worked out a successful immigration program in São Paulo, the Prados gradually dropped their opposition to abolition, opening up communication with a leading abolitionist (and Liberal), Joaquim Nabuco. In the early 1880s Martinico Prado wrote to Nabuco that he shared his views on abolition, not only on humanitarian grounds, but also because "I yield, most of all, to an economic conviction that this country will be truly rich only on the day when there are no more slaves."[43] Later, in 1887, when the gradualist approach to abolition which the Prados supported had failed, and when slaves began to defect from Paulista plantations *en masse,* the Prados joined a planter association, the Associação Libertadora, which lent its support to growing demands for abolition.[44]

Shortly thereafter, Eduardo Prado wrote to Nabuco informing him of the Associação Libertadora's plans and attempting to enlist Nabuco's support for the Paulista planters' effort: "If it should happen that the great majority of the farmers of São Paulo province promise to free all their slaves by the end of '89, will your party [the Liberal abolitionists] be satisfied? Can it limit itself to exerting pressure on the slaveowners of Rio de Janeiro to get them to imitate the example of the Paulistas?" Nabuco agreed to this approach, because it split the formerly solid opposition of southern coffee planters to abolition and drove a wedge between Antônio Prado and more retrograde Conservative leaders, such as the baron of Cotegipe, João Maurício Wanderley. In an audience with Pope Leo XIII on 10 February 1888, Nabuco drove home the point that abolitionism had become "pre-eminently a movement of the landowning class itself," citing the recently adopted stance of Antônio Prado as proof. Subsequently Nabuco praised Antônio's statesmanship as a key factor in ending Brazilian slavery.[45]

The Prados' approximation to Nabuco and other evidence cited above make it clear that family solidarity was a significant element in the Prados' politics, one that transcended Conservative and Republican party affiliations many times. Were there any limits to the politics of family? A comparison of Antônio's and Martinico's political styles as a function of family influence brings us closer to understanding the role of politics in the family.

Connectedness and Disconnectedness: The Limits of Family Politics

Alfred Adler's thought provides a guide to analyzing the psychology of political behavior among siblings. Adler posited that first sons will tend to be conservative, to follow the parental example, while younger sons tend to be rebellious and to believe there is no power on earth that cannot be overturned.[46] More recently, the psychiatrist Irving D. Harris has advanced the hypothesis that first- and later-born politicians differ essentially in the "connectedness" and "disconnectedness" of their approach to politics.[47] Harris's hypothesis provides a suggestive tool for examining the political orientations and styles of the two principal Prado politicians, Antônio and Martinico.

Antônio was much more clearly linked to the Prado family's political conventions than was Martinico. In family tradition, Antônio is the heroic expression of the family's political status at its height, while Martinico is the militant dissident. Though both expressed considerable skepticism about the game of politics, Antônio's misgivings did not lead him outside the empire's established framework. Martinico, in contrast, repudiated Brazil's entire political history as absolutist oppression of liberal democracy.[48] Antônio rose to power within the Conservative party by styling himself initially as a "faithful soldier" of that party. As a politician, Martinico had to connect himself to the electorate also. He did so by pledging to adhere to the *mandato imperativo*, the principle binding politicians to reflect their constituents' views, but he reserved the right to disconnect himself at any moment. "I will do only that which the electorate wishes," he said in 1882, "as long as its aspirations are in harmony with my way of thinking."[49]

Because of the connections Antônio enjoyed, those of family prestige and of establishment politics, it was unnecessary for him to cultivate the electorate, as limited as it was during the monarchy. Antônio's constituents knew what they could expect of the baron of Iguape's grandson, Martinho Prado's son, and Antônio da Costa Pinto e Silva's son-in-law. Antônio's public manner, and his parliamentary bearing in particular, were the epitome of the expressionless quality Brazilians know as *casmurrice*, the pursuit of an inner set of goals behind a cold, stony façade.[50] Antônio's style was that of the established de facto aristocrat, the noble and heroic type who inspires confidence by his station in life rather than by an infectious personality.

In contrast, Martinico Prado, disengaged from family political traditions and allegiances, developed a militant style that capitalized on his flamboyant personality, his human relations talent, his keen sense of satire, and his rapport with the electorate. An appreciative assessment of Martinico's campaign style, written in the early 1880s, pictured him as a "political Columbus" who had abandoned "lying" written programs in favor of live speeches delivered almost in the style of the New England town meeting. Following Martinico from town to town in the Ninth Assembly District, Victor Malin observed the great success of this approach, which was more remarkable in that Martinico addressed predominantly Conservative and Liberal audiences. "In place of backroom intrigues, of ambiguous political pamphlets, of clandestine negotiations," Malin wrote, "Dr. Martinho Prado Júnior is going to inaugurate among us the system of the *meeting*, of the conference, of the full and openly debated demonstration of . . . political ideas."[51]

It is clearly necessary to take this with a grain of salt. The ideological in Martinico, as in any politician, was tempered by the practical. To be elected and to ensure the election of other Republicans, Martinico had traded votes with Conservatives. He had to negate the threat Republicanism inspired in Conservative and Liberal constituents by denying that he was radical: "I am a law-abiding, level-headed, obliging Republican. Therefore what I will do, if elected deputy, will flow from those characteristics like the coffee bean from the hulling machine."[52] Martinico also made porkbarrel appeals, promising to fight for needed public works and services in the neglected Ninth District.[53] When he sought national office in 1884, when the emancipation of sexagenarians was the chief controversy, however, he expressed his commitment to open, representative politics. Martinico noted that Liberals and Conservatives (he exempted his brother's Conservative Union from the latter) failed to say how they would vote on the project, a violation of his sense of political ethics: "The politician owes respect and deference to his fellow citizens, to the point of the most complete frankness in relating his plans. Only thus can . . . [politicians] be considered representatives of a party and thus of an idea. Acting otherwise, they are nothing more than buyers of votes, pirates in the hands of politics under the inspiration of private interests, in opposition to public ones."[54] Martinico took an open stand in favor of the sexagenarian emancipation project, and his subsequent clear defeat[55] showed that his constituents were not ready then for even gradual abolition, though they returned him to the Provincial Assembly to represent their less controversial interests.

Martinico's republicanism, despite its compromises with political reality and with common family economic interests, placed strain on immediate family ties. In 1881 one of his brothers, Caio or Eduardo, writing under the pseudonym "Piff," covered Martinico's reception as guest of honor at the law school's Republican club, the Clube Republicano Acadêmico. "Piff" treated the whole affair with condescension: when Martinico took his seat, "never was there seen such enthusiasm for such a simple feat."[56] During his speech Martinico removed his frock coat, symbol of the Establishment, invoked the image of the eighteenth-century revolutionary Tiradentes,[57] and urged young Republicans not to become turncoats (*virar casaca*) if offered posts by the established parties. Later, in a poem written under the conjunctive pseudonym "Peff-Piff," Eduardo and Caio implied that Martinico was the real traitor:

> In Yesteryear the Tooth-
> Puller sang, now he pulls
> Teeth for the Republic, oh Lie
> Yesterday Shirtsleeves sang
> The Turncoat who
> Exhausts the patience of his family.[58]

Eduardo Prado was later to characterize the Republicans of which his brother was a prominent spokesman as privileged malcontents and "slavocrats . . . [who], out of hatred for the empire, made themselves Republicans."[59]

The Prados' political role in the late Empire was, at first glance, paradoxical: highly skeptical of the political system, they nonetheless achieved considerable influence in it, particularly in the critical years from 1885 to 1889, when Antônio Prado was minister of agriculture and Caio Prado served as president of two provinces. The paradox dissolves when it is recalled that the Prados' rising political fortunes coincided with the disintegration, after 1870, of what has been called Brazil's "mandarin" system of national administration. Though Antônio and Caio qualify as members of the mandarin class that governed imperial Brazil, they entered it at a point when the centralizing national role of that class was ceasing to function.[60] Antônio was primarily a regionalist mandarin, especially concerned with the economic needs of São Paulo. And Caio, it will be recalled, had been placed in a high post of the national administration not so much for political reasons as for family ones: Veridiana wanted to remove him from the allegedly dispersive life he led in São Paulo. In Caio's case, the politics of family had double meaning.

While there is considerable evidence that family ties strongly affected the Prados' politics in the Second Empire, the family does not appear to have functioned as a family oligarchy in the manner of, for example, the Feitosas, who dominated the interior of Ceará in northeastern Brazil. Caio Prado explicitly rejected traditional politics in Alagoas, though he was less successful in doing so in Ceará. Moreover, São Paulo's society was more complex and was experiencing more rapid change than the Brazilian northeast. In addition, the national and provincial arenas in which the Prados operated were less amenable than the rural município to family control. Finally, the Prados aimed not so much at political dominance itself as at influencing those areas of provincial and national politics that impinged on regional economic growth. In the last analysis, the family's political solidarity was an expression of common economic interest, the best evidence of which is Antônio's and Martinico's broad cooperation (seasoned with brotherly quibbling over tactics) on the abolition-immigration question.

Paulista republicanism, based on a necessary compromise between committed abolitionists and anti-emancipation fazendeiros, and characterized by vote trading between its adherents and provincial Conservatives, lacked the pungency one might expect of a supposedly "radical" movement that aimed at overthrow of the monarchy. Nonetheless, the purely political aspects of Martinico Prado's republicanism did strain family ties. It should not be overlooked that other Prados viewed his republicanism as a heresy against the very traditions of Conservative party loyalty that had assisted the Prados' rise to power. In contrast to Antônio, Martinico received no assistance from the immediate family in his maverick political career. Finally, his flamboyant rhetoric added to the discontent that helped to discredit the regime in which his brother was a high and influential leader. When the monarchy fell during the height of Antônio's personal and political powers, he was forced into political retirement for a decade and never regained his former influence.

The Prados were not one of the monolithic political families pictured in the traditional literature as typical of Brazilian politics. Politics was, in fact, an element contributing to the decline in the Prado family's solidarity. The general conditions of the monarchy and the overwhelming importance of the abolition issue muted this tendency before 1889. After that date, political friction within the family became more pronounced. Moreover, individualistic responses to the new political environment after the fall of the monarchy became more characteristic of the Prados than were corporate political strategies.

❧ CHAPTER VI ❧

FAMILY LIFE IN THE

FIRST REPUBLIC,

1889–1930

Traditionally, the Brazilian First Republic has been regarded as a period of declining family influence. In Gilberto Freyre's synthesis, the era was marked by a "process of disintegration of the patriarchal and semi-patriarchal societies in Brazil."[1] The collapse of the monarchy and the deportation of Dom Pedro II have been interpreted as a kind of national patricide that was followed by filial guilt and a resurgence of reverence for the departed father.[2] In chapters 1 and 2, I argued that in São Paulo the patriarchal tradition may not have had the deep foundation characteristic of the more conventional Brazilian northeast, and in fact Republican sentiment was very strong in São Paulo, which was among those states that played leading roles in the First Republic. In the case of the Prados, we have already seen that there were many exceptions before 1889 to the supposed patriarchal norms of family life. The result was a family that was, if not egalitarian, at least strongly individualistic. These trends, combined with the unsettled atmosphere of the First Republic, resulted in a further weakening of the Prados' family structure and an increase in intrafamilial conflict after 1889.

Extended Family and Parentela

The fifth generation of the Prado-surname extended family, that which matured in the late nineteenth century, consisted of fifty members in ten nuclear groups, a near-doubling of the extended family in one generation. A significant measure of the weakening of the extended family structure is the changing pattern of marriages, summarized in Table 4.

Most fourth-generation marriages were arranged by parents, and practical economic and political considerations took precedence over romantic love. This may also have been true in the fifth generation, but under the influence of social and cultural change the level of "rational," nonromantic decision may have declined. In the fifth generation, endogamous marriage was relatively rare. Interestingly, however, it was in the most successful family branches—the descendants of Martinho and Veridiana Prado—that marriage between cousins continued. With one exception (Eduardo Prado's marriage to his cousin Carolina), these marriages involved Prados and non-Prado cousins. There were thus almost no unions between the ten nuclear groups of the Prado-surname extended family in the fifth generation. This reflected the differentiation that occurred within the extended family during the nineteenth century as a result of economic factors, differences in cultural attainments, and even miscegenation. The successful Prados were based in the provincial (after 1889, the state) capital, and their economic and political strength grew in the nineteenth century under the monarchy as that city tightened its control of the province. In contrast, the more obscure family branches continued to reside in secondary towns like Jundiaí; their modest economic and political status offered little marital incentive to their richer, more powerful, more urban cousins. In addition, miscegena-

TABLE 4

Marriage Patterns in the Prado Family

Relationship of Spouse	4th Generation	5th Generation
Other Prado	5	1
Other Relatives	6	4
Nonrelatives	11	36
Total	22	41

Sources: Frederico de Barros Brotero, *A família Jordão,* 57–167; Brotero, *Queirozes,* 11, 19, 69; *In Memoriam: Martinho Prado Júnior* [392]–[402]; and Luiz Gonzaga da Silva Leme, *Genealogia Paulistana* 7:26–39, 39–42.

tion removed one family branch from the possibility of intermarriage with the others.

Thus the incidence of exogamous marriages increased greatly. In the less prominent Prado branches, most of these were with persons of obscure origins and accomplishments, including several whose names—Fiori, Joly, Storiani, and Mayer—indicate that they may have been recent immigrants. Especially in the leading family branches, however, many new ties were also established with other important families: with fazendeiros and businessmen of the Alves de Lima, Junqueira, Cunha Bueno, Pires Ferreira, and Aranha families; and with political and military figures from various Brazilian regions and from the Melo e Franco, Araújo de Oliveira, Mendonça, and Gomes Guimarães families (see Appendix B). Thus the prominent branches enhanced their status while further increasing the gap separating them from their country cousins. One of the main new alliances was formed by multiple unions with the family of Count Leite Penteado (Antônio Alvares Leite Penteado, 1852–1912). For many Paulistas, Antônio Prado and Antônio Leite Penteado symbolized the financial and industrial surge in São Paulo during the First Republic.[3] Another important alliance was between Martinico's son Fábio Prado, who became mayor of São Paulo in the 1930s, and Renata, the daughter of the leading immigrant industrialist, Rudolfo Crespi. The Prado-Crespi union is evidence of the merger of planter and immigrant elites in São Paulo.[4] Less well known is the fact that members of the traditional but tattered elite families of the Brazilian northeast married into successful southern families like the Prados. This was the social counterpart of the economic and political shifts that occurred in late-nineteenth-century Brazil.[5]

In sum, the tendency in the extended family was toward greater internal differentiation, while the leading Prados strengthened their parentela by making new alliances outside the initial family network. Several Prado branches never escaped obscurity, and they were ignored for marital purposes by the more successful elements of the clan. There was a clear trend from endogamous to exogamous marriage. In one extended family there were many nuclear families of unequal status, and the bonds of family often proved weaker than those of residence, wealth, talent, class, and race. While not entirely abandoning the practice of cousin-marriage, the leading Prados showed little interest in it as a goal in itself. Meanwhile, within the leading branch the tendency toward individualization and conflict continued.

The Growth of Conflict

The most prominent Prados found the social and political environment of the First Republic to be, at best, unfriendly to their traditions and ideals. They tended to devote themselves more exclusively to economic activities and withdrew from or rebelled against the Republic's politics. Antônio Prado and his family made five trips to Europe in the 1890s, largely because of their distaste with events in Brazil. In October 1891 Maria Catarina Prado wrote to a son that Antônio, whose loyalty to his native city was legendary, had only bad things to say about it.[6] Between escapes to Europe, the couple spent many nights in São Paulo "completely alone," and in November Maria wrote to her son Paulo, "You cannot imagine how different São Paulo is: everything is lacking. There is much talk that we will return [to Europe] in September of '92 and I hope to God this happens."[7] As Maria Catarina observed, Dom Pedro II's death in exile on 5 December 1891 emphasized the family's sudden isolation in Paulistano society:

> We have felt our emperor's death strongly. In Rio, they say, the sorrow was immense, but here in São Paulo it was absolutely nothing, so that the [state] President let the normal Thursday concert go on and it lasted all afternoon and night and there was a very well attended performance. Your father is one of the frequenters of these concerts, but this night he did not go because Nazareth, who felt [the emperor's death] strongly, formally opposed it.[8]

Escaping to the mountain resort at Caxambú did little to ease the isolation the Prados felt. They found only a few old friends there; the other vacationers were "something ghastly." Antônio Prado, who may have preferred the odds of roulette to those of politics and life, was one of the most enthusiastic players and biggest winners.[9]

The family of Antônio and Maria Catarina found more genuine refuge at their fazenda, Santa Veridiana. Antônio plunged into the construction of a large new house there, and Maria reported in June of 1892 that it was "splendid and is well furnished (even luxurious) and the front garden is very pretty and it does not even seem that we are on a fazenda in São Paulo."[10] The younger children's studies with their tutors—the padre Garrand for the boys and Mademoiselle Ruling, who was with the family for fifty years, for the girls—provided an air of normality. Young Luíz Prado was fascinated by the work and stories of the fazenda's blacksmith, the former slave Firmino. Life was enlivened by the visits of relatives like Dr. Eulálio da Costa Carvalho, Elias Fausto Pacheco Jordão, Nabor Jordão, Inácio Monteiro de Barros, and Francisco Pacheco e Silva. If he was home from Europe and not feuding with Antônio over politics, Eduardo Prado came from his adjoining fazenda, Brejão, often bringing with him foreigners such as the Belgian chemist August Collon or the American geologist Orville Derby.[11] The saint's-day festivals in June and July were always occasions for large family reunions, one of which was briefly described by Maria Catarina: "There was much dancing and Gabriel Coutinho did stunts with Almeida[.] They found a young girl, the wife of the administrator of Brejão, who is very uninhibited, and danced the *fado* a great deal, . . . so that we spent all night of São João's eve much entertained. There were bonfires and the band here at the fazenda already plays very well."[12]

In the city, however, Maria Catarina remained at times shut up in the house for days, something she said never happened in Europe.[13] Antônio went out with his cousin Elias Fausto Pacheco Jordão, his brother-in-law Elias Antônio Pacheco e Chaves, and, less frequently perhaps, his brother Martinico. The men dined at a new restaurant, the "Rotisserie Sportsman," which Antônio said was the equal of the restaurants of Paris, and sometimes made trips alone to their seaside resort at Guarujá.[14] There were also extravagant rites like the marriage of Martinico's son Plínio to his first cousin, Lucila Pacheco e Chaves, to add color to what was otherwise a disturbing and unsettling time for the family.[15] These fêtes, as in this case, were too often followed by family tragedies like the death of Antônio's and Maria's daughter Marina Prado Aranha, who died on 20 December 1896, after giving birth to her second child.[16]

More significant yet was the generational conflict that overtook the Prados. The graduation of Paulo Prado, Antônio's and Maria Catarina's oldest son, from the São Paulo law school in 1889 coincided

with the fall of the monarchy. This juxtaposition of events symbolized the difficulties of coming of age in a changed political and
social atmosphere: "Paulo saw the doors of the career that he would
have followed if Dom Pedro II's reign had continued for some years
more close on him."[17] Deeply personal factors were at work as well.
Had Paulo followed the elite tradition for first sons, he would have
married fairly early (after the mandatory European sojourn), brought
up a large family, and assumed his role as principal heir to the family
political and economic fortunes. Instead, he had a stormy, willful,
and even irresponsible life as a young man and settled down to the
responsibilities of his position only during the World War I era.[18]

In 1891 Paulo's mother wrote to him about his personal difficulties, advising him to regularize his life.[19] Paulo's years of traveling—
more escape from family control than mere post–law school sojourn—troubled his family as much as Eduardo's had earlier. Veridiana complained that Paulo, her grandson, was an ingrate and for a
while would not speak of him.[20] In 1894, as Paulo's absence continued, Maria Catarina wrote him of her concern: "I believe you are
enjoying yourself too much; it is necessary to be cautious. Your father, who is very good, is angry, but promised that he would send you
money."[21] Two years later, when Paulo asked to go to Japan, Antônio
was very annoyed and reminded Paulo that he was needed in the
family businesses, a complaint Antônio renewed the next year when
he accused Paulo of abandoning the Prado-Chaves Export House.[22]
Rather than inclining his head before paternal authority, Paulo shot
back an angry reply alleging that he was losing his company position
to a more industrious rival.[23] Antônio Prado, who was reputed to be
a strict disciplinarian, was unable to control his oldest son and continued to finance a style of life that displeased him.

To understand this clash it is necessary to appreciate moral conflicts of the era as the Prados experienced them. Elements of the
traditional Prado morality have already been mentioned: Antônio's
commitment to hard work and steadfastness, Veridiana's concern
when Eduardo had been spirited away from God and family by "impious folk," and Maria Catarina's feeling that it was dangerous to
enjoy oneself too much. Maria's letters to Paulo provide further examples. In February of 1892 she wrote him of one of the samba
"schools" that was to compete in that year's Carnival, "which could
win a prize for the indecency of the women who were all almost

naked. I never saw such immorality as now here in São Paulo!!"[24] From Lisbon in 1893 Maria sent Paulo this description: "Lisbon is very lively and I believe that it ought to be very agreeable to men, because all the *demi-monde* that I saw in [Paris] is here and in all places calling one's attention. For families this is very insipid."[25] As Maria Catarina reckoned, young, unattached men like Paulo would indeed be attracted to the demi-monde, which a proper family could only regard as tasteless at best.

Paulo's younger brother Luíz later thought that of that generation only he, Luíz, had led a normal life; the others were involved in *brigas de família*, family fights.[26] Many of them adopted *belle époque* life-styles that contrasted sharply with their fathers' careers as planters and politicians. Before he became mayor of Rio de Janeiro in the late 1920s, Antônio Prado Júnior showed little sign of settling down to traditional family life. In 1906 he was styled as "one of Paulista society's most brilliant young men and one of the most active organizers of the elegant and sporting life" of São Paulo.[27] In his yellow Panhard he made an 8,500-mile trip through France, Switzerland, Austria, Germany, Holland, and Belgium in twenty-two days, and was later credited with making the first trip from São Paulo to Rio by auto. With his wife, Eglantina Penteado Prado—"an almost-Parisienne Paulista who is one of the most beautiful ornaments of our feminine society"[28]—Antônio Júnior enjoyed a life of conspicuous consumption based on the hard-earned wealth of his father rather than on adherence to the paternal work ethic.

Nor were changes in society and their reflection in family life limited to Prado sons. Nazareth Prado, Antônio's and Maria Catarina's oldest daughter, eschewed the traditional marriage ceremony when she married Oduvaldo Pacheco e Silva, substituting for it "an entirely new thing, . . . very common in Europe."[29] After her marriage Nazareth withdrew from her parents and thereby prompted numerous complaints from her mother, who (like Antônio with Paulo) found herself powerless to remedy the situation: "Nazareth does not come here because Oduvaldo wants to go to his fazenda and since mothers-in-law ought not to mix in their sons-in-laws' life, I do not say anything, [but] suffer silently."[30] Nazareth later separated from Oduvaldo, became a "disciple" of the diplomat-writer Graça Aranha, a free spirit of the 1920s avant-garde, and according to some, a black sheep of the family.[31]

In a different form, generational conflict also afflicted Martinico Prado, the "radical" of the fourth generation. The permissiveness he advocated in the 1880s did not extend to relations with sons-in-law. Martinico's chief problem was Alberto de Oliveira, son of a rich Recife merchant who had committed suicide two years after Alberto's birth; Alberto was married to Martinico's eldest daughter, the docile, innocent Lavínia whom Ina von Binzer had liked so well. Alberto's doings included a fraudulent business venture, gambling, late hours, and a generally dissolute life, all of which left Martinico livid with fury.[32] Having none of Maria Catarina's scruples about the role of in-laws, Martinico intervened to correct the errant Alberto, whose affairs nonetheless went from bad to worse.[33]

In addition to conflict between generations, the tense political situation of the 1890s (see chapter 9) caused the heightening of sibling rivalry within the older generation. The Brazilian civil war of 1893 and the divergent political loyalties of Antônio, Martinico, and Eduardo Prado caused one such episode. Eduardo became chronically angry with Martinico and "very mistrustful" of Antônio, who in turn would not speak to Eduardo.[34] The differences between Antônio and Eduardo were resolved, but it is unlikely that Eduardo and Martinico were ever able to bridge the gap created by their sharply opposed monarchist and Republican allegiances.

Another type of conflict, less open but equally characteristic of changing times and family mores, is evident in the marriage of Eduardo and Carolina Prado, which Veridiana finally pushed to a less than ideal conclusion in 1892. The marriage was a ritual in which Eduardo sacrificed his freedom and instincts on the altar of filial duty. Immediately after the ceremony, he left for his fazenda, leaving his bride in São Paulo city as he had earlier left her in a convent while he was globetrotting.[35] Temperamentally, Eduardo and Carolina were opposites: he was generally voluble, sociable, and expansive; she was cold and withdrawn. When fourteen-year-old Luíz Prado visited his uncle and aunt in Paris in 1899, Eduardo was absent and Carolina declined to greet her nephew personally.[36] On another occasion, when Eduardo invited Joaquim Nabuco to stay at Brejão, he referred to Carolina as simply "the silent lady of the house."[37] Eduardo and Carolina had no children in their nine years of marriage (Eduardo died in 1901), a further suggestion of the coolness between them.

While Veridiana's role in doggedly arranging Eduardo's marriage suggests the force of tradition in the family, in other respects her behavior does not. Unlike the baron of Iguape decades earlier, Veridiana was a remote figure to her grandchildren. Two of them recalled that she preferred the company of young people and foreigners to that of family members. Appearing before her as children to receive the ritual *benção* (blessing), they recall her saying to a servant: "Rita, give a cookie to these children and send them away. Children are prized in their absence."[38]

In describing several dimensions of conflict that indicate the changing nature of the Prado family, it is important not to lose sight of those areas of cooperation that continued to exist. In the 1920s the Prados continued to serve as historical example and as present support for certain members of their parentela. In writing to her own wayward son, Miguel, Alzira Chaves often invoked morals drawn from the lives of Martinho Prado and his son Eduardo.[39] Alzira's husband, Fernando, had suffered a series of economic reverses, and his family was rescued by close relatives. Martinico's son Caio, father of the historian, was especially active in the cause.[40] In 1923, when a cyclone damaged Fernando Chaves's fazenda, old quarrels were put aside. Alzira explained how relatives had come to the rescue:

> Uncle Mendonça proposed to your father's friends and relatives that each of them give a *conto* to help us with our indispensable expenses. . . . Uncle Antônio Prado, when he found out about this, said, "I too will enter into this, because the fight I had with Miguel is finished, and I will have great pleasure in helping Fernando." It is on these occasions that true friends are known.[41]

In addition, despite their relative political eclipse in the First Republic, the Prados were still called upon by relatives for political favors, though their capacity to deliver these was much reduced by circumstances.[42]

In part, of course, the changing nature of the family was due simply to the passing of the older generation. Before Martinho Prado died in 1891, he had purchased a block of houses in the city, evidently so that several branches of the family could live near each other.[43] Martinico suffered a serious cerebral malady in 1894, a stroke left him an invalid in 1900, and he died in 1906. Antônio's wife, Maria Catarina, died in 1899. Two years later, Eduardo succumbed to yellow fever. In 1910 Veridiana, the matriarch, died at the age of eighty-five. This left Antônio Prado, who lived until 1929, as the remaining family elder, but his influence was felt mainly among his own children. In the 1920s he came to depend more and more on his sons Luíz and Paulo, and was cared for by his daughter Nazareth.

In the 1970s family members dated the decline in the traditional closeness of the family from about the time of World War I.[44] The origins of this decline, as we have seen, reached back much farther, and it had many facets. The family members themselves gradually came to feel that there were not one but many Prado families, each with its own personality. In place of the unifying figure of the nineteenth century, the baron of Iguape, the most prominent Prados of the twentieth century had before them two contrasting types—the conservative, correct Antônio and the revolutionary, flamboyant Martinico—a fact crystallized in the publication of separate commemorative histories by the two family branches. The origins of this division lie in the marked individuality of the leading Prados and, as we shall see, in factors such as race. To understand it we must make an exploration, however difficult and tentative, of the collective and individual traits of the family's leading members.

Labyrinths of the Mind: Family, Personality, and Race

The easy generalities applied to some Brazilian families[45] do not seem adequate for the Prados. For one thing, while Paulistas may not have displayed in extreme form withdrawn, brooding introspection sometimes attributed to the Mineiros and other inhabitants of Brazil's remote interior, they were neither the stereotypical free-living sensualists of the northeast nor the fun-loving, expansive *Cariocas* of Rio de Janeiro. One observer, commenting on the difficulty of treating Eduardo Prado's complex personality, observed that "Eduardo Prado, as a good Paulista and a good Prado, never was a friend of confidences. He kept his intimate life for himself. He never was a man of the diary nor of memoirs."[46] The gifted Portuguese novelist Eça de Queiroz, who knew Eduardo as well as anyone, pronounced his biographical article on Eduardo "the worst article of all my bad articles" and begged Eduardo for "some idea, or even some adjective" to improve it.[47] The comment suggests the pronounced reticence that seems to have been part of the Prado family ethic. Or, as Paulo Prado said in a different context, "dirty laundry is washed in the family."[48]

Nonetheless, with due caution one may plausibly identify certain strands of the Prado family ethic. First, a devotion to work was evident in the family's extraordinary economic and political achievements. A second ingredient was an aggressive individualism that was always tolerated if not condoned by the family; that characteristic is best shown in the lives of Veridiana, Martinico, Eduardo, and Paulo Prado, but present in some degree in many other family members. This independence, as subsequent chapters will show, often resulted in the Prados' opposition, frequently at great personal cost, to dominant trends in Brazilian society. Antônio stood against the reactionaries of his own party in the climax of abolitionism and later against his class in the early coffee-subsidy schemes; Martinico opposed the monarchy and Eduardo the Republic; Veridiana rebelled against the ascriptive status of Paulista women; Paulo Prado attacked the bourgeois culture and political malaise of the 1920s; and, later, Caio Prado Júnior advocated Marxist change to correct the inequities of Brazilian society in the post-1930 era. A third characteristic was the Prados' public aloofness, particularly in politics, where Antônio, his brothers Caio and Martinico, his son Antônio Júnior, and his nephew Fábio, politicians all, claimed to be above the dirty business of the game. Aloofness, combined with a fourth characteristic, intellectual curiosity, led the Prados on many occasions to criticize the very society, the very class, of which they were prominent members; they often seemed to have the uncanny knack of standing simultaneously in the center of events and above them. This attribute can be explained partly by the family's unusually cosmopolitan exposure; its long involvement with European culture provided a set of experiences against which to evaluate Brazilian society. In addition, the Prados valued modern ideas and things and collected "firsts" as others might collect stamps and coins, while they clung to certain values of the land and of the rural fazenda, which was an important vehicle of their success. Tristão de Ataíde argued that the common Prado family trait was "the *spirit of antici-*

pation of the future, of risk, of adventure, that is so typical of the bandeirante spirit, so closely tied to Paulista tradition itself."[49] In sum, the family ethic encompassed the value of work, aggressive individualism, public aloofness (and private reticence), a critical social outlook, and a high degree of cosmopolitanism and modernism tempered by respect for the land and its traditions. This was an ethic that allowed for highly idiosyncratic interpretation, as evidenced by the three brothers, Antônio, Martinico, and Eduardo, who form the core of this study.

Alfred Adler has argued that irrespective of an ostensibly common family environment, each child is formed in a different psychological situation. Adler developed a paradigm of sibling development which is strikingly applicable to the Prado brothers. The oldest child, he observed, may acquire a great capacity for organization, generally favors his father, reveres power, respects authority, and has a strong tendency toward conservatism. The second child, in contrast, may mature more rapidly than his older sibling but tends to set goals so high that he may suffer from lack of fulfillment. He is rarely able to endure the strict leadership of others or to accept "eternal laws." The youngest sibling has so many chances for competition, so many siblings to learn from, that he may develop in an extraordinary way. Sometimes he will not admit to a single ambition; he wants to excel in everything and be unlimited and unique. Eternally the youngest, he may also suffer extreme inferiority feelings.[50]

In many ways, Antônio Prado exhibited the traits that Adler posited for oldest siblings. Brazilian tradition accorded the oldest son special recognition and powers. Antônio's unusual capacity for organization and his political conservatism are well known.[51] In public testimonials he was lauded as courageous, self-sacrificing, dedicated, persevering, tenacious, energetic, upstanding, loyal, progressive, incorruptible, and civic-minded;[52] he was the perfect big brother, it would seem. He was also the extreme of cold efficiency in public, "always glum, seeming to be of bad humor or to have come from a funeral; he spoke as if it was against his taste, [as if] angry with the audience."[53] This, the public Antônio Prado, is the one whose memory has been preserved in history.

There was a different, a private man, from whom the public figure developed only after years of anguish and doubt. There is scattered evidence of his nervousness as a child and as a man in his fifties.[54]

His letters from Europe in the 1860s showed profound skepticism about orthodox Catholicism, about Brazilian politics and Brazilians generally, and about his own life and fate, sentiments especially remarkable in view of his later economic and political accomplishments.[55] After he returned to Brazil he continued for years to have such doubts but found solace in his parents' example.[56]

Even to his children Antônio presented two sides. To Luíz Prado he seemed hard and severe. On the other hand, he continued to finance Paulo's gallivanting, even though he disapproved of it. His eldest daughter, Nazareth, later denied that he was the "rigid and dried-up man that he appeared to strangers." To her, perhaps his most characteristic quality was his extreme simplicity: his bedroom was like the "modest retreat of a monk," with simple, even rustic furnishings.[57]

Perhaps because he could relate warmly only to a few intimates, Antônio found release in his affection for horses. No enemy of business, he lost his liking for horseracing, as he explained, "when it stopped being the sport it was and took on a certain character of business."[58] Antônio's unusually close friendship with a previously unknown youth, Everardo Vallim Pereira de Sousa, began with an encounter on horseback—almost as if the common bond of horses inspired in him a certain confidence. The relationship gave Pereira de Sousa enough insights to attempt a "psychological" analysis of Antônio Prado.

To Pereira de Sousa, Antônio's lack of affect, his seemingly fixed granite face, were "defensive arms" used against "undesirable" persons. These included those who tried to approach him on a personal level, who spun endless tales of hunting, fishing, and their friends' personal lives. Antônio used his severe myopia as a first line of defense to avoid such people. If this barrier was breached, he put on his stone mask and maintained it until people took the hint. Possessed of a strongly utilitarian outlook and a morality that stressed "correctness," Antônio regarded small talk as completely futile and, if it touched on others' private lives, improper. However, with people who understood and respected his values, such as his sons-in-law Luis Aranha and Afonso Arinos, he loved to talk and even to be contradicted. In his later years he welcomed controversy as an opportunity to bring his rusty skills as parliamentary debater into practice.[59] The death of his wife, Maria Catarina, in 1899 appears to have affected him strongly. That he reentered politics shortly thereafter, after a decade of retirement, illustrates the powerful link between his private and public lives.

There is more circumstantial and less direct evidence upon which to base a psychological sketch of the second brother, Martinico, yet Adler's theoretical construct seems to fit him well. Martinico apparently felt a rivalry with his older brother; he was unable to accept strict leadership; he set his goals so high that he could not possibly realize them and thus became disillusioned. At one level, Martinico's rebellion was only political; he followed the family economic patterns, acting as his father's protégé and later his partner. His political rebellion, however, was also a revolt against control by his family, which was strongly tied to the Conservative party and to the monarchy.[60]

In childhood Martinico, unlike his serious, highstrung brother Antônio, was boisterous and full of tricks. Later, as a law student in the early 1860s, he expressed admiration for such rebels as Martin Luther and the nineteenth-century revolutionaries of Russia and Italy and announced that he had become a Mason.[61] Although the family viewed all of this with alarm, they tended to regard it as a passing fancy. Antônio wrote condescendingly of his brother (who was, after all, only three years younger) that "the news of Martinico's liberalism does not surprise me; it is proper to his age and proof that he has studied or at least read something."[62] In refusing to accept Antônio's advice that he study medicine or engineering in Europe and in his hunger strike to force his parents to give him permission to go to war in Paraguay, Martinico brought rebellion home. Coming from a fazendeiro-merchant family, Martinico succeeded in creating a personal counterimage: thin, with intensely burning eyes, a long sword at his side, and an outsized revolver tucked carelessly under his belt, he was a warrior ready for battle.[63]

Martinico's "revolutionary" tendencies continued throughout his political life. One outcome of them was his mercurial disillusionment with the Republic once it was not a distant ideal but rather a sordid present fact. In October 1891 he spent much time in Rio de Janeiro, "very enthusiastic about the federal capital"; a week later, he was placed on a governmental proscription list and fled Rio in haste.[64] A successful local Republican leader during the monarchy, he was unable to accept party discipline (and the role of the military) when events moved to the national stage.

Even less is known of the private Martinico than of the private Antônio. Ina von Binzer's observations suggest that in private there were severe limits on the idealism he so forcefully projected in public. A proponent of permissive child-rearing and of abolition, he reacted angrily and vindictively when those ideals led to unwanted results.[65] It might be argued that his Republican idealism was only a pose, but his long-term commitment to it, even though it caused him anxiety and considerable notoriety both in public life and within the family, suggests otherwise. It is more likely that his political rebellion was also a personal revolt against the family and thus could be carried out only to certain limits. Beyond those limits, in the parent-child and master-slave relationships, Martinico acquiesced in traditional patterns of authority.

Unfortunately, there is insufficient evidence upon which to base a psychological picture of the third brother, Caio (often called the most brilliant of the four), or of the sisters Anézia and Ana Blandina. The youngest brother, Eduardo, appears to have been the most complex of all, perhaps simply because so much has been written of him. Like the Adlerian type, Eduardo was extravagant and multifaceted, adept at many things but master of none. Like Martinico, Eduardo was a rebel, albeit a conservative one. In a way, Eduardo's life-style was a mockery of those of his older brothers: they were planter-politicians, he was a footloose *litterateur;* they were savers, he was a spender. Both Eduardo and Caio contributed to a satirical law-school review, *A Comédia.* Among the victims of their satire was Martinico Prado.[66]

Assessments of Eduardo's character stress his sociability, stout-heartedness, iconoclasm, and sometimes-malicious sense of humor, and they also point out that he possessed a certain degree of pride and "pose."[67] An anonymous friend recalled that "Eduardo Prado cried only rarely and with difficulty." More revealing was his analysis of the inner Eduardo: "He did not have a clear understanding of himself. He knew that he was worth something, that he had weight, but he did not see distinctly what it was."[68] Combining this observation with the fact that Eduardo lived in the shadow of two more illustrious older brothers, one can detect the feelings of uncertainty or even inferiority that Adler posits as sometimes characteristic of the youngest son.

Behind the public image of the happy, healthy, robust man, there was the private reality: Eduardo had suffered a good deal and harbored malice unrelieved by his well-known sense of humor. Behind Eduardo's image as that classic stereotype, the rich South American planter disporting himself in Europe's capitals, was the fact that he was forever in financial trouble, dependent on his mother's pocketbook.[69] Eduardo suffered from gout and lived in fear of yellow fever, which claimed his brother Caio's life in 1889 and took his own in 1901. In 1894, after publication of his anti-Republican book *A ilusão americana* (1893), Eduardo was forced into exile. In 1896, his strident monarchism unabated, Eduardo received a threat written in blood; his sister-in-law said she had never seen "so fearful a person," and he was soon forced into exile again.[70] Moreover, Eduardo's secular tastes and religious faith were frequently in conflict, and as the twentieth century dawned, despite a decade of rededication to Catholicism after his supposed derelictions of the 1880s, he feared losing his faith altogether and becoming nothing but a "miserable epicure."[71]

This spiritual doubt was matched in its intensity only by his anti-Semitism. According to his godson, Edmundo Navarro de Andrade, Eduardo's anti-Semitism was "as unique as it was infantile," but it also reached the level of "true rancor." On his fazenda, Eduardo had an engraving of the English House of Lords; carefully, with a pin, he had put out the eyes of all the Jewish parliamentarians. Eça de Queiroz thought that Eduardo's anti-Semitism was not simply economic, but social: "Prado, in the Jews, detested not only their financial despotism, but their social advent as well. . . . He detested that they had come out of the sordidness of the ghetto, that they did not use the infamous saffron-colored badges on their clothing, and that they never died in Christian fires." According to Eça, Eduardo had learned his anti-Semitism not in the France of the 1890s, but "in the fourteenth century with the Dominicans."[72] Nonetheless, when the Brazilian Academy of Letters convened in 1898 to elect Emile Zola an honorary member for his courageous defense of Dreyfus, Eduardo refused to join the effort.[73] Eduardo's involvement in European finance may have contributed to his anti-Semitism, though he enjoyed excellent relations with the Rothschilds.[74] More likely, the fervent Catholicism of his later years and his monarchism predisposed him to prejudice against the Jews, though there were probably deeper personal reasons why it possessed him so virulently.[75]

Eduardo's anti-Semitism is more puzzling in light of his views on a much more gripping question for late-nineteenth-century Brazil: race-mixture. By comparison, in Brazil anti-Semitism was not a real issue.[76] Unlike his older brothers, Eduardo had never been a slavemaster. Moreover, he condemned European colonial barbarity in Africa, praised Ibero-American society for its capacity for race-mixture a generation before Gilberto Freyre's popularization of the idea, and regarded the mixed-race *caboclo* as the real Brazilian.[77]

The subject of race sheds additional light on the complexity of family ties. Eleutério Prado (1836–1905) was Antônio's first cousin, his traveling companion in Europe, and his close friend until the late 1870s. At about that time Eleutério, frustrated and rebellious because the family refused to permit him to marry the woman of his choice, began to live openly with two black cooks. As a result he was snubbed by most of the older Prados, who called him *o negreiro* ("the slavetrader").[78] Eleutério educated his mulatto children, and the oldest, Armando (b. 1880), became valedictorian of the law school, a newspaper publisher, the director of the state archive, an amateur historian, and a state and federal deputy.[79] Several younger white Prados, most notably Paulo and Antônio Júnior, were friendly with Armando and his siblings and thus regularized somewhat the strange position that Eleutério's children occupied as brown Prados.

Some clues about Armando's personal feelings can be found in his published writings. In a speech delivered in 1903, when he graduated from law school, he referred to threats posed to "family organization" by racism and injustice in the Western world at large, but without mentioning his own situation. A degree of Prado family solidarity was present in Armando's reliance on Eduardo's *A illusão americana* for his views on the "workers' question" and Brazil–United States diplomacy. Elsewhere, Armando treated themes related to his status, but with characteristic Prado detachment. Thus he stressed the humble origins of Padre Diogo Antônio Feijó, a Brazilian regent in the 1830s, and the struggle of the historian Adolfo de Varnhagen to be recognized as a Brazilian citizen.[80]

As slaveowners until 1888 and as cosmopolitan citizens of the world, the Prados were ambiguous about race, as were many members of Brazil's educated classes.[81] When slavery was at its height, the Prados regarded it as a "tragic necessity" and were fully aware of its enormous injustice. In later years, Eduardo Prado praised race-mixture as a strength of Brazilian society. The Prados maintained friendships with several talented mulattoes: the abolitionist José do Patrocínio, the brilliant writer Machado de Assis, and the Paulista historian and ethnographer Teodoro Sampaio, a long-time family friend. Yet when miscegenation touched the family directly, the race issue was difficult to handle. There were slurs about Eleutério the "negreiro," and one family-sponsored genealogy failed to recognize his common-law marriage and the existence of his children.[82] So different in many ways from other elite families, the Prados evidently shared the belief that "purity" of blood was necessary to maintain elite status.[83]

A family story indicates just how convoluted race and family in Brazil could be. In the early 1900s Antônio Prado Júnior, acting as manager of what is reputed to have been the first Brazilian soccer team to compete abroad, took the team to play in Europe. One of the stars was Antônio's mulatto cousin Joaquim Prado, Armando's brother. A French cousin of the Prados, a descendant of Ana Blandina Prado Pinto, came to watch the team and, pointing out Joaquim, asked Antônio who "that monkey" was. "That is no monkey," replied Antônio, "that is your cousin."[84]

This story dramatizes how much intra-familial differentiation and conflict within the extended family and parentela and within the most prominent nuclear components of them increased during the First Republic. Endogamous marriage, once common, diminished greatly. Conflict, earlier on an individual basis, assumed generational proportions in the late nineteenth and early twentieth centuries. Though patterns of cooperation were still evident in the parentela in the 1920s, they seem to have come into play in times of economic crisis, rather than as a result of more broadly operative family affection. Thus, though "disintegration" of the family network is too strong a word, the Prado experience does lend support to Gilberto Freyre's broad thesis of decline in the familial basis of Brazilian society after 1889.

The sibling rivalry and markedly individual personality development traced here, as my use of the Adlerian paradigm implies, might be assumed to be Brazilian manifestations of wider patterns of psychological dynamics. However, the changing nature of Brazilian society produced the specific conditions under which modifications in family structure and dynamics occurred, once the rural, agricultural basis of Brazilian society began to yield to more urban, commercial-industrial patterns. Political strife after 1870 stimulated family conflict and helped family members to express it. European cultural influence played an ambiguous, fundamentally unsettling role in the Prado family. In turning to cultural, economic, and political themes in subsequent chapters, we may expect that the Prados' behavior was the result of not only the family ethic and individual variations from it, but of general social conditions as well.

❧ CHAPTER VII ❧

EDUARDO AND PAULO

REDISCOVER BRAZIL

In the nineteenth century many members of the Brazilian elite class felt that Brazil must look abroad for models to follow in closing the gap that separated it from the more developed nations. This sentiment facilitated what some have depicted as the cultural reconquest or recolonization of Brazil, a trend that has continued to the present day, though not without provoking a nationalist response.[1] Returning from Europe, many Brazilians confronted their homeland and its problems with indifference or dismay. Others were impelled by the contrast of European society with what they saw as the "Brazilian reality"— widespread poverty, ignorance, apathy, political corruption, economic underdevelopment, and social inequality—to question whether imitating European (and, after 1889, North American) models could provide answers to such problems. The *belle epoque* ended in a world war that shattered the image of Europe as master of its progressive destiny; and as North American influence in Brazil grew, the "defensive nationalism" of the nineteenth century gave way to the "offensive nationalism" of the twentieth.[2] Brazil— with its modern cities and its traditional hinterlands; its sophisticated urban elites, disaffected middle class, and impoverished lower classes; and its strongly marked cultural, political, and economic regionalism—is a complex nation. That very complexity produced a "tension between the need for roots and the urge for modernity."[3]

Although no single movement or event can capture the era's moral and intellectual flux, São Paulo's modernist movement, given shape in the Modern Art Week of 1922, expresses some of the cultural ferment that occurred during the First Republic. According to Mário de Andrade, a modernist leader, "the modernist movement was clearly aristocratic. By its character of a game of chance, by its extreme adventurist spirit, by its modernist internationalism, by its ferocious nationalism, by its antipopular gratuitousness, by its preponderant dogmatism, it was an aristocracy of the spirit. Very natural, then, that the high and low bourgeoisie feared it."[4]

The movement took place in the city where physical and psychological change were taken for granted. In the 1920s the old colonialist Rudyard Kipling visited São Paulo and marveled at its automobile traffic, its bustling commerce, and its immense hydroelectric plants.[5] Massive European immigration had altered not only the demography of São Paulo, but many of its traditional mores as well. Along with such developments, in part as a result of sheer growth, the dominance of old elite families had weakened. A Prado relative wrote of attending the theater in 1923 and not seeing anyone she knew, something that could not have happened a generation before.[6]

In the Prado family the clash of modern and traditional forces increased during the First Republic, but it was also an extension of similar conflicts experienced during the monarchy. Antônio Prado's perceptions of the variety of European culture in the 1860s and Martinico's first adopting and later rejecting European political models are important examples of the interplay of modern and traditional, of foreign and Brazilian experiences before 1889. Their generation was able to seek "progress" through economic and political endeavor; during the First Republic, however, many of the younger Prados encountered a different situation which made economic careers less inspiring and political ones all but impossible, as we shall see in subsequent chapters. Thus while Antônio Prado continued as the economic and political chief of the family, his much younger brother Eduardo and Antônio's oldest son, Paulo, devoted much of their energies to re-evaluating foreign cultural influence in Brazil. Ultimately, both attacked the imitation of models from abroad and the distortion of what they saw as "the Brazilian reality."

Eduardo Prado and the Foreign Illusion

The group of leaders who came of age in about 1880 in São Paulo has been seen as "revolutionary" in politics and culture.[7] Preoccupied with republicanism and abolition, the members of that generation also came to regard the literature of Brazil's romantic school as a coarse joke. Employing European critical methods, they attacked traditional Portuguese literary canons. The innovative, irreverent works of Eça de Queiroz found ready audiences. The thought of Charles Darwin and Herbert Spencer, of the German evolutionist Ernst Haeckel and the French surgeon-anthropologist Paul Broca entered the still-traditional São Paulo law school. Cafés became forums for discussions of Auguste Comte's positivism and Ludwig Buchner's materialism.[8] French enjoyed a near-monopoly as the language of the intellectuals: well-stocked bookstores carried British and German works in French translation. The Paulista elite also favored French hairdressers, dressmakers, tailors, art and photography studios, newspapers, social clubs, governesses, and teachers.[9]

A supposed "conservative" in "revolutionary" times, Eduardo Prado nonetheless was influenced by the trends that led many of his fellows along more radical paths. In 1875, at the age of fifteen, he entered the law school, and in 1878 he joined the editorial board of O Constitucional, the organ of the school's Conservative Club.[10] By 1880 he had established a reputation as an "implacable adversary of the Liberals."[11] While Eduardo's general outlook was formally conservative, he also demonstrated considerable independence. In an essay written in law school, he argued against his professor's view that the human sense of justice comes from divine revelation.[12] A confirmed Catholic, he attacked the newly formed Catholic party in São Paulo on the grounds that "Catholic" meant "universal" while "party" implied "fragmentation."[13] Eduardo's reaction to European ideas was thus governed by a thoughtful and independent mind, the dominant characteristic of which, as later defined by Eça de Queiroz, was "curiosity."[14]

Eduardo graduated from law school in 1881 and spent most of the 1880s in globe-circling travels. Speaking and writing French, German, and English more or less fluently, Eduardo seems not to have felt the isolation abroad that Antônio had felt twenty years before. Like Antônio, however, he was strongly aware of the contest between "civilized" and "backward" cultures, and he frequently sympathized with the latter. In Italy he disapproved of Englishmen and North Americans who protested against "the very irregularity of an ignorant and backward country, . . . where there are abuses which would never be tolerated in England nor in progressive America." In

Egypt, Eduardo thought ridiculous the indignation of travelers who wished to see that country administered like England or France: "Certain tyrannies of the Egyptian government revolt sensitive temperaments, but Western reformers, who have plagued the country for forty years, have not improved the state of the fellah." In Cairo, Eduardo found "the coexistence of the civilized banality of the West with the remains of Oriental life" lamentable. At the same time, he approved of the British regime in Malta, for there local customs had been respected while the English, on contact with "southern joviality," had lost "the sadness of men of the North."[15] Eduardo sympathized with the less "advanced" countries because he knew that those Englishmen and North Americans would no doubt consider Eduardo's Brazil to be little more than a Western version of Egypt or Italy.

The United States was an unpleasant stop in Eduardo's travels, perhaps because he encountered it during the height of the Gilded Age. Arriving in New York in August 1886, he wrote that the city seemed "dirty and ugly for him who comes from Paris."[16] "Chicago," he wrote to a friend, "is the most brutal city of the world." The high point of this trip was Salt Lake City, where Eduardo was well treated and where he sympathized with the Mormons, persecuted by "the Yankee element." In San Francisco, Eduardo decided that "of the world, [the best is] Europe; of Europe, France; of France, Paris; of Paris, all the perimeter of the *pavé du bois [du Boulogne]!*"[17]

Thus Eduardo's globetrotting was a prologue to his fixing a Parisian residence. At his apartment at 119 rue Rivoli in the city's noisy center, he surrounded himself with the marvels of nineteenth-century technology—the telephone, the typewriter, and the phonograph—and was served by an English butler who was said to have worked for Charles Darwin.[18] Eduardo mounted an impressive library which became a research center for fellow Brazilians such as the baron of Rio Branco, José Maria de Silva Paranhos Júnior, who soon emerged as a giant of Brazilian diplomacy. It was in Paris that Eduardo's most famous friendship, with Eça de Queiroz, blossomed. His intellectual circle also included Portuguese friends such as José Francisco de Oliveira Martins and Ramalho Ortigão and Frenchmen such as the economist-historian Emile Levasseur, the anarchist and geographer Elisée Reclus, and Joseph Frederick Sant'Anna Nery.

Eduardo collaborated with these men and others on scholarly works about Brazil.[19]

An important result of Eduardo's long residence in Paris was that his European friends often challenged his view of Brazilian events. In 1888 Eça de Queiroz wrote Eduardo that he considered Brazil "still a colony . . . of the *Boulevard.* Its letters, sciences, customs, institutions: none of this is national." Eça went on to say that he would like to see "a natural, spontaneous, genuine Brazil, a national, Brazilian Brazil, and not this Brazil that I see made of old pieces of Europe, brought by steam-packet and put together in haste."[20] A year later, Eduardo characterized Brazil as "an undisciplined country in which everything is flaccid and disunited," a country lacking the puritan discipline of Britain and the United States and the military discipline of Germany; but while he tended to judge Brazil by foreign standards, he also warned against the imitation of foreign models.[21]

The military-Republican coup of 15 November 1889, which destroyed the Brazilian monarchy, changed Eduardo's attitudes toward what he had recognized as the failings of imperial Brazil. The early Republican regime's press censorship, suppression of dissent, and violence drove him to the view that the Empire had been liberal while the Republic was reactionary. But Eduardo continued to receive the opinions of European friends who, while deferring to his knowledge of Brazil, still questioned whether the monarchy ever could have governed effectively and reckoned that the coup had been good for Brazil.[22]

Thus Eduardo's European experiences, combined with events in Brazil, produced in him a division of spirit. Eça de Queiroz parodied it in the novel *As cidades e as serras (The Cities and the Mountains).* The protagonist of the novel, Jacintho, was supposedly based on Eduardo.[23] Jacintho—a *belle epoque* dilettante swept up in the Age of the Machine, confusing progress with civilization— was clearly a caricature, departing in many ways from his real-life model. Nonetheless, Jacintho symbolized the most important aspect of Eduardo's relationship to European culture, that his predilection for the "city" (Europe) conflicted with his roots in the "mountains" (Brazil). As a critic observed, Eduardo was one of the Brazilians who "lived between Brazil and the world, between the fazenda and the *boulevard.*"[24]

A recurring theme in Eduardo's writings is the relationship of people to their native land. He disapproved of the Portuguese generation of Eça de Queiroz and Ramalho Ortigão because they had forsaken Lisbon for Paris, and he praised a volume of poetry that expressed the author's loyalty to his homeland.[25] This, of course, was a personal theme, since Eduardo shared the blame that he assigned to Eça and Ortigão. In part, Eduardo attempted to resolve the conflict by exporting Europe to Brazil, by establishing a magnificent library on his fazenda deep in the Paulista interior, and by strengthening his contacts with his *caboclo* workers.[26]

A more definitive resolution of the conflict was stimulated by the Brazilian civil war of 1893. In that conflict the Republican regime Eduardo opposed prevailed partly because the naval "neutrality" of the United States was implemented so as to strengthen the government's position. A monarchist who sensed that the survival of the Republic depended to some extent on strengthening its ties with the United States, Eduardo seized the opportunity to write his most famous book, *A illusão americana* (1893).

The book has two main aspects. Its first, often-overlooked, dimension is its attack on the Brazilian Republic.[27] Its second, more obvious, significance is as a statement of cultural nationalism; the book is said to have set "the tone, the phrasing, the themes" of subsequent anti-American nationalism in Brazil.[28] With *A illusão americana (The American Illusion)* Eduardo thus accomplished for Brazil what the Uruguayan José Enrique Rodó did for Latin America as a whole with his essay *Ariel* (1900). *Ariel* is the more universal work, based on the conflict between materialism and spiritualism, and avoiding the internal conflicts that divided the Latin American nations. *A illusão americana*, with its attacks on nearly all the Latin American republics, is exclusivist and is cast in more specific, more material terms.[29] For Eduardo, as for many elite Brazilians steeped in European culture, the United States was an unprecedented, seemingly inexplicable culture. As he wrote to Teodoro Sampaio on his impressions of the United States: "I passed from a bound volume in my classical collection to a book with no classical meaning whose pages still needed to be cut apart in order to be read!"[30]

Eduardo was unusually successful in that effort, and many of his conclusions about North American society in the Gilded Age would not be challenged today by liberal or leftist scholars. If, upon scanning the pages of North American experience, he drew a different lesson than would his friends Joaquim Nabuco, the baron of Rio Branco, and Rui Barbosa—leaders in the strengthening of Brazilian-American relations—it is important to remember that Eduardo's message was tailored to attacking, by association, the Republic of Brazil. In *A illusão* once Eduardo had used the supposed glories of the Yankee founding fathers to discredit by contrast the Brazilian Republic's founders, he was really interested only in the dark side of the United States. Contemporary North American society, he wrote, appealed only to those with a materialist conception of life. Extermination of Indians, lynching, and suppression of the working class were practiced to the highest degree there. The United States had had only a pernicious effect on Brazil. Compared to the many Europeans who had analyzed Brazilian life and had enriched its scientific literature, with few exceptions (Eduardo's friend Orville Derby was one), Americans had little genuine interest in Brazil, and had instead introduced to the country that American pastime, lynching. Brazilians who studied in the United States—these included a nephew and a cousin of Eduardo's, who took degrees at Cornell and at Harvard—were "those who know the least and have the least preparation," who judged the United States the best country in the world because it had "much electricity and good *water closets.*" The rub was that Brazilian leaders had great affinity for electricity, good water closets, *and* the North American form of government. Eduardo rightly recognized that institutions require a cultural base; they could be right for their native countries and "bring confusion and disorder in countries where they are arbitrarily transplanted": "Let us copy, let us copy, think the foolish, let us copy, and we will be great! We ought rather to say: Let us be ourselves, let us be what we are, and only thus will we be something."[31]

Since Eduardo always harbored a distaste for the United States, it was easy for him to begin his critique of foreign cultural influence in Brazil with the northern giant. But once he had started on a line of thought that emphasized the futility of copying foreign customs and institutions, it inevitably carried over to Europe as well: "the American illusion" became "the foreign illusion." This development originated in Eduardo's own earlier observations, such as those he had made in Egypt, and in the criticisms of the Paris community in the

1880s, and was heightened by Eduardo's fear of a possible United States–British alliance, which would bring the force of Anglo-American energy down on supposedly "indolent" Latin America.[32]

Under the inspiration of Rio Branco and the tutelage of the historian Capistrano de Abreu, Eduardo devoted himself increasingly to historical research in the last years of his life. His main efforts were to discover the Brazilian past through research on religious figures like the Jesuit founder of São Paulo city, Joseph de Anchieta; the seventeenth-century Jesuit minister of state, Antônio Vieira; and the religious apostate Manuel de Morais. However, had Eduardo not died of yellow fever at the age of forty-one, perhaps he would have pursued history along the lines Capistrano himself did, examining the social, cultural, and psychological roots of Brazilian civilization.[33] The germ of such an approach was evident in the speech Eduardo gave at the conference he organized in 1897 to commemorate Anchieta's life and works. In addition to denouncing the barbarities of European colonialism in Africa, Eduardo attributed the strength of Ibero-American culture to its capacity for race-mixture and came to the conclusion, unexpected given his social origins and erstwhile affinity for European culture, that the mixed-race caboclo was "the true Brazilian."[34] A year later, Eduardo gave another address in which he spoke of the destructive effects of European culture on Brazilian traditions. Those effects included the dispersion of the Brazilian home and family and the "denationalization of the habits of daily life," symbolized by the exchange of the "solid family silver" for the "vile tableware of Paris."[35] In order to preserve Brazilian culture, the most Europeanized Prado of his generation was saying, it was necessary to protect Brazilian life from the destructive impact of modern influences from abroad.

Paulo Prado's Rediscovery of Brazil

The concerns that developed late in Eduardo's life were reactivated some twenty years afterward by his nephew Paulo Prado, who was only nine years Eduardo's junior. As in Eduardo's case, it was necessary for Paulo to submerge himself rather fully in European culture before he could begin to feel its deleterious effects on Brazil. Paulo graduated from the law school in 1889, only days before the military coup of 15 November ended the monarchy. He soon joined Eduardo in Paris, collaborating with him in the European agency of the *Jornal do Comércio*. Paulo had been prepared for Europe by long talks with his maternal grandfather, Antônio da Costa Pinto e Silva. These reportedly dwelled on the customs separating Brazil from Europe: the work, sacrifice, and simplicity of people and things in Brazil; the leisure, luxury, and refinements of culture in Europe.[36] For a long while, leisure and luxury appealed more to Paulo than sacrifice and simplicity. In 1892 Eça de Queiroz wrote of "genteel Paulo, who is coming here [to Paris] to train his dilettantism."[37] Paulo was assigned the task of keeping the Prados abreast of French culture by arranging subscriptions to *Figaro* and *Revue illustrée*.[38] Once ensconced in Paris, Paulo showed little inclination toward serious work, and the family was at pains to get him back to the family businesses in São Paulo.

As compared to the preceding generation, Paulo's seemed to lack a compelling mission in life. Despite political misfortunes, the family's social and economic standing was assured, as lavish testimonials in contemporary magazines showed.[39] In contrast to the more provincial and spartan days of the mid-nineteenth century, during the *belle epoque* the new Prado generation indulged itself in whirlwind European auto tours, high-society life, and conspicuous consumption. It was a time for spenders, not savers. When the literary critic Tristão de Ataíde saw Paulo at the Carlsbad spa in 1913, he described him as a type characteristic of a bred-out race: "Neurasthenic to the roots of his hair. Played out."[40]

Meanwhile, colonialism had changed the European image in Brazil. In 1903 Armando Prado had drawn a grim picture of a world beset by imperialism and the Western nations' disrespect for law and justice.[41] World War I, in part an outcome of colonial rivalries, changed Paulo Prado's outlook and activities. Supposedly a played-out neurasthenic, Paulo saw the war as Brazil's opportunity to restructure its commercial and cultural relations with the Old World.[42] As will become evident, the changing social environment in São Paulo itself also had much to do with Paulo's reawakening.

In 1916 Paulo was one of the discontented Paulista intellectuals who organized the *Revista do Brasil*, a journal devoted to the critical analysis of Brazilian affairs. In 1918 Paulo, like Eduardo earlier, came under the guidance of Capistrano de Abreu, and in Paulo's case this influence had full opportunity to develop. Four years later, at the age of fifty-three, Paulo became a leading promoter of the Modern Art Week, a movement primarily of young artists and writers in São Paulo who sought to free the Brazilian arts from the restricting forms officially sponsored by the Brazilian Academy of Letters, which had dominated the arts from 1890 to 1920.[43] The rather schizoid combination of "modernist internationalism" and "ferocious nationalism" that Mário de Andrade pictured as characteristic of Brazilian modernism, along with Paulista regionalism, dominated Paulo's work.

Paulo's concern for the proper relation between Europe and Brazilian intellectuals came out clearly in his 1923 preface to a biography of Joaquim Nabuco. For Paulo, Nabuco was part of "that very beautiful group which was perhaps the last depository of the intellectual greatness of . . . the Empire," a circle which also included Rio Branco, José Carlos Rodrigues, and Eduardo Prado. This group "purified and strengthened its life in Europe by its continuous and religious preoccupation with Brazilian affairs." Such Brazilians had rediscovered Brazil in Europe (Paulo let that irony pass without comment), and Paulo denied the assertions of "cheap nationalism" that "whoever lived in Europe, and came from there with knowing airs and the light-colored flannels of Poole, ought to read only *The Times* and *Figaro*, and scarcely know of the existence of these exotic Brazils which shame him in his pretensions of parvenu dandyism."[44] Thus did Paulo differentiate Nabuco, Rio Branco, Eduardo Prado, and, by implication, himself from those Brazilians who were guilty of shallow imitation of European modes.

Paulo's literary development was greatly affected by the turbulent political situation of the 1920s. In 1922 and 1924 there were barracks revolts in Rio and São Paulo, and in 1926 Antônio Prado gave voice to his long-standing discontent with the Republic's malaise by founding the Partido Democrático in São Paulo. In several articles titled "O momento" ("The Moment"), published in 1923 and 1924, Paulo identified the political situation as the greatest problem in Brazilian society. Politicians and fazendeiros came in for much of the blame, but Paulo reserved special vehemence for a third group: the indifferent "gregarious mass," composed of not only the "newcomers, the recently arrived, the cosmopolitans, [and] the rapidly enriched," but of "the descendants of past greatness, the anemic fruits of the decadence of the race" as well.[45] Paulo's analysis was remarkable not only for its xenophobia, but also for its critique of the very sectors of which he was a member. He was able to adopt this stance partly because his vision of politics transcended the mere machinations of office; it included what he referred to in his introduction to the modernist Oswald de Andrade's *Poesia Pau Brasil* (1924) as the "deformation of reality from which we [Brazilians] have not yet liberated ourselves." In 1924 Paulo dated this deformation from Brazilian independence. To him, only two nineteenth-century Brazilian writers, Casimiro de Abreu and Catulo Cearense, were truly Brazilian in language and style: "The others are Lusitanians, Frenchmen, Spaniards, Englishmen, and Germans, versifying in a foreign tongue which is the Portuguese of Portugal."[46]

Paulo was reacting to the very forces and things which, decades before, his family and others had seen as the longed-for remedies for Brazilian backwardness. Attempting to catch the feeling of Brazilian chaos in 1924, the "delicious cocktail" of foreign influences and domestic nature that had inspired Oswald de Andrade's poetry, Paulo summed it up like this:

> Brazil, Brazilians, whites, reds, and blacks; landscapes of the most revolting bad taste, skies like the blue of a chapel with little stars of gold, earth of vermilion and purple; . . . electric posts on skeleton trees, telephones in the virgin forest, the red disks of railroads surging like moons in coconut groves, airplanes landing on desert beaches, motor boats honking on the rivers of the backlands; Italian bandeirantes, Syrian conquistadores—all the disordered life of a new and rich land, in full and ardent puberty, offering herself to the fecundation of first desire.[47]

In his books *Paulistica: historia de São Paulo* (1925) and *Retrato do Brasil: ensaio sôbre a tristeza brasileira* (1928), Paulo broadened his search for the deformation of Brazilian reality, tracing it to factors inherent in the Portuguese colonization, the nineteenth-century re-Europeanization, and the incipient twentieth-century Americanization of Brazil.

Paulistica was Paulo's first attempt to probe the "dark jungle" of Brazilian history. Perhaps because of the size of the task, he chose a regionalist point of departure. He strove to follow a path between scientific and romantic history, to give "to the aridity of the archives the blood and life necessary for understanding the psychology of the past."[48] He had to wrestle as well with the conflict between his own internationalism (and polyglot pretensions) and his nationalist instincts. Capistrano wrote him during the composition of *Paulistica* that in Brazil it was common "to eat French and belch German" and advised Paulo, "You have to choose now: either get to know German well enough to read it with facility, or pull the baubles [from your work]."[49] Paulo himself acknowledged that in his youth "only Europe interested us," and he recalled the many "injustices" he had committed in abandoning Brazil for Europe.[50]

Paulo's view of São Paulo's past emphasized what he depicted as the positive effects of its isolation from the colonial mainstream behind the Serra do Mar, that mountainous "bastion of resistance against the pretensions of metropolitan control." Though he recognized the brutality of slave- and gold-hunting bandeirismo, he nonetheless regretted the reassertion of royal control in the latter half of the eighteenth century, a control that eroded Paulista independence while gradually integrating the captaincy into the colonial regime. With national independence in 1822, "unanimity" (one of Paulo's prime devils) and "adhesionism" had become the Paulista's chief characteristics. *Paulistica* also foreshadowed themes, such as sexual license, that would become central three years later in his *Retrato do Brasil*. Paulo concluded the first edition of *Paulistica* by stating that the Paulista was "the saddest of the inhabitants of a sad country."[51]

Retrato do Brasil explored the central paradox of Brazilian life, as Paulo perceived it and phrased it in the book's opening sentence: "In a radiant land lives a sad people." *Retrato* is divided into four parts: "A Luxúria" ("Licentiousness"), "A Cobiça" ("Greed"), "A Tristeza" ("Sadness"), and "O Romantismo" ("Romanticism"). The first three constitute Paulo's explanation of the introductory paradox, as summed up in the formula "Luxúria, cobiça: melancólia." Uncontrolled, brutal sexuality combined with unrestrained lust for gold were the root causes of Brazilian sadness: "The history of Brazil is the development of these obsessions, subjugating the mind and body of their victims." The fourth part of the book asserts that romanticism, a late-colonial import, became a nineteenth-century "infection" incubated particularly at the São Paulo law school and spread by *bacharéis* (like Antônio and Martinico?) throughout the Brazilian body politic, fur-

ther deforming the "Brazilian reality." In the book's postscript, Paulo
made clear that the influences he sought to diagnose as deformers of
Brazilian society included the twentieth-century United States. He
depicted the world as caught in a life-and-death struggle among "Capitalism, Communism, Fordism, [and] Leninism," while Brazil re-
posed in its "colonial sleep," "in complete ignorance of what is happening in the outside world." After a long catalogue of Brazil's
problems, Paulo asserted that "one national vice, however, domi-
nates: the vice of imitation." From this situation, there were only two
ways out: war or revolution. Brazil seemed to have adopted the latter
course—though not precisely in the form Paulo wished—two years
later, when the Revolution of 1930 brought Getúlio Vargas to power.[52]

Paulo claimed that he was surprised by the success of *Retrato do
Brasil*, by the controversy it generated, and by the fact that it was (as
it still is) interpreted as a pessimistic view of Brazilian history. As he
wrote in 1929 to his son Paulo Caio Prado, who evidently shared the
third reaction:

> It is curious that you do not understand everything that I put in
> the book which several critics . . . perceived perfectly: namely,
> the patriotic anxiety of him who wants good for his country and
> points out the errors and crimes of the moneylenders in the
> temple. . . .
>
> You are intoxicated by certain aspects of American life. There
> are many things in the world other than Wall Street, Fordism,
> and money. Read, from time to time, the *Nation*, Mencken's
> articles, and his *Americana*. There are also pessimists in the
> United States.[53]

Like *A illusão americana*, *Retrato do Brasil* has become a fundamental landmark in the literature of Brazilian historiography, nationalism, and national psychology.[54] It has been labeled as "the
pessimistic extreme of nationalism," an excessive first attempt at
historical analysis (a first attempt it was not), and the product of
"deep bitterness" as the result of a "reexamination of the past, in a
seizure of the present."[55] But these phrases do not fully explain the
book's success nor its importance: it touched on matters buried deep
in the national elite's subconsciousness and sensitivities, and it
symbolized the crisis in Brazil's ruling circles at the end of the First
Republic. Even though sexual lust, greed, and *tristeza* were only part

of the nation's formative process, the open recognition of them as such (and, to be sure, the reader's vicarious pleasure in sharing that recognition) accounts, in part, for the book's perennial success. The book raised questions of national identity and challenged the national motto, "Ordem e Progresso," by suggesting one perhaps closer to the reality of things: "Luxúria, Cobiça: Tristeza." In more personal terms, viewed in the context of Paulo's earlier writings, *Retrato do Brasil* extended his disenchantment to the entire process of the absorption of foreign culture in Brazil. It was also Paulo's culminating effort to rediscover his homeland.

The deep concern of Eduardo Prado and Paulo Prado for the nature of Brazilian culture and its place in the world was not, of course, "typical" of the Prado family at large. There were probably many family members, as Paulo's letter to his son implies, who merely shifted their allegiance from the *belle epoque* to Fordismo. *A illusão americana* and *Retrato do Brasil* were more important as individual statements that linked their authors to dissident movements such as monarchism, modernism, and nationalism—and as indicators of the crisis afflicting São Paulo's old elite—than as signs of tendencies in the Prado family generally.

At the same time, Eduardo's and Paulo's critiques of foreign influence did flow out of an important strain of thought long evident in the leading Prado branch. Antônio's European letters in the 1860s and Martinico's developing political philosophy in the 1870s and 1880s stressed the complexity of European culture, the advantages it offered, and the threats it posed. The very extremism of *A illusão* and *Retrato* indicates as well that the conflict of cultures reached new heights during the First Republic. Many Prados experienced this clash, though on more mundane levels than those at which Eduardo and Paulo addressed it. The city of São Paulo itself became a more hostile environment for the family, partly because of changes from abroad. Maria Catarina Prado described a brawl between Italians and Brazilians in 1892.[56] Events like the strike against the Paulista Railway in 1906, ostensibly fostered by immigrant "anarchists," marked the rise of labor conflict in the city and inexorably affected family life; forced to contend with the strike, Antônio Prado was unable to attend Martinico's funeral.[57] Foreign entrepreneurs, the "Italian bandeirantes and Syrian conquistadores" of Paulo's lexicon, imperiled the economic dominance of the native Paulista elite. That

Eduardo and Paulo, members of that elite, were driven in their analyses of foreign influence to attack elements of their own class (and, by implication, of their own families) indicates the degree of the threat posed to them by the broad panorama of social change. Traditional social cohesiveness and the family itself were not adequate shelter against such a threat. As we shall see, Eduardo's and Paulo's cultural critiques reflected the Prados' difficulties in the economic and political realms as well.

Ultimately, *A illusão americana* and *Retrato do Brasil* are at the same time parts of the Prado patrimony and of the Brazilian public domain. They are, perhaps, the most important legacy left by the Prados to contemporary Brazil. More recently, the historian Caio Prado Júnior applied more rigorous Marxist analysis to the symptomatology offered by Eduardo, Paulo, and others. With the passage of time, the historical eye is surer and the diagnosis of the cultural recolonization of Brazil has become more knowledgeable. Nonetheless, the fundamental dilemma perceived by Antônio Prado in the 1860s and restated and elaborated by Eduardo Prado in 1893 and Paulo Prado in 1928—how to benefit from foreign influence without being dominated by it—remains a crucial problem today.

❥ CHAPTER VIII ❦

ENTREPRENEURS AND

FAZENDEIROS

São Paulo's economic history during the First Republic is largely that of two interrelated sectors, coffee and industry. Both were subject to broad patterns in the national economy and to Brazil's role in the world market. The advent of the Republic in 1889, says Caio Prado Júnior, "unchained a new spirit and social tone much more in accord with the phase of material prosperity in which the country engaged itself."[1] The first symptom of this new economic climate was a period of wild speculation, the *encilhamento* (1890–91), which brought Brazil near financial ruin and foreshadowed both the promise and the problems of the period.[2] A second phase of the Republic's economic history dates from 1898, when President Manuel de Campos Salles made it his first task to restore national finances. During this stage, which lasted until 1910, Paulista coffee interests became predominant in national politics, serious problems arose in the coffee economy, and the industrial labor force grew restless. Many analysts point to the World War I years as a third phase in Brazilian economic history during the First Republic, a period of further difficulty for coffee but one of forced growth in industry because of the disruption of European imports and markets.[3] The postwar period constitutes another phase, one of readjustment to peacetime economic conditions and of initial promise and subsequent troubles in both the coffee trade and in industry; the period ended with the crash of 1929.[4]

The lack of complete data before 1920 lends an impressionistic quality to descriptions of Brazilian industry's growth, but by that year São Paulo had become Brazil's leading industrial center.[5] The reasons for São Paulo's industrial emergence are well known. The state's coffee economy had stimulated the necessary capital formation and the creation of an efficient rail network. Abolition in 1888 released capital for industrial investment. Increasing urbanization and a rapid growth in population—from 64,934 to 1,074,877 for the city of São Paulo in the years 1890–1934, from 1,384,753 to 6,433,327 for the state—created Brazil's largest internal market. São Paulo had abundant hydroelectric resources. European immigration brought not only farmworkers but skilled workers and technicians of urban background as well. Both immigrants and planters possessed the entrepreneurial skills to respond to new economic stimuli.[6]

There were also limits to the early industrialization process in São Paulo. As in the rest of Brazil, industry in São Paulo depended on foreign machinery, technology, and, to some extent, capital. Moreover, industry grew "parasitically" under high tariffs and continual exchange depreciation. At first these factors made it possible for industry to grow without foreign competition, but when protectionism ceased to be official policy in the 1920s, Paulista industry was vulnerable to more efficient foreign rivals. "Brazilian industrialists," it has been said, "lived as in a family, a peaceful family in which opportunities were distributed fraternally."[7] Corporations in Brazil were often personalistic, whereas in the northern hemisphere they tended to be faceless conglomerations of capital. In Western Europe and the United States industrial capitalism, starting from similar familistic bases, had evolved relatively slowly in the midst of sweeping social changes. In Brazil the techniques of industrial and entrepreneurial capitalism were imported in a relatively brief period of time and grafted onto a traditional social structure which was changing only slowly. Industrialization occurred in São Paulo in the context of the national export economy, often called a dependent, colonial element of the world economy. These factors, and what Richard Morse calls the historical Catholic-agrarian cultural ethos of São Paulo, did not prevent industrialization but did give it a special character.[8]

A relatively recent addition to São Paulo's economy and its cultural ethos was the coffee economy itself, which combined a modern market-economy outlook with traditional patterns such as exploitive land use, latifundia, and paternalistic labor relations. The health of the coffee economy and that of infant industrialism were directly related during the First Republic. More generally, it has been observed that the great weakness of Brazil's early industrial growth was its dependence on foreign commerce and on the international balance of trade, matters in which the state of the coffee economy was paramount, as the repeated coffee valorization plans, beginning in 1906, emphasize.[9]

During the First Republic coffee was a troubled crop. Growth in the sector tended to be quantitative rather than qualitative, a recurrence of a centuries-old agricultural pattern in Brazil. Overproduction became the key problem. Exports from Santos rose from 2 million bags in 1889–90 to nearly 14 million in 1906–7, after which they fluctuated between 7 million and 10 million bags yearly, with a trend toward the higher figure in the 1920s. Generally, because of saturated markets abroad, prices fell as production rose, particularly from 1896 to 1918. The nominal value of coffee exports, therefore, showed no consistent pattern of growth during those years. After World War I both production and prices tended to rise, but the apparent benefits of this were offset by the declining exchange rate of the milreis and by general increases in the cost of living.[10]

The interplay between coffee and industry, and the developments in both sectors within the context of family capitalism, are revealingly demonstrated by the Prados' experience during the First Republic. Family capitalism, of course, is not unique to Brazil. Daniel Bell goes so far as to assert that "the story of the rise and fall of social classes in Western society . . . is that of the rise and fall of families. Without understanding that fact, . . . [by] viewing class position in individualistic terms, . . . one cannot understand the peculiar cohesiveness of dominant classes in the past, or of the sources of the break-up of power in contemporary society today."[11] The decline of family capitalism, which Bell dates from about 1880 and attributes to the rupture of ties between property and "dynastic" marriage, clearly applies in less absolute manner in Brazil than in Western society as a whole. Nonetheless, as previously demonstrated, in the late nineteenth and early twentieth centuries a variety of causes served to weaken the solidarity of the Prado family. An additional factor is that after 1889 the Prados' political influence was greatly reduced.[12] How the Prados fared in facing a new economic environment in the First Republic is thus a crucial aspect of the family's history.

New Opportunities in a Changing Economy

Shortly after the coup of 1889, the Prados moved with typical flexibility to take advantage of the economic climate created by the advent of the Republic. In January 1890 Antônio Prado opened in São Paulo the Bank of Commerce and Industry, which he headed until 1920 and which became the fiscal arm of the family conglomerate. Antônio's role as banker recalls that of his grandfather, the baron of Iguape, although by the 1890s banking was losing some of its intimate, small-town character. The Bank of Commerce and Industry soon became the leading private credit institution in São Paulo, with average assets of about 100,000 contos ($24,000,000), or from one-fourth to one-third of recorded private bank assets in the state, in the period from 1900 to 1910.[13] The establishment of the bank presumably represented the institutionalization of funds previously held in family hands. Some measure of the leverage the bank gave the Prados may be gained from the fact that, as late as 1887, the total assets of the eight banks which operated in São Paulo city, Santos, and Campinas were only 91,000 contos.[14] By March 1928 the Rio de Janeiro branch of the Bank of Industry and Commerce had cash reserves of over 102,000 contos ($12.5 million), second only to the Bank of Brazil.[15]

Eduardo Prado's activities in Europe, though personally unproductive, also reflected the new economic climate. As critic of the Republic and partner and European manager of the *Jornal do Comércio*, Eduardo occupied an important position. He opposed the growing commercial ties of Brazil with the United States and encouraged British interests to resist that new menace. As a journalist and financial agent, he gathered economic data and arranged for its dissemination. As a Brazilian whose patriotism (and financial interests) transcended his anti-Republicanism, Eduardo also suppressed some news which would have sorely affected Brazil's credit rating in the early 1890s, as he wrote to José Carlos Rodrigues, his *Jornal do Comércio* partner, on 28 February 1892:

> Some time ago I found out that, at the time [Brazilian bonds] arrived at 55, the Rothschilds kept them from falling again to 50, buying all that appeared at 55 on behalf of the [Brazilian]

government. This would be sensational news, but I did not send it because it would create difficulties for the government and reveal that "in reality" our credit in London was below 55, since the treasury itself maintained that quotation as a minimum.

This startling information probably came to Eduardo from the Rothschilds themselves, with whom he had established personal relations.[16]

Though it was useful to the Prados to have a family member so closely in touch with the London money market, Eduardo rendered more directly valuable services as agent for the Paulista Railway, the presidency of which his brother Antônio assumed in 1892. In that year Eduardo negotiated the Paulista's purchase of the English-owned Rio Claro Railway. Eduardo strengthened his hand by obtaining financial information directly from the Brazilian minister in London, Antônio Correia.[17]

The Prados had been involved in promoting, administering, and financing the Paulista Railway since its inception. Antônio Prado's long presidency of it, lasting until 1928, was the most important entrepreneurial activity of the family during the First Republic. The Rio Claro purchase inaugurated Antônio's presidency, and he was soon criticized because profits declined in the 1890s, when the first payments on the Rio Claro bonds coincided with the falling exchange rate of the milreis. The Rio Claro decision, however, had been as much strategic and personal as economic, since the Paulista, with Antônio's domain at Santa Veridiana as an exposed salient, sought to break out of its encirclement by the Rio Claro and Mogiana lines. Even when the Rio Claro bonds became due, the Paulista remained a basically sound venture.[18]

The abortive extension of the Paulista's lines to Piracicaba, where Antônio had inherited agricultural interests from his father-in-law, illustrates the entrepreneurial and personal qualities that Antônio Prado brought to the railroad and shows as well the corporate ruthlessness of railroad competition in São Paulo. On 30 April 1902 the Paulista signed a contract with Piracicaba's town council for the projected extension. A local newspaper exulted that Antônio Prado was going to free the town from the "tyranny" of the existing line, the Sorocabana and Ituana Company, "by giving us the Paulista, which is life, which is Progress and which will be, in short time, the salvation of our industry, our commerce, and, principally, our fortunate agriculture."[19] In June of 1903, however, Antônio Prado wrote to his agent in Piracicaba, his brother-in-law João Conceição, that the project no longer interested him because the Sorocabana-Ituana railroad had declared bankruptcy and was going to be reorganized. Antônio asked Conceição to get the contract canceled, offering "a small guarantee, perhaps twenty-five contos [$6,000]" to the town.[20] Conceição quickly refused in words Antônio Prado was not used to hearing from a business associate or a family member:

> In the position in which I stand with the people here [in Piracicaba], who so trusted in me and in my relations to obtain, even with the sacrifice of the municipal coffers, the wide gauge of the Paulista, . . . I am without courage to communicate the deception [needed] to make any request in the sense [you ask], and even more, to offer the ridiculous indemnification of 25 contos, . . . thanks to which the Paulista will receive the large sum of 2 or 3 thousand contos de reis.[21]

In view of the bankruptcy and pending reorganization of the Sorocabana-Ituana railroad, which soon was bought by first the federal and then the state government,[22] the Paulista's and Antônio Prado's decision to renege on the contract made good business sense. However, there is no denying the hardship suffered by Piracicaba's residents, who had their hopes raised and then dashed. As they and João Conceição learned, family relations could cut two ways. Traditional family ties based on loyalty and mutual services were hard pressed to survive in a developing capitalist economy where profit and competition were the rules of the game.

Under Antônio's management the Paulista extended its lines and introduced important innovations such as reforestation for ties and fuel, electrification, all-steel passenger cars on regular first- and second-class service, and modern locomotives, all of which helped ensure its profitability while maintaining a high level of services. In its first fifty years of operation, 1872 to 1922, the last thirty under Antônio Prado's direction, the line paid a dividend of not less than 7 percent in every year save one, with a yearly average of over 10 percent. Unlike most Brazilian railroads, it was able to avoid heavy indebtedness. An opponent of foreign economic control who styled himself an economic "Jacobin,"[23] Antônio only twice had to seek outside financing for the railroad: in 1892, when a £2,750,000 bond issue was floated for double-tracking its mainline, and in 1922, when a $4,000,000 bond issue was negotiated to finance electrification. Moreover, though the Paulista had begun as a coffee railroad, by 1920 only 38 percent of its revenues came directly from coffee.[24]

The Paulista Railway was not, of course, strictly a family venture, but for a generation the line bore the heavy and progressive stamp of Antônio Prado's influence. When Antônio assigned his son Luíz to work as a lathe operator during the latter's vacation from engineering studies at São Paulo's Polytechnic School, a fellow worker told Luíz what the initials of the railroad, C.P.V.F.F. (Companhia Paulista de Vias Ferreas e Fluviais), really stood for: "Conselheiro Prado vai ficar furioso"—"Councilor Prado is going to be furious."[25] Moreover, many Prados and their relatives served on the railroad's directorate: Antônio's sons Paulo and Antônio Júnior; Elias Fausto Pacheco Jordão, Antônio's cousin; Elias Antônio Pacheco e Chaves, his brother-in-law; and Luis Tavares Alves Pereira, father-in-law of Martinho Prado Neto. In this way the Prados were able to ensure that the railroad's policies would coincide with their other interests.

Commerce and Industry

The Prados' production of coffee and shipping of it to port via the Paulista Railway was complemented by another major enterprise, the Prado-Chaves Export Company. The firm originated in the Central Paulista Company, founded by Martinho, Antônio, and Martinico Prado in the mid-1880s, possibly because of dissatisfaction with existing exporters. On 15 November 1887 the Central Paulista was reorganized as Prado-Chaves and Company with an initial capital of 500 contos ($230,000). Elias Antônio Pacheco e Chaves and Elias Fausto Pacheco Jordão were added as partners. In the 1890s the company's capital was raised to 4,000 contos ($800,000) and other relatives joined its management.[26]

Initially, Prado-Chaves handled the coffee exports of the interrelated Prado, Chaves, Monteiro de Barros, Conceição, and Portella families. Under the direction of Paulo Prado, Martinico's son Plínio (a Harvard Ph.D.), João Machado Portella, and Ernesto Ramos, the

Antônio da Silva Prado, baron of Iguape (1788–1875)

Veridiana Valeria da Silva Prado (1825–1910)

Maria de Moura Leite da Silva Prado, baroness of Iguape

Martinho da Silva Prado (1811–1891)

Clockwise from top left:
*Antônio Prado (1840–1929), Martinho Prado Júnior (1843–1906),
Eduardo Prado (1860–1901), Caio Prado (1853–1889)*

Antônio Prado (1840–1929), at the age of twenty

Antônio Prado as a provincial deputy, 1870   *Antônio Prado in 1890*

Antônio Prado as mayor of São Paulo, 1899

Antônio Prado (1840–1929)

*Martinho Prado Júnior ("Martinico," 1843–1906),
as a twenty-year-old student*

Martinho Prado Júnior in Argentina
during the Paraguayan War, 1865

Martinho Prado Júnior as district attorney, 1867

Martinho Prado Júnior (1843–1906)

Martinho Prado Júnior establishing the fazenda Guatapará, 1885

Albertina Pinto da Silva Prado, wife of Martinho Prado Júnior

*Martinho da Silva Prado Júnior, Dona Albertina Prado,
and their twelve children*

company gradually became the most important Brazilian-owned coffee export house in Santos. From a negligible share of that port's coffee exports in the 1890s, the company increased its share to 16.82 percent in 1912–13. Between 1908 and 1923, Prado-Chaves founded subsidiaries in London, Hamburg, and Stockholm.[27]

This growth occurred during a worsening crisis of overproduction and falling prices that was first evident in 1896. With the adoption of government price supports, the coffee valorization agreements of 1906, Prado-Chaves became a semiofficial arm of the state government. Immediately before the agreements were announced, the government had Prado-Chaves inform its foreign agents of the news, a move planned to stimulate an immediate price rise. Once valorization was adopted (over the objections of Antônio Prado, as we shall see), Prado-Chaves played a significant role as the leading Brazilian exporter in a sector dominated by foreigners. In 1907 it handled about 10 percent of the eight million bags of coffee bought and stored by the government. In the same year, Prado-Chaves and Antônio Prado's Bank of Industry and Commerce received 15,633 contos ($4,846,230) for government-purchased coffee, nearly all the funds paid out in Brazilian currency.[28]

The coffee valorization of 1906 affected different groups in different ways and illustrates important facets of the political economy of coffee in the dependent economy of São Paulo. The scheme allowed the industry to survive its greatest crisis up to that time; Brazilian fazendeiros thus realized a short-term success from the plan. For German, French, and North American trading houses, a windfall resulted from profitable legitimate and illegitimate manipulations related to coffee valorization. Consumers ultimately paid most of the costs. For São Paulo the valorization program was a qualified success, as the state gained relative to other Brazilian states and the federal government but lost relative to foreign financial and commercial interests, whose dominance, in any event, did not concern the liberal state very much. São Paulo did accept a significant departure from the dominant laissez-faire ideology, but its valorization plan treated the superficial aspects of the coffee economy's problems, while letting deeper difficulties go untouched.[29]

Prado-Chaves profited not only from its privileged position in the valorization scheme, but from the misfortunes of bankrupt fazendeiros, many of whom preferred to deliver their plantations to a Bra-

zilian firm rather than a foreign one. By 1909 the company had acquired seventeen such properties (Appendix D). The best were re-
stored by rigid economy and modern methods and sold to the firm's
partners. Others were replanted in grapes and figs and sold at handsome profits.[30] At least two were subdivided and sold to immigrant
and Brazilian farmers, thus fulfilling in some measure the Prados'
old interest in promoting small-farm agriculture. A plantation near
Campinas was subdivided into five- and ten-alqueire parcels including, where possible, pasture, woodland, and water. It was reported
that this plantation was "surrounded by happy farms established by
more or less independent colonos." Another thousand alqueires on a
second plantation owned by Prado-Chaves was subdivided, and
within six months three hundred alqueires had been sold to Italians,
Austrians, Germans, and native Brazilians. Thus Prado-Chaves
demonstrated a willingness permanently to alienate portions of
large landholdings, an advance over the standard practice of granting
temporary use of land for foodplots.[31]

The disruption of European markets during World War I was a
near-disaster for the coffee company. Prado-Chaves's exports fell
from nearly 1.5 million bags in 1912–13 to one-third that total in
1916–17, while its proportion of Santos exports dropped from 16.82
to 5.47 percent. Paulo Prado, as São Paulo's representative on the
federal coffee board, negotiated the government's purchase of two
million bags of coffee in 1916, using his ties with international trade
circles to overcome what Prado-Chaves saw as "interests contrary to
those of the country as a whole." In 1918, with the end of the Great
War, Prado-Chaves enjoyed its greatest year, exporting 2.2 million
bags of coffee, 28.25 percent of Santos's total. This, however, was an
artificial event probably caused by the temporary absence of European exporters. Soon afterward, the firm's absolute volume of exports and its share of the market dropped drastically and never returned to prewar levels.[32] The growth of Prado-Chaves had coincided with its privileged relationship with government, and its decline evidently resulted from the loss of that status, as well as from
the recovery of foreign firms after the war.

Another Prado line developed during the First Republic was the
cattle business. In 1895 Antônio Prado founded a tannery near São
Paulo city, the Cortume Agua Branca. Combined with his railroad
and exporting interests, the tannery led to his establishment, in

1910, of the first Brazilian-owned refrigerated meat-packing plant, the Frigorífico Barretos, begun as a partnership with the immigrant entrepreneur Alexandre Siciliano. The Paulista Railway held a prior concession to construct such a plant at Barretos, its northern terminus, but this obviously was no obstacle to Antônio Prado. He himself went to Europe to get technical advice and materials, and he recruited experienced labor from Argentina and from the United States. Using the Paulista Railway's rail and river system, Antônio was able to obtain cattle from Minas Gerais, Mato Grosso, and Goiás. Original plans called for production only for domestic consumption, but local demand could supposedly satisfy only one-third of the Barretos plant's capacity. Thus, in 1914, 1.5 tons of meat were exported. Despite the war, exports to Europe expanded greatly, to 3,500 tons in 1915 and to approximately 5,850, 7,700, and 11,050 tons in the years 1916 through 1918.[33]

Antônio Prado's decision to export meat was not without its critics. During the war years the cost of basic foodstuffs in Brazil rose sharply, partly because of the emergence of a class of capitalists who exerted a near monopoly over such commodities. Afonso Henriques de Lima Barreto wrote in 1917 that Brazilian sugar was being sold abroad for half its price in Brazil. A similar situation, Lima Barreto said, existed with regard to beans, "with [Francisco] Matarazzo in the lead," and with respect to meat, "with the butcher Antônio Prado and his traveling salesman, Graça Aranha, both at the head of the indecent speculation in frozen meats furnished at low cost to foreigners, while we here pay double for a kilo of the same product."[34] In 1919, when the unusual situation created by the war had ended and traditional suppliers of meat in Rio Grande do Sul, Uruguay, and Argentina regained the market, the frigorífico was leased to another firm and passed from direct Prado control.[35]

Other Prado ventures departed from the coffee-meat-exporting-railroad conglomerate. One of the most important was the Santa Marina Glassworks, founded in 1895 by Antônio Prado and Elias Fausto Pacheco Jordão to supply bottles for the beer-making concerns Companhia Antártica and Cervejaria Germânica. Two-fifths of its original capital of 1,000 contos ($200,000) was subscribed by Antônio. In 1919, he acquired three-fourths of the stock, and six years later its capital was raised to 5,000 contos ($600,000). Originally, 200 French and Italian glassblowers produced some 8,000 bottles daily.

With the addition of modern equipment in the late 1920s, production was increased to 140,000 bottles a day.[36]

Several of Martinico Prado's descendants were involved in industrial activities not directly tied to the export economy. The most successful was Cícero Prado, who established an important paper factory still in family hands. Fábio Prado, who became São Paulo's mayor in 1934, married a daughter of the Italian industrialist Rudolfo Crespi and became Crespi's principal assistant in his cotton-textile manufacturing business. Caio Prado, father of the historian, served as assistant to his father-in-law, Antônio Alvares Penteado, a leading Paulista industrialist, in the latter's jute-manufacturing concern. Two other sons of Martinico pursued nonindustrial careers: Martinho Prado Neto was a fazendeiro and a pioneer in citrus growing and packing, and Cássio was an unsuccessful resort-hotel operator.[37] Though detailed information about this branch of the family is lacking, there appears to have been a clear trend toward business rather than agricultural careers. More intriguing is that evidently there were no group ventures among the brothers; either they pursued individual careers or, as sons-in-law, were partners in firms whose controlling members were outside the immediate Prado family.

"The Martyrdom of Coffee"

While the Prados presided over a variety of financial, transportation, processing, and manufacturing enterprises—activities which, as a whole, seem to have reached their peak in the pre-1914 period—the family had to contend with the increasing ills of the coffee economy after 1896. Most of the Prados' businesses depended directly or indirectly on coffee, and the family expanded its coffee plantings greatly from 1889 to 1900, when a ban on further planting was imposed by the state for a decade. Coffee, historically the vehicle of the Prados' success, became a heavy burden. It may well have placed a limit on their other entrepreneurial activities.

In the early 1890s coffee seemed to have a limitless future. Diseases afflicted competing Asian coffee plantations. Republican decentralization offered the promise and partial reality of planter-class control over the government. Credit inflation opened up sources of capital for acquiring new lands while it raised coffee prices in the local market because of monetary devaluation.[38] However, over-production soon became chronic; depreciation of the milréis was a mixed blessing for those, like the Prados, who depended on foreign consumer items and manufacturing equipment; and the Republican regime proved to be less responsive than the Prados would have liked.

When Martinho Prado died in 1891, a new company, Veridiana Prado and Sons, was set up to operate the old fazendas Campo Alto and Loreto in Mogi-Mirim and the family's newly acquired giant, São Martinho. Antônio Prado served as its manager and still directed his private fazenda, Santa Veridiana. Martinico ran another giant, Guatapará, which after his death in 1906 was managed, along with his other interests, by his son Plínio.[39] Another plantation, Brejão, was deeded to Eduardo Prado, evidently in order to induce him to settle down.[40] Other fazendas, as mentioned previously, were later acquired from Prado-Chaves or were held in partnership in that concern (Appendix D).

Within this impressive array of family holdings there existed considerable variation. From 1889 to 1899, before the state ban on planting, 1,268,000 trees were planted at São Martinho, the gem of the Prado properties.[41] Much of the work was evidently done by independent Italian contractors who had formerly been field hands. In 1908 São Martinho was incorporated with a capital of 5,000 contos ($1,550,000). Antônio Prado was its president, and 99 percent of the stock was held by the Prado-Chaves Export House. Eventually it boasted 3.4 million coffee trees and was a self-contained world for its four thousand workers.[42]

Eduardo Prado's Brejão was much more modest, though impeccably maintained and productive. Eduardo was called to the planter profession at a most untimely point. Attempting to re-enact the successes of his older brothers a generation earlier, his efforts to expand his holdings by investing in virgin coffee lands had no prospect of immediate success. Moreover, in 1897 he was forced to withhold part of Brejão's coffee from market because of falling prices.[43]

Because of different economic situations Antônio and Eduardo Prado reacted quite differently to the price crisis. Much more vulnerable, Eduardo was quick to realize the necessity of government intervention. Viewing the situation of coffee in the late 1890s as "simply terrifying," Eduardo bent his political principles and repeatedly asked his former adversary Rui Barbosa to sponsor a plan in the federal congress to declare a moratorium on the debts fazendeiros owed to coffee commissaries and exporters.[44] Since Antônio, through the Prado-Chaves house (in which Eduardo had no interest), was one of these exporters, he probably resented Eduardo's notions.

There were other grounds for disagreement. Antônio consistently opposed government intervention in the coffee crisis and recommended common-sense measures to his fellow fazendeiros to ease the crisis, if indeed, he said, a crisis existed at all. In 1903, when the crisis had become chronic, Antônio expressed his faith that "economic laws" would end overproduction.[45] Two years later, he admitted that government action might be necessary to aid "the economic laws of production and consumption" but lashed out at the ban on new planting as "anti-economic and anti-liberal, a negation of riches acquired by work, offensive against property, and an arbitrary application of the right of levying taxes." Though negatively expressed, this was Antônio's classic nineteenth-century economic liberalism reduced to its essence. When the coffee valorization plan passed in 1906, Antônio remained hostile to it, warning that a rapid solution could not be expected to a problem rooted in Brazilian "traditions, vices, and customs."[46]

Antônio's opposition to a price-support scheme widely supported by the coffee-planter "class" is not only evidence of his faith in classical economics, but an indication of the extent to which he had transcended that class. He was no ordinary fazendeiro solely concerned with obtaining a good price in Santos. Rather he managed a large conglomerate, giving credit, running fazendas, managing a railroad whose profits depended to a high degree on coffee production, and depending on equipment imports to tool his fledgling industries. Thus Antônio Prado stood at the center of the countervailing forces of economic change in São Paulo: fazendeiro versus exporter, planter versus industrialist, debtor versus creditor, capital versus labor, private versus public interest,[47] economic nationalism versus internationalism. In this rather exquisite position, imbued with classic economic liberalism, Antônio advocated increased production, increased immigration, modern methods and efficiency, propaganda to stimulate foreign consumption of coffee, and, for the suffering fazendeiro, "patience" rather than government intervention with its uncertain effects.

The crisis in coffee raises the difficult, complex question of Antônio Prado's role vis-à-vis the foreign companies which dominated the coffee-export economy in the early twentieth century. Joseph Love notes that Antônio was a business partner of a representative of one of the two foreign enterprises dominating coffee export, the German-based Theodor Wille company. Antônio was also a member of the board of Wille's British rival, the Brazilian Warrant Company. Paulo Prado served as director of the Companhia Registradora de Santos, a coffee-warehousing concern owned by Edward Greene of the Brazilian Warrant Company; the Companhia Registradora "obtained a guaranteed interest rate (6 percent) from the state on capital they invested in their operations, to the detriment of Brazilian exporters and commissários." Love maintains that Wille and Brazilian Warrant succeeded partly because of " 'cutting in' men like Antônio Prado." During World War I, Antônio "pulled political strings for British businesses in exchange for having his concerns removed from the British blacklist." Moreover, the one thing that in Love's view kept São Paulo's elite from being "mere domestic agents of foreign enterprise"—coffee valorization—was opposed by Antônio Prado out of fear of its monetary, fiscal, and exchange consequences, and, perhaps, its impact on his profits as an exporter.[48] Elsewhere, it is reported that a federal senator accused Antônio Prado of acting for European bankers in negotiating a valorization consolidation loan in 1908.[49]

Yet it would be wrong to see Antônio as a "mere domestic agent of foreign enterprise." Indeed, a leading historian has called him one of Brazil's first economic nationalists.[50] The truth probably lies in the middle. Since the 1860s Antônio had been a believer in economic liberalism, the ideological cover under which foreigners increased their control of Brazil's dependent economy. But for Antônio, as for most of his generation of the elite, economic liberalism meant "progress," the means by which Brazil, led by São Paulo, was supposedly to join the club of "advanced" nations. Only the Great Depression of the 1930s dispelled this view, bringing economic nationalism to the fore. Economic nationalism was really associated with a later generation, though Antônio was generally aware of the threat of foreign domination and concerned about it. His brother Eduardo and his son Paulo were cultural nationalists. He himself had been conscious, since the 1860s, of the ambivalent impact of Europe on Brazil, as model and threat. He criticized President Campos Sales' financial policy toward foreigners as "servile."[51] Seen properly, Antônio Prado in his sixties and seventies, during the first two decades of the twentieth century, was a transitional figure in a transitional era between economic liberalism and economic nationalism.

By the 1920s a series of circumstances combined to threaten seriously the Prado economic conglomerate. The flow of immigrant workers had not been adequately guaranteed by the Republican government, despite its supposed attentiveness to Paulista coffee interests. The Prados were continuously preoccupied with the labor situation, but eventually, because of improved conditions in Mussolini's Italy, the flow of immigrants dried up at its source.[52] The refusal of the government of São Paulo to approve Antônio's own extraordinary attempt at personal immigration diplomacy—the abortive "Ouchy Agreement" he signed with the Italian government in 1921—left him in a bitter mood.[53] Frosts, a flu epidemic among workers, a locust plague, and the effects of the war—the four g's of 1918: *geada, grippe, gafanhotos,* and *guerra*—wreaked havoc on the family's plantations.[54] The Barretos frigorífico was leased out, and Prado-Chaves was in irreversible decline.

In these circumstances, a rapid liquidation of the Prados' coffee properties and reinvestment into industry might have seemed appropriate. However, though there were other indicators that compromised them—the declining exchange rate of the milréis and inflation—rising coffee prices in the early 1920s once again held out the promise of a prosperous future for coffee. Thus, instead of shifting decisively from agriculture to industry, Antônio Prado's sons specialized ever more narrowly in coffee production and exporting. Luíz Prado took over the management of Santa Veridiana and São Martinho, but his efforts were mainly a holding action against heavy economic and natural odds. Though his situation was fraught with difficulties, Luíz later wrote that the best advice he received from his father was "to dedicate myself to agriculture, thus giving a logical continuance to the traditions of our family."[55] The erudite, polished modernist Paulo Prado came to style himself, somewhat ingenuously, as "a simple producer, factor, and exporter." Each thus defined himself primarily in the context of the troubled coffee economy and more narrowly than his capitalist-industrialist father. Despite his resentment of its political apathy, Paulo became a defender of the planter class. He accepted the valorization concept to an extent his father never did, but protested against the high costs borne by planters and against the ineptitude of the government's coffee policies.[56]

Paulo's essay "The Martyrdom of Coffee," published in 1927 when coffee production and prices were soaring, presented the fazendeiro as trapped in an inexorable economic system leading toward a "fatal crash." An insightful and irreverent amateur historian, Paulo recognized the 1920s schemes of coffee valorization and monetary devaluation as "an old system that Brazil knew since colonial times, when in the seventeenth century sugar was valorized with devalued money."[57] Paulo's reaction was no doubt more extreme than that of other family members. The fazenda Guatapará, run by Martinico Prado's heirs, was more profitable in the 1920s than in the previous decade, though its profits dropped drastically in the 1930s.[58] The Paulista Railway continued to be profitable, and the Santa Marina glassworks was expanding. Nonetheless, Paulo's essay emphasized the family's continuing partial dependence on agriculture and the export economy, and in a footnote added to the essay after the crash of 1929, he had no occasion to retract his earlier views.[59] The main adjustments made by the family in the 1920s and 1930s were to diversify agricultural production, replacing coffee partly with oranges and sugar and expanding cattle production.[60] In 1935 the Prado-Chaves Company began to export cotton, controlling 9.5 percent of Santos exports by 1942,[61] an adjustment which nonetheless failed to bring the company back to its pre–World War I status.

The Planter-Entrepreneur and the Immigrant-Entrepreneur

The early industrialization of São Paulo, as Warren Dean has described it, was in part the work of two types: the planter-entrepreneur, symbolized by Antônio Prado, and the immigrant-entrepreneur, exemplified by Francisco Matarazzo. Even before 1914 there is some evidence that the immigrant tended to wrest control of industry from the planter. Later, when the two entrepreneurial elites began to merge, the process was governed by a revealing equation: immigrant industrialists provided money and the planter elite provided the prestige and political control that went with their social standing.[62] An impressionistic study suggests that by the 1940s immigrant families had superseded those of Brazilian origin in controlling Brazilian industry.[63] Thus, a comparison of the Prados' economic role and that of the leading immigrant entrepreneur, Francisco Matarazzo, helps interpret the economic experience of the Prado family as well as the early process of industrialization in São Paulo generally.

Francisco Matarazzo (1854–1937) arrived in São Paulo from Italy in 1881. From a modest beginning as a pushcart vendor in the interior town of Sorocaba, he eventually built Latin America's largest industrial empire. Matarazzo's career falls into four stages: rural commerce and, secondarily, the production of lard (1881–90); urban trade and importing (1890–1900); industrial activities developed from commerce (1900–1930); and the predominance of industrial production (1930 on). Three features of the development of the Matarazzo empire are especially important. The first is Matarazzo's early specialization in importing and later in producing products such as lard and wheat for domestic consumption. The second is the vertical integration of his interests; importing wheat, for example, he soon acquired plants and raw materials to manufacture sacking, then purchased his own shipping fleet and built his own docks to avoid the congestion on the public wharves. Finally, although Matarazzo started as a merchant and acquired fazendas as a source of raw material, the final result was a manufacturing empire.[64]

In contrast, the Prado conglomerate was based on the coffee-export trade. Unlike the import sector, the export economy encountered a chronic condition of oversupply in the twentieth century. Moreover, while some vertical integration existed in the Prados' fazenda–railroad–export house–European outlet chain, they did not acquire interests in related areas such as agricultural machinery or chemicals, and they were content to rely on public docks and foreign shipping. Finally, manufacturing, though it constituted the primary endeavor of some individuals, continued to occupy a secondary role in the family at large.

The Prado and Matarazzo experiences may be compared on the

level of organization and institutionalization as well. José de Souza Martins depicts the following stages in the development of the Matarazzo empire: Francisco's individual enterprises (1881–90); his partnerships with his brothers (1891–1911); the period "in which the company became a corporation and absorbed the second generation . . . in administrative posts" (1911–24); and a subsequent period when the capital of Francisco and his descendants, already dominant, became almost exclusively influential in the company (1924 on).[65] This marked trend from individual to highly integrated, unitary corporate structure had no equivalent in the Prado conglomerate. The Prado-Chaves company tended to act as a holding company for some family concerns, and family-owned fazendas tended to become corporate agribusinesses (without, however, losing their character as family enterprises). But this movement was fragmentary and partial, businesses were organized on the basis of fluctuating family ties, and "the Prado conglomerate" was not embodied in any single corporate entity. The São Martinho and Guatapará agricultural corporations, for example, were controlled by the heirs of Antônio and Martinico Prado, respectively, and those two branches of the family increasingly regarded themselves in competitive terms.[66] The Prado conglomerate, in sum, was more a loose federation with a strong sense of "states' rights" than an empire.

At the personal level, there were also contrasts between the Matarazzo and Prado experiences. Whatever his own complexities may have been,[67] Francisco Matarazzo was able to give his principal heir, Francisco Matarazzo Júnior, the strength to resist parceling out the family fortune after his death. The last effective unifying economic figure of the Prado family was Martinho Prado, who died in 1891. Antônio Prado provided a unifying figure for his branch of the family, and, because of the extraordinary force of his character, he was able to resolve the incipient conflict in his dual roles as fazendeiro and capitalist-entrepreneur; but his two most trusted heirs came to define themselves primarily in terms of the coffee trade. Antônio Prado himself had long preached the virtue of fathers' instilling in sons the love of agricultural traditions,[68] and this, ironically, may have limited the Prados' ability to adapt to the emerging industrial order in São Paulo, which after 1930 was left increasingly to the immigrant-entrepreneur.

The point is not that the immigrant-entrepreneur was, by virtue of his immigrant status, more intelligent, more capable, or more naturally inclined toward industrial capitalism. Antônio Prado's own career, and the less dramatic industrial careers of other Prados and other Brazilian entrepreneurs demonstrate the contrary. Rather, I suggest that the differing historical and sociocultural conditions of the two groups affected their response to industrialization occurring in the context of an export economy. As a recent arrival, the immigrant-entrepreneur had greater need for family solidarity and was less subject to the cultural and political factors that tended to erode such solidarity in native Brazilian families like the Prados. To the immigrant, the fazenda was a secondary phenomenon, acquired for raw materials or social prestige; to the planter-entrepreneur and his family, it was a primary reference point, not only economically, but socially and psychologically.

The Prados' economic activities contain some hints that shed fresh light on our understanding of the nature of the Brazilian-born sector of Brazil's "capitalist class" during the First Republic. Even within the limited confines of the family, diversity of interests rather than unity marked the Prados' economic endeavors, reminding us of the complexities hiding in the simple word *class*. Antônio and Eduardo clashed over state intervention in the coffee economy, and Paulo eventually accepted valorization, although his father never did. Differences in levels of economic security and in age thus led to family schisms in the economic realm.

During the First Republic the dominant economic ideology, liberalism, began to show signs of obsolescence. This was fundamentally important in weakening the ideological justification of the Prados' class power base. Moreover, Antônio, the only economic strategist capable of guiding a familistic capitalist empire, was unalterably wedded to the ideology that would become defunct in 1929, the year—ironically enough—when Antônio Prado died. Liberal social values promoted the individualism that strained the bonds of family capitalism. The Prados thus faced two alternatives. They could become individualistic entrepreneurs, perhaps becoming prominent local agents for foreign multinationals, as in the case of Martinho Prado Neto. Or they could retrench defensively on the plantation, making a psychological as well as economic return to their roots which assumed almost talismanic qualities in troubled economic times.

Prado family capitalism depended on the vicissitudes and contradictions of a neocolonial export economy. The bulk of the Prados' businesses, and the most important of them—the Paulista Railway and the Prado-Chaves Export House—were directly linked to exports. Imports for industries and for consumers' goods were purchased with export earnings. As Eduardo and Paulo knew, the capitalist world market economy could destroy even the rich and powerful. The Prados' economic interests, moreover, required that they remain on good terms with foreign capital, but this requirement often conflicted with their pride and nationalism. For the Prados, nationalism more often expressed itself in a cultural rather than an economic idiom, but it nonetheless expressed deep dissatisfaction with the evolving world system in which "culture" blended imperceptibly into "economics." Not until the crash of 1929 did economic nationalism move to the fore.

The structure of the Prado family—weakened by liberal notions— ultimately could not cope with the organizing and planning tasks required by modern capitalism. After 1840 the highest degree of family economic (and personal and political) solidarity coincided with the simplest form of economic organization significant in the family's history, the slave-labor fazenda of the mid-nineteenth century. The family's sponsorship of railroads, immigration, factories, and international finance required it to enter ever more complex spheres of economic and political life at the provincial and state, national, and international levels. Initially the Prados were successful in these broader arenas and overcame opposition. The immigration program and the São Paulo loan of 1888 are good examples. However, the economic cooperation between Martinico and Antônio Prado in the 1880s had no important sequel among their descendants in the twentieth century. Meanwhile, the essentially personalistic methods with which the family had been able to influence broad economic forces and the relevant political organs before 1889 resulted in ignominious defeats, such as the Ouchy Agreement affair, during the First Republic. The organization skills of this family—inheritor of the supposedly superfamilistic Brazilian tradition—proved unequal to those of such hungry immigrant clans as the Matarazzos, an irony that did not escape the attention of the pro-immigration Prados.

The "capitalist class" in Brazil should not be depicted only in narrow economic terms. At one level, the family's organizational and planning abilities were undermined by the loosening of family life highlighted in generational and gender conflicts. At another level, Eduardo Prado and Paulo Prado wrote classic books analyzing regional, national, and international conflicts; these books challenged simple notions of "progress" via models imported from advanced capitalist countries and thus weakened the ideological foundations of liberal capitalism. At yet another level, despite their power, prestige, and individual wealth, the Prados found themselves politically marginal during the First Republic. This surprising marginalization challenges those who would predict that talent, social prestige, and capitalist economic power automatically translate into political dominance.

ᛥ CHAPTER IX ᛤ

AT THE MARGINS

OF POLITICS

During the First Republic (1889–1930), while countries like Argentina and Mexico were following the path of increasing centralization, Brazil experimented with political decentralization. Brazil's course was largely affected by the desires of the coffee growers and exporters of São Paulo, usually allied with those in neighboring Minas Gerais. The First Republic was dominated by Brazil's rural oligarchies and state governors who supported the central government in foreign affairs and national finances in return for patronage and a free hand in state and local rule.[1] The national electorate remained small—never more than 3.5 percent of the population[2]—and was manipulated by monolithic state parties, local *coronéis* (strongmen) and state governors. The Empire's national parties disappeared and no true national parties were formed. The growing middle and working classes were generally barred from politics. As one historian and self-styled "militant politician" of the era has noted, "the representative system was a vast hoax, as it had been during the Empire."[3]

Nonetheless, significant structural changes accompanied the advent of the Republic. In place of the poder moderador, there arose the "politics of the governors," caucuses of state bosses and the incumbent president, to determine presidential succession. *Coronelismo* (local rule by coronéis) took the place of the imperial parties as a means of integrating localities and regions into the nation, however loosely. Decentralization and states' rights replaced the centralization of the Empire. Unlike the imperial leadership, the masters of the First Republic gave political recognition to the geographical shift in the economy caused by the growth of the coffee complex in south-central Brazil. With only three exceptions, Brazil's presidents in the period 1894–1930 were from either São Paulo or Minas Gerais, and until the 1920s national policy often favored the needs of coffee interests.[4]

Given the First Republic's notable decentralization, a periodization based on its presidential administrations is a vast oversimplification and is used here only to provide a broad context against which to examine the Prados' political behavior during the era. From 1889 to 1894, Brazil was ruled by the army under Generals Deodoro da Fonseca (1889–91) and Floriano Peixoto (1891–94). This dictatorship consolidated the regime and created a modicum of order under which civilians could rule. The heyday of the First Republic, from 1894 to 1910, encompassed the presidencies of the Paulistas José Prudente de Morais e Barros (1894–98), Manuel Ferraz de Campos Sales (1898–1902), and Francisco de Paula Rodrigues Alves (1902–6) and the Mineiro Afonso Pena (1906–9). This was an era of further political and then financial consolidation. During a third phase, 1910 to 1922, political stagnation set in. This period began with a contested, and thus atypical, national election in 1910, in which the liberal spokesman for "civilian" interests, Rui Barbosa, was defeated by the official, military-endorsed candidate, Marshal Hermes da Fonseca, nephew of Deodoro. The administrations of Venceslau Brás (1914–18) and of Epitácio Pessoa (1919–22) saw civilians returned to power but also witnessed, especially under Pessoa, ruptures in the coalition of state oligarchies that controlled national politics. In the final period, the administrations of Artur Bernardes (1922–26) and Washington Luís Pereira de Sousa (1926–30), the Republic was attacked from the outside by middle- and working-class groups, disaffected junior officers (the *tenentes*), and planters who resented the abandonment of procoffee policies. In addition, the Republic suffered an internal breakdown when rival state bosses could not agree on presidential succession in 1930.[5]

In São Paulo, the First Republic continued some traditional features of politics. The political elite of the state—263 persons including 6 Prados, according to Joseph Love—"tended to come from a small circle of families, closely linked by blood and marriage; went to the same schools or the same sorts of schools; and were wont to adopt European cultural values."[6] Although family ties became a less common characteristic of the elite political generation born after 1889 than of that born before, family solidarity underlay disputes and factions in the dominant political party, the Paulista Republican party (PRP). The PRP, like the imperial political parties, was essentially opportunistic. The leaders of its most viable opposition, the Democratic party (PD), formed in 1926, did not differ much in background from those of the PRP. As Love noted, "The control of state politics by traditional ruling groups was not seriously threatened by inteɪnal challenges representing new social forces."[7]

Despite continuities with the defunct Empire, the First Republic was a changed political environment. Relations between nation and states (the former provinces) changed drastically, of course, as São Paulo continued to champion state autonomy and liberal constitutionalism even under the centralizing rule of Getúlio Vargas in the 1930s and 1940s. Less well known—and more relevant to this study—was the changed relation between São Paulo's state government and its municípios and local governments. During the First Republic governors of São Paulo gained "immense power," especially during the administrations of Jorge Tibiriçá (1904–8), who vastly strengthened the state police force, and Washington Luís (1920–24), who modernized the state judiciary and lessened its dependence on local power.[8] State governors came into conflict with urban groups. The state had extensive powers over municípios, and despite the fact that cities grew rapidly, the urban mayor played only a peripheral role in the political system.[9] Only two of São Paulo's municípios—São Paulo and Santos—were overwhelmingly urban, and they furnished only 20 percent of the state's voters in 1927. Urban groups were kept from having much influence in politics. In response to their plight, some city dwellers sponsored a revival of *municipalismo,* a movement for more local autonomy that had originated in São Paulo during the Empire. Other urbanites challenged the dominant PRP—which depended on rural coronéis in the frontier regions—by joining the PD.

It is some measure of the Prados' political fate after 1889 that their chief successes were as mayors. This gave a certain continuity to their tradition of political participation and public service, but they were, in fact, removed from the mainstream of politics. From the margins of politics the Prados often criticized the new regime. The family's political protests typified the Prados' troubled adaptation to the First Republic. They also cast unflattering light on the First Republic itself, as perceived by an elite family closely connected with Brazilian modernization.

Continuity or Withdrawal?

After the collapse of the monarchy the Prados never recovered their former political influence, and family ties began to weaken more quickly. These tendencies, however, were far from clear in 1889. Antônio Prado could have joined the republican leadership as many former imperial leaders did. Had he done so, he might have played a far more constructive role than he did, given his very great prestige in São Paulo and his capacity for politics and administration. Martinico Prado was a historical (pre-1889) Republican and, like other Paulistas of his party, might have come into great power, but political idealism and, eventually, failing health prevented that. Had either or both brothers become political leaders, Eduardo Prado's monarchism might have been muted. But facing a new political situation, the brothers—so different in formal political identification and in personality—could not forge a common political front. They thus came to represent three variations of the politics of the elite who remained outside the mainstream in the First Republic: progressive conservatism, idealistic republicanism, and unregenerate monarchism.

It has been said that Antônio Prado, the progressive conservative, was one of those imperial political chiefs who contributed to political continuity during Brazil's transition from monarchy to republic.[10] This is misleading insofar as it implies an active, continuous, and wholehearted role during the 1890s and afterward. Antônio's chief concern in 1889 was to avoid major disruptions in Brazilian society. Five months before the Republican coup of 15 November 1889, a Liberal ministry led by the viscount of Ouro Prêto, Afonso Celso de Assis Figueiredo, was named to resist demands for sweeping reform being voiced by members of all parties. Antônio Prado interpreted the situation as pre-revolutionary, with the Conservatives caught between the surging tide for reform and the Ouro Prêto ministry's intransigence. Faced with parliamentary elections in São Paulo, he decided that the Conservatives had to run on a platform of decentralization, and he convinced Paulista and national leaders to accept his strategy. The primary elections in São Paulo resulted in the Conservatives' defeat in eight of nine general-assembly districts and forced runoffs between Liberals and Republicans in two districts. Antônio then threw Conservative support to the Republicans, since the two parties agreed on decentralization. The subsequent Liberal victory may have made the military-Republican coup of 15 November more acceptable to Antônio than the aborted prospect of Liberal dominance.[11]

At any rate, Antônio Prado became Brazil's first major imperial leader to urge acceptance of the new regime. A careful reading of his famous editorial appearing in the *Correio Paulistano* three days after the coup, however, reveals his reservations and sets the conditions for his later withdrawal from politics. His main concerns were to preserve public order and to see the Republic legitimized by some expression of popular will, primarily through the creation of a national party that would include not only historic Republicans but members of the Conservative and Liberal parties as well. His endorsement of the new regime rested to a great extent on the latter points.[12]

Antônio's own activities in late 1889 and early 1890 betrayed a wait-and-see attitude. São Paulo's Republicans decided on 15 November to form a provisional state government of leaders from the three parties and asked Antônio to join the junta. He declined on several grounds: he was against a collective executive; the Republicans had made the "revolution" and ought to implement it; and, finally, he could not abandon the trust of those who had elected him imperial senator. In declining the Republicans' invitation, however, Antônio promised his unofficial cooperation and advised the Republican leader and future president of Brazil, Manuel Ferraz de Campos Sales, that if the states were to "permit the central government to intervene in the organization of the states, we will never have a Federative Republic."[13]

Antônio clearly supported federalism, and he hoped that a national party would develop to provide overall coherence to the nation, which many felt would fly apart under a federalist regime. In December 1889 Antônio toyed with the idea of an active political career.[14] He was elected to the national Constituent Assembly in 1890 but never took up his seat, probably because he foresaw the submissive role that Deodoro da Fonseca and his civilian advisers planned for that body.[15] His abandonment of politics soon extended even to his pet project of immigration, which he had regarded earlier as transcending politics. In 1890 Antônio was nominated by General Francisco Glicério to become superintendent of European immigration. Antônio declined for "compelling motives of a private nature" and advised the baron of Rio Branco, who later took the post, of his "sorrow at not being able to place my weak services at Your Excellency's disposition."[16] Antônio remained outside politics until 1899, growing more disheartened with events in Brazil and in São Paulo.

Martinico Prado, the idealistic republican, was among those Paulista Republicans who greeted the coup of 15 November enthusiastically. He helped negotiate the transfer of the provincial government from monarchist to republican control, though the secondary role he played indicates that he had already been outstripped by other Republican leaders.[17] In January 1890 the Republic experienced its first political crises, over banking reform and press freedom. In February Martinico left for Europe to survey the prospects for immigration. Returning to Brazil, he was elected to the Constituent Assembly convened on 15 November 1890 to pass on the constitutional draft prepared by the Deodoro administration. Tremendous tension existed between the authoritarian, politically inexperienced Deodoro and the Constituent Assembly, which was jealous of its independence. Deodoro's cabinet, seemingly more loyal to the assembly than to Deodoro, resigned en masse on January 21, 1891. Deodoro named as a new cabinet leader an old monarchist, the baron of Lucena, who appointed a new cabinet with only one historic Republican. In this atmosphere, the final debates on the Constitution of 1891 were held. It was approved on 21 February, the Constituent Assembly reconstituting itself as a two-house congress. According to Aureliano Leite, Martinico's role in the constitutional debates was limited: he was little interested in the debates, he offered a half-dozen amendments on economic matters, and he failed to sign the constitution.[18] Approval of the nation's organic law did not end the infighting in the young Republic. In a speech in the Chamber of Deputies in August 1891, Martinico characterized the Deodoro administration as "nothing more than a government of compadres."[19] On 3 November Deodoro dissolved the Congress, surrounded it with military forces, and declared a state of siege.[20] Most legislators returned to their states; a minority, including some Paulistas, remained in Rio to conspire with Deodoro's successor, Marshall Floriano Peixoto. Martinico was placed on a governmental proscription list and had to flee the capital.[21] Floriano Peixoto took power in a coup on 23 November.

Meanwhile, the Republican movement in São Paulo had divided.

After the federal cabinet resigned on 21 January 1891, Deodoro had appointed the Republicans' grand old man, Américo Brasiliense, governor of São Paulo.[22] Brasiliense engineered a coup within the PRP, dissolving its executive committee and filling most of the vacated seats with former monarchists, and thus alienating the historical Republicans.[23] Martinico, however, was in the pro-Brasiliense faction and was selected for the reconstituted PRP executive committee. Opposing Brasiliense were several powerful men—future governors of São Paulo and presidents of Brazil, among whom were Prudente de Morais, Campos Sales, and Bernardino de Campos.[24] Brasiliense, already in a tenuous position because of the split in Paulista Republican ranks, fatally damaged his authority by his highly unpopular endorsement of Deodoro's 3 November closing of Congress. Three weeks after Deodoro was deposed, Brasiliense was pressured to resign the governorship. A purge of Brasiliense supporters in 1892 removed Martinico. Thus ended the political career of one of the founders of Paulista republicanism and one of its most charismatic and successful politicians.

Martinico Prado withdrew from politics because of disillusionment with the sordid politics of the early Republic, not, as his son claimed, because of the needs of family and business, nor because of health, the reason given by Paulista Republicans who were anxious to explain any breach in the ranks.[25] Martinico had always had business and family concerns, as did most politicians. He was healthy enough to make five trips to Europe after his political withdrawal. On the first of these postpurge trips—"almost an exodus," according to the political historian José Maria dos Santos[26]—Martinico and his large family left São Paulo on 9 February 1892 and arrived in Genoa seventeen days later. A month afterward, Martinico led the family to Paris, where, despite his fabulous wealth, he took quarters in the Hotel Bedford, a second-class hotel in a bourgeois, commercial district. It was the hotel in which the exiled Dom Pedro II had died a year earlier; the choice could scarcely have been accidental. From October 1892 until the following February, Martinico returned to do business in Brazil, leaving the family in Paris. In February he returned to France and brought his family home in May 1893. In early 1894, two years after his purge from the PRP, Martinico apparently suffered a minor stroke that temporarily deprived him of his speech and left him greatly shaken.[27] In 1895 he had recovered sufficiently to take the family to Europe again. Two years later, a relative reported that "Martinico continues with his mania of speaking badly of everything and everyone."[28] Further trips to Europe were made in 1899 and 1900. Returning from Europe in 1900, Martinico suffered a stroke in Bahia. He was so ill that the family avoided making the trip by sea from Bahia to Rio de Janeiro, for fear he would die on board the ship and have to be buried at sea. Both Martinho Prado Neto and José Maria dos Santos date the onset of Martinico's serious illness to 1900. Because of the family's aversion to burial at sea, it is not likely that Martinico became seriously ill earlier than that year. A second son who set ideals high and suffered corresponding disillusionment, Martinico believed to his death in 1906 in the ideal of the Republic but withdrew from its less-than-ideal practices and politicians.

Eduardo Prado's Monarchist Reaction

The words *monarchist, reactionary,* and *conservative* have been applied to Eduardo as if synonymous. The first is clearly appropriate; he opposed the Republic and strove to restore the monarchy with all means possible from 1889 until his death in 1901. Eduardo was also a "reactionary" in the literal sense; he reacted against the Republic and sought to reinstitute Brazil's previous form of government. But Eduardo's reaction was based on the conviction that the monarchy had been liberal while the Republic was itself reactionary, a reasonable view in the 1890s. Finally, if Eduardo was a conservative, he was so primarily in desiring to conserve what he found valuable in Brazilian traditions. On contemporary issues this supposed conservative fought for civil rights and freedom of the press under a regime hostile to both; he called attention to the poverty and neglect of Brazil's *sertanejos* (backlanders); he expressed genuine concern with what Brazilians called the "social question" and with capitalism's abuse of workers; and he condemned military rule and the narrow base upon which the First Republic rested, all regarded as liberal or leftist concerns now. In 1894 Eduardo proposed to Rui Barbosa, a leading liberal, that they edit an oppositionist newspaper to deal with Brazilian affairs "in a liberal and civilized way."[29] The political coloration of the First Republic and the inadequacy of the political lexicon distorted much of Eduardo's message. In more recent times the writings of this "reactionary conservative" have been adopted by left-wing nationalists.[30] Eduardo's reaction to the entry of the United States into the Cuban-Spanish war in 1898 makes it clear why:

> The exceedingly rich, exceedingly strong government of the United States is itself a slave of its monopolistic, soulless, impious plutocracy, which crushes the poor and buys senators, diplomats, and presidents. This tyrannical plutocracy . . . survives only through the toleration of the workers it oppresses. All observers see clearly, in the near future of the United States, a tremendous reaction by the suffering workers, who are already grumbling and indignant. When all that mass of millions and millions of men, erect and united, protests and takes justice into its own hands, it will be, in its time, stronger than everything and everyone, and the great gutted Republic, the incarnation of monopoly, fraud, and hypocrisy, will be drowned in blood, consumed in flames, the greatest and most just of punishments History will have registered.[31]

Eduardo believed in the superiority of monarchism over republicanism. Like his brother Martinico, who argued just the opposite, Eduardo tailored the evidence to fit his ideas and never explained the wide divergencies in nations under both forms. In his mind monarchy meant Great Britain,[32] but he also repeatedly urged the general preëminence of European monarchies over American republics in resolving the "social question" to provide for the proletariat's legitimate aspirations. Hidden behind his views, however, was a line of thought, common in his era, which Eduardo never allowed himself to develop: the natural advantages of resources and of "race" (nationality) explained national prominence, not form of government.[33] Eduardo did not doubt the virtues of Brazil's natural resources, and though he had some reservations about the reliability and energy of the Brazilian "race,"[34] this was not his fundamental concern. Brazilian malaise in the 1890s stemmed from the fact that the able (that is, monarchist) leadership had been driven from authority at sword point by military strongmen, aided by their unscrupulous bacharel allies.[35]

Until 1894 Eduardo's greatest concern was Brazil's external relations, because these bore on the survival of the military republic itself. These were the years of his *Fastos da dictadura militar no Brazil* (1890) and *A illusão americana* (1893). By habit Eduardo placed great emphasis on the European reaction to the 1889 coup, especially the British response. Probably with the assistance of his London financial contacts, Eduardo documented the disastrous effect of the advent of the Republic on Brazil's national finances and foreign credit rating.[36] The economic issue, he wrote in private and with considerable dissimulation, was "all there is to my monarchism."[37] Eduardo noted as well that while the American republics had readily recognized the new regime, the United States had been the last to do so, and thus recognition had come "exactly in inverse proportion to the importance and seriousness of the nations," an interesting observation from the author whose fame rests chiefly on his supposed anti-Americanism. Moreover, in his haste to discredit the Republic, Eduardo asserted that the press of the United States— "that great country where law rules, where liberty breathes, where the people govern"—had viewed unfavorably the arbitrary dictatorship, the banishment and imprisoning of monarchist leaders, and the lack of popular representation characteristic of the new regime.[38]

Eduardo's *Fastos da dictadura militar* had a significant impact on Brazil's politics during the early First Republic. One of its articles containing criticism of Deodoro was published in the 28 November 1890 issue of Rio de Janeiro's *A Tribuna*, a monarchist journal. On the following night, with the evident approval of Deodoro, government troops assaulted *A Tribuna*, leading to a crisis in which the cabinet almost resigned en masse, a prelude to its resignation on 21 January 1891.[39] Ironically, Campos Sales in this crisis defended freedom of the press; later, as state governor in 1896, he would close down Eduardo's monarchist journal in São Paulo. Politics strains ideals.

Until 1893 Eduardo had viewed Brazilian developments from Europe, except for brief returns home for family reasons. The outbreak of civil war in Brazil's southernmost state, Rio Grande do Sul, in early 1893 drew Eduardo back from Europe and soon provided occasion for a revised estimate of the role of the United States in Brazil. Until he tested the winds, Eduardo sought to conceal the links of monarchists to the *Gaúcho* opponents of the Republic, a loose alliance known as Federalists.[40] The Federalist revolt was not explicitly monarchist, but it might have served as a vehicle for restoration.[41] When a navy rebellion broke out in Rio de Janeiro on 6

September, Eduardo added fire to the cause with *A illusão americana*. Whatever hopes Eduardo had for the success of the civil war, he was outraged at the effects of American naval "neutrality" in Rio de Janeiro, which benefited the Republican forces. He thus saw the United States not as a critic, but as an ally of the regime he despised.

Having done what he could in *Fastos da dictadura militar* to undermine European support for the Republic, Eduardo set about destroying the multifaceted "American illusion," the chief dimension of which perhaps was that Brazil was somehow tied to the other American republics. Rather, Eduardo urged, Brazil was an "immense island," separated by language, culture, and even primordial geology from the rest of America.[42] Eduardo had little difficulty destroying the illusions of Latin American republicanism and inter-American fraternity, the latter encouraged by United States Secretary of State James C. Blaine, that "almost great man, . . . a type of Hamilton, of Clay, of Webster, or of Seward," but "incomplete, . . . unequal, and unbalanced." The "republicans" of Latin America were military *caudilhos* (strongmen), and each republic quarreled violently with its neighbors.[43] The source of these illusions was, of course, the United States, whose constitution had been widely aped by the Latin American republics, and most recently by what Eduardo earlier called "the more or less United States of Brazil."[44]

Like many Latin Americans of his time, Eduardo had a love-hate relationship with the United States. At times he expressed great admiration for the northern colossus and its institutions, and he was especially attracted by George Washington and his compatriots. He recognized as well that the United States was a *sui generis* culture and that its foremost realities were rich resources and energetic people. However, the revolutionary, republican heritage of Washington and Jefferson that Eduardo praised had deteriorated into the immoral excesses of the Gilded Age. In phrases that recall those of an earlier "Marx of the master class," John C. Calhoun, Eduardo denounced the United States of the Gilded Age as "a regime of oppressive monopoly and of cruel plutocracy."[45] The plight of the working class in the United States was far worse than in Europe, because of "bourgeois ferocity against the proletariat." In no one person was this aspect of the American illusion of progressive republicanism better exemplified than in Andrew Carnegie, whose paean to the American Way, *Triumphant Democracy* (1886), was followed by the brutal crushing of a strike at Carnegie's Homestead steel works in 1891. The foreign component of the American illusion was represented by Secretary of State Blaine, who, as overseas spokesman for a plutocratic society, allied himself with the capitalist "millionocracy" that wished to extend its domain abroad by means of trade treaties. A republic, after all, was nothing more than "a corporation of limited responsibilities," while a monarchy was "a solid firm" interested in protecting its workers' welfare, if only to avoid revolution.[46]

A illusão americana was a dangerous book written by a monarchist suspected of having aided armed rebellion.[47] It attacked the Brazilian republic by assaulting its most ready and powerful ally, thus threatening a cornerstone of republican foreign policy and the stability of the regime itself. It was immediately confiscated, but the few numbers of its first edition that circulated, together with its many subsequent editions, went far toward fixing the antipathy with which many literate Brazilians—not those in power before 1930, clearly—began to regard the "blond giant" of the north.[48] Six months after its publication, when the insurgents had been defeated, Eduardo's arrest was ordered. To escape prison and possibly worse, Eduardo fled overland through the *sertão* (backlands) of Minas Gerais and Bahia and witnessed its endemic poverty and hunger. Arriving in Europe via British steamer, he added the plight of the rural masses to his indictment of the Republic, although the accusation was unfair because this poverty was the product of centuries, not years, of neglect and oppression. With the Canudos affair in later years, discussed below, the situation of Brazil's rural folk acquired special meaning for the evolution of the Republic. Eduardo's experience in the sertão helped shift his attention from Brazil's external relations to its internal problems.[49]

In exile in 1894, Eduardo began his friendship with Rui Barbosa, who had been a strong critic of Antônio Prado's ministerial policies in the 1880s and whom Eduardo had attacked vigorously and with some injustice when Barbosa was the Republic's first minister of finance.[50] Barbosa's own fall from power because of his criticism of the regime's abuse of civil rights, followed by Rui's own exile, rehabilitated him in Eduardo's eyes. Eduardo sought Barbosa's aid in publishing an opposition newspaper and in aiding monarchist political prisoners.[51]

The inauguration of civilian government under the Paulista, José Manuel Prudente de Morais, in November 1894, created the opportunity for Eduardo to return home. Restoration of the monarchy remained his chief goal and led him to become a leading ideologue and organizer of the Monarchist party in São Paulo. On 15 November 1895, the party issued its manifesto, written either by Eduardo or by João Mendes de Almeida,[52] the ultramontane Catholic and despised enemy of Antônio and Martinico Prado a few years earlier, who now became their younger brother's close ally. The manifesto began by lamenting that the "Republic repudiated God, judging him of no use to the new institutions" and ended with a plea for the "divine sentence" that combined with the monarchists' "wishes and forces" would result in restoration. Among the defects of the Republic were listed two with special meaning for Eduardo: "misery in the population, [and] disorganization in the family." The monarchists set about recruiting adherents, and Eduardo claimed to have received many letters of support.[53] But as time went on and as his own brothers—representing precisely the uncommitted former imperial leaders and disaffected idealistic Republicans whom the monarchists hoped to attract—remained indifferent or hostile to monarchism, Eduardo must have realized the odds against which the crusade struggled. Moreover, as Eduardo would soon learn, the civilian republic was no less draconian in its suppression of dissent than the military republic had been.

While pursuing the long-range goal of restoration, Eduardo set about his immediate task of criticizing the Republic's abuses. From October 1895 until March 1897, he wrote at least fifty-five articles in *O Comércio de São Paulo,* which he purchased in 1896 with Veridiana's backing. About half of them, with titles such as "Violence of the Government," "Governmental Anarchy," and "Outside Civilization," were explicitly political. Another fourth dealt with the "financial pathology" of the Republic and especially with the problems in the coffee economy. Other articles attacked the government's ineptitude in combating epidemics in São Paulo and its suppression of freedom of the press.[54] In retaliation, Eduardo was condemned in the Republican press.[55]

Unable to abandon his strident journalism, Eduardo began to search for more respectable allies. Rui Barbosa remained friendly but was unwilling to involve himself directly. In 1896 Eduardo turned to Joaquin Nabuco, a more moderate monarchist, much as Eduardo and his brothers had turned to Nabuco during the abolition crisis. Nabuco responded with some interest and more caution.[56] He cannot have been reassured about Eduardo's invitation for him to become editor of *O Comércio* when Eduardo wrote him, "I am expecting an attack at any moment. The fury of the Republicans against the 'Commercio' is irreducible. . . . One threat follows another. In order to live, we have to surround ourselves with a thousand precautions."[57] The one precaution Eduardo did not take was silence.

In late 1896 and early 1897, Eduardo's monarchism immersed him in momentous, tragic, and bloody events that washed over Brazil. In September and October 1896 he published articles dealing with the Republic's "financial pathology," with its "affliction of agriculture," and with the desirability of monarchist participation in pending general elections, despite the probability of governmental electoral fraud.[58] In late October the governor of São Paulo, Campos Sales, decided to crush the Monarchist party. In a letter to Bernardino de Campos, he confided that he "never gave importance to restorationist pretensions, . . . especially here in São Paulo," but that he feared that monarchist activities "would frustrate my attempt to get a foreign loan" for São Paulo. Therefore he had decided to "hurl the police" on the monarchists and "not permit them to have more than the slightest liberty of movement."[59] Eduardo Prado, whose involvement in Paulista, Brazilian, and European financial matters stretched back to the 1880s and involved him with many influential people, undoubtedly was a principal target of Campos Sales's repression. State police were used to break up peaceful monarchist meetings of handfuls of people in private dwellings. This activity placed the Republic "outside of civilization," wrote Eduardo, but monarchist judicial appeals were fruitless.[60] As late as March 1897, Campos Sales complained to the president of Brazil, Prudente de Morais, of the monarchists' "pernicious effects on the credit, the finances, and the politics of the Republic."[61]

The famous rebellion at Canudos in the northeastern backlands of Brazil added mass hysteria to the political elite's financial fears. The Canudos rebels had embarrassed the Republic by defeating army expeditions in November 1896, and January and March 1897. Word of the third defeat, involving the death of the popular soldier Moreira César on 2 March, reached São Paulo city on Sunday, 7 March. The authorities, perhaps on purpose, had falsely depicted the rebellion as a plot organized and armed by monarchist outsiders, since, as Campos Sales wrote, "it seems to me that simple yokels or fanatics, no matter how numerous, could not completely rout a force organized, prepared for war, and commanded by a leader of the most solid prestige and proven capacity."[62] As reported in the *Correio Paulistano*, events took an ugly turn. A crowd gathered before the government palace. Campos Sales addressed it, advising calm but also stating "that the death of Coronel Moreira César would have to be avenged." The crowd proceeded to the offices of the *Correio Paulistano*, where it shouted "Long live the republic, death to monarchy." The mob became more agitated with each moment, and "from the midst of the crowd a youth surged forth and screamed, 'To the *Comércio*, to the *Comércio*,' and everyone ran there amidst enormous confusion." The *Comércio* was within sight of the government palace, and the authorities had posted a cavalry picket in front of the monarchist journal, but the guard could not, or would not, stop the mob. "Furniture was flung into the street, boxes of type were thrown on the ground; the destruction was complete; the only thing saved was a flag . . . bearing the motto 'Love and Charity,' which was taken away by the police." Cavalry reinforcements arrived late.[63] Worse could have happened. In Rio de Janeiro, Gentil de Castro, editor of two newspapers, the *Gazeta da Tarde* and *Liberdade*, was lynched. The offices of those two and of a third, *Apóstolo*, were sacked and burned, and their contents piled for a huge bonfire on the principal street of commerce, fashion, and politics, the Rua do Ouvidor.[64] As the great chronicler of the Canudos rebellion, Euclides da Cunha, noted: there was "a certain similarity between the scene in the Rua do Ouvidor and [the] disturbance . . . [at Canudos], one equaling the other in savagery."

Backlands lawlessness was precipitately making its entrance into history; and the Canudos revolt, when all is said, was little more than symptomatic of a malady which, by no means confined to a corner of Baia, was spreading to the capitals of the seaboard. The man of the backlands, that rude, leather-clad figure, had partners in crime who were, possibly, even more dangerous. Is it worth while to be more explicit?[65]

Certainly not for Eduardo Prado, who after the destruction of *O Comércio* found himself exiled again, this time by the civilian Republic. In exile, he blamed the regime's defeats at Canudos—later avenged by a bloody assault in September and October 1897—on the Republican administration itself, where responsibility rightly rested.[66]

This was the beginning of the end of Eduardo's overt monarchist activities. Although in 1899 he published a pamphlet designed to exploit rivalry between civilian Republicans and the military,[67] it had become obvious that restoration was impossible. Moderate monarchists like Nabuco were disheartened. He wrote to Eduardo in January 1899 that "I am a *drifted man* [sic]. . . . In fact, I am withdrawn from the world."[68] Nabuco soon accepted a diplomatic post, a decision excoriated by many monarchists but defended by Eduardo Prado. Eduardo himself pursued a different course, redirecting his energy into scholarship, his refuge for the man of honor.[69]

More than any other Prado, Eduardo had seen the moral, philosophical, and even familial roots of his world shaken by the advent of the Republic. He saw the very cultural foundations of Brazil undermined; God, home, and family were abandoned. His older brothers had acquiesced in the events of the 1890s, and, in thinly disguised phrases, Eduardo directed some of his most scornful words at such adhesionists. Nephews and cousins had fallen under the alien tutelage of North American universities. The Republic was like a household that had lost the ability to rule itself according to supposed domestic norms.[70]

Until his monarchist advocacy Eduardo had no "career," no standing when measured against his brothers. The fact that his career was notorious and that it angered his brothers (while evidently pleasing Veridiana, who continued to support him) does not detract from his efforts. They withdrew from a difficult situation; he faced it head on. Moreover, Eduardo left behind a lasting critique of the Republic which could have come only from one at its outer limits, an indictment which, in its broad outlines, is still as compelling and perceptive as when it was written.

Pragmatism and Protest: Antônio Prado, 1899–1929

While Eduardo self-consciously made himself an enemy of the Republic, Antônio Prado was repeatedly lauded as one of the high-minded former monarchist leaders who had lent his support to the Republic, though in fact he did so negatively by not opposing it. The Republican organ, O Estado de São Paulo, made the contrast explicit. In successive issues in 1895 it praised Antônio's declaration of 18 November 1889 urging acceptance of the Republic and derided the "elegant but futile exotic pessimism of Dr. Eduardo Prado."[71] While Antônio let himself be used thus as a buttress of the new regime, there is little question that he had only disdain for its politics, as his refusal to participate in the Constituent Assembly of 1890 clearly demonstrated. This disaffection continued, and when Antônio re-entered politics in 1899 it was as an "apolitical" independent whose appeal was founded, in part, on his lack of ties with the Paulista Republican party.

Antônio was chosen mayor of São Paulo in that year and served four terms, leaving office in 1910. A rare press interview he gave to the Italian journalist Alexandre d'Atri in 1903 reveals his continuing aloofness from politics and the broad lines of his political thought. As in 1889 he gave general but significantly qualified support to the Republic. Antônio's special national concerns were immigration, where he saw his old programs being abandoned, and finances, where he alleged that Brazil was becoming the victim of "a servile financial policy, in relation to the foreigner, imposing upon us difficulties of all sorts." On political matters—d'Atri noted that Prado had to overcome "his habitual reluctance for everything that smells of politics"—Antônio likened the Republic to a ship navigating on rough seas with dark clouds surging on the horizon: "The command is in able hands educated in a good school of administration, but the discipline on board leaves much to desire and the passengers are apprehensive."[72] He lamented the growth of a class of politicians concerned mainly with the scramble for jobs but saw restoration of the monarchy as "a chimera, a utopia." What Antônio Prado seemed to want was a republic that would tend toward the supposed stability of the monarchy. In particular, he thought the four-year presidential term too short: a new president spent the first year setting his policies; during the second he began to implement them; the third was given over to jockeying for the next election; and the fourth year, presumably, was taken up with the election itself. As a result, "the President, received with flowers on the day of taking office, always leaves the Catete palace discredited."[73]

By serving eleven years as an apolitical mayor, Antônio managed to avoid that fate, but he was confined to a smaller ship of state and had little, if any, impact on issues he judged to be of capital national importance. As captain of a more modest vessel, he looked primarily to the good repair and renovation of the ship itself, demanded greater discipline from its crew, sought to reassure first-class passengers, and confined steerage voyagers below decks. Antônio's mayoralty, during the heyday of the First Republic, represented the return of an *ancien régime* figure, progressive, pragmatic, and conservative at the same time, who would put the troubled 1890s to rest and provide the city with at least the basic accoutrements and atmosphere of orderly, literally businesslike growth. As the head of several prosperous businesses, Antônio was looked upon to apply his commercial techniques to civic administration and thus to shore up public confidence as São Paulo faced the twentieth century. In his daily schedule as mayor he visited municipal works projects and dropped in at the Agua Branca tannery, the Santa Marina glassworks, the Bank of Commerce and Industry, and the Paulista Railway.[74] One of his first projects was overseeing the paving of the city's main streets. On 7 May 1900, he personally inaugurated the city's first line of electric trolleys, driving the first coach from the Largo São Bento in the city center to the end of the Alamêda Barão de Limeira, where his mansion, the Chácara do Carvalho, stood.[75] The route recalls the extension of the Paulista Railway to Antônio's fazenda, Santa Veridiana, in 1892. Antônio also promoted the much-needed beautification of the city's parks and plazas, and the central Praça da República remains today as one of the landmarks of his administration.

Antônio received high marks from the Paulistano elite and from foreign entrepreneurs for his honest, efficient, and energetic administration.[76] The limitations of his stewardship of the city are clearer now than they were at the time. According to Richard Morse, "the prefecture of Antônio Prado . . . left little more than a few isolated monuments, such as a new market and the imitative and pretentious Municipal Theater."[77] A city engineer, while providing the basis for that judgment, also pointed to its cause, a lack of resources.[78] Moreover, the elite and middle class benefited most from Antônio's administration, a fact inherent in the social values and social structure of the time. This was dramatically demonstrated in Antônio's forceful suppression of the Paulista Railway strike in 1906, when he was both mayor and railroad president.[79] As time went on, Antônio, approaching seventy, also ran afoul of a younger generation of politicians that he claimed was more devoted to private interests than the public good as he perceived it. It was this development, supposedly, that led him to leave his municipal office in 1910.[80] A further symptom of Antônio's continuing alienation from politics is the fact that he took no part in Rui Barbosa's campaign swing through São Paulo in 1909, which attracted great support, particularly among the younger generation of voters.[81]

Antônio Prado was again in political retirement after 1910, but despite his general dissatisfaction with politics, his instincts died hard. He kept up his contacts by hosting seven national deputies on a tour of the Paulista Railway, the Barretos meat-packing plant, and the fazenda São Martinho during World War I.[82] Later he supported Rui Barbosa and Nilo Peçanha in their campaigns against orthodox Republican candidates for president.[83] His tendency toward reinvolvement in politics increased after his eightieth birthday with his personal diplomacy of 1921, the abortive Ouchy Agreement. Governor Washington Luís's rejection of the agreement widened the gap between Antônio and state and national leaders, and came at a time of rising national discontent, evident in the feuding of the state machines that controlled national politics and in an unsuccessful barracks revolt in Rio de Janeiro in July 1922.

Meanwhile, in late 1922 or early 1923, Paulo Prado, Antônio's oldest son, took over the editorship of the *Revista do Brasil*.[84] Paulo expressed much of the concern his father felt about political life in Brazil. In an article that recalled the tone of his uncle's *A illusão americana*, Paulo pictured the Venezuelan dictatorship of Juan Vicente Gómez as interested only in money and pleasure and concluded that "there is an air of kinship between all the Republics of Latin America." Like Eduardo earlier, Paulo was chagrined at the benign acceptance of political corruption by Paulistas who had forgotten the supposed regional traditions of liberty. Paulista politicians, he asserted, were untroubled by the lengthy state of siege declared in Rio after the barracks revolt, and fazendeiros were happy as long as "the paternal and omnipotent" government kept coffee prices high. In early 1924 Paulo noted that the arrival of a few foreign accountants in Rio de Janeiro had been enough to restore the value of the milréis and had produced general optimism in spite of widespread and chronic political disorder.[85]

In March 1924, three months before a military rebellion broke out in São Paulo with considerable civilian support, Paulo identified the political question as the most important in Brazil. He likened the national political process to a boxing match held in an empty arena while the populace stood outside muttering, "This is a fight of politicians; they will work it out." The tragedy was, Paulo continued, that politics intervened in everyone's life, yet was governed by a small clique, which "according to the iron organization of the oligarchies, [is] brought to power by the system of electoral nominations in which Pedro names João, João later names José, in order for . . . [José] in his turn to name the original Pedro, who becomes the lock on the door of the little partisan church."[86] Paulo's sponsorship of the Modern Art Week in 1922 gave rise to his political critique, and by the late 1920s he was calling for an "insurrection both moral and material."[87]

Paulo's attitudes help explain why his father, at the age of eighty-six, led the formation of the reformist Democratic party in 1926. Contributing to the situation was Antônio Prado's rancor for Washington Luís, who became president of Brazil in that year. This feud may have led Washington Luís to attempt to mend his fences with Antônio by means of the "nonpolitical" appointment of Antônio Prado Júnior as mayor of the federal district (Rio de Janeiro).[88] If that was the new president's intention, it was not fulfilled. His neglect of São Paulo's coffee interests exacerbated the grudge Antônio Prado held against him, despite the fact that both men were opponents of valorization. In 1929 Afrânio de Melo Franco wrote to the former president of Brazil Epitácio Pessoa that Antônio had "always affirmed that if Dr. Washington Luís became president of the Republic, his vanity, his obstinacy, his scorn for the opinions of others, and his lack of vision would provoke a bloody revolution in the country."[89]

Personal, economic, and political motives were intermixed in the foundation of the Democratic party. Clearly, at Antônio Prado's age only the greatest of frustrations could have led him back into political partisanship after what he referred to as thirty years of retirement. The party's manifesto, written by Antônio Prado, listed as its chief concerns the lack of meaningful political parties and the resultant drift in national affairs. Although the party did not intend direct political action at first "because of the intensive commotion in which the country finds itself," it did set out its essentially middle-class, reformist goals: defense of the "liberal principles" of the Brazilian constitution; reform of the electoral laws, especially through provision for the secret ballot; the guarantee of "the influence to which they are entitled" to agriculture, commerce, and industry; an independent judiciary; and even a vaguely worded provision to "sustain and defend all measures of interest to the social question."[90]

The manifesto was worded to attract the broadest support from Paulista dissenters, but the Democratic party was primarily an expression of the discontent of the upper middle class and allied coffee planters. Of the 601 signers of the manifesto, 42.6 percent were middle-class professionals, 23.4 percent were white-collar functionaries, 15.5 percent were planters or other property-owners, and 14.5 percent represented commerce, finance, and industry (see Appendix F). The ten-man party directorate consisted of Antônio Prado, who listed himself as a fazendeiro, three other fazendeiros, three law professors, and three other lawyers. Thus representatives of the other professions and of business and white-collar groups that made up the majority of the party were not included in its initial leadership.[91]

The chief political goal of the party was to broaden political participation in a system dominated exclusively by orthodox Republican state parties. Naturally, its members had in mind chiefly the participation of the middle-class sectors they represented, but the party rhetoric also made reference to involvement of "all the Brazilian people." The original name proposed for the party by Antônio Prado, the Paulista Popular party, however, was immediately dropped in favor of the more innocuous label, Democratic party.[92] In 1927 the party succeeded in electing three federal deputies, but though its membership grew, it failed the following year to elect state and local officials.[93] This was evidence of its shallow roots in the state and of the power and patronage of the entrenched Paulista Republicans.

Electoral fraud and other pressures by the Paulista Republican party led the more radical elements of the Democratic party to seek alliances with dissident elements in other states, particularly the *Partido Libertador* (Liberation Party) of Rio Grande do Sul, forerunner of the Liberal Alliance which carried Getúlio Vargas to power via revolution in 1930. Curiously, the octogenarian Antônio Prado played an active role among these "radicals," one similar to his support of Paulista Republicans in the months before the coup of 1889. He argued in 1926 that his withdrawal from politics earlier had been due not simply to the advent of the Republic, but to the fact that no national Republican party had been formed. As for the Paulista Republican party, it was only "a simple group of politicians, who practice a system of government without ideas to carry out and having only the possession and conservation of power in their hands as a goal."[94] Antônio thus advocated the creation of a national opposition party based on the Democratic party's principles and supported by "popular action," in which he voiced full confidence. He viewed the insurgent movement in Rio Grande do Sul enthusiastically and praised the efforts of a Gaúcho leader, J. F. de Assis Brasil, to convert other states to it. After Antônio Prado's death in April 1929, Getúlio Vargas, attempting to fortify the Rio Grande do Sul–São Paulo axis, praised the coffee policies of Antônio, which had been ignored in orthodox Republican circles.[95]

Whether Antônio would have supported the revolutionary means Vargas used to gain power is a moot point, but one suspects that he would not have opposed them, given his deep disillusionment with the First Republic and his enmity for Washington Luís, whose effort to impose a Paulista successor as president was the final catalyst to Vargas's revolution in 1930. According to one contemporary account, as Antônio lay dying in Rio de Janeiro, his family and friends heard him clearly profess his ultimate belief in the Democratic party's victory and in the possibility that it might become a revolutionary movement.[96]

During the First Republic, the Prados dwelt uneasily at the margins of politics. While they retained their social prestige and much of their economic power, they were unable or unwilling to capitalize on these assets politically and were reduced to firing verbal broadsides and manifestos from the sidelines. This decline in power, moreover, occurred precisely when São Paulo and the coffee economy gained considerable influence in national politics, a development in which the Prados—who were boosters of their state and among the most successful of coffee entrepreneurs—could not share. The patterns of family political behavior described here cannot be adequately explained strictly in social or economic terms. Rather, the Prados' political alienation takes on an almost psychological cast.[97] Martinico's lodging at the Hotel Bedford in Paris, where the deposed Emperor Pedro II died, was a poignant clue.

Although to the orthodox Republicans they may have been Jeremiahs forecasting doom, the Prados represented much of value in Brazilian political tradition. Antônio Prado was a spokesman for the classical economic liberalism that had done much to modernize the economy of São Paulo in the nineteenth century, as it also planted the seeds of economic dependency against which Antônio warned. As the First Republic advanced he saw a good deal of his former program abandoned and his advice ignored. Martinico Prado saw the historical idealism of the Republican movement (always well tempered, to be sure, by political expediency) dropped in the name of the machinations of political power. The psychology of loyalty to prior commitments and the consequent unwillingness to compromise thus explains part of the older Prados' withdrawal from a political system they perceived as rejecting the best of Brazil's political past.

As Richard Morse has observed, the nineteenth-century traditions of romanticism and crusading liberalism were no longer adequate preparation for the complexities of the dawning urban age. Men of the rural-urban aristocracy like Antônio and Martinico, Rio Branco, Joaquim Nabuco, and Rui Barbosa, necessarily gave way to a younger generation of leaders, often of foreign origin, "traditionless, opportunist, generated by the city."[98] But what of the younger Prados, like Eduardo and Paulo Prado, formed in the city when the influence of romanticism and crusading liberalism had waned? In Eduardo Prado, the merits of the Brazilian past were broadly defined, encompassing the entire imperial tradition and the deep cultural roots of Brazilian society. Eduardo's unrelenting attacks on the Republic scandalized Antônio's sense of pragmatic, Victorian responsibility and offended Martinico's continuing and perhaps romantic devotion to Republican ideals. Nevertheless, the younger brother's moral outrage during the early First Republic accurately reflected, in exaggerated but revealing form, the alienation of an entire family, revived anew in Paulo Prado's essays in the 1920s.

The Prados' moral outlook was a mixture of traditional and modern features, and perhaps because of that, the family was suspended between its socioeconomic position, which traditionally would have led to political leadership, and the necessity to repudiate the Republic, which fell far short of "modern" political standards. Under such circumstances, the family had only restricted political alternatives. One of these was withdrawal, the course pursued by Antônio and Martinico in the 1890s. A second was the "apolitical" mayoral role first assumed by Antônio, later practiced by his son, Antônio Prado Júnior, and still later adopted by his nephew, Fábio Prado, as mayor of São Paulo from 1934 to 1937.[99] A final alternative was open protest. This response, developed first by Eduardo Prado and revived by Paulo and Antônio in the 1920s, had its historical aftermath in the career of Caio Prado Júnior as Marxist scholar and Communist state deputy in the 1940s.

This last reaction, the Prados' political protest, has the most interesting implications for the political evolution of São Paulo and of Brazil. Eduardo's monarchism was based on cultural nationalism that would eventually develop into economic and political nationalism after 1930 and 1945, respectively. Antônio Prado's founding of the Democratic party indicated a new alliance between some elements of the old coffee elite, the Paulista "aristocracy" some have perceived, and new middle-class sectors. That Antônio, at the age of eighty-six, was still the commanding voice of protest in the Prado family, indicates as well the failure of the younger Prados, with one notable exception, to inherit the tradition of political activism so notable in the family in the nineteenth century.

Operating at the margins of the First Republic, the Prados were more adept at diagnosing the Brazilian political malaise than at remedying it. Their perceptions and activities were shaped by their planter and upper-class status, but like Brazilians of less-favored classes, they found themselves politically alienated. One may reasonably doubt the extent to which Eduardo Prado's celebration of the caboclo and the downtrodden proletariat or Antônio Prado's call for "popular action" implied the necessity of social revolution. But, however paternalistically, their critiques of the First Republic encompassed the feared lower class and the neglected middle class. As of 1930, it remained for another Prado to move from bourgeois dissatisfaction with Brazil's ruling oligarchies to advocating the cause of proletarian revolt. The intellectual and political development of Caio Prado Júnior belongs to a different era of Brazilian life, but it can be noted here that in his own formation he followed and recast the Prado family traditions of political skepticism and forthright protest.

❧ CONCLUSION ❧

This study began by emphasizing the prime reality of Brazil past and present, the many poor and the few rich. It was suggested that among several major causes of this distressing reality is the role of elite families. The power of the supposedly "patriarchal" elite family has been stressed by Gilberto Freyre and by many other Brazilian and foreign observers. However, in the last generation a "new family history" has subjected the older patriarchal model to rigorous examination and has begun to formulate more complex interpretations of the role of the family in Brazilian life, though it has yet to produce a comprehensive new vision. This qualitative case study reminds us of the complex, multifaceted, and sometimes contradictory nature of an elite Brazilian family. To understand such a family—and by extension the "ruling class" or "capitalist class" of which its leading members were a part—it is necessary to consider *all* its dimensions, not simply its economic or political behavior. Thus, this study has focused on family structure and dynamics, cultural influences from abroad and the reaction to them, economics, politics, and even the literary achievements of the family. In the process, it was discovered that individualism also played an important role in the Prado family.

Time and place created the Prados' opportunities and set limits on their achievements. São Paulo between 1840 and 1930 was in many ways unique, even within the Brazilian context. Thus, by comparison to the elite families of the northeast sugar coast (at least as depicted in traditional accounts), Paulista elite families were less tradition-bound and more opportunistic, adventuresome, acquisitive, and capitalistic. The Spartan environment of the eighteenth century encouraged hard work and savings. The Prados began their ascent with modest farming, livestock trading, and far-flung urban capitalism. In the early nineteenth century, expanding opportunities and the rising political fortunes of São Paulo during the independence era provided the baron of Iguape with the basis for his financial and commercial career, which left a heavy urban capitalist imprint on the family. The coffee boom of the Paulista west in the latter half of the century—an event unique in its specifics to that particular region—clearly was the central economic opportunity in Prado family history. The slave-labor plantation became a major force in the Prados' lives. It did so, however, after and in partial competition with a longstanding urban-capitalist, mercantile tradition, and at a time when the Prados knew that slavery itself was a doomed and disgraceful social institution. Thus, in São Paulo, even slavery—so intimately linked to the northeastern patriarchal plantation milieu depicted in Freyre's works—was a far different condition than elsewhere and earlier in Brazil. The slaves and coffee financed participation by the Paulista elites in European culture, which introduced both inspiring and disquieting forces into Brazilian life. European influence was felt more intensely in sober-minded São Paulo than in most, if not all, other Brazilian regions. Cosmopolitan international exposure, wealth, and the desire for political power led the Paulista coffee elite to play a leading role in the nation's politics from the 1880s to 1930. Curiously, however, while their state became a dominant force during the First Republic, the Prados' power waned. Their collective portrait between 1889 and 1930 is not one of an element of the "ruling class" ruthlessly dominating society, but rather one of an element of the elite in sullen withdrawal or open and articulate rebellion against its class. Some of the themes of the last four chapters of this study are conflict, illusion, martyrdom, and marginalization. To understand both the nineteenth-century achievements and the twentieth-century frustrations of the Prado family, it is necessary to summarize the salient features of their family life, exposure to European culture, economics, and politics, as well as to consider their individualism.

Between 1840 and 1930 the Prado extended family consisted of a line of rich, influential, urban cousins who owned rural fazendas but were based in São Paulo city, and various branches of poorer cousins in the interior. Throughout the period, economics and politics, geographic mobility, cultural interests, and even miscegenation weakened existing family solidarity. Endogamous marriage between Prado cousins declined significantly. Meanwhile, the rich and influential Prados, while refusing to marry their poorer cousins of the interior, restructured and broadened their parentela by marriage with other families of similar status and interests: the Pacheco Jordão, the Queiros Teles, the Chaves, the Monteiro de Barros, the Penteado, and other clans. At the same time, within the principal Prado branch there occurred an increasing differentiation of outlook, so much so that in the twentieth century some branches began to identify each other as "conservative" or "radical." In the present, so great are the perceived and real differences between the various Prado branches that those who bear the Silva Prado surname can be regarded as a "family" only in the narrow genealogical sense. The most significant aspect of Prado family structure, then, was its flexibility: the Prados responded to changing conditions by abandoning old family ties and by forging new ones, an almost continuous process. This flexibility itself was an important component of the family's "modernity."

In its intrafamilial dynamics, the Prado family experience contains major departures from the supposed patriarchal norms of male dominance. As early as the late eighteenth century and early nineteenth century, Ana Vicência Rodrigues de Almeida, a Prado matriarch, participated actively in the family businesses, and her urban residence was the principal symbol of the solidarity of the extended family. Her granddaughter, Veridiana, was an even more independent family member, influential in the family's cultural and economic affairs. Veridiana was much more famous than her husband, Martinho, from whom she separated in 1877, when separation was very rare and required a correspondingly strong will. Later, Veridiana's own granddaughter, Nazareth, abandoned her marriage. Nazareth participated in the cultural avant-garde of the 1920s and became a "black sheep" of the family.

Similarly, in parent-child relationships, the Prado history includes much evidence of divergence from the patriarchal ideal of docile, submissive children. The baron of Iguape, the closest approximation to the patriarchal type in the family, was an indulgent, tolerant, involved, and protective father and grandfather. His grandson Martinico advocated "revolutionary" causes that violated the family conservatism, yet his activities were long tolerated by the family though they eventually became an important source of family disunity during the heightened political tensions of the 1880s and 1890s. As a father, Martinico used permissive childrearing techniques that violated the norms of the elite class and presided over a chaotic brood that shocked the German governess, Ina von Binzer. Antônio Prado, despite his public aloofness and reputation as a man of hard discipline, was reluctant to exercise full control over his wayward son Paulo. These relationships prepared the ground for more general intergenerational conflict after 1889.

These "modern" features of Prado family life can be attributed partly to the disturbing, ambivalent role of European culture in the family after 1860. Antônio's, Eduardo's, Veridiana's, and Paulo's trips to and residences in Europe required independence and a loosening of family and community bonds. The European trips of the Prado sons produced tensions in their relationships with their parents, who accused them of neglecting Christian and filial duty, of abandoning Brazilian patriotism, and of disregarding family business interests. Nonetheless, Europe was irresistible to Prado youths and elders alike, and they introduced European customs, ideas, machines, and immigrants into the Paulista milieu as hoped-for remedies for Brazilian "backwardness." Perhaps the most influential import was classical liberalism, which, with its exaltation of personal liberty, individualism, and private acquisitiveness, justified the erosion of traditional corporate familism. Ultimately, as Eduardo Prado perceived, European cultural hegemony weakened elite Brazilian family life itself.

Politics tended also to fragment family unity, particularly after 1889. Before then there existed considerable political solidarity in the Prado family, though one imagines republican Martinico did not cheerfully endure the taunts of his conservative monarchist brothers, Eduardo and Caio. After 1889 the inability of Antônio, Martinico, and Eduardo to forge a common front against the machine politics of São Paulo and Brazil was striking. The unrepentant monarchist Eduardo was totally unable to convince his own flesh and blood to join his crusade. Thus the family's skepticism and protest expressed themselves primarily in individualistic outbursts or in various movements, but not in a united family strategy.

There was even decline and disunity in the family's economic activities. Until the First World War, these showed a high degree of coordination and corporate purpose. The difficulties of the coffee economy, however, affected Antônio, Eduardo, and Paulo differently, and they responded differently. After the war, corporate family endeavor declined and was replaced by more pluralistic economic behavior. This placed the Prados at a relative disadvantage when facing competition with immigrant-entrepreneur families such as the Matarrazzos.

Families are composed of individuals, and the notable individualism of leading Prado family members was encouraged by economic opportunities and liberal values. Some of the sharpest, most compelling images from this history are those of Prados challenging the dominant values and behavior of their class. The list is a long one: the baron of Iguape stacking his cash fortune in the street to dispel rumors of bankruptcy; Martinico's flamboyant republicanism and extravagant attacks on the monarchy; Eduardo's monarchist crusade, fiery attacks on the Republic, and appeal that the "monopolistic, soulless, impious plutocracy" of the United States be overthrown by its "suffering workers"; Veridiana's departures from Paulista bourgeois morality; Nazareth's avant-garde behavior a generation later; Paulo Prado's revisionist views of official Brazilian history, questioning of "Fordismo," and critique of Brazilian politics; Antônio's disgust at everything that smelled of politics, his bitter quarrel with the Paulista governor and Brazilian president Washington Luís, and his call late in the 1920s for "revolution." Class loyalties were no absolute, and sophisticated class analysis should ponder the significance of individuals departing from their presumed "class interests," rejecting such norms in unexpected and decisive ways. Classes are composed of real, specific people who act sometimes in apparently contradictory human ways, who pursue public roles and private agendas not always mutually consistent, who are motivated not just by economic accumulation, but also by acceptance or rejection of the dominant political game, by the interplay of international with national culture, by such family concerns as parenthood, sibling rivalry, youth rebellion, and the need for individual identity and purpose.

The Prado experience can be understood further by reference to a variety of explanations of the transformation of São Paulo and Brazil during the years 1840 to 1930. Modernization theory helps account for the new ideas and practices that were notable features of the Prado experience. Dependency theory helps to explain the ideological and economic neocolonialism of the times. The concept of "associated-dependent development" reminds us that significant positive changes occurred in Brazil at the same time that foreign power grew and took on new forms. What emerges from this study is the paradoxical nature of the process of "transformation" (to choose the most neutral word), as experienced by one family. On the one hand, there were many features said to be "modern" in the Prado family experience: a general acceptance of secular-rational norms; considerable social, physical, and psychic mobility; and the growth of striving, achievement-oriented personalities. The international economic and cultural experiences of the Prados, while exposing them to "modern" Europe and North America, also carried over-tones of neocolonialism and dependency, which in turn generated nationalistic responses. Politics remained a particularly "tradi-tional" sphere during the years 1840 to 1930; perhaps for this reason, it was a particularly frustrating one for the modernizing Prado family.

Above all, the reality of few rich and many poor remained sub-stantially unaltered in Brazil, although widespread access to the means of production by São Paulo's immigrants was one important advance. In the Prado parentela itself, only a few achieved great wealth; many languished in obscurity. The Prados were aware of the rich-poor gap and of its undesirability. In the 1860s Antônio Prado contrasted the industrious Swiss peasant with his "indolent" Brazilian counterpart but without inquiring into the roots of indo-lence. Antônio also lamented the human suffering caused by the highly "perfected" large-scale agriculture of Scotland. As slavemas-ters, a role they inherited as birthright, Antônio and Martinico sincerely regretted the "tragic necessity" of slavery and worked to substitute a free immigrant labor force; class-, family-, and self-in-terest certainly modulated their behavior in the heated context of 1880s São Paulo, but Martinico repeatedly argued that decent wages and the colonos' happiness were the best advertisements for immigra-tion. He and Antônio favored an intermediate landowning class be-tween rich and poor. They saw that dream realized in São Paulo to an important extent, thanks to the demands and struggles of the colo-nos and the willingness of members of the elite such as the Prados to respond to such agitation. As her family duties and interests waned, Veridiana created a domestic circle of favored lower-class retainers and, defying custom, sold grapes in the street to benefit the poor. Eduardo, in his harried political and cultural crusade of the 1890s, hailed the *caboclo* peasant as the true Brazilian, publicized the sufferings of the *sertanejos*, and attacked Yankee exploitation of workers. In 1906 Antônio Prado suppressed a railway workers' strike but later granted the workers concessions. Still later, Antônio helped found the Democratic party, a liberal bourgeois organization that proposed, however timidly, to address the "social question." Late in his life, Antônio endorsed "popular action" to resolve the prolonged political and economic crisis of the First Republic.

Clearly, the frustrations and estrangement of the leading Prados were of a different order from the hunger, ill-paid labor, unemployment, sickness, illiteracy, and daily indignities suffered by the poor majority in Brazil. But the Prados' reversals were real, their alienation profound and painful, their protests often courageous, costly, and rooted in broadly nationalist concerns. They frequently inveighed against the leadership of their own class, helping to expose its foibles and undermining its confidence in its ability to rule. As a dominant entity, the coffee-capitalist family elite of São Paulo passed from the scene in Getúlio Vargas's revolution of 1930. The passage of a half-century since then reveals to us how resistant to change is the prime reality of Brazilian life. Industrialization, urbanization, multinational corporations, science and technology, democracy and military dictatorship only seem to make the rich richer and the poor poorer. The substantial urban middle sectors that have evolved between the traditional haves and have-nots have complicated the picture but have not fundamentally altered it, nor are they likely to do so, given the middle groups' divisions, precarious position, and distaste for workers and the marginally employed. Paulo Prado's imagery of 1928 remains painfully apt for many: "In a radiant land lives a sad people."

The Prado family's efforts to end the gross inequalities of Brazilian society were limited by the traditional paternalism of their class and their country, by the imported classical liberalism of the pre-1929 era which may well have widened the rich-poor gap, and by their understanding of events which, after all, are clearer in historical perspective than they were when they were happening. After the Great Depression revealed Brazil's economic dependency beyond reasonable doubt and highlighted the flaws and contradictions of liberal economics and politics, Caio Prado Júnior added Marxist historical analysis to the Prado family legacy of trenchant critiques of their society. Although in an obvious sense his work departed markedly from the earlier analyses of Martinico and especially Eduardo and Paulo, in another way Caio Prado Júnior's historical investigations represented the continuation of the family's longstanding skepticism, alienation, and social criticism. Responding in their best moments to concerns higher than individual, family, or class interests, the Prados documented and attacked many injustices of the elite establishment, both national and international. *A illusão americana* and *Retrato do Brasil* deserve places alongside Caio Prado's histories as the leading Prado legacy to Brazil, an intellectual tradition that criticized imperialism, exposed the inequities of the existing order, and urged the necessity of fundamental change.

⋙ APPENDIX A ⋘

PRINCIPAL KIN OF THE

PRADO FAMILY

First Generation: Mid-Eighteenth Century

José Dias Ferreira
   Capitão-mór of Jundiaí; links to old do Prado family. Father-in-law of Raymundo and the first Martinho Prado.

Second Generation: Late Eighteenth Century

Manuel Rodrigues Jordão
   Made fortune in goldmining and commerce; linked to prestigious Camargo family. Father-in-law of the second Antônio Prado (d. 1793).

José de Moraes Leme
Antônio de Queiros Teles
Luís José Pereira de Queiros
   The third-named, and descendants of all three, were important fazendeiro-politicians. All three were husbands of Ana Joaquina Prado.

Third Generation: Early Nineteenth Century

José Manuel da Fonseca
   Fazendeiro-politician; imperial senator (1854). Husband of Ana Brandina Prado, his cousin.
Dr. Lucas Antônio Monteiro de Barros
   Visconde de Congonhas do Campo (Minas Gerais); first post-independence president of São Paulo (1824–27). Father-in-law of Maria Marcolina Prado.
João da Silva Machado
   Politician; vice-president of São Paulo (1837–38); barão de Antonina (1843); led separation of Paraná from São Paulo; imperial senator (1854). Father-in-law of Joaquim Prado.
Elias Antônio Pacheco e Silva (1779–1835)
   Wealthy sugar planter; militia officer. Father-in-law of Francisco Prado.

Fourth Generation: Mid-Nineteenth Century

Dr. Elias Antônio Pacheco e Chaves
Fazendeiro-businessman-politician; national deputy for São Paulo; police
chief, São Paulo city (1876). Husband of Anézia Prado; father-in-law of
Plínio Prado.

Antônio da Costa Pinto (e Silva)
Politician-fazendeiro; six-time national deputy for São Paulo; president
of Paraiba, Rio Grande do Sul, São Paulo, Rio de Janeiro; imperial
minister (1875). Father-in-law of the fourth Antônio Prado (1840–1929).

José da Costa Carvalho
Marquês de Monte Alegre (1854). Founder of *O Farol Paulistano* (1827);
regent of Brazil (1831–35); minister of Empire (1848); president of the
council of ministers (1849). Godfather of Antônio Caio Prado.

Antônio Leme da Fonseca
Fazendeiro-politician, Jundiaí; alderman; lieutenant-colonel in national
guard. Husband of Emília Prado.

Antônio Pereira Pinto
Jurist-politician; president of Espírito Santo and Sergipe. Father-in-law of
Ana Blandina Prado.

Antônio de Queiros Teles (1789–1870)
Barão de Jundiaí; fazendeiro-politician. Father-in-law of Etelvina Prado.

Fifth Generation: Late Nineteenth and
Early Twentieth Centuries

Antônio Manuel Alves de Lima (1873–1944)
Fazendeiro; manager of fazenda Guatapará for thirty years; state
secretary of agriculture, São Paulo (1931). Husband of Julita Prado.

Dr. Osório Junqueira (1883–1943)
Fazendeiro-businessman; his father was important nineteenth-century
Paulista politician. Son-in-law of Evangelina Prado Uchôa.

Afonso Arinos de Melo e Franco (1868–1916)
Lawyer, monarchist journalist, author. Son of important *Mineiro*
politician. Husband of Antonieta Prado.

Antônio Augusto Monteiro de Barros
Fazendeiro; co-founder of Prado-Chaves Export Company. Father-in-law
of Hermínia Prado.

Joaquim da Cunha Bueno
Fazendeiro (Cravinhos); exporter. Son of Tomás da Cunha Bueno (d.
1883), "opulent" fazendeiro and Liberal party chief. Father-in-law of Luíz
Prado.

Antônio Alvares Leite Penteado (1852–1912)
Conde Penteado; capitalist, pioneer in textile industry in São Paulo. Father-in-law of Antônio Prado Júnior, Caio Prado, Martinho Prado Neto.

Oduvaldo Pacheco e Silva
Diplomat (Argentina, France). Husband of Nazareth Prado.

Manuel Carlos Aranha
Barão de Anhumas. Fazendeiro (Campinas). Father-in-law of Marina Prado.

Felisberto Inácio de Oliveira
Barão de Cruangi (Pernambuco?). Father-in-law of Lavínia Prado.

Dr. Inácio José de Mendonça Uchôa
Supreme court minister. Father-in-law of Evangelina Prado.

Joaquim Jacinto Mendonça
"Eminent and prestigious" imperial councilor. Father-in-law of Cornélia Prado and of Corina Prado.

Rudolfo Crespi
Conde Crespi; leading Paulista industrialist. Father-in-law of Fábio Prado.

Jorge da Fonseca
Admiral in Brazilian navy. Father-in-law of Cícero Prado.

Firmino Pires Ferreira
Paper-industry magnate. Grandfather of wife of Cícero Prado.

Dr. José Inácio Gomes Guimarães
Judge and president of appellate court, São Paulo. Father-in-law of Maria das Dôres Prado.

Sources: Frederico de Barros Brotero, *A família Jordão e seus afins,* 66–67, 84–88, 91–97, 103, 109, 113–14, 337, 347–48, 373, 386; Brotero, *Barão de Antonina,* 6; Brotero, *Brigadeiro Jordão (Manuel Rodrigues Jordão),* 3; Brotero, *A família Monteiro de Barros,* 115–23; Brotero, *Queirozes: Monteiro de Barros (ramo paulista),* 14, 18, 36, 47, 49; Warren Dean, *The Industrialization of São Paulo,* 73–74; *In memoriam: Martinho Prado Junior,* 12, [399]; Luiz Gonzaga da Silva Leme, *Genealogia paulistana,* 2:235, 275, 3:429, 4:474, and 7:40; Pedro Luis Pereira de Sousa, *Meus cinqüenta anos na Companhia Prado Chaves,* 51–55.

➤ APPENDIX B ⬅

ACCOUNTS OF MARTINHO PRADO, 1856–64

	INCOME			EXPENSES				PROFITS
Year	Fazenda	Dividends/ Interest	Total	Fazenda	Interest	General	Total	
1856	46.2	1.3	47.6	5.1	21.1	—	26.2	21.3
1857	62.5	3.9	66.5	6.3	16.2	—	22.5	44.0
1858	39.8	7.7	47.4	7.6	6.2	5.6	19.3	28.1
1859	115.7	8.0	123.7	14.8	2.2	12.9	29.9	93.9
1860	77.4	12.0	89.4	11.8	—	13.7	25.5	63.9
1861	82.2	21.6	103.8	9.1	—	4.7	13.8	90.0
1862	86.6	26.6	113.3	15.0	—	12.2	27.2	86.1
1863	79.6	31.9	111.5	11.5	—	11.3	22.8	88.6
1864	115.2	36.8	151.9	21.9	—	15.6	37.5	114.4

Source: Martinho Prado, MS account book, 1856–1864, LSP.

Note: Figures are rounded to nearest tenth of a *conto,* causing some discrepancies in totals. The *conto*'s highest value in the period was $560 (1856); its lowest value was $510 (1859). Dashes indicate zero.

⇒ APPENDIX C ⇐

IMMIGRANTS' EARNINGS AT TWO

PRADO FAZENDAS, 1888

Martinho Prado's Fazenda, Campo Alto

	Amount (Milréis)	Number	Cumulative Percentage
Debts	200–0	4	6.3
Profits	0–199	35	61.0
	200–399	15	84.0
	400–599	5	92.0
	600–799	3	97.0
	800–999	1	98.5
	over 1,000	1	100.0

Martinico Prado's Fazenda, Albertina

	Amount (Milréis)	Established Immigrants			Recent Arrivals				Cumulative Percentage
		a	b	c	d	e	f	no.	
Debts	100–149	0	0	0	0	0	1	1	0.9
	50–99	0	1	0	0	0	5	6	6.2
	1–49	0	0	0	0	2	7	9	14.2
No Debt or Profit		0	0	0	0	2	0	2	15.9
Profits	1–199	7	10	4	0	9	6	36	47.8
	200–399	5	6	1	0	7	2	21	66.3
	400–599	5	3	1	3	8	0	20	84.0
	600–799	4	2	0	1	4	0	11	93.8
	800–999	0	0	2	0	1	0	3	96.5
	over 1,000	0	1	2	0	1	0	4	100.0
	Totals	21	23	10	4	34	21	113	

The 113 recorded immigrants on Albertina included both those established for an unspecified time and very recent arrivals. Six separate groups, ranging from that longest established (group a) to that which arrived in late 1888 (group f) are identified, though dates of arrival for the earlier groups are unspecified.

Source: Alfred Marc, *Le Brésil,* 349–55. The value of the milréis in 1888 was U.S. $.51.

Note: All sixty-four immigrants recorded for Campo Alto arrived in 1888. Sixty showed profits by the year's end.

❧ APPENDIX D ❧

AGRICULTURAL PROPERTIES OF THE PRADO

FAMILY

Principal Family Properties, 1904–5

Name and Location	Owner	Area Cultivated/Total (*Alqueires*)		Coffee Trees	Production (*Arrobas*)	Work Force Brazilian/ Immigrant		Nominal Value (*Contos*)
Campo Alto, Araras	Veridiana	450	1,700	322,988	15,000	50	120	500
Mattão, Mattão	Antônio	108	388	200,000	12,000	26	78	200
Guatapará, Ribeirão Prêto	Martinico	1,111	6,268	2,112,700	160,000	56	1,610	6,616
São Martinho, Sertãozinho	Veridiana and sons	1,588	13,988	1,268,000	190,000	100	800	1,000
S. Veridiana, S. Cruz das Palmeiras	Antônio	350	600	600,000	40,000	28	261	1,300
Totals		4,107	32,944	4,503,688	417,000	260	2,869	9,616

Source: São Paulo (Estado), *Estatistica agricola e zootechnica, municípios* of Araras, Mattão, Ribeirão Prêto, Sertãozinho, and Santa Cruz das Palmeiras. My thanks to Thomas Holloway for use of this document.

Note: The *alqueire* was equal to about six acres; the *conto* was worth about U.S. $320 in 1905; the *arroba* weighed between twenty-five and thirty-two pounds, varying regionally.

AND OF THE PRADO-CHAVES EXPORT

COMPANY

Prado-Chaves Company Properties, 1906–9

Name or Location	Area (*Alqueires*)	Coffee Trees
1. Campinas	130	130,000
2. Dourado	550	200,000
3. Jundiaí	300	116,000
4. Santa Rita	150	142,000
5. Santa Rita	79	90,000
6. Ventania	650	247,000
7. Tieté	500	175,000
8. Santa Silveria	456	385,000
9. Campo Alegre	436	160,000
10. Dourado	600	128,000
11. Floresta	236	290,000
12. Visconde do Pinhal	200	132,000
13. Louveira	160	124,000
14. Dourado	160	68,000
15. Itahiquara	163	170,000
16. Ribeirão Prêto	120	230,000
17. Brodowski	65	90,000
Totals	4,955	2,877,000

Sources: São Paulo (Estado), *Estatistica agricola e zootechnica,* *municípios* of Campinas, Dourado, Jundiaí, and Santa Rita do Passo Quatro; *Companhia Prado Chaves Exportadora.*
Note: Obvious duplications were eliminated.

CONTRACT FOR THE PLANTING OF 200,000

COFFEE TREES

By this contract[1] made between the contracting parties, the Sivelli Brothers as contractors and Dona Veridiana Prado and Sons as owners of the Fazenda São Martinho, situated in the município of Ribeirão Prêto,[2] the following is established:

1st

The contractors, the Sivelli Brothers, obligate themselves to plant this year, at the latest by the middle of November, 200,000 coffee trees, by seeds, with a distance of 16 *palmos*[3] between seed-holes, in deep holes, and covered with good wood shavings, clearing and felling the bushes and trees on their own account as well as performing the burning and then making the alignment of the plantation;

2nd

With the planting and construction of workers' houses completed, the contractors may plant a row of corn between each row of coffee plantings and can renew this planting one more time with the condition, however, that they may do this only after performing all the work of cultivating the coffee and maintaining the houses;

3rd

The contractors will be responsible for the care of the said plantation of coffee during 4 years, terminating at the end of November, 1901, being obligated to keep it always cultivated and to replant dead trees, as well as to open and to maintain cart-paths, which shall be made equal to those already existing on the fazenda, soon after the planting is concluded;

4th

No planting other than corn will be permitted in the coffee grove;

5th

The contractors cannot employ workers or friends that have left the employ of the fazenda, and subject themselves to the inspection and orders of the Administrator, which cannot be contrary to the clauses of the contract;

6th

The contractors will also pull from the planting-holes all seedlings in excess of two, as well as suckers which appear;

7th

Dona Veridiana Prado and Sons obligates itself to perform the tree-killing [*picada*] necessary for clearing the land and to furnish the necessary seeds for the planting, as well as to furnish a small dwelling-house for the contractors and to furnish roofing-tiles, boards, and door jambs necessary for the construction of dwellings [*ranchos*] sufficient for their personnel;

8th

[Dona Veridiana Prado and Sons] obligates itself to pay the contractors 1$500 réis for each four-year-old coffee tree, or the quantity of 300:000$000 (three hundred contos de réis)[4] which will be paid in the following installments: the first of 20:000$000 (twenty contos de réis) after the burning is completed; the second of 40:000$000 (forty contos de réis) after the planting is concluded and roads constructed, and from then on in tri-monthly installments of 15:000$000 (fifteen contos de réis);

9th

From all payments 10% (ten percent) will be deducted to guarantee the faithful execution of the contract, which will be delivered at the end of the contract, on the occasion of the liquidation of accounts;

10th

The contractors will replant all coffee [trees] that die or are lost by fire or frost, except that this service shall not exceed the period of this contract;

11th

[The coffee] produced during the four years will belong to the owners of the fazenda and the harvest will be carried out by the contractors at the going rate on the fazenda;[5]

12th

The contractors have the right to furnish to their personnel the supplies they need;

13th

This contract will run for four years; however, in the event of the death of one of its two parties, the parties obligate themselves to have it respected by their heirs or by the new owners in case of sale;

14th

At the end of this contract, when the existing coffee trees are counted, missing trees will be discounted at the rate of 2$000 (two milréis) per tree.

> S. Paulo, 20 March 1897
> /s/ Antônio Prado, for
> Veridiana Prado
> and Sons
> /s/ Sivelli Brothers

[1] "Contracto de empreitada para o plantio de 200.000 pes de cafe," 20 March 1897, uncataloged papers of Fernando Chaves, Museu Paulista, São Paulo.

[2] The area in which the fazenda was located became part of the new município of Sertãozinho one month later.

[3] A *palmo* (*palma*) or "palm" was a traditional measure roughly equivalent to nine inches.

[4] The value of the *conto de réis* was U.S. $160 in 1897; thus the total value of the contract was U.S. $48,000.

[5] Coffee trees generally began producing in three years and reached full maturity in another two or three years.

⋙ APPENDIX F ⋘

Partido Democrático

CLASS COMPOSITION (1926)

	Number	Group Total	Group Percentage
Middle-Class Professionals		256	42.6
Lawyer (*advogado*)	139		
Engineer (*engenheiro*)	42		
Doctor (*médico*)	28		
Newspaperman (*jornalista*)	10		
Dentist (*dentista*)	8		
Pharmacist (*pharmaceútico*)	6		
Law professor (*professor da Faculdade de Direito*)	6		
Teacher (*professor*)	3		
Professor of pharmacy (*professor da Escola de Farmácia*)	3		
Dental surgeon (*cirurgião-dentista*)	2		
Professor, polytechnical school (*professor da Escola Politécnica*)	2		
Military officer (*militar*)	1		
Legal agent (*solicitador*)	1		
Artist (*pintor*)[1]	1		
Priest (*sacerdote*)	1		
Music professor (*professor do Conservatório*)[2]	1		
Chemist (*químico*)	1		
Medical professor (*professor da Faculdade de Medicina*)	1		
White-Collar Employees		141	23.4
General ("*commercio*," "*do commercio*")	80		
Bank employee (*funcionário bancário*)	48		

(*continued*)

APPENDIX F (*Continued*)

	Number	Group Total	Group Percentage
Bookkeeper (*guarda-livros*)	7		
Notary (*tabelião*)	2		
Accountant (*contador*)	2		
Clerk (*escrevente*)	2		
Propertied Classes		93	15.5
Planter (*lavrador*)	59		
Property owner (*proprietário*)	34		
Business, Finance, and Industry		87	14.5
Businessman (*comerciante*)	68		
Industrialist (*industrial*)	10		
Broker (*corretor*)	8		
Factor (*commisário*)	1		
Miscellaneous and Status Uncertain		24	4.0
Student (*estudante*)	18		
Railroad employees, unspecified (*ferroviário, funcionário ferroviário*)	4		
Unspecified (*empregado, funcionário*)	2		
Totals		601	100.0

Source: Nazareth Prado, *Antonio Prado no imperio e na república*, 392–408.
[1] José Wasth Rodrigues.
[2] Mário de Andrade, musicologist and author.

➋ NOTES ➋

In citing works in the notes, short titles have generally been used. Works and collections frequently cited have been identified by the following abbreviations:

AAMB   Archive of Antônio Augusto Monteiro de Barros Neto
IM:MJP   *In memoriam: Martinho Prado Junior*
JPC   *Coleção Jorge Pacheco e Chaves,* Instituto Histórico e Geográfico de São Paulo
LSP   Archive of Luíz Prado

Full titles and publication data may be found in the Bibliography, where Luso-Brazilian authors' names are alphabetized under the *final* name.

INTRODUCTION

1 Frederick B. Pike, *Spanish America, 1900–1970,* chaps. 1–3.
2 Elizabeth W. Dore and John F. Weeks, "Economic Performance and Basic Needs."
3 Immanuel Wallerstein, *The Modern World-System.*
4 Elizabeth Anne Kuznesof, "Household Composition and Headship as Related to Changes in Mode of Production."
5 Ibid.; E. Bradford Burns, *The Poverty of Progress.*
6 Fernando Henrique Cardoso, "Associated-Dependent Development."
7 E. Bradford Burns, *A History of Brazil,* chap. 8.
8 Different definitions of the term *development* abound. A fundamental distinction should be made between growth and development. Growth is merely quantitative process—that is, an increase in gross national product, bananas exported, miles of railroad track—which usually ignores the distributional impact of such events on different social classes and groups. While most Latin American economies have grown, the growth has benefited the haves more than thè have-nots. For me, development implies sustained movement toward a more just society, a value judgment I readily confess. Many recent studies point to the comprehensive and indivisible nature of authentic development. Economically, development ought to ensure that everyone receives "basic needs"—decent food, housing, water and sanitation, health care, and education. Human, political, and civil rights are needed to gain and

protect economic rights. Most difficult of all, a restructuring of the international political and economic order seems necessary if "national development" is to occur.

9 Alfred C. Stepan, *The Military in Politics.*

10 Prado is used as an abbreviation for Silva Prado throughout. The Silva Prados should not be confused with two other São Paulo families of similar names, the Almeida Prados and the do Prados. Early eighteenth-century ties existed between the do Prados and the Silva Prados, but links between the two families later became unimportant.

Published works on the Prados include Maria Thereza Schorer Petrone, *O Barão de Iguape;* Cândido Motta Filho, *A vida de Eduardo Prado;* and the following commemorative family-sponsored volumes: Nazareth Prado, comp., *Antonio Prado no imperio e na republica; Primeiro centenário do Conselheiro António da Silva Prado;* and *In memoriam: Martinho Prado Junior, 1843–1943.* The best genealogy is Frederico de Barros Brotero, *A família Jordão e seus afins.*

11 The most influential, comprehensive, complex, and sometimes contradictory work is Gilberto Freyre's trilogy, *Casa grande e senzala* (1933), *Sobrados e mucambos* (1936), and *Ordem e progresso* (1959), which in later editions bears the collective subtitle "An Introduction to the History of Patriarchal Society in Brazil." The trilogy is translated in abridged form as *The Masters and the Slaves, The Mansions and the Shanties,* and *Order and Progress.* Though Freyre professes to a "sociological" rather than a historical conception of time—a fact that tends to blur his treatment of discrete historical epochs—the three volumes treat the rise of rural patriarchy in the colonial era, its decline and replacement by urban "semi-patriarchy" in the nineteenth century, and the "disintegration" of both forms after approximately 1889, respectively. For a brief but perceptive analysis of Freyre's methodology, see Richard M. Morse, "Crosscurrents in New World History," 53–55.

Works consistent with and influenced by Freyre's work but concerned more with the political ramifications of family influence include: Luíz Aguiar da Costa Pinto, "Lutas de família no Brasil"; José Francisco de Oliveira Vianna, *Instituições políticas brasileiras,* esp. vol. 1; and Nestor Duarte, *A ordem privada e a organização política brasileira.* Two brief accounts by North Americans accept Freyre's treatment of the colonial era in *Casa grande e senzala* while ignoring the changes Freyre describes in *Sobrados e mucambos* and *Ordem e progresso:* Charles Wagley, *An Introduction to Brazil;* and T. Lynn Smith, *Brazil: People and Institutions,* 459–61.

Antônio Candido's "The Brazilian Family" is a valuable, mildly revisionist account of nineteenth-century elite family life, drawing on the author's own background as a member of an elite family in south-central Brazil. An important but neglected methodological article containing an implicit challenge to views that urge the underlying unity of family life in diverse Brazilian regions is Roger Bastide, "A monografia familiar no Brasil."

While they do not challenge Freyre on historical grounds, several analyses of contemporary patterns point to class and regional differences in family structure and function. See Emílio Willems, "The Structure of the Brazilian Family"; Thales de Azevedo, "Family, Marriage, and Divorce in Brazil"; and Manoel Tosta Berlinck, *The Structure of the Brazilian Family in the City of São Paulo.*

12 Vianna, *Instituições políticas,* 1:243.

13 Wagley, *An Introduction to Brazil,* 168.

14 Clovis Bevilaqua, *Direito da família,* 392. See also Pinto, "Lutas de família," 119, and Tristão de Alencar Araripe, "Pater-familias no Brazil nos tempos coloniaes." For colonial legislation on the family, see Portugal, *Ordenações filipinas,* vol. 1, títulos 79, 88, and 94; vol. 2, títulos 9, 35, 37, 45, 59, 62; and vol. 3, títulos 5, 9, 12, 18, 21, 29, 31, 41–42, 47–48, 56, 70, 86, and 99; and Portugal, *Ordenações do senhor rey D. Affonso V,* vol. 2, título 28; vol. 3, títulos 45–46; vol. 4, títulos 11–18, 37, 41, 82–84, 87, 89–93, 95, 97–102, 105–8, and 112; and vol. 5, títulos 6–25 and appendix, "Sobre os adulterios," 418–20.

15 Bevilaqua, *Direito da família,* 392.

16 Lafayette Pereira, *Direitos de família,* 5.

17 Brotero, *Família Jordão,* 60. Linda Lewin's research disputes this; see below, p. 13.

18 Candido, "The Brazilian Family," 294–95; Araripe, "Pater-familias."

19 Candido, "The Brazilian Family," 295.

20 Charles Expilly, *Mulheres e costumes no Brasil,* 401. *Goiabada* is a sweet made from guava.

21 Ramalho Ortigão, "Carta a Eduardo Prado," 8.

22 Joaquim Nabuco, *Minha formação,* 28. The oppression of women in slave societies was more general; for the United States case, see William R. Taylor, *Cavalier and Yankee,* 172–76.

23 Manoel de Oliveira Lima, *Memórias,* 9.

24 "O ministerio familiar," 214.

25 Willems, "Brazilian Family," 341; Azevedo, "Family, Marriage, and Divorce," 293–96; Bernard C. Rosen, "Socialization and Achievement Motivation in Brazil," 615. See also the report on the first national women's congress in Brazil, "The Women," *Time* (international ed.), 12 June 1972, 15. The *Jornal do Brasil* of 27 April 1972 carried an article headlined "Psychiatrist Finds That the Brazilian Woman Still Lacks

Preparation for Freedom." In 1983 it was reported that men who kill their wives or female companions can expect light punishment; see Warren Hoge, "Machismo Murder Case."

26 Freyre, *Sobrados e mucambos*, 1:68ff.

27 Expilly, *Mulheres e costumes*, 374–79.

28 James C. Fletcher and D. P. Kidder, *Brazil and the Brazilians Portrayed in Historical and Descriptive Sketches*, 176.

29 Candido, "Brazilian Family," 294–95.

30 Fletcher and Kidder, *Brazil and the Brazilians*, 176, 164. A *collegio* is a secondary school.

31 Freyre, *Sobrados e mucambos*, 1:68ff.

32 Freyre, *Casa grande e senzala*, 1:424 and note.

33 Graciliano Ramos, *Infância*, 66.

34 Wagley, *An Introduction to Brazil*, 176; Billy Jaynes Chandler, *The Feitosas and the Sertão dos Inhamuns*.

35 Duarte, *Ordem privada*, 138–69; Willems, "Brazilian Family," 345.

36 Gerald L. Soliday, ed., *History of the Family and Kinship*.

37 Tamara K. Hareven, "Postscript," 454. Hareven's articles cited below and in the bibliography provide an excellent introduction to the field.

38 Ibid., 455–56.

39 Francesca M. Cancian, Louis Wolf Goodman, and Peter H. Smith, "Capitalism, Industrialization, and Kinship in Latin America," 319–20.

40 Kuznesof, "The Role of the Female-Headed Household in Brazilian Modernization, São Paulo, 1765–1836," 559.

41 Edward Shorter, *The Making of the Modern Family*, 14; Hareven, "Postscript," 455–56.

42 Formal marriage was not widespread. Kuznesof included as married "male accompanied by adult female not listed as a blood relative (or in-law) or servant, even if both list their marital status [in census] as 'unmarried.'" "Household Composition," 86, table 1, n. 1.

43 Kuznesof, "Female-Headed Households," p. 608.

44 Donald Ramos, "City and Country," 374. Minas Gerais is popularly regarded as one of the most traditional of Brazilian regions, especially as regards the family and religion.

45 Donald Ramos, "Marriage and the Family in Colonial Vila Rica," 205ff. See also his "Vila Rica."

46 Tamara K. Hareven, "Family as Process," 322, 326.

47 Edward Shorter notes these disadvantages and attempts a compromise between them and "the narrowness of quantitative analysis and the possibly atypical descriptions of concrete places in fixed times." He bases his research on three sources: medical typographies, minor bureaucrats, and local intellectuals; see his *Modern Family*, 10–11.

48 Kuznesof, "Clans, the Militia, and Territorial Government," and "The Role of Merchants in the Economic Development of São Paulo, 1765–1850."

49 Alida C. Metcalf, "Marriage, Inheritance, and Family Structure in Eighteenth-Century Brazil."

50 Linda Lewin, "Some Historical Implications of Kinship Organization for Family-based Politics in the Brazilian Northeast," 272; see also 285–86.

51 A. J. R. Russell-Wood, "Women and Society in Colonial Brazil"; quotations on pp. 2, 33.

52 Susan A. Soeiro, "The Social and Economic Role of the Convent," quotations on pp. 219, 225.

53 June E. Hahner, "Women and Work in Brazil, 1850–1920."

54 Susan K. Besse, "When the Public Becomes Private and the Private Becomes Public," 17.

55 For lower-class family life in the teeming slums of Brazil in the 1950s, see Carolina Maria de Jesus, *Child of the Dark*.

56 For a general treatment, see Raymond T. Smith, "Family." For Brazilian variations see Berlinck, *Structure of the Brazilian Family*, 25–34.

CHAPTER I. ORIGINS, 1700–1840

1 As an adjective *Paulista* means of or pertaining to the São Paulo region; as a noun it means a native or resident of the area.

2 The basic work on the bandeirantes is Afonso de Escragnolle Taunay, *História geral das bandeiras paulistas*. For a more thematic survey, selected documents, and readings, see Richard M. Morse, ed., *The Bandeirantes*.

3 C. R. Boxer, *The Golden Age of Brazil, 1695–1750*, chap. 3.

4 Caio Prado Júnior, *The Colonial Background of Modern Brazil*, 69.

5 A classic statement of this thesis is Paulo Prado, *Paulística*, xxv. See also Caio Prado Júnior, *Colonial Background*, 68, where, however, the tendency for São Paulo to rally in the last quarter of the eighteenth century is also noted.

6 Richard M. Morse, *From Community to Metropolis*, 16–17, and Gilberto Leite de Barros, *A cidade e o planalto*, 1:152–63, are among those works that reinterpret the eighteenth century in São Paulo. For demographic evidence challenging the "decadence thesis," see Maria-Luiza Marcílio, *La ville de São Paulo*, esp. 118.

7 Barros, *A cidade e o planalto*, 1:171–79.

8 Kuznesof, "Household Composition," and "Female-Headed Household."

9 Barros, *A cidade e o planalto*, 213–27.

10 Ibid., 165.

11 Vianna believed that primogeniture was more strictly adhered to in the north of Brazil than in the south; see his *Instituições políticas brasileiras*, 1:240.

12 Metcalf, "Marriage, Inheritance."

13 Barros, *A cidade e o planalto*, 167–68.

14 Maria-Luiza Marcílio, *La ville de São Paulo*, 126–45.

15 Unless otherwise specified, genealogical data in this and subsequent chapters are from Brotero, *Família Jordão*, 57–147. The sergeant-major (*sargento-mór*) was a militia position of some responsibility and prestige.

16 Alberto Prado Guimarães, "Eduardo Prado," 586. Determined searches by Prado family members in the late nineteenth century were unable to shed light on the family's European origins; interview with Luíz Prado, 12 May 1972.

17 Alfredo Ellis, *Raça de gigantes*, 142.

18 On the do Prados see Pedro Taques de Almeida Paes Leme, *Nobilarchia paulistana historica e genealógica*, vol. 2, and Francisco de Assis Carvalho Franco, *Dicionário de bandeirantes e sertanistas do Brasil*, 305–15.

19 Brotero, *Família Jordão*, 616–19; cf. Luiz Gonzaga da Silva Leme, *Genealogia paulistana*, 7:26.

20 "Escritura de dívida e obrigação que faz o Sargento-mór Antonio da Silva do Prado," 15 May 1730, in Brotero, *Família Jordão*, 611–14. The *oitava*, or dram, equaled one-eighth ounce. A rough idea of its eighteenth-century purchasing power can be had from the following examples of the excessively high commodity prices in gold from Minas Gerais in 1703: for six pounds of beef, one oitava; for an ordinary pistol, ten oitavas; for a little cask of brandy, one hundred oitavas; for a Brazilian-born black, a good craftsman, five hundred oitavas; see Boxer, *Golden Age*, 330–32, 354–56. Evidently either the price level in São Paulo in 1730 was considerably lower, or Antônio da Silva do Prado's mortgaged slaves and new slaves were of less than prime character.

21 "Procuração bastante que faz Francisca de Siqueira Morais," in Brotero, *Família Jordão*, 614–16.

22 Martinho's four sisters married into important families, most notably the Nunes Paes and Oliveira Lima clans. His brother, Raimundo, became a militia captain in São Paulo, but Raimundo's male descendants migrated to Mato Grosso and thus play no subsequent role in this study.

23 Manuel Eufrásio de Azevedo Marques, *Apontamentos históricos, geográficos, biográficos, estatísticos e noticiosos da província de São Paulo*, 2:109; Portugal, Arquivo Histórico Ultramarino, *Catálogo de documentos sôbre a história de São Paulo*, 5:161, 6:65, 7:46 and 354–55, cited hereafter as "Portugal, *Documentos*." The Portuguese league varied between 5,555 and 6,000 meters. The land grant thus probably measured a minimum of 5.9 square miles or about 3,800 acres. The capitão-mór at this time was "the governor of an unincorporated settlement and/or commandant of a company of second-line militia"; Dauril Alden, *Royal Government in Colonial Brazil*, xxii.

24 Brotero, *Família Jordão*, 9, 55–58; Frederico de Barros Brotero, *Brigadeiro Jordão*.

25 Portugal, *Documentos*, 11:246.

26 Receipt signed by Bento José de Souza, Jundiaí, August 1790; letters of José Ignacio Ferreira Campos to Antônio Prado, Meia Ponte (Goias), 2 April 1792 and 7 March 1793; José Pedro Alexandre Pereira Salgado to Joaquim Prado, Natividade, 12 August 1795; receipt signed by Antônio Coelho, 6 June 1800; "Clareza do Snr. Antônio Castro de Azevedo," undated, ca. 1800; all in Archive of Antônio Augusto Monteiro de Barros, São Paulo (hereafter, *AAMB*). Also, Portugal, *Documentos*, 10:66.

27 Barros, *A cidade e o planalto*, 1:185–88. In Barros's view, this coronelismo, the predecessor of the better-known nineteenth- and twentieth-century forms of local strongman rule, was part of the consolidation of patriarchalism in São Paulo, which he says occurred only in the late eighteenth century. Patriarchalism is usually presumed to have occurred much earlier in areas such as Bahia and Pernambuco.

28 "Omenagem q. presta o Cap. mor Joaquim Antônio Guimarães pela Villa de Jundiaí por seu bastante procurador o Cap. mor Eleutério da Silva Prado," 12 February 1814, *AAMB*; Afonso de Escragnolle Taunay, *História do café no Brasil*, 3:69; Maria Thereza Schorer Petrone, "Um comerciante do ciclo do acucar paulista," 129; "Termo que assigna o Capitão Joaquim da Silva Prado," 17 May 1839, *AAMB*.

29 John Mawe, *Travels in the Interior of Brazil*, 81–84.

30 Augusto de Saint-Hilaire, *Viagem à provincia de São Paulo*, 103–4, 124, 130, 137–38.

31 Ibid., 187–88.

32 Ibid., 172–73, 180–81, 187–88. As a noun, *Mineiro* refers to residents or natives of Minas Gerais; as an adjective, it means of, or pertaining to, that area.

33 Portugal, *Documentos*, 10:376; receipt signed by Antônio Prado, Villa Bôa, 28 May 1807, and letter, Ana Vicência to Antônio, São Paulo, 3 January 1815, both in *AAMB*.

34 Petrone, "Um comerciante," 36:117; 37:326; and 39:127.

35 Ibid., 36:117 and 37:340, 326. For an exhaustive treatment of Antônio's cattle dealings and tax collecting see Petrone, *O Barão de Iguape.*

36 Petrone, "Um comerciante," 37:343, 324; the quote is from 39:127.

37 Ibid., 39:124.

38 São Paulo (Cidade), Arquivo Municipal, *Registo geral da Camara Municipal de S. Paulo,* vol. 16 (1820–22); Brotero, *Família Jordão,* 59; Leopoldo de Freitas, *A Sra. Dona Veridiana Prado,* 6–7.

39 Morse, *From Community to Metropolis,* 50–51.

40 São Paulo (Cidade), Arquivo Municipal, *Registo geral da Camara Municipal,* 16:443–49.

41 Francisco de Castro Couto Mello, "Memoria sobre a declaração de independencia," 339–51. For an excellent revisionist essay on Brazilian independence, see Emilia Viotti da Costa, "Introdução ao estudo da emancipação política do Brasil."

42 Brotero, *Família Jordão,* 59.

43 Actually half-siblings, half-cousins, because of the marriages of their mother, Ana Vicência Rodrigues de Almeida, to the brothers, the second Antônio and Eleutério Prado.

44 Morse, *From Community to Metropolis,* 54–55; Barros, *A cidade e o planalto,* 2:349–50.

45 Frederico de Barros Brotero, *A família Monteiro de Barros,* 117, 120, 121.

46 Ibid., 122; the quotation more accurately describes the prestige of the Prados in the second half of the nineteenth century than in the late 1820s.

47 Ibid., esp. pp. 5, 8–9, 122–23.

48 Brotero, *Família Jordão,* 60, 66–75, and Frederico de Barros Brotero, *Barão de Antonina,* 6, 70.

49 Antônio Prado to Antônio Rodrigues de Almeida Jordão, São Paulo, 31 May 1827, and Antônio Prado to Gertrudes Galvão de Moura Lacerda, São Paulo, 16 October 1827, in Brotero, *Família Jordão,* 632–34; see also pp. 514–18 and 620.

50 In one history of eighteenth-century São Paulo replete with the exploits of the do Prados, the only Silva Prado mentioned is a twentieth-century family member; see Afonso de Escragnolle Taunay, *História da cidade de São Paulo no seculo XVIII.*

CHAPTER II. FAMILY LIFE IN THE SECOND EMPIRE

1 Freyre, *Sobrados e mucambos,* esp. chaps. 3 and 4.

2 Brotero, *Família Jordão,* 611. Genealogical data for this chapter is

drawn from Brotero, *Família Jordão*, 57–167; Frederico de Barros Brotero, *Queirozes*, 11, 19, 69; *IM:MPJ* [392]–[402]; and Leme, *Genealogia paulistana*, 7:26–29, 39–42.

3 No claim was made in the various family-sponsored commemorative volumes to link the Prados to the early colonial period.

4 For my definition of "Prado-surname extended family," see above, p. 16.

5 Costa Pinto (1826–87) was six times national deputy from São Paulo and four times appointed president of Brazilian provinces. In 1877 he was named minister of empire, and he held large properties in Piracicaba, São Paulo. For more details see Eugenio Egas, *Galeria dos presidentes de S. Paulo*, 441–49, and J. L. Almeida Nogueira, *A academia de São Paulo*, 1:105f.

6 The elder Pereira Pinto (1819–80) served in the Paulista provincial assembly and in the national parliament, representing the province of Espírito Santo. He also was president of the latter province and of Sergipe. He is best known for his collection of treaties, *Apontamentos para o direito internacional*. See Nogueira, *A academia de São Paulo*, 4:143–44.

7 Martinho Prado, MS diary (1838–60), Archive of Caio Prado Júnior, São Paulo, fols. 121–29. Source cited hereafter as "Martinho Prado, MS diary."

8 Born in Bahia in 1796, Costa Carvalho was educated at Coimbra, Portugal, was appointed crown magistrate (*juiz de fóra*) in São Paulo in 1821, and founded the city's first newspaper, *O Farol Paulistano*, in 1827. After serving as Brazilian regent, he headed the São Paulo Law School, served as minister of empire (1848), and became president of the Council of Ministers (1849). He approved the law that ended Brazil's foreign slave trade in 1850. He was named successively baron (1841), viscount (1843), and marquis of Monte Alegre (1854). See Brasil Bandecchi, Leonardo Arroyo, and Ubiratan Rosa, eds., *Nôvo dicionário de história do Brasil*, 419.

9 Brotero, *Família Jordão*, 73–74, 472. Prados whom I interviewed in 1972 had no knowledge of this branch.

10 Prado to Fonseca, Rio, July 1838, *AAMB*.

11 Martinho Prado, MS diary, fol. 121.

12 Alzira Pacheco e Chaves to Miguel Chaves, 17 March 1924, Miguel Chaves Papers (uncataloged), Museu Paulista, São Paulo. Collection cited hereafter as "Miguel Chaves Papers."

13 Luíz da Silva Prado, "Biografia de D. Veridiana Valeria da Silva Prado," MS dated 1949, 3, *LSP*; Freitas, *A Sra. Dona Veridiana Prado*, 5–6; Adalzira Bittencourt, *A mulher paulistana na história*, 178–80. Müller was the author of a statistical study of the province, *São Paulo em 1836*.

14 Undated interview notes of Artur de Cerqueira Mendes, "Segundo as declarações de D. Antonieta Arinos e Dr. Luiz Prado," in an uncataloged file marked "D. Veridiana Prado," Instituto de Estudos Brasileiros, Universidade de São Paulo. Document subsequently cited as "Declarações de D. Antonienta Arinos e Dr. Luiz Prado"; file cited hereafter as "Cerqueira Mendes file." Cerqueira Mendes apparently never published his study of Veridiana.

15 Martinho Prado, MS diary, fols. 121–29.

16 Luiz Prado, "Biografia de Veridiana Prado," 4.

17 Child discipline in mid-nineteenth-century São Paulo is described in Maria Paes de Barros, *No tempo de dantes*, 21, 26, 29–30, 33–34, 49, 58–59.

18 "Termo que assigna o Comendador Antonio da Silva Prado, procurador do Tenente Coronel José de Almeida Leme, nomeado Comandante Superior das Legiões de Itú e Sorocaba," MS dated 28 April 1842, and "Termo que assigna o Comendador Antonio da Silva Prado, procurador do Capitao-mor Manoel Jozé de Mello, nomeado Comandante Superior das Legiões de Taubaté," MS dated 2 May 1842, both in *AAMB*. The documents were endorsed by José da Costa Carvalho, former regent of Brazil and then baron of Monte Alegre, later named as godfather of Antônio Caio Prado, the baron of Iguape's grandson.

Caio Prado Júnior, a great-great-grandson of the baron of Iguape, calls the period from 1837 to 1849 the most reactionary in Brazilian history, though with no mention that his forebears stood on the side of reaction; see his *Evolução política do Brasil*, 164–68.

19 Brotero, *Família Jordão*, 59; "Carta de nomeação para Sindico do Recolhimento de Sta. Theresa em São Paulo," MS dated 1861, *AAMB*.

20 Antonio de Castro Alves, *Obras completas*, 2:555.

21 "Declarações de D. Antonieta Arinos e Dr. Luiz Prado."

22 Baron of Iguape to Veridiana Prado, São Paulo, 23 September 1852 (copy), Archive of Ana Candida Ferraz Sampaio, São Paulo. Collection cited hereafter as "Sampaio Archive."

23 *IM:MPJ*, 10. *A Província de São Paulo*, 18 April 1875, 3:2.

24 "*Pois observo que elle anda com humores alvoroçadas.*" Baron of Iguape to Veridiana Prado, São Paulo, 1 December 1851, *AAMB*.

25 Baron of Iguape to Veridiana Prado, São Paulo, 29 August 1852, *AAMB*.

26 Baron of Iguape to Veridiana Prado, São Paulo, 23 September 1852 (copy), Sampaio Archive.

27 Veridiana Prado to baroness of Iguape, Mogi-Mirim, 10 August 1861 (copy), and n.p., n.d. (original), both in Sampaio Archive.

28 Nogueira, *A academia de São Paulo*, 4:275. The traditionalist spokesman was Antônio Pereira Pinto Sénior, Ana Blandina Prado's

future father-in-law. In traditional Japan, divorce was easy for a man to obtain, and marriage was regarded neither as a sacrament nor as a concern of the state; see Goode, *World Revolution*, pp. 358–59.

29 Antônio Prado to Veridiana Prado, Lisbon, 28 July 1862, *AAMB*.

30 Antônio Prado to Veridiana Prado, Paris, 24 November 1862, *AAMB*.

31 Martinico Prado to Alfredo Chaves, Elias Chaves, and "Sodré," Montevideo, 29 October 1865, Coleção Jorge Pacheco Chaves, Instituto Histórico e Geográfico de São Paulo, file 920/512d/A1. Collection cited hereafter as *JPC*. For Martinico's hunger strike, see *IM:MPJ*, 14.

32 Martinho Prado to Antonio Correia Pacheco, São Paulo, 3 July 1866, Sampaio Archive; italics added.

33 Caio Prado to Elias Chaves, São Paulo, 8 December 1867, *JPC*, 920/512co/A1; original italics.

34 *IM:MSP*, 14.

35 Caio Prado to Elias Chaves, São Paulo, 2 March 1868, *JPC*, 920/512co/A1; original italics.

36 Anézia Prado Chaves to Veridiana Prado, São Paulo, 8 July 1871, *JPC*, 920/C512/A1.

37 This despite the fact that there was a consistent surplus of women in São Paulo city and many unmarried females in their twenties and thirties; see Marcílio, *La ville de São Paulo*, 126–45.

38 See chap. 2, n. 6.

39 *A Província de São Paulo*, 18 May 1876, 3:2, and 19 May 1876, 2:2.

40 "Escriptura de venda e compra de terreno," MS dated 18 April 1878, *AAMB*.

41 São Paulo, 2 September 1882, *AAMB*; original italics. Here Veridiana used one version of the spelling of her name; I have adopted the more usual version except in direct quotes. The importance of religion in the Prado family seems to have varied from person to person. Veridiana and Eduardo were quite religious. Antônio Prado's early disillusionment with formal Roman Catholicism is discussed in the next chapter. Martinico Prado became a Mason during his law school days— although Masonry in Brazil lacked the anti-Catholicism of European Masonry—and apparently was an agnostic. Antônio Caio Prado's daughter, Ana Abiah, founded the first abbey of contemplative nuns in Latin America, in Buenos Aires in 1911.

42 See José Lins do Rego's essay "Eduardo Prado" in *A casa e o homem*, 15–34. According to Lins do Rego: "[Veridiana] fought with her husband, travelled alone, raised her children as she wanted, brought artists into her home, and had no fear of the tongues which cut her life to pieces. She did what she wanted how she wanted to do it. She was a Victorian without the angelic morality of Victoria. For her love was not

a crime. . . . This was the mother who seemed to many the germ of the bourgeoisie's dissolution, a scratch on the Christian vase of the sacred family" (p. 17) and "Veridiana was the best expression of the worldly spirit of the nineteenth century. It was in contact with his revolutionary mother that Eduardo reacted with the fury of an Oedipus with opened eyes" (p. 21). Unfortunately, Lins do Rego offers no evidence for these assertions. Later in his life, Eduardo did bemoan the passing of traditional family life, but to account for this in oedipal terms seems far-fetched.

43 A series of five paintings depicting the parable was acquired by the Prados in the mid-nineteenth century and in 1972 hung in the dining room at the Fazenda Santa Veridiana.

44 For the Rudge family, see Brotero, *Família Jordão*, 128, and *Barão de Antonina*, 14.

45 Unpublished research notes of Artur Cerqueira Mendes, Mendes File. Facts confirmed in letter of Caio Prado Júnior to author, 4 December 1973.

46 Paulo (1869–1943), Nazareth (b. 1875), Marina (d. 1896), Antonieta (dates unknown), Antonio, Júnior (b. 1880), Herminia (dates unknown), Luiz (b. 1885), and Sílvio (dates unknown). None of the available sources gives full dates of birth and death.

47 Interview, Luíz Prado, São Paulo, 7 August 1972.

48 João Fernando de Almeida Prado, "Paulo Prado e a época de sua formação," 97.

49 Maria Catarina Prado to Paulo Prado, Petrópolis, 30 December 1885, Rio, 4 January 1886, 22 and 30 December 1885, and 5 December 1886, *LSP*; Petropólis, 22 [December 188-?] and 7 January 1886, *AAMB*.

50 Everardo Vallim Pereira de Sousa, "Reminiscências," in *Primeiro centenário*, 196–97.

51 Lavínia (b. 1870), Caio (b. 1872), Plínio (1873–1918), Evangelina (1874–1915), Clélia (1876–1913), Cornélia (1878–1908), Julita (b. 1879), Martinho Prado Neto (b. 1881), Cássio (b. 1883), Corina (b. 1885), Fábio (1887–1963), and Cícero (b. 1888).

52 *O Estado de São Paulo*, rotogravure, sec. 1, November 1943.

53 Ina von Binzer, *Alegrias e tristezas de uma educadora alemã no Brasil*, 76. The role of the foreign governess in Brazil is a significant but unexplored topic in the study of elite family life. On a governess's role in another elite family, see Barros, *No tempo de dantes*, 15, 92ff.

54 Von Binzer, *Alegrias e tristezas*, 78–79. The Caio in question is the future father of the historian Caio Prado Júnior.

55 Ibid., 83. Gaius Gracchus (154–121 B.C.) and his brother Tiberius (163–133 B.C.) were radical statesmen of the Roman Republic and advocates

of agrarian reform. Martinico named two other sons Cássio (Cassius) and Cícero. The giving of classical names, relatively rare in the 1870s and 1880s, later became more common in Brazil; see Freyre, *Ordem e progresso*, 1:cliv. Martinico himself had a slave named Tibério (Tiberius), whose escape and Martinico's tantrumlike reaction to it are described in von Binzer, *Alegrias e tristezas*, 80–81.

56 Von Binzer, *Alegrias e tristezas*, 86–87. Cf. Antônio Candido's remarks, pp. 7–8 above.

57 Ibid., 95. The "permissiveness" Ina von Binzer described in Martinico's household may possibly represent her own culturally biased point of view rather than the eccentricity of Martinico's family; however, she makes little point of it in discussing other Brazilian families she served. Caio Prado Júnior has posited the view that indiscipline was more the rule than the exception in colonial times. Empirical studies of this question are lacking, however, and the history of child-rearing and discipline in Brazil is an almost completely unexplored topic.

58 Luíz Prado, "Biografia de D. Veridiana," 7–8. A different version of the story was told me by Caio Prado Júnior, Martinico's grandson. According to him, upon learning the identity of his young assailant, the emperor did not smile but became truly angry. Interview, Caio Prado Júnior, São Paulo, 13 April 1972. The two versions, the former from the "orthodox" side of the family and the latter from the "radical" side, show the persistence of attitudinal and ideological splits in the family long after the event in question.

59 Luíz Prado, "Biografia de D. Veridiana," 7.

60 "Testamento de D. Viridiana Valesia [*sic*] da Silva Prado," São Paulo, 25 September 1888, *LSP.*

CHAPTER III. EUROPE DISCOVERED

1 Freyre, *Sobrados e mucambos*, 1:309–10; Emília Costa Nogueira, "Alguns aspectos da influência francesa em São Paulo na segunda metade do século XIX," 340. Additional sources on nineteenth-century cultural developments include Freyre's *Ingleses no Brasil*, and, for São Paulo, Morse, *From Community to Metropolis*, chaps. 7–8, 11, and 13.

Portions of this chapter and chapter 7 were previously published as "The Prado Family, European Culture, and the Rediscovery of Brazil, 1860–1930," in State University of New York, *Proceedings of Conference at Brockport, New York* (Buffalo, 1973), 135–63, and in the *Revista de História* 52, no. 104 (October–December 1975): 803–24.

2 For an excellent comparison of Brazil and Britain in 1850, see Richard Graham, *Britain and the Onset of Modernization in Brazil,* 1–22.

3 Among numerous examples are: Luis Viana Filho, *A vida do Barão do Rio Branco;* Nabuco, *Minha formação;* Manuel de Oliveira Lima, *Memórias;* and André Rebouças, *Diário e notas autobiográficas.*

4 See above, pp. 24–25.

5 Barros, *No tempo de dantes,* 11; *Primeiro centenário,* 223; Caio Prado to Elias Chaves, São Paulo, 7 February 1868, *JPC* 920/C512/CO/A1.

6 Fletcher and Kidder, *Brazil and the Brazilians,* 364–65. Decades later, however, in 1882, Ina von Binzer wrote her German correspondent about São Paulo: "We are a university city. But don't think of Bonn or Heidelberg, because the academy here is only a law school"; von Binzer, *Alegrias e tristezas,* 77. São Paulo did not have a full-fledged university until 1932.

7 Nogueira, "Influência francesa," 333.

8 Ibid., 322–23.

9 MS account book of Martinho Prado, 1856–64, *LSP.* On 2 April 1856, Martinho entered an expenditure of one conto ($560) for an imported piano. Other entries were made for dancing masters, imported wines, books, and picture frames.

10 His father's account book entry of 24 July 1862 shows that Antônio's passage to Lisbon cost 1:492$250. Antônio's expenses in Europe in 1864 were 15:250$730.

11 Antônio Prado to Veridiana and Martinho Prado, Paris, 7 November 1862, *LSP.*

12 Antônio Prado to Veridiana Prado, Paris, 24 November 1862, *AAMB.*

13 Antônio Prado to Veridiana Prado, Lisbon, 28 July 1862; London, 8 September and 24 November 1862; Paris, 24 February 1863; Frankfurt, 3 August 1863, *AAMB.*

14 Antônio Prado to Veridiana Prado, London, 8 September 1862, *AAMB.*

15 Antônio Prado to Veridiana and Martinho Prado, London, 23 September 1862, *LSP.*

16 Antônio Prado to Martinho Prado, London, 8 October 1862, *AAMB.* Four years later, as a deputy in the provincial assembly of São Paulo, Antônio introduced measures to promote cotton growing, which he saw as a small-farm alternative to the dominance of large-property coffee agriculture; São Paulo (Província), Assembléia Legislativa, *Anais* (1866), 230–34. Largely because of preferential tariffs favoring coffee production, Brazil failed to profit much from the cotton crisis; see Frank Lawrence Owsley, *King Cotton Diplomacy,* 137, 143, 265.

17 Antônio Prado to Veridiana Prado, Paris, 23 October 1862, *AAMB.*

18 Antônio Prado to Veridiana and Martinho Prado, Paris, 7 November 1862, *LSP.*

19 Probably Marie Alfred Jules Girardin (1832–88), professor of literature and novelist.

20 Antônio Prado to Veridiana Prado, Paris, 24 January 1862 [*sic*, for 1863], *AAMB*. In this letter, in response to Veridiana's direct inquiry, Antônio also observed that London's women were "in general very pretty; . . . on the other hand, French women are rarely pretty, and one does not see any but are painted white and with their hair powdered, which is horrible."

21 Antônio Prado to Veridiana Prado, Rome, 14 April 1863, *AAMB*. Antônio made similar observations in Germany, interpreting the situation there as a struggle to overcome the feudal past; Antônio Prado to Veridiana Prado, Frankfort, 3 August 1863, *AAMB*.

22 Antônio Prado to Veridiana Prado, Paris, 7 June 1863, *LSP*. Although no proof exists, it is likely that Antônio read the *Life of Jesus*, which prompted hundreds of press articles in praise and damnation within a year of its publication. For Renan, see Harold William Wardman, *Ernest Renan*. Renan's work had a significant impact in Brazil; see Nabuco, *Minha formação*, chap. 7; and Motta Filho, *A vida de Eduardo Prado*, 109–14.

23 Antônio Prado to Veridiana Prado, Paris, 7 June 1863, *LSP*. As minister of agriculture in the late 1880s, having grudgingly moved to an abolitionist stance, Antônio adopted a modification of part of this slogan to symbolize his policy: "Free labor in a free country."

24 Antônio Prado to Veridiana Prado, Paris, 24 May 1863, *LSP*.

25 Richard Graham, "Os fundamentos da ruptura de relações diplomáticas entre o Brasil e a Grã-Bretanha em 1863."

26 Antônio Prado to Martinho Prado, Paris, 7 March 1863, *AAMB*.

27 Antônio Prado to Veridiana Prado, London, 22 June 1863, *AAMB*.

28 Antônio Prado to Veridiana Prado, Brussels, 7 July 1863, *AAMB*.

29 Antônio Prado to Veridiana Prado, Paris, 24 October 1863, *AAMB*.

30 Antônio Prado to Veridiana Prado, Paris, 7 November 1863, *AAMB*.

31 Antônio Prado to Veridiana Prado, Paris, 24 December 1863, *LSP*.

32 Ibid. Antônio did evidently translate some verses of the Brazilian poet Antônio Gonçalves Dias (1823–64) into French; see Nazareth Prado, *Antonio Prado*, 19.

33 Antônio Prado to Veridiana Prado, Paris, 24 March 1864, *AAMB*.

34 *IM:MPJ*, 15, 265–69.

35 Interview, Caio Prado Júnior, São Paulo, 13 April 1972.

36 *IM:MPJ*, 313–14. Louis-Nathaniel Rossel was the first professional soldier hired by the commune, became its military commander, resigned over civilian interference in the commune's military matters, was captured and shot by royalists; see Roger L. Williams, *The French Revolution of 1870–1871*, 143–44.

37 São Paulo (Província), Assembléia, *Discurso proferido . . . em sessão de 28 de fevereiro de 1878 por Martinho Prado Junior*, 22–23.

38 São Paulo (Província), Assembléia, *Discurso proferido . . . em sessão de 19 de março de 1879 por Martinho Prado Junior*, 27–28. Martinico's knowledge of English history was based in part on Sir Thomas Erskine May's *Constitutional History of England* (1861–63), cited in this speech.

39 São Paulo (Província), Assembléia, *Discurso proferido na sessao de 20 de março de 1879 por Martinho Prado Junior*, 12.

40 São Paulo (Povíncia), Assembléia, *Discurso proferido . . . em sessao de 19 de março de 1879*, 44–45.

41 *IM:MPJ*, 257.

42 São Paulo (Província), Assembléia Legislativa, *Os deputados republicanos na Assembléia Provincial de São Paulo*, 60.

43 Maria Catarina Prado to Paulo Prado, Paris, 10 September 1897, *AAMB*.

44 Freyre, *Sobrados e mucambos*, 1:333–34.

45 "Declarações de D. Antonieta Arinos e Dr. Luíz Prado."

46 Brotero, *Família Jordão*, 115; *IM:MPJ*, [393], [396]. Three of Ana Blandina's four daughters married into the defunct French aristocracy, establishing lines of French cousins who continue to visit their Paulista kin today.

  Ana Blandina, known in the family as "Chuchuta," was described to me as a rather severe, traditional, and moralistic woman. After his first wife, Eudoxia da Cunha Bueno, died in 1922, Luíz Prado married a French woman in Paris in 1924. When he sent his aunt, Ana Blandina, a visiting card announcing this marriage, she sent him a note saying, in effect, "When you come to see me, bring certificates of religious and civil marriage; otherwise don't come." Interview, Luíz Prado, Santa Veridiana, 12 March 1972.

47 Ricardo Gumbleton Daunt, ed., *Diário da Princesa Isabela*, 37.

48 Wanderly Pinho, *Salões e damas do segundo reinado*, 103. Originally a small farm, *chácara* here means a large suburban house with extensive grounds. For the chácara's distinctiveness as a Paulista residential style, see Barros, *A cidade e o planalto*, 1:230–42.

49 Ortigão, "Carta a Eduardo Prado," 9.

50 Luíz Prado, "Biografia de D. Veridiana," 8.

51 See chap. 7.

52 Queiroz, *Obras*, 3:1618, 1629. Photos of the Prado family taken on this occasion are reproduced (and incorrectly dated) in Motta Filho, *A vida de Eduardo Prado*, between xxiii and 1.

53 Interview, Luíz Prado, São Paulo, 23 February 1972.

54 Luíz Prado, "Biografia de D. Veridiana," 10.

55 Even within São Paulo province, there may have been considerable variety; Warren Dean writes of the planters of the município of Rio Claro that they "were not much given to literature—'three books, one of domestic medicine, a work by Jesus Christ, and *Duas horas mariannas.'*" See Dean, *Rio Claro*, 45.

CHAPTER IV. COFFEE CAPITALISTS

1 See Alfred W. Crosby, Jr., *The Columbian Exchange*, esp. chap. 3.
2 Paulo R. Pestana, "A expansão de lavoura cafeeira em São Paulo," 110–14. An *arroba* weighed between twenty-five and thirty-two pounds, varying regionally.
3 For a particularly critical view of the coffee boom and the planter class see Dean, *Rio Claro*, which attempts to rectify traditional proplanter historiography. A more balanced account is Thomas Holloway, *Immigrants on the Land*. Other sources in the extensive literature include Celso Furtado, *The Economic Growth of Brazil*; Taunay, *História do café*; Pierre Monbeig, *Pionniers et planteurs de São Paulo*; Paul Singer, *Desenvolvimento econômico e evolução urbana*; Emília Viotti da Costa, *Da senzala à colônia*; and Paula Beiguelman, "A grande imigração em São Paulo."
4 Petrone, "Um comerciante," 126–27.
5 "Diário da Caixa Filial do Banco do Brasil" (1858), MS in *Coleção Antônio da Silva Prado*, vol. 1, fols. 6–7. Making up 8.5 percent of the stockholders, the Prados held 25 percent of the stock. Stockholders related to them included members of the Sousa Queiros, da Silva, de Morais, da Fonseca, Queiros Teles, Pacheco, and Silva Teles families.
6 "Declarações de D. Antonieta Arinos e Dr. Luiz Prado."
7 Martinho Prado, MS diary, fol. 123.
8 *IM:MPJ*, 10. The *alqueire* in São Paulo equaled about six acres. For the chaotic conditions of land occupation and ownership in São Paulo, persisting well into the twentieth century, see Holloway, *Immigrants on the Land*, chap. 5.
9 Martinho Prado, MS account book, 1856–64, *LSP*. For detailed figures, see Appendix B.
10 *IM:MPJ*, 11; Monbeig, *Pionniers et planteurs*, 123. The exchange rate of the milreis dropped from fifty-four cents in 1889 to thirty cents in 1891, so that the foreign exchange value of Martinho's fortune was nearly twice as much in the late empire.
11 Luíz Prado, "Fazenda Santa Veridiana," 1–2.
12 Taunay, *História do cafe*, 7:376, 170, 185.

13 C. F. van Delden Laërne, *Brazil and Java*, 325–27, 334–35.

14 For families involved in the coffee expansion in the Paulista west, see Alfredo Ellis Júnior, *O café e a paulistânia*, 352; and Antônio Machado Sant'Anna, "Cidadãos do mundo," 1.

15 *IM:MPJ*, 335, 343–44, 347–48.

16 Ibid., 345–46. Note Antônio Prado's plan to promote small-farm cotton agriculture, p. 218, n. 16 above.

17 Holloway's *Immigrants on the Land* documents the acquisition of substantial rural property by immigrants and thus severely challenges the thesis of other scholars that the advent of free labor in São Paulo merely resulted in the substitution of debased white workers for black slaves.

18 *IM:MPJ*, 24; see also "Bandeirantes do café: Dr. Martinho Prado Junior." Twenty years after its foundation, Guatapará was evaluated at ninety times its purchase price. See Appendix D.

19 The locale of São Martinho was later included in the new município of Sertãozinho, brought into existence by a law of 5 December 1896 and formally organized on 21 April 1897; Instituto Brasileiro de Geografia e Estatística, *Enciclopédia dos municípios brasileiros*, 30:293–94.

20 *IM:MPJ*, 22–23; *Companhia Prado Chaves Exportadora*, 43–45; Luiz Bueno de Miranda, "Ilustre família," *Primeiro centenário*, 138. For acreage and other statistics, see Appendix D.

21 Dean, *Rio Claro*, 1.

22 Ibid., 51, 68, 117, 123.

23 Washington Prado, *Historia de uma cidade bandeirante*, 73–76. One judge disqualified himself because he was a Prado relative.

24 Antônio Prado to Veridiana Prado, Paris, 7 March 1864, *LSP*.

25 MS diary of Antônio Prado, December 1867–January 1868, typed copy, Archive of Caio Prado Júnior, p. 4. Portions of this diary were published in Hélio Viana, "Um diário de mocidade do Conselheiro Antònio Prado," *Primeiro centenário*, 155–62.

26 Dean, *Rio Claro*, 86.

27 Provincial Assembly speech, 16 March 1882, *IM:MPJ*, 184.

28 Martinico Prado to Elias Chaves, Santa Cruz, 26 December 1876, Sampaio Archive.

29 Von Binzer, *Alegrias e tristezas*, 80–81.

30 A cousin, João Elias Pacheco Chaves Jordão, had a large force of 180 immigrants working on his fazenda in Rio Claro in 1854; Costa, *Senzala á colônia*, 83.

31 See p. 58 above.

32 Beiguelman, "A grande imigração," 103.

33 MS contract of Martinho Prado with the Associação Auxiliadora de Colonisaçao e Emigração [*sic*, for "Imigração"] na Província de São Paulo (n.d., ca. 1872–73), *JPC*, 920/C512d/A1.
34 Provincial Assembly speech, 16 March 1882, *IM:MPJ*, 190–92. Martinico still opposed importing slaves for sale.
35 Antônio Prado, "Notas sobre a colonisação em S. Paulo," 195. Although in 1884 Martinico apparently argued the unprofitability of free labor as an incontestable fact, on another occasion he claimed that one free worker produced as much as three slaves, a contradiction explainable in terms of crude accounting techniques as well as political exigencies of the moment; see Dean, *Rio Claro*, 140; and [Maria] Teresa Schorer Petrone, "Imigração assalariada," 3:275, n. 1. Dean argues that free labor was more profitable, although most slaveowners of the time believed otherwise.
36 Michael M. Hall, "The Origins of Mass Migration in Brazil, 1871–1914," 90–93.
37 *Correio Paulistano*, 9 April 1886, 3:4, and 1 July 1886, 3:3.
38 Ibid., 4 July 1886, 2:3. Of the twenty-one members of the society listed here, six were members of the titled nobility and several were former presidents or vice-presidents of São Paulo. Numerically most prominent, with five signers of the contract, was the Sousa Queiros family, Prado cousins.
39 Petrone, "Imigração assalariada," 281; *IM:MPJ*, 233–34, 365–67.
40 São Paulo (Província), Assembléia Legislativa, *Os deputados republicanos*, 47.
41 Petrone, "Imigração assalariada," 281.
42 Robert Brent Toplin, *The Abolition of Slavery in Brazil*, 106, 133, 139, 163, 230–33, 237, 242, and 244; and Robert Conrad, *The Destruction of Brazilian Slavery, 1850–1888*, 103, 228–35, 249–54. A more recent, extremely careful account is Thomas H. Holloway's "Immigration and Abolition."
43 Hall, "Origins of Mass Migration," 103.
44 Rui Barbosa, *Obras completas*, vol. 16, *Queda do Império*, 3:101–7, 113–16.
45 Laërne, *Brazil and Java*, 359–60. Laërne is not clear on this matter, but it appears that before the wage reduction immigrants were paid six hundred *reis* (twenty-six cents) per forty-five liters of coffee picked and that after it they received five hundred *reis* per fifty liters. In addition to wages, the immigrants at Santa Veridiana received: (1) free lodgings; (2) the right to plant beans, but not corn, in the coffee groves for their subsistence; (3) free pasture for two animals; (4) free arable land near

their houses for other subsistence crops; (5) advances on wages at 6 percent interest; and (6) free Portuguese-language schooling for their children in reading, writing, and arithmetic.

46 Louis Couty, *Le Brésil en 1884*, 162–63; Laërne, *Brazil and Java*, 360–61. Such profits, however, were far from common.

47 Couty, *Le Brésil en 1884*, 163, 329–30.

48 Pedro Brasil Bandecchi, "Documento sobre a imigração italiano em Ribeirão Prêto," 601–5.

49 The otherwise careful study by Holloway, *Immigrants on the Land*, 98 and 191 n. 53.

50 Ibid., chap. 4.

51 Alfred Marc, *Le Brésil*, 2:348; *A província de São Paulo no Brazil*, 50–55. My thanks to Thomas Holloway for calling this source to my attention. Holloway notes that in 1887 "in some areas of high demand, landowners offered de facto freedmen wages of 20 to 25 milreis per month plus food, but a more common wage rate was 15 milreis for men and 6 to 10 milreis for women, with food provided"; immigrant day workers could get 1 to 3 milreis per day and 15 to 25 per month. See Holloway's "Immigration and Abolition," 170–71. For additional information on immigrants' wages, see da Costa, *Da senzala á colônia*, 195–200; Dean, *Rio Claro*; and Holloway, *Immigrants on the Land*.

52 Marc, *Le Brésil*, 348–55; for details see Appendix C. According to Marc, immigrants were generally furnished, free, a house, pasturage for a horse and a cow, and two hectares (five acres) of land for food crops (cf. n. 45 above). Marc reported that Italians had acquired property worth 5,233,518 francs (about $1.2 million) by the late 1880s, as estimated by the Italian consul in São Paulo.

53 Max Leclerc, *Cartas do Brasil*, 83–87. Pictures of colono houses in Holloway's *Immigrants on the Land*, 80–81, bear a strong resemblance to those I observed at Fazenda Santa Veridiana in 1972, except that when I saw them television antennas sprouted from every rooftop.

54 "Contracto de empreitada para o plantio de 200.000 pés do café," MS in Fernando Chaves Papers; see Appendix E.

55 São Paulo (Estado), Secretaria de Agricultura, *Estatistica agricola e zootechnica no anno agricola de 1904–1905*, municípios of Araras, Mattão, Ribeirão Prêto, Sertãozinho, and Santa Cruz das Palmeiras. See Appendix D.

56 Baron of Iguape to Queiros Teles, São Paulo, 8 October 1863, *AAMB*.

57 *A Província de São Paulo*, 8 August 1876, 2:1, and 9 May 1876, 3:1. Antônio received rental rights for fifteen years and stood to make a large profit even if he rented the theater only once a week.

58 Adolfo Augusto Pinto, *História da viação pública de S. Paulo*, 32.

59 Robert H. Mattoon, Jr., "Railroads, Coffee, and the Growth of Big Business in São Paulo, Brazil," 274–75. The São Paulo Railway was also known as the Santos-Jundiaí and the Companhia Inglêza (English Company). For Mauá, see Anyda Marchant, *Viscount Mauá and the Empire of Brazil.*

60 Robert H. Mattoon, Jr., "The Companhia Paulista de Estradas de Ferro," 63–66, 92, and appendix D, where in various years between 1869 and 1900, Prados are shown as owning from 3 to 9 percent of the railroad's stock.

The Paulista Railway was formally known at different times as the *Companhia Paulista de Estradas de Ferro* (Paulista Railroad Company) and as the *Companhia Paulista de Vias Ferréas e Fluviaes* (Paulista Rail and Water Lines Company).

61 *A Província de São Paulo*, 3 August 1876, 1:5, and 4 August 1876, 2:2. For details of the Mato Grosso route controversy see Mattoon, "Companhia Paulista," chap. 4.

62 Ibid., 99; Pinto, *História da viaçao pública*, 44; Mattoon, "Railroads, Coffee, and Big Business," 285. Dean notes that the viscount of Rio Claro and the count of Três Rios used their political influence to have personal sidings located at their fazendas on the Rio Claro Railroad (Dean, *Rio Claro*, 43). For Antônio's presidency of the Paulista Railway see chap. 8 below.

63 Eduardo Prado to Pedro Vicente de Azevedo, president of São Paulo, London, 17 October 1888, in Eduardo Prado, *Copiadoras de cartas*, vol. 1, looseleaf insert, fols. 2–12. Collection cited hereafter as Eduardo Prado, *Copiadoras.*

64 Penedo was a director of the English-owned São Paulo Railway; see Marchant, *Viscount of Mauá*, 238.

65 Renato Mendonça, *Um diplomata na côrte de Inglaterra*, 412–16.

66 The classic statement is Friedrich Engels, *The Origin of the Family, Private Property, and the State.*

67 Dean, *Rio Claro*, 197. Cf. Holloway, *Immigrants on the Land*, 167: "Only the income potential of the large-scale agricultural enterprise could attract the initial investment and transport infrastructure without which the productive capacity of the São Paulo hinterland would have remained only potential."

CHAPTER V. THE POLITICS OF FAMILY, 1868–1889

1 José Maria Bello, *A History of Modern Brazil, 1889–1964*, xvi. General treatments of the era's politics include: Bello, *History of Modern*

Brazil, chaps. 1–3; C. H. Haring, *Empire in Brazil;* Burns, *A History of Brazil*, chaps. 3–4; and Sérgio Buarque de Hollanda, *Do império à república*, vol. 5, tome 2 of his *História geral da civilização brasileira*. More specialized are: Victor Nunes Leal, *Coronelismo, enxada e voto;* Maria Isaura Pereira de Queiroz, *O mandonismo local na vida política brasileira;* and Emília Costa Nogueira, "O movimento republicano em Itú." An analysis of the political elite is Eul-Soo Pang and Ron L. Sickinger, "The Mandarins of Imperial Brazil." See also the introductory essay and readings in Alfred C. Stepan, "The Continuing Problem of Brazilian Integration."

2 For excerpts from the 1824 constitution, see E. Bradford Burns, ed., *A Documentary History of Brazil*, 211–18.

3 See the discussion in Hollanda, *Do império à república*, vol. 5, tome 2, 70–73.

4 Fletcher and Kidder, *Brazil and the Brazilians*, 183. The Liberals claimed a remote connection to the republican movements of the late colonial period, the First Empire (1822–31), and the Regency (1831–40), but this had no operative significance in the Second Empire. *Conservative* and *Liberal* are capitalized in the text only to identify parties; when lowercased the words denote broad ideological stances.

5 Caio Prado Júnior, *Evolução política do Brasil*, 193.

6 See Nogueira, "O movimento republicano em Itú." Fewer than 20,000 slaves of an estimated 1.5 million in 1872 were freed under the Law of the Free Womb; see Rollie E. Poppino, *Brazil: The Land and the People*, 174.

7 Caio Prado Júnior, *Evolução política do Brasil*, 171–95.

8 This, of course, was true of Martinico Prado.

9 Costa, *Da senzala à colônia*, 464.

10 Brasil, Ministério da Justiça e Negócios Interiores, Arquivo Nacional, *Organizações e programas ministeriais*, 231–33, 239, 352, 359, 386, 395.

11 Brasil, Câmara dos Deputados, *Anais*, 1888, 1:22.

12 João Fernando de Almeida Prado, "Paulo Prado e a época de sua formação," 103; Pinto, "Lutas de família," 35–36.

13 See, for example, Chandler, *Feitosas*, chap. 3, "Families and Parties: Government and Politics in the Time of Pedro II," which also contains a good description of provincial and local government.

14 For summaries of the careers of Antônio and Martinico Prado, see Rubens do Amaral, "Antônio Prado"; and José Maria dos Santos, "Martinho Prado Junior," in *IM:MPJ*, 69–84.

15 The baron was a member and occasional president of São Paulo's municipal council from 1849 to 1854. In late 1852 a clash occurred

between some members of that body and the provincial president. The council alleged that the president had exceeded his powers in revoking an election sanctioned by it and defied his orders to revise the election results. The president dismissed the council and selected the baron to form a new one more to his liking. See São Paulo (Cidade), *Registo geral da Câmara Municipal*, vols. 34–37, esp. 35:157–75 and 36:5–14.

16 Antônio Prado to Veridiana Prado, London, 8 October 1862, *LSP.*
17 Antônio Prado to Martinho Prado, Paris, 7 June 1863, *LSP.*
18 Ibid.
19 Antônio's exposure to English liberalism came at its height in the period 1850 to 1875; see David Thomson, *England in the Nineteenth Century*, 224–31.
20 Antônio Prado to Martinho Prado, Paris, 8 March 1864, *AAMB.*
21 Senate speech, 19 September 1887, reprinted in Nazareth Prado, *Antonio Prado*, 236.
22 Telegram, Joaquim Nabuco to Antônio Prado, Petrópolis, 24 February 1889, *LSP*; Carolina Nabuco, *The Life of Joaquim Nabuco*, 173; *Gazeta da Tarde* (Rio), 22 June 1889, quoted in Nelson Werneck Sodré, *História da imprensa no Brasil*, 275. Antônio steered clear of the separatist solution urged by some Paulistas but may have been influenced by some of their arguments. A close friend and future father-in-law of Nazareth Prado, Francisco Eugénio Pacheco e Silva, was author of the separatist pamphlet *A zona paulista.*
23 Senate speech, 2 September 1886, reprinted in Nazareth Prado, *Antonio Prado*, 124–25.
24 Presidential message, quoted in Jayme de Altavila, "Antônio Caio da Silva Prado em Alagoas (1887–1888)," 191; see also p. 194.
25 José Aurélio Saraiva Câmara, *Fatos e documentos do Ceará provincial*, 273–74.
26 Caio Prado to Veridiana Prado, Fortaleza, 11 October 1888 (copy), Cerqueira Mendes file, Instituto de Estudos Brasileiros; original italics.
27 Eduardo Prado, "Destinos politicos do Brazil," 473; see also 481–91. Eduardo, however, cautioned against "a servile imitation of forms, an error which has cost the other Latin nations of America, where traditions of local government have not existed and where education is lacking, so much" (487).
28 São Paulo (Província), Assembléia, *Discurso proferido . . . em sessão de 28 de fevereiro de 1878*, 17ff.
29 São Paulo (Província), Assembléia, *Discurso proferido . . . em sessão de 19 de março de 1879*, 35–45.
30 See chap. 3 above.
31 *IM:MPJ*, 301–4, where Silva Bueno's attack is also reproduced.

32 "Cópias fac-similares de circular em que o Cons. A. Prado apresenta-se
    como candidato a deputado," Rio, 20 August 1868, *JPC*,
    324.81/P896c/A1.

33 "Circular apresentando chapa de deputados provinciais, por Joaquim
    Octavio Nebias, Anto. da Costa Pinto e Silva, e Antônio da Silva
    Prado," Rio de Janeiro, 25 September 1869, *JPC*, 324.81/C578/A1.

34 Antônio Prado, "Discurso contra exclusão da Assembleia Provincial
    como representante do 3º districto," MS in *AAMB*; *IM:MPJ*, 300.

35 Nazareth Prado, *Antonio Prado*, 20; Costa, *Da senzala à colônia*, 382;
    Conrad, *The Destruction of Brazilian Slavery*, 103; *IM:MPJ*, 310–12.

36 Nogueira, *A academia de São Paulo*, 1:60; Howard Allen Marcus,
    "Provincial Government in São Paulo," 88–90. Perhaps because of
    political warfare in São Paulo, Antônio's record in the national
    Chamber of Deputies from 1869 to 1875 was undistinguished. He was
    often absent from its sessions and, except for filibustering against the
    Law of the Free Womb, took no significant part in its deliberations.
    Brasil, Camara dos Deputados, *Anais*, 1869–75.

37 *A Província de São Paulo*, 6 December 1876, 2:5. Martinico said later
    that he rejected Mendes because of the Republicans' repugnance for the
    latter's "religious fanaticism"—the phrase recalls Antônio Prado's
    reaction to Rome—"which could cause such evil." Personally,
    Martinico saw Mendes as a "dangerous man, capable of lighting
    inquisitorial fires." *A Província de São Paulo*, 8 December 1876, 2:2.

38 In an attack on the corruption of Paulista Conservatives, Martinico
    excepted Francisco Alves dos Santos, who he said acted out of
    misunderstanding, not bad character. Ibid., 30 March, 31 March, and 4
    April 1876.

39 Rodrigo Silva to Antônio Prado, São Paulo, 11 November 1885; Prado to
    Silva, Rio de Janeiro, 14 November 1885, *AAMB*. Between them, these
    two Paulista Conservatives kept the crucial Ministry of Agriculture in
    Paulista hands from 1885 to 1889.

40 See above, p. 47.

41 Afonso Celso, *Oito anos de parlamento*, 82.

42 Unidentified newspaper clipping, file 24.710, Archive of *O Estado de
    São Paulo*.

43 Quoted in Carolina Nabuco, *Life of Joaquim Nabuco*, 80. Martinico's
    approach to abolition was still gradualist, however; see *IM:MPJ*, 201–2.
    His attitude toward the role of blacks in Brazilian society was
    romanticized and somewhat condescending, though still progressive for
    the time; see Martinho Prado Júnior, *Circular de . . . candidato
    republicano à assembleia geral pelo 9º districto da provincia de São
    Paulo*, 8–9.

44 *IM:MPJ*, 373–78.

45 Quotes from Carolina Nabuco, *Life of Joaquim Nabuco*, 158, 162–63; see also Joaquim Nabuco, *Minha formação*, 195, 207.

46 Adler, *The Individual Psychology of Alfred Adler*, 376ff.

47 Irving D. Harris, *The Promised Seed: A Comparative Study of Eminent First and Later Sons*, esp. 10–11, where the hypothesis is stated. The youngest Prado brothers, Caio and Eduardo, were, of course, Conservatives. Neither was a career politician in the sense that Antônio and Martinico were, however. Their rebellion took the form of dabbling in "bohemian" circles. Harris discusses the "heroic" and "militant" types characteristic of first- and later-borns, respectively, in chap. 4.

48 Provincial Assembly speech, 8 March 1888, *IM:MPJ*, 247ff.

49 Provincial Assembly speech, 16 March 1882, *IM:MPJ*, 196.

50 Everardo Vallim Pereira de Sousa applied the term *casmurrice* directly to Antônio; see his "Reminiscências," *Primeiro centenário*, 224. The syndrome of casmurrice is most sensitively elaborated in Machado de Assis's novel *Dom Casmurro*.

51 Victor Malin, "Colombo politico," *A Comédia*, 21 May 1881, 1. "Meeting" in English in original.

52 Ibid.

53 São Paulo (Província), Assembléia Legislativa, *Anais*, 1885, 71–73.

54 Martinho Prado Júnior, *Circular de . . . candidato republicano*, 3–4.

55 Martinico finished a poor third in the election, receiving only 237 of 1,368 votes; Brasil, Câmara dos Deputados, *Anais*, 1886, 1:36.

56 *A Comédia*, 22 April 1881, 2–3.

57 Joaquim José da Silva Xavier (1746–92), whose nickname, "Toothpuller," reflected his part-time profession.

58 "Outr'oura cantava o Tira / Dentes, hoje tira dentes / Á Republica, o Men-Tira / Outr'oura cantava, o Tira / Casaca, casaca vira / E enche a pausa dos parentes." *A Comédia*, 7 May 1881.

59 Eduardo Prado, "Destinos politicos do Brazil," 471, and his *Collectaneas*, 2:8.

60 Pang and Seckinger, "Mandarins of Imperial Brazil," 239–44.

CHAPTER VI. FAMILY LIFE IN THE FIRST REPUBLIC

1 Freyre, *Ordem e progresso*. The quotation is from the book's subtitle.

2 Luis Martins, "O patriarca e o bacharel."

3 "In truth, the Prados and the Penteados exercised their hegemony, even outside the country, for a period of almost forty years [1880–1914?]." Paulo Cursino de Moura, *São Paulo de outrora*, 56.

4 Warren Dean, *The Industrialization of São Paulo*, 73.

5 Freyre, *Ordem e progresso*, 2:391.
6 Maria Catarina Prado to Paulo Prado, São Paulo, 19 October 1891, *LSP*.
7 Maria Catarina Prado to Paulo Prado, São Paulo, 25 October 1891, *AAMB*, and 8 November 1891, *LSP*.
8 Maria Catarina Prado to Paulo Prado, São Paulo, 8 December 1891, *AAMB*.
9 Maria Catarina Prado to Paulo Prado, Caxambú, 13 March and 8 April 1892, *AAMB*, and 26 March 1892, *LSP*.
10 Maria Catarina Prado to Paulo Prado, Santa Veridiana, 6 June 1892, *LSP*.
11 Luíz Prado, "Fazenda Santa Veridiana," typescript (1944), 7, *LSP*.
12 Maria Catarina Prado to Paulo Prado, Santa Veridiana, 25 July 1892, *LSP*.
13 Maria Catarina Prado to Paulo Prado, São Paulo, 25 October 1891, *AAMB*.
14 Maria Catarina Prado to Paulo Prado, 6 August 1892, *AAMB*. The resort was founded in 1892, and Elias Fausto Pacheco Jordão, who had studied civil engineering at Cornell University from 1869 to 1874, served as its president. He imported for it a complete fifty-room hotel, a church, a casino, and forty-six houses made of Georgia pine. Pedro Luis Pereira de Sousa, *Meus cinqüenta anos na Companhia Prado Chaves*, 67.
15 The *Correio Paulistano* of 10 April 1896 contains a full description of the reception.
16 Interview, Luíz Prado, São Paulo, 7 August 1972. A year later, Maria Catarina, who blamed the doctors for her daughter's death, still wrote of her "assassination." Maria Catarina Prado to Paulo Prado, São Paulo, 20 December 1897, *LSP*.
17 J. F. de Almeida Prado, "Paulo Prado," 96–97.
18 Brotero implies that Paulo had an illegitimate but subsequently recognized son, Paulo Caio Prado, who later became a manager of the Prado-Chaves Export House; see *Família Jordão*, 92–93. It may have been with this in mind that the historian Capistrano de Abreu later wrote teasingly to Paulo, "According to the philosopher [Herbert Spencer], the perfection of the future family will consist of the growing love of sons for parents. For my part I would add to that the veneration of widows and the prenuptial virginity of males." João Capistrano de Abreu, *Correspondência*, 2:397.
19 Maria Catarina Prado to Paulo Prado, 22 January 1891, *LSP*.
20 Maria Catarina Prado to Paulo Prado, São Paulo, 20 May 1892, *AAMB*.
21 Maria Catarina Prado to Paulo Prado, Caxambú, 26 April 1894, *AAMB*.
22 Maria Catarina Prado to Paulo Prado, São Paulo, 23 March 1896, and Paris, 18 June 1897, *AAMB*.

23 Paulo's reply is summarized in Maria Catarina Prado to Paulo Prado, Paris, 6 August 1897, *AAMB.*

24 Maria Catarina Prado to Paulo Prado, São Paulo, 21 February 1892, *LSP.*

25 Maria Catarina Prado to Paulo Prado, Lisbon, 22 July 1893, *AAMB.*

26 Interview, Luíz Prado, São Paulo, 19 March 1972.

27 *Sao Paulo "Magazine"* 1, no. 2 (15 June 1906): 67–69.

28 Ibid. The description of elite women as "ornaments" was typical of the time.

29 Maria Catarina Prado to Paulo Prado, São Paulo, 5 September 1892, *AAMB.*

30 Maria Catarina Prado to Paulo Prado, Santa Veridiana, 11 November 1893, *LSP.*

31 Interview, Ana Cândida Ferraz Sampaio (Nazareth's daughter), São Paulo, 5 July 1972. See also Joel Silveira, "Graça Aranha e o 'Diario Íntimo' de D. Nazareth Prado," in *Grã-finos em São Paulo e outras notícias do Brasil.*

32 Maria Catarina Prado to Paulo Prado, São Paulo, 8 January 1892, *AAMB.*

33 Maria Catarina Prado to Paulo Prado, Santa Veridiana, 7 July 1892, *AAMB.*

34 Maria Catarina Prado to Paulo Prado, São Paulo, 30 September 1893, *LSP.*

35 Maria Catarina Prado to Paulo Prado, 3 October 1892, quoted in Motta Filho, *A Vida de Eduardo Prado,* 136, n. 7.

36 Interview, Luíz Prado, São Paulo, 12 March 1972.

37 Eduardo Prado to Joaquim Nabuco, "Brejão," 11 January 1899, quoted in Nabuco, *The Life of Joaquim Nabuco,* 206, n. 2.

38 "Declarações de D. Antonieta Arinos e Dr. Luiz Prado." One of the young people whose company Veridiana preferred and who became her protégé has left his account of her; see Navarro de Andrade, "Dona Veridiana Prado."

39 Alzira Chaves to Miguel Chaves, 21 December 1923, 17 March 1924, and 8 August [192-], Miguel Chaves Papers. These and other letters in this collection reveal a loss of parental control similar to that in the Prado family.

40 Alzira Chaves to Miguel Chaves, single letter dated 8 and 16 September 1925, Miguel Chaves Papers.

41 Alzira Chaves to Miguel Chaves, São Paulo, 21 September 1923, Miguel Chaves Papers.

42 Luís de Assis Pacheco Júnior to Fernando Chaves, São Paulo, 27 September 1930, Fernando Chaves Papers, Museu Paulista. Martinho Prado Neto to Miguel Chaves, São Paulo, 23 May 1923, Miguel Chaves Papers.

43 "Escriptura de compra e venda de caza," 11 November 1890, and "Escriptura de compra e venda de predios," 29 October 1891, *AAMB*.
44 Interviews, Antônio Augusto Monteiro de Barros Neto, São Paulo, 3 August 1972, and Luíz Prado, Santa Veridiana, 18 June 1972.
45 See above, p. 8.
46 Tristão de Ataíde, "Eduardo Prado," consulted in Archive of *O Estado de São Paulo,* file 10.040.
47 Eça de Queiroz to Eduardo Prado, Paris, 15 August 1898, reprinted in Plínio Barreto, "Eduardo Prado e seus amigos," 194.
48 J. F. de Almeida Prado, "Paulo Prado," 106.
49 Tristão de Ataíde, "Os Prado"; original italics.
50 Adler, *Individual Psychology,* 376–82.
51 Morse, *From Community to Metropolis,* 174; Amaral, "Antônio Prado."
52 Tancredo do Amaral, *História de São Paulo ensinada pela biographia dos seus vultos mais notaveis;* Neves Junior, "Dr. Antônio Prado"; and "Dr. Antonio Prado," 1.
53 Afonso Celso de Assis Figueiredo (Afonso Celso), *Oito anos de parlamento,* 82.
54 See chap. 2 above; also, Maria Catarina Prado to Paulo Prado, Paris, 17 May 1891, *AAMB.*
55 These letters are discussed fully in chap. 3.
56 MS diary of Antonio Prado, December 1867–January 1868 (typed copy), p. 3. Archive of Caio Prado Júnior.
57 Article from *Diário da Noite,* 27 February 1940, reprinted in *Primeiro centenário,* 256–59; see also Edmundo Navarro de Andrade, "Antônio Prado," *Primeiro centenário,* 61.
58 Quoted in Everardo Vallim Pereira de Sousa, "Reminiscências," *Primeiro centenário,* 222.
59 Ibid., 224.
60 On the relation of personal and political rebellion, see Carl E. Schorske's superb article "Politics and Patricide in Freud's *Interpretation of Dreams.*"
61 *IM:MPJ,* 15, 265–69.
62 Antônio Prado to Veridiana Prado, London, 8 October 1862, *LSP.*
63 Photograph (1865), *IM:MPJ,* between 24 and 25.
64 Maria Catarina Prado to Paulo Prado, São Paulo, 31 October and 8 November 1891, *LSP.* Martinico's disillusionment with the Republic is discussed more fully in chap. 9.
65 Von Binzer, *Alegrias e tristezas,* 80–81, 95.
66 *A Comédia,* 22 April 1881, 2:3.
67 Guimarães, "Eduardo Prado," 587; Coelho Netto, "Eduardo Prado como

uma visão"; [Luís] Batista Pereira, *Eduardo Prado*, 13; Max Fleuiss, article in *A Manhã*; Daniel Bicudo, "Eduardo Prado, humorista."

68 Article signed "Syl," *O Comércio de São Paulo*, 2.

69 Luiz Viana Filho, *A vida do Barão do Rio Branco*, 182–83, 207, 253, 268. According to Luíz Prado, Veridiana was "nearly ruined by Eduardo"; Interview, Santa Veridiana, 12 March 1972. Despite his money problems, Eduardo felt compelled to pay for a gift of wine from Alexandre d'Atri, the Italian journalist, overcoming d'Atri's protests with "two military 'nos.' " Letter, d'Atri to an unknown correspondent, Paris, 10 July 1898, *JPC*, 920/P896cp/A1.

70 Maria Catarina Prado to Paulo Prado, São Paulo, 8 February 1896, *LSP*.

71 Guimarães, "Eduardo Prado," 591.

72 Andrade, "Páginas vívidas: Eduardo Prado," 48–49; Queiroz, *Obras*, 2:1624–25.

73 Josué Montello, "Um pouco de Eduardo Prado." In part, Eduardo's refusal was based on the academy's failure to offer support to writers, like Eduardo, who suffered official repression in Brazil.

74 See below, chap. 8.

75 It was Catholic fervor and reactionary politics that led to the Dreyfus affair in France; see David Thomson, *Europe Since Napoleon*, 344. Jean-Paul Sartre's *Anti-Semite and Jew* deals with anti-Semitism in the French setting which, Eça de Queiroz's disclaimer notwithstanding, so powerfully affected Eduardo. Sartre says of the anti-Semite: "He is a man who is afraid. Not of the Jews, to be sure, but of himself, of his own consciousness, of his liberty, of his instincts, or his responsibilities, of solitariness, of change, of society, and of the world— of everything except the Jews" (53).

76 Eduardo tried to get the Portuguese writer Oliveira Martins to do an article on anti-Semitism for Rio's *Jornal do Comércio*; the latter declined on the basis that the subject did not have much interest for the Brazilian public. Oliveira Martins to Eduardo, letter dated only "Lisbon, 21 [March 1891?]," *JPC*, 920/P896cp/A1. See also Prado to Martins, Paris, 24 March [1891] and Prado to J. C. Rodrigues, 31 March 1891, in Eduardo Prado, *Copiadoras*. On the relative absence of anti-Semitism in Brazil before the 1930s, see Robert M. Levine, "Brazil's Jews During the Vargas Era and After," 46–47.

77 Eduardo Prado, "O Catholicismo, a Companhia de Jesus, e a colonização do Brasil," 55–56.

78 Interview, Luíz Prado, São Paulo, 7 August 1972.

79 Brotero, *Família Jordão*, 78–82; João Francisco Velho Sobrinho, *Dicionário bio-bibliográfico brasileiro*, 1:555.

80 Armando Prado, *Discurso proferido no acto da collação de gráo aos*

bacharelandos em direito, 13–14, 18, 26–27, "Discurso," 56, and "Francisco Adolpho de Varnhagen," 139–40.

81 Thomas E. Skidmore, *Black into White*.

82 *IM:MPJ*, [393].

83 The Prados' sensitivity to this issue may have been heightened by the fact that they were subject to rumors of miscegenation beyond the fact of Eleutério's common-law marriage. See Freyre, *Ordem e progresso*, 1:clix, and "O que seria aquela coisa?" 3–6. I found no evidence to confirm either rumor and, in lieu of such, regard them as the malicious gossip characteristic of a society that was, after all, very conscious of "racial purity."

84 Interview, Antônio Augusto Monteiro de Barros Neto, São Paulo, 3 August 1972.

CHAPTER VII. EDUARDO AND PAULO REDISCOVER BRAZIL

1 The broad cultural mosaic of the period is elaborated in Freyre, *Ordem e progresso*. Briefer treatment of cultural developments in Brazil, set in the general Latin American context, is in Jean Franco, *The Modern Culture of Latin America*, 108–16, 292–97. For São Paulo's cultural ferment in the twentieth century, see Morse, *From Community to Metropolis*, chaps. 17 and 20.

2 E. Bradford Burns, *Nationalism in Brazil*, 8–9. For a brief survey of the recent literature and an analysis of the issues of Brazilian nationalism, see Darrell E. Levi, "Brazilian Nationalism: An Introduction," and "Brazilian Nationalism: Perspectives, Problems, Perplexities."

3 Franco, *Modern Culture*, 293.

4 Mário de Andrade, *O movimento modernista*, 28–29.

5 Rudyard Kipling, *Brazilian Sketches*, chaps. 3 and 6.

6 Alzira Chaves to Miguel Chaves, São Paulo, 25 March 1923, Miguel Chaves Papers.

7 Ataíde, "Eduardo Prado: sempre vivo."

8 Ibid., citing article of Gonzaga Duque in *Revista Contemporánea*, October 1900.

9 Nogueira, "Influência francesa em São Paulo," 326–34.

10 Lafayette de Toledo, "Imprensa paulista," 399. Examination of the paper, however, revealed no signed articles by Eduardo, though he was an editor of it.

11 Fernando Mendes, *Estudos de crítica*, 80.

12 Eduardo Prado, "Primeira dissertação do aluno no. 42 da Faculdade de Direito de S. Paulo."

13 *A Comédia,* 19 April 1881, 1.

14 Queiroz, *Obras,* 2:1617.

15 Eduardo Prado, *Viagens: A Sicilia, Malta, e o Egypto,* 5, 131–32, 140, 65.

16 Eduardo Prado, *Viagens: America, Oceania, e Asia,* 191.

17 Plínio Barreto, "Eduardo Prado e seus amigos," 187–89; Eduardo Prado, *Viagens: America, Oceania, e Asia,* 195–97.

18 Clodomiro Vianna Moog, *Eça de Queirós e o século XIX,* 295–96.

19 Levasseur, who wrote a history of French industry and the working classes as well as *The American Workman* (Baltimore, 1900), was the general editor of *Le Brésil* (Paris, [1899]), an extract from *La Grande Encyclopédie* (1886), to which Eduardo contributed essays on Brazilian art, literature, and immigration. These essays were also reprinted in F. J. de Sant'Anna Nery's *Le Brésil en 1889.* Reclus, best known for his monumental *Nouvelle Géographie Universelle* (Paris, 1876–94), was guided by Eduardo on a tour of the Paulista interior.

20 Queiroz, *Obras,* 2:1106, 1108.

21 Eduardo Prado, "Destinos politicos do Brasil," 476, 482, 488. For the influence of England on Eduardo see the essay "Victoria, R.I.," in his *Collectaneas,* 1:244–56, 261, 265.

22 Ramalho Ortigão to Eduardo, Lisbon, 19 November 1889, *JPC,* 920/P896cp/A1. See also Ortigão's "O quadro social da revolução brazileira," 81–90; and Moniz Barreto's review of Eduardo's *Fastos da dictadura militar no Brazil.*

23 For critical opinion, see João Alves das Neves, "Eça e Eduardo Prado," and Luis Martins, "Eduardo Prado: panfletário."

24 Ataíde, "Eduardo Prado: sempre vivo." See also Pereira, *Eduardo Prado: o escriptor, o homem.* Cf. Joaquim Nabuco, *Minha formação,* 39–42, 45.

25 Eduardo Prado, *Collectaneas,* 1:295, 306–19.

26 A rough analysis of the library's auction catalog, *Catalogue de la Bibliothèque Eduardo Prado,* reveals that 38 percent of its books were on history, followed by arts and literature (19 percent), politics (10 percent), social science (8 percent), reference works (7 percent), economics (6.4 percent), religion (5.8 percent), and physical science (5.8 percent). Eighteen French journals were listed, as well as sixteen British, seven Brazilian, two each from Germany and the United States, and one from Switzerland.

　　For Eduardo's relationship with his fazenda workers, see João Capistrano de Abreu, *Ensaios e estudos,* 347–48, and Raimundo de Menezes, "Curiosidades biográficas." The *caboclo* is Brazil's mixed-race "peasant."

27 See chapter 9.

28 Burns, *Nationalism in Brazil*, 91; see also Freyre, *Ordem e progresso*, 1:clix, 151, 155, 268. For additional assessments, see Abreu, *Ensaios e estudos*, 343, and his *Correspondência*, 1:262. At least seven Portuguese-language editions of *A illusão* exist (São Paulo, 1893; Paris, 1895; São Paulo, 1902; São Paulo, 1917; Rio de Janeiro, 1933; São Paulo, 1958; and São Paulo, 1961) as well as one Spanish-language edition (Madrid, [1918]). The Spanish edition and the more recent Brazilian editions coincide with periods of rising anti-Americanism; the last two were published by Editôra Brasiliense, owned by Caio Prado Júnior. All citations are from the fourth Portuguese-language edition of 1917.

29 For a brief synopsis of and background to *Ariel*, see Gordon Brotherston's introduction to *Ariel*, by José Enrique Rodó. Whereas Rodó cited only three sources (*Ariel*, 5), Eduardo, in revisions made to the confiscated first edition of *A illusão* while he was in European exile, cited about fifty different sources, including government documents from the United States and several other nations, Jefferson's *Works*, Henry Clay's *Speeches*, and liberal magazines such as *Harper's* and the *North American Review.*

30 Quoted in Motta Filho, *Vida de Eduardo Prado*, 210.

31 *A illusão americana*, 234; preceding quotation, 247–48 ("water closets" in English in original); see also 236–44.

32 Prado, *Collectaneas*, 2:161–74.

33 José Honório Rodrigues, "Capistrano de Abreu and Brazilian Historiography"; and Katherine Fringer, "The Contribution of Capistrano de Abreu to Brazilian Historiography." For Abreu's opinion of Eduardo's historical research, see his *Ensaios e estudos*, 339–48. According to Gilberto Freyre, even Eduardo's polemics "combine the admirable talent of almost a political sociologist and . . . the notable erudition of a social historian"; *Ordem e progresso*, 1:32.

34 Prado, "Catholicismo," 55–56.

35 Eduardo Prado, "Discurso de anniversário da fundação do Instituto Histórico de São Paulo," 527.

36 J. F. de Almeida Prado, "Paulo Prado," 100.

37 Quoted in Geraldo Ferraz, "Paulo Prado," 141–42.

38 Maria Catarina Prado to Paulo Prado, on board the *La Plata*, 7 September 1893, *AAMB*.

39 For example, *Sao Paulo "Magazine"* 1, no. 2 (15 June 1906).

40 Quoted in Ferraz, "Paulo Prado," 142.

41 Armando Prado, *Discurso proferido*, 13–14.

42 Ferraz, "Paulo Prado," 142.

43 Mário de Andrade, *O movimento modernista*, 23. For the role of Paulo's sister, Nazareth, in getting Graça Aranha to participate in the

Modern Art Week, see Silveira, *Grã-finos em São Paulo,* 199–200. For a concise survey of the modernist movement and selected readings, see Antônio Candido and J. Aderaldo Castello (eds.), *Presença da literatura brasileira,* vol. 3.

44 Paulo Prado, "Prefácio," ii–v. Eduardo is mentioned four times in the seven-page preface.

The idea of being shamed before the foreigner appears several times in the Prados' history. In 1862, Martinico spoke of slavery as a "sad necessity which degrades us so much in front of the foreigner." Antônio referred to the brutal treatment of draftees for the Paraguayan War, which "shames us before the foreigner and gives a wretched idea of our customs." After the 1889 coup, Eduardo reportedly burned his Brazilian newspapers so that his English butler would not form a bad impression of Brazil. *IM:MPJ,* 268; *O Paiz,* 5 October 1865; and Sebastiano Pagano, *Eduardo Prado e sua época* (São Paulo, 195-?), 22.

45 *Revista do Brasil* 8, no. 89 (May 1923): 3.

46 Paulo Prado, "Poesia Pau Brasil," 59, 60.

47 *Revista do Brasil* 8, no. 100 (April 192?).

48 *Paulistica,* 2d ed., xxiii. This edition contains seven new essays added to those of the first edition and reflects Paulo's historical and contemporary concerns.

49 Capistrano to Paulo, Gigante de Pedras, 20 November 1924; Capistrano to Paulo, dated only "Ash Wednesday," 1925, in Abreu, *Correspondência,* 2:459, 464.

50 *Paulistica,* xx.

51 Quotes from *Paulistica,* xxvi and 226.

52 *Retrato do Brasil,* 6th ed., 3, 103, 99, 145, 181, 173, and "Nota do autor a 4a. edição," 2.

53 Rio, 1 January 1929, reprinted in *Retrato do Brasil,* 6th ed., 184–85.

54 José Fernando Carneiro, *Psicologia do brasileiro,* 19.

55 See the essays by Pedro Moacyr Campos, José Honório Rodrigues, and Sérgio Buarque de Hollanda, in *Perspectives on Brazilian History,* ed. Burns, 80–82, 107, 185, 192; and Burns, *Nationalism in Brazil,* 64.

56 Maria Catarina to Paulo, Santa Veridiana, 7 July 1892, *AAMB.*

57 On rising labor conflict, see Dean, *Industrialization of São Paulo,* chap. 9; Morse, *From Community to Metropolis,* 209–12; and S. Fanny Simon, "Anarchism and Anarcho-Syndicalism in South America," 53–55.

CHAPTER VIII. ENTREPRENEURS AND FAZENDEIROS

1 Caio Prado Júnior, *História econômica do Brasil,* 219.

2 *Encilhamento* denotes a place where horses are saddled for a race and,

hence, the speculative nature of the period. For standard views, see Bello, *History of Modern Brazil,* 72–76, and Edgard Carone, *A republica velha: instituições e classes sociais,* 100–107. Paul Singer applies the term to the entire period of liberal monetary policies from 1889 to the financial "crack" of 1900; see his *Desenvolvimento econômico e evolução urbana,* 45, n. 46.

3 For a summary and critique of this view, see Dean, *Industrialization of São Paulo,* chap. 6.

4 The periodization used here is derived from that in Poppino, *Brazil,* 200–204, 238–41.

5 Cf. Caio Prado Júnior, *Histórica econômica do Brasil,* 267, and Dean, *Industrialization of São Paulo,* 92–93.

6 Dean, *Industrialization of São Paulo,* chaps. 1–3. See also Singer, *Desenvolvimento econômico e evolução urbana,* 41–58, and Morse, *From Community to Metropolis,* chap. 18 and p. 338.

7 Caio Prado Júnior, *História econômica,* 270.

8 Morse, *From Community to Metropolis,* 224–34.

9 Dean, *Industrialization of São Paulo,* 85–88, 113–14, 141; Singer, *Desenvolvimento econômico e evolução urbana,* 53–54; Caio Prado Júnior, *História econômica,* 272–73; Furtado, *Economic Growth of Brazil,* 193–202.

10 Yearly figures on coffee production, exports, prices, and the exchange rate from 1889 to 1927 are in São Paulo (Estado), *O café em São Paulo,* 22–23. For other sources on coffee, see chap. 4, n. 3, above. For estimates of inflation, see Dean, *Industrialization of São Paulo,* 92, 106.

11 Daniel Bell, "The Break-up of Family Capitalism," 317.

12 On the critical role of the government in Brazilian economic development, see Singer, *Desenvolvimento econômico e evolução urbana,* 47.

13 São Paulo (Estado), *Annuario estatistico,* 1900–1910.

14 Singer, *Desenvolvimento econômico e evolução urbana,* 34.

15 Francisco Guimarães, *Annuaire du Brésil: economique et financier,* 89.

16 Eduardo Prado to London and Brazilian Bank, Paris, 2 and 4 March 1891; Eduardo Prado to "Sr. Feijo," 9 March 1891; Eduardo Prado to Oliveira Martins, 20 April 1891; Eduardo Prado to Rodrigues, Paris, 28 February 1892, 19 April 1891 (telegram), and 5 January 1892, all in *Copiadoras,* 1:162–63, 168, 183–84, 310, 315, 424, and 3:55–56. For the Rothschilds' role in Brazil, see J. F. Normano, *Brazil,* 150–63.

17 Eduardo Prado to the directors of the Paulista Railway, 19 November 1891, and Eduardo Prado to N. B. Megan [undated], in *Copiadoras,* 2:enclosure between 10 and 11, 3–5, and 20–21; Correia to Eduardo

Prado, London, 8 December [1892?] and 19 December 1892, on Brazilian legation stationery, *JPC*, 920/P896cp/A1. Megan was a director of the Rio Claro. See also Mattoon, "Companhia Paulista," 123–25, and Pinto, *História da viação pública*, 194–209.

18 Notarized balance sheet, "Movimento financeiro das linhas da Companhia Paulista de Vias Ferreas e Fluviais," 1 October 1899, *AAMB*. Antônio Prado's policies are defended by a former employee in Pinto, *História da viação pública*, 200–209.

19 *Jornal de Piracicaba*, 1 May 1902, 1.

20 Antônio Prado to Conceição, São Paulo, 22 June 1903, *JPC*, 920/P896ca/A1.

21 Conceição to Antônio Prado, Piracicaba, 24 June 1903, *JPC*, 920/P896ca/A1.

22 Julian Smith Duncan, *The Public and the Private Operation of Railways in Brazil*, 58–64.

23 Alexandre d'Atri, *Entrevista concedida pelo Exmo. Snr. Conselheiro Dr. Antonio da Silva Prado*, 10.

24 An informative summary of the Paulista Railway's operations, prepared by Antônio Prado, is in the offering statement of the $4 million bond issue published by the firm of Ladenburg, Thalman, and Co. (1922), Sterling Memorial Library, Yale University. See also Duncan, *Railways in Brazil*, 130–46, 175. Cumulative statistics are in São Paulo (Estado), *Annuario estatistico*, 1900–1918.

25 Interview, Luíz Prado, São Paulo, 19 March 1972. The title *"Conselheiro"* (councilor) was used by members of the Imperial Council of Ministers, and was employed by Antônio long after the monarchy's demise.

26 Antônio Prado to Elias Chaves, Rio, 10 July 1887, *JPC*, 920/C512co/A1; *Companhia Prado Chaves Exportadora*, 5–9, 15.

27 *IM:MPJ*, 23; *Companhia Prado Chaves Exportadora*, [28]–[29].

28 Taunay, *História do café*, 10:126, 136, 183 and 11:57. Foreign exporters were paid in pounds and francs, so that the Brazilian treasury's payments to Prado-Chaves saved it considerable foreign exchange. The relative disadvantage to Prado-Chaves in receiving depreciated Brazilian currency is evident, but the company may have been able to use the funds for domestic expenses.

29 Thomas H. Holloway, *The Brazilian Coffee Valorization of 1906*, 76–84. Holloway notes (p. 39) that between 1895 and 1906, the twenty largest Santos exporters handled 87.3 percent of coffee exports; of these Prado-Chaves was the only Brazilian firm, with a mere 3.9 percent of exports. Eighteen other Brazilian firms handled only 2.7 percent of exports in those years.

30 *Companhia Prado Chaves Exportadora*, 9; Sousa, *Meus cinqüenta anos*, 8–13.
31 Holloway, *Immigrants on the Land*, 125.
32 *Companhia Prado Chaves Exportadora*, 13, [28]–[29].
33 Roberto Cochrane Simonsen, *The Meat and Cattle Industry of Brazil*, 5–6. Export tonnage calculated from heads of cattle exported as reported in Nazareth Prado, *Antonio Prado*, 478–79.
34 Afonso Henriques de Lima Barreto, *Marginália*, 191–94. José Pereira da Graça Aranha (1868–1931) was a diplomat and writer best known for his novel, *Canaã* (1902). A long-time friend of the Prados, he wrote the introduction to Nazareth Prado's *Antonio Prado*.
   Increased prices for food were due, in addition to monopoly capitalism, to foreign exchange depreciation and the effects of the war since much of Brazil's food was imported; Furtado, *Economic Growth of Brazil*, 186ff.
35 Roberto Simonsen (n. 33 above) was part of the group that leased the meat-packing plant.
36 Nazareth Prado, *Antonio Prado*, 480–81; Jacob Penteado, *Belenzinho, 1910*, 78; Roberto Capri, *Album comemorativa*. The glassworks was managed in 1972 by Antônio Prado's grandson, Antônio Augusto Monteiro de Barros Neto.
37 Caio Prado Júnior to the author, 22 January 1974.
38 Furtado, *Economic Growth of Brazil*, 193.
39 Pedro Luís Pereira de Sousa, *Casa Barão de Iguape*, 121.
40 Veridiana Prado to Eduardo Prado, São Paulo, 29 November 1891, *JPC*, 920/P896f/A1.
41 São Paulo (Estado), *Estatistica agricola e zootechnica*, município of Sertãozinho, passim. My thanks to Thomas Holloway for the use of this little-known agricultural census.
42 "Contracto de empreitada para o plantio de 200.000 pés de café," São Paulo, 20 March 1897, Fernando Chaves Papers. (See Appendix E.) For more details, see *Companhia Prado Chaves Exportadora*, 43–45; *Primeiro centenário*, 138; and Sousa, *Meus cinqüenta anos*, 63–66.
43 Fortunato Morais to Eduardo Prado, São Paulo, 7 September 1897, *JPC*, 920/P896cp/A1; R. Correia to Veridiana Prado, Rio Claro, 22 November 1896, *AAMB*.
44 Eduardo Prado to Rui Barbosa, São Paulo, 23 April 1901 (copy), *LSP*. See also Hélio Viana, "Rui Barbosa e Eduardo Prado."
45 Taunay, *História do café*, 9:163–66; d'Atri, *Entrevista*, 10.
46 Quotes in Taunay, *História do café*, 10:46–52, 130.
47 As mayor of São Paulo, Antônio forced his son Luíz to abandon a promising brick business because it used sand from the Tietê River belonging to the city. Interview, Luíz Prado, São Paulo, 7 August 1972.

48 Joseph L. Love, *São Paulo in the Brazilian Federation, 1889–1937*, 190, 205–6, 269, 271, and 342, n. 42.

49 Holloway, *Brazilian Coffee Valorization*, 99, n. 33.

50 José Honório Rodrigues, *Notícia de vária história*, 88.

51 See below, p. 175.

52 *Gazeta de Notícias*, 24 May 1890, 1; Beiguelman, "A grande imigração," 145; d'Atri, *Entrevista*, 9; Felix Buscaglia to Antônio Prado, Biella, Italy, 1 December 1923, *AAMB*.

53 Antônio Prado to Washington Luís Pereira de Sousa, 25 October and 8 November 1921 (copies), *AAMB*. Washington Luís, then governor of São Paulo and later president of Brazil (1926–30), refused to sanction the agreement on the grounds that it violated Brazilian sovereignty. For Antônio's embittered, sarcastic reaction, see his "Notas sobre a colonisação em S. Paulo," 199.

54 *Companhia Prado Chaves*, 45; Luíz Prado, "Fazenda Santa Veridiana," 9.

55 Luíz Prado, "Fazenda Santa Veridiana," 9. In a similar vein, a Prado relative wrote to her wayward son: "I am anxious to see my children settled. I have faith that God will permit them to begin life in an environment as good as agriculture is. Our fathers were planters, and I would like our sons to be planters too." Alzira Chaves to Miguel Chaves, 24 May 1923, Miguel Chaves Papers.

56 Paulo Prado, "O martyrio do café," in his *Paulistica*, 209–17.

57 Ibid., 212.

58 A financial summary for Guatapará in the years 1912–41 is in *IM:MPJ*, [379]. In the 1930s Martinho Prado Neto, as coffee planter and federal deputy (1934–37), came to share Paulo's deep concerns about the coffee economy, referring at one point to the National Department of Coffee as the "No. 1 enemy of coffee"; see his *Pró lavoura*, esp. 171–77.

59 Paulo Prado, *Paulistica*, 217 n.

60 A secondary response may have been investment in urban real estate. In the late nineteenth and early twentieth centuries, some members of the Prado *parentela* were involved in such activity, and in 1972 Martinho Prado Neto headed a real estate firm that included among its clients Ford-Willys, Esso, Shell, IBM, Kodak, RCA, Union Carbide, Mead-Johnson, and large Brazilian firms. "Planta dos terrenos do Dr. Elias Chaves" (1885), *JPC*, 620/P713/A1; Oduvaldo Pacheco e Silva, "Recordações da infancia e da mocidade" (88-p. MS in Sampaio Archive), 62; Dean, *Industrialization of São Paulo*, 113; advertisement, *O Estado de São Paulo*, 14 May 1972.

61 *Companhia Prado Chaves*, 36, 45.

62 Dean, *Industrialization of São Paulo*, 68 and chap. 5. For an acerbic picture of the new Paulista elite formed from planter and immigrant

groups, emphasizing the social prestige of the former and the latter's wealth, see Silveira, *Grã-finos em São Paulo,* 13–45.

63 Henry William Spiegel, *The Brazilian Economy,* 228–29.

64 José de Souza Martins, *Empresário e emprêsa na biografia do conde Matarazzo,* 30–33, 40; Dean, *Industrialization of São Paulo,* 60–66; Morse, *From Community to Metropolis,* 228–29.

65 Martins, *Empresário e emprêsa,* 40.

66 In interviews with Prado family members in 1972, I was repeatedly informed of the differences between the various branches. One informant said that each of the many branches had its own "personality" and that the rural Prados, for example, are impecunious and incapable of planning. Members of the "conservative" branch, descendants of Antônio Prado, stressed that the "radical" Prados, descendants of Martinico Prado, were visionaries incapable of constructive action and "against everything," while the "radicals" emphasized the bourgeois style of their "conservative" counterparts. Such attitudes, of course, may or may not be a strict reflection of reality, and I was impressed by elements of a "Prado family ethic" common to Prado "conservatives" and "radicals" alike, but the mere existence of divergent perceptions of the family is an important indicator of intrafamily differentiation.

67 See Martins, *Empresário e emprêsa,* 41ff., on Matarazzo's conflicting images as Italian nobleman and "the number one worker of São Paulo."

68 Taunay, *História do café,* 9:166.

CHAPTER IX. AT THE MARGINS OF POLITICS

1 Bello, *History of Modern Brazil,* pp. 168–69.

2 Stepan, "Continuing Problem of Brazilian Integration," 244 n. 3. In São Paulo the suffrage expanded from 15,000 in 1886 to 31,000 in 1892; by 1936, after the First Republic, it had reached 485,000, still only 7 percent of the population. However, in São Paulo, voter participation did grow three times faster than population. See Love, *São Paulo in the Brazilian Federation,* 140.

3 Bello, *History of Modern Brazil,* 255.

4 Carone, *República velha: instituições e classes sociais,* 153–55; Burns, *History of Brazil,* pp. 305–13. For a critical view of the coffee-dominance thesis, see Love, *São Paulo in the Brazilian Federation,* 177ff.

5 Adopted from Carone, *A república velha: evolução política.*

6 Joseph L. Love, *São Paulo in the Brazilian Federation,* appendix B and p. 152.

7 Ibid., table 5.2 and pp. 161, 145.

8 Ibid., 126.

9 The Constitution of 1891 left the definition of municipal authority to state legislatures; see Morse, *Community to Metropolis*, 238–39.

10 Freyre, *Ordem e progresso*, 1:142–43; see also p. 175 below.

11 João Morães, "Proclamação da república em S. Paulo," pp. 189–94. Morães was an eyewitness to the events described.

12 *Correio Paulistano*, 18 November 1889, 1.

13 Morães, "Proclamação da república," 197–99.

14 Calling card of Antônio Prado to José Vicente de Azevedo, 27 December 1889, inviting Azevedo to a meeting "for electoral ends." Archive of Olinto Moura, São Paulo.

15 José Maria dos Santos, *Bernardino de Campos e o partido republicano paulista*, 190, n. 79.

16 Undated letters (1890) from Antônio to Manuel Joaquim Albuquerque Lins and to Rio Branco, *AAMB*.

17 Santos, *Bernardino de Campos*, 104, 114, 117.

18 *IM:MPJ*, 43, 49.

19 Quoted in Love, *São Paulo*, 175.

20 Bello, *History of Modern Brazil*, 77–88.

21 Maria Catarina Prado to Paulo Prado, São Paulo, 8 November 1891, *LSP*.

22 Américo Brasiliense de Almeida Melo (1833–96) was eulogized by Eduardo Prado, no friend of Republicans, as the purest and most illustrious of them; see Prado's *Collectaneas*, 2:136–44.

23 Love, *São Paulo*, 110–11.

24 Célio Debes, *Campos Salles*, 2:350.

25 *IM:MPJ*, 23, 383–88.

26 *IM:MPJ*, 82, where the date of the trip is incorrectly given as 1893. Santos's account of Martinico's political withdrawal is the best published version, although it contains some small factual errors.

27 Maria Catarina Prado to Paulo Prado, São Paulo, 27 March 1894, *LSP*.

28 Francisco de Assis Pacheco Júnior to Elias Chaves, São Paulo, 5 November 1897, *JPC*, 920/C512co/A1.

29 Quoted in Hélio Viana, "Rui Barbosa e Eduardo Prado," 72.

30 See, for example, Pontes de Moraes, "A illusão americana," 112–28, where a review of *A illusão americana* serves as a vehicle for an attack on United States military influence in Brazil.

31 "A Hespanha," in *Collectaneas*, 1:383–84.

32 See his essay "Victoria, R.I.," in *Collectaneas*, 1:249–65.

33 Eduardo Prado, *A illusão americana*, 176ff., 231–32.

34 Eduardo Prado to José Carlos Rodrigues, Paris, 31 March 1891, in Eduardo's *Copiadoras*, 1:248. These reservations did not, however,

extend to Brazil's mixed-race caboclo majority, which, if anything, Eduardo tended to over-romanticize.

35 Eduardo Prado [pseud. Frederico de S.], *Fastos da dictadura militar no Brazil*, 22ff.; see also Motta Filho, *A Vida de Eduardo Prado*, 153–70. *Fastos da dictadura militar* consists of six articles written for Eça de Queiroz's *Revista de Portugal* (December 1889–June 1890). It should be read with the more balanced, precoup "Destinos politicos do Brasil," and with Eduardo's "Practicas e theorias da dictadura republicana no Brazil," *Revista de Portugal* 3 (1890): 74–120, neither of which was reprinted in *Fastos*. A ninth article in the series, "Physiologia politica e sul americana: o Deodorismo e alguns dos seus phenomenos" (MS, 1890 or 1891, *LSP*), was never published, probably because of its unrestrained tone and because Eça de Queiroz had experienced pressure, through diplomatic channels, because of the earlier articles.

36 Eduardo Prado, *Fastos da dictadura militar*, 24–25, 164–282.

37 Eduardo Prado to José Carlos Rodrigues, Paris, 28 February 1892, in *Copiadoras*, 3:56.

38 Eduardo Prado, *Fastos da dictadura militar*, 160–66.

39 Debes, *Campos Salles*, 1:322–25.

40 Eduardo Prado to Ellis T. Powell of London's *Financial News*, 18 March 1893, in *Copiadoras*, 3:424. As a noun, *Gaúcho*, in this context, means natives or residents of the state of Rio Grande do Sul; as an adjective, it means of, or pertaining to, the state or region.

41 Bello, *History of Modern Brazil*, chaps. 8–10; and Carone, *A república velha: evolução política*, 80–128.

42 Eduardo Prado, *A illusão americana*, 5.

43 Ibid., 3–5, 110–16; quotation from 110.

44 Eduardo Prado, *Fastos da dictadura militar*, 21.

45 Eduardo Prado, *A illusão americana*, 232–33, 53. See Richard Hofstadter, "John C. Calhoun: The Marx of the Master Class," in *The American Political Tradition*, 68–92. Both Eduardo's and Calhoun's reactions were those of men of planter origins facing the threat of an industrializing society.

46 Eduardo Prado, *A illusão americana*, 169–91.

47 Eça de Queiroz to Oliveira Martins, Paris, 17 April 1893, in Queiroz, *Obras*, 3:361; Eça discounted the rumor, but see n. 49 below.

48 Freyre, *Ordem e progresso*, clix, 151, 155, 268.

49 Eduardo Prado, "Fragmento a proposito da viagem atraves dos sertões da Bahia e Minas," in *Collectaneas*, 3:172–80; [Eduardo Prado], *Eduardo Prado e a república no Brasil*, 18–19. Following Eduardo's departure from Brazil, he was named as a plenipotentiary to try to gain support from European nations for the rebels; see June Hahner, *Civil-Military Relations in Brazil*, 105.

50 Eduardo Prado, *Fastos da dictadura militar,* 22–26, 241ff.

51 Hélio Viana, "Rui Barbosa e Eduardo Prado."

52 Authorship is attributed to Eduardo in Carone, *A república velha: instituições e classes sociais,* 383, n. 18. Eduardo wrote that the manifesto was edited (*redigido*) by João Mendes; Eduardo Prado, *Collectaneas,* 2:57.

53 Afonso Celso de Assis Figueiredo, visconde do Ouro Prêto, *Contradictas monarchicas,* pp. 93–98, 112–13.

54 The articles are reprinted in Eduardo Prado's *Collectaneas,* vols. 2 and 3.

55 *O Estado de São Paulo,* 1–20 November 1895.

56 Hélio Viana, "Rui Barbosa e Eduardo Prado," 75–77. Joaquim Nabuco to Eduardo Prado, 30 January 1896, in *Cartas a amigos,* by Nabuco, 1:263–64.

57 Quoted in Americo Palha, "Grandes figuras de nossa história: Eduardo Prado," *Diário Carioca,* 22 October 1944. Refusing the editorship, Nabuco did agree to write a political column for *O Comércio.*

58 *Collectaneas,* 2:315–51.

59 Campos Sales to Bernardino, 1 November 1896, reprinted in Debes, *Campos Salles,* 2:415–17.

60 *Collectaneas,* 2:352–59 and 3:36–71.

61 Campos Sales to Prudente, 5 March 1897, reprinted in Debes, *Campos Salles,* 2:419–21.

62 Ibid. The classic account of the Canudos rebellion is Euclides da Cunha's *Os sertões* (1902), translated as *Rebellion in the Backlands.* For a perceptive analysis, emphasizing the conflict's crucial ties to local and national politics, see Ralph Della Cava, "Brazilian Messianism and National Institutions." For the Republican response in São Paulo, including apparently manufactured evidence "proving" Eduardo's conspiratorial activities, see *O Estado de São Paulo,* 1–20 March 1897.

63 *Correio Paulistano,* 9 March 1897, quoted in Debes, *Campos Salles,* 2:418.

64 Debes, *Campos Salles,* 2:421; and da Cunha, *Rebellion in the Backlands,* 279.

65 Ibid.

66 *Collectaneas,* 3:111–13.

67 Eduardo Prado [pseud. Graccho], *Salvemos o Brazil;* see Hahner, *Civilian-Military Relations,* 170.

68 Joaquim Nabuco to Eduardo Prado, Rio, 3 January 1899, Archive of Olinto Moura, São Paulo. "Drifted man" in English.

69 *O Comércio de São Paulo,* 6 April 1899, quoted in Carolina Nabuco, *Life of Joaquim Nabuco,* 243; Eduardo Prado, "Em defesa," 10 January 1897, in *Collectaneas,* 3:33–36.

70 For examples of domestic metaphors used by Eduardo in criticizing the Republic, see *Collectaneas*, 3:18, 68–69, 403–4. One of his complaints against the early Republic, however, was the Fonseca family's nepotism; see Eduardo Prado, "Practicas e theorias," esp. p. 83.

71 *O Estado de São Paulo*, 14–15 November 1895.

72 Unlike his predecessors Prudente de Morais and Campos Salles, President Francisco de Paula Rodrigues Alves was not a historic republican. The "good school of administration" was the same as Antônio's, São Paulo's Conservative party during the monarchy.

73 D'Atri, *Entrevista*, 7–11; the quotes are d'Atri's paraphrases of Antônio's remarks.

74 Graça Aranha, "A vida realista de Antonio Prado," in *Antonio Prado*, by Nazareth Prado, 43–44.

75 Penteado, *Belenzinho, 1910*, 294.

76 *O Estado de São Paulo*, 8–9 January 1905; São Paulo Tramway, Light and Power Co., Ltd., *Annual Report, 1904*, 10.

77 Morse, *Community to Metropolis*, 239–40.

78 Vitor da Silva Freire, "Melhoramentos de S. Paulo." A more appreciative view of Antônio's mayoralty, written apparently by the same Vitor da Silva Freire in 1929, appears in Nazareth Prado, *Antonio Prado*, 363–80, and in *Primeiro centenário*, 113–39.

79 Antônio was lauded by establishment sources for his firmness in opposing labor "anarchy"; see, for example, *Sao Paulo "Magazine"* 1, no. 2 (15 June 1906): 38. Shortly after the strike some reforms, such as the eight-hour day and widows' pensions, were "spontaneously" implemented by the railroad; see *O Estado de São Paulo*, 25 February 1940.

80 João Fernando de Almeida Prado, "Paulo Prado e a época da sua formação," 104.

81 Although he was still mayor at the time, Antônio is not mentioned in Rui Barbosa's *Excursão eleitoral ao Estado de S. Paulo*.

82 Letter from César Lacerda Vergueiro, Nicanor Nascimentos, et al., on stationery of the Câmara dos Deputados, Rio, 9 August 1916, *AAMB*.

83 Rui Barbosa to Antônio Prado, [15 May 1919], in Ruy Barbosa, *Correspondência*, 404–5; Prado to Peçanha, December 1921, reprinted in Nazareth Prado, *Antonio Prado*, 806–8.

84 Abreu, *Correspondência*, 2:435.

85 Paulo Prado, "O momento."

86 Ibid., no. 99 (March 1924), 193–94.

87 Afonso Arinos de Melo Franco, *Um estadista da República*, 3:1306.

88 The "nonpolitical" nature of the appointment is affirmed in Bello, *History of Modern Brazil*, 258 and in Franco, *Um estadista da*

República, 3:1277. As mayor, Antônio Prado Júnior devoted his attention primarily to the physical modernization and beautification of Rio, much as his father had earlier in São Paulo. He also commissioned the first aerial survey of the city. For some details of his administration, see Fernando Nascimento Silva, ed., *Rio de Janeiro em seus quatrocentos anos*, 145–46; Cicero Marques, *O último dia de governo do Presidente Washington Luis*, 84–85; and Francisco Guimarães, *Annuaire du Brésil*, 448–49. My thanks to Michael Conniff for bringing the first two sources to my attention.

89 Franco, *Um estadista da República*, 3:1329.

90 The manifesto is reprinted in Carone, *Primeira república: texto e contexto*, 240–42. Carone characterizes it as "timid" and singles out the secret ballot as "the magic formula of the bourgeoisie."

91 Boris Fausto, "A revolução de 1930," in *Brasil em perspectiva*, 235; Nazareth Prado, *Antonio Prado*, 414. Love (*São Paulo*, 164–66) concludes that the leadership of the PRP and the PD were very much alike.

92 Democratic party literature, reprinted in Nazareth Prado, *Antonio Prado*, 412, 410.

93 Carone, *A república velha: evolução política*, 399. However, Antônio Prado's son-in-law, Luís Queiros Aranha, was at some point elected state deputy on the Democratic party ticket; see Nazareth Prado, *Antonio Prado*, 512.

94 Antônio Prado, "Carta aos Campineiros," 7 July 1926, in Nazareth Prado, *Antonio Prado*, 428–31.

95 Getúlio Vargas, "A successão presidencial e a defeza do café," [1929], reprinted in Nazareth Prado, *Antonio Prado*, 804–6.

96 Nazareth Prado, *Antonio Prado*, 591, where it is noted that among those who offered their public sympathies to the family on the death of Antônio Prado was the revolutionary and future leader of the Communist party of Brazil, Luís Carlos Prestes.

97 Cf. Luís Martins, "O patriarca e o bacharel."

98 Morse, *Community to Metropolis*, 171.

99 For Fábio's mayoralty, see Fábio Prado, *Mensagem do prefeito Fábio Prado à Camara Municipal de S. Paulo*; Paulo Duarte et al., *Fábio Prado*.

⋙ GLOSSARY ⋘

Alqueire. A unit of territorial measurement, approximating six acres in nineteenth-century São Paulo.

Arroba. A unit of weight, varying regionally, between twenty-five and thirty-two pounds.

Bacharel (pl. *bacharéis*). Holder of a bachelor's degree from a law school or university.

Bandeirante. The slave- and gold-hunting frontiersman of São Paulo during the sixteenth to the eighteenth centuries. In modern usage, a synonym for *paulista*.

Caboclo. Brazil's mixed-race "peasant."

Caipirada. An elite word for an ignorant or inappropriate act; *caipira* is a regional word for *caboclo*.

Capitão-mór. Captain-major; the commanding officer of a district in the colonial militia.

Casa grande. The patriarchal plantation house.

Chácara. A large suburban house with extensive gardens.

Cidade. City.

Comendador. Commander; an honorific title in royal military-religious orders.

Compadres. Persons bound to one another by *compadrio*.

Compadrio. Godparenthood; ritual kinship.

Coronel (pl. *coronéis*). Colonel; either a formal military title or an informal title used by local strongmen.

Coronelismo. Local strongman rule.

Colonos. Immigrant farmworkers.

Conto, conto de réis. In the period studied, a large unit of Brazilian currency, consisting of 1,000 *milréis*, written 1:000$000.

Caudilho. Strongman; equivalent to the Spanish-language *caudillo*.

Fazenda. Plantation.

Fazendeiro. Owner of a *fazenda*.

Frigorífico. Refrigerated meat-packing plant.

Gaúcho. As a noun, a native or resident of the province or state of Rio Grande do Sul; as an adjective, of or pertaining to the province or state.

Juiz de fora. Royal magistrate with legal training.

Juiz ordinário. A lower-court judge without legal training.

Mestiço. Mixed-race person.

Milréis. Unit of Brazilian money, written 1$000, the common unit for small transactions.

Mineiro. As a noun, a native or resident of the province or state of Minas Gerais; as an adjective, of or pertaining to that province or state.

Município. County.

Oitava. One-eighth of an ounce, a measure of gold.

Padrinho. Godfather.

Paulista. As a noun, a native or resident of the province or state of São Paulo; as an adjective, of or pertaining to that province or state.

Paulistano. As a noun, a native or resident of the city of São Paulo; as an adjective, of or pertaining to the city.

Poder moderador. Moderating power; during the Brazilian Empire (1822–89), the "fourth branch" of government exercised by the emperor.

Quinhentista. An adjective applied to elite families tracing their Brazilian origins to the 1500s.

Sargento-mór. Sergeant-major; a post of considerable authority in the colonial militia.

Sertanejos. Impoverished backlanders.

Sertão (pl. *sertões*). Interior or backlands area.

Sítio. Farm.

Sobrado. Town house of the elite.

Terça. The third of people's property which they could freely dispose of through inheritance.

Vila. Town or village.

➤ BIBLIOGRAPHY ➤

UNPUBLISHED SOURCES

Private Archives
 Ana Candida Ferraz Sampaio. São Paulo.
 Antônio Augusto Monteiro de Barros Neto [*AAMB*]. São Paulo.
 Olinto Moura. São Paulo.
 Luíz da Silva Prado [*LSP*]. Fazenda Santa Veridiana, Santa Cruz das
  Palmeiras, State of São Paulo.
 Caio da Silva Prado Júnior. São Paulo.

Public Archives
 Instituto de Estudos Brasileiros, Universidade de São Paulo.
  Miscellaneous documents, originals and copies, and research notes
  of Artur de Cerquiera Mendes, in uncataloged file marked "D.
  Veridiana Prado."
 Instituto Histórico e Geográfico de São Paulo.
  Eduardo Prado, *Copiadoras de Cartas.* 3 vols. 1888–96.
  Coleção Antônio da Silva Prado. 27 MS vols. 1810–73.
  Coleção Jorge Pacheco e Chaves.
 Museu Paulista.
  Miguel Chaves Papers. Uncataloged, ca. 1890–1930.
  Fernando Chaves Papers. Uncataloged, ca. 1900–1930.

OTHER SOURCES

Abreu, João Capistrano de. *Correspondência.* Edited by José Honório
 Rodrigues. 3 vols. Rio de Janeiro: Ministério de Educação e Cultura,
 Instituto Nacional do Livro, 1954–56.
———. *Ensaios e estudos, critica è historia.* 1st ser. Rio de Janeiro:
 Briguiet, 1931.
Adler, Alfred. *The Individual Psychology of Alfred Adler.* Edited by Heinz
 L. Ansbacher and Rowena R. Ansbacher. London: George Allen and
 Unwin, 1956.
Aires, Leopoldo. "Eduardo Prado." *A Gazeta,* 27 February 1960.
Alden, Dauril. *Royal Government in Colonial Brazil, With Special
 Reference to the Administration of the Marquis of Lavradio, Viceroy,
 1769–1779.* Berkeley and Los Angeles: University of California Press,
 1968.

Altavila, Jayme de. "Antônio Caio da Silva Prado em Alagoas (1887–1888)." *Revista Brasiliense* 21 (January–February 1959): 184–94.

Alves, Antônio de Castro [Castro Alves]. *Obras completas*. Edited by Afranio Peixoto. Livros do Brasil, vol. 1. Rio de Janeiro: Editôra Nacional, 1938.

Amaral, Rubens do. "Antônio Prado." In *Homens de São Paulo*. São Paulo: Martins, 1955.

Amaral, Tancredo do. *Historia de São Paulo ensinada pela biografia dos seus vultos mais notaveis*. 2d. ed. Rio de Janeiro and São Paulo: Alves, 1895.

Andrade, [Edmundo] Navarro de. "Dona Viridiana Prado." *Revista de Academia Paulista de Letras* 2, no. 8 (12 December 1939): 34–38; and 3, no. 9 (12 March 1940): 32–37.

————. "Pagínas vívidas: Eduardo Prado." *Revista de Academia Paulista de Letras* 2, no. 5 (12 March 1939): 11–17; and 2, no. 6 (12 June 1939): 45–51.

Andrade, Mário de. *O movimento modernista*. Rio de Janeiro: Casa do Estudante do Brasil, 1942.

Araripe, Tristão de Alencar. "Pater-familias no Brazil nos tempos coloniaes." *Revista do Instituto Histórico e Geográfico Brasileiro* 55 (1892): 15–23.

Assis, Joaquim Maria Machado de (Machado de Assis). "Eduardo Prado." In *Obra Completa*. 2 vols. Rio de Janeiro: José Aguilar, 1959.

Ataíde, Tristão de (Alceu Amoroso Lima). "Eduardo Prado." *Comentário*, April–June 1961.

————. "Eduardo Prado: sempre vivo." *A Manhã*, 31 August 1941.

———— (Tristão de Athayde). "Os Prado." *Jornal do Brasil*, 16 July 1976.

Azevedo, Aroldo de. *Cochranes do Brasil: a vida e a obra de Thomas Cochrane e Ignacio Cochrane*. Brasiliana, vol. 327. São Paulo: Editôra Nacional, 1965.

Azevedo, Thales de. "Family, Marriage, and Divorce in Brazil." In *Contemporary Cultures and Societies of Latin America*, edited by Dwight B. Heath and Richard N. Adams. New York: Random House, 1965.

Bandecchi, Pedro Brasil. "Documento sobre a imigração italiana em Ribeirão Prêto." *Revista de História* 72 (October–December 1967): 601–12.

Bandecchi, Brasil, Leonardo Arroyo, and Ubiratan Rosa, eds. *Nôvo dicionário de história do Brasil*. São Paulo: Melhoramentos, 1970.

"Bandeirantes do café: Dr. Martinho Prado Junior." *Revista da sociedade rural brasileira* 31 (January 1923): 15–21.

Barbosa, Rui. *Excursão eleitoral ao Estado de S. Paulo*. São Paulo: Casa Garraux, 1909.

————. *Obras completas*. Vol. 15, *Trabalhos diversos*. Revised, with a preface, by Hélio Viana. Rio de Janeiro: Ministério da Educação e Cultura, 1965.

————. *Obras completas*. Vol. 16, *Queda do império*. Rio de Janeiro: Ministério da Educação e Saúde, 1947–49.

Barbosa, Ruy. *Correspondencia*. Collected, revised, and annotated by Homero Pires. São Paulo: Livraria Academica, 1932.

Barreto, Afonso Henriques de Lima. *Marginália: artigos e crônicas*. 2d ed. With a preface by Agrippino Grieco. Obras de Lima Barreto, vol. 12. São Paulo: Brasiliense, 1961.

Barreto, Moniz. Review of *Fastos da dictadura militar no Brazil*, by Eduardo Prado. *Revista de Portugal* 3 (1890): 763–68.

Barreto, Plínio. "Eduardo Prado e seus amigos (cartas ineditas)." *Revista do Brasil* 1, no. 2 (February 1916): 173–97.

Barros, Gilberto Leite de. *A cidade e o planalto: processo de dominância da cidade de São Paulo*. São Paulo: Martins, 1967.

Barros, Maria Paes de. *No tempo de dantes*. São Paulo: Brasiliense, 1946.

Barros Neto, Antônio Augusto Monteiro de. Interviews. São Paulo, 3 July and 3 August 1972.

Bastide, Roger. "A monografia familiar no Brasil." *Revista do Arquivo Municipal* 78 (August–September 1941): 6–39.

Beiguelman, Paula. "A grande imigração em São Paulo." *Revista do Instituto de Estudos Brasileiros* 3 (1968): 99–116; 4 (1968): 145–57.

Bell, Daniel. "The Break-up of Family Capitalism." *Partisan Review* 34, no. 2 (Spring 1957): 317–20.

Bello, José Maria. *A History of Modern Brazil, 1889–1964*. Translated by James L. Taylor. Stanford, Calif.: Stanford University Press, 1966.

Berlinck, Manoel Tosta. *The Structure of the Brazilian Family in the City of São Paulo*. Latin American Studies Program Dissertation Series, no. 12. Ithaca, N.Y.: Cornell University, 1969.

Besse, Susan K. "When the Public Becomes Private and the Private Becomes Public: Women and the Family in Early Industrial São Paulo." Paper presented at the American Historical Association meeting, Washington, D.C., 28 December 1982.

Bevilaqua, Clovis. *Direito da família*. 1896. 5th ed. Rio de Janeiro: Livraria Editôra Freitas Bastos, 1933.

Bicudo, Daniel. "Eduardo Prado, humorista." *A Tribuna*, 10 April 1960.

Binzer, Ina von. *Alegrias e tristezas de uma educadora alemã no Brasil*. Translated by Alice Rossi and Luisita da Gama Cerqueira. São Paulo: Anhembi, 1956.

Bittencourt, Adalzira. *A mulher paulistana na história*. Rio de Janeiro: Livros de Portugal, 1954.

Blake, Augusto Victoriano Alves Sacramento. *Diccionario biographico brazileiro.* 7 vols. Rio de Janeiro: Typographia Nacional, 1883–1902.
Boxer, C. R. *The Golden Age of Brazil, 1695–1750.* Berkeley and Los Angeles: University of California Press, 1969.
Brasil. Parlamento. Câmara dos Deputados. *Anais.* 1869–75, 1884–89.
————. Parlamento. Senado. *Anais.* 1885–89.
————. Ministério da Justiça e Negócios Interiores. Arquivo Nacional. *Organizações e programas ministeriais: regime parlamentar no império.* 2d ed. Rio de Janeiro: Departamento de Imprensa Nacional, 1962.
Broca, Brito. "A posição de Eduardo Prado." *A Gazeta,* 8 August 1953.
Brotero, Frederico de Barros. *Barão de Antonina: apontamentos genealógicas.* São Paulo: Salesiana, [1940].
————. *Brigadeiro Jordão (Manuel Rodrigues Jordão): esboço genealógico.* São Paulo: Gráfica Paulista, 1941.
————. *A família Jordão e seus afins: Pereira Mendes, Silva Prado, Monteiro de Barros, Queiroz Teles, Queiroz Ferreira, Queiroz Lacerda, Queiroz Aranha, Pereira de Queiroz, Fonseca, Prates, Mendes Pereira, Assis Pacheco Jordão, Pacheco e Silva, Pacheco e Chaves, Rodrigues Jordão, Araujo Ribeiro, Ribeiro Jordão, Pompeo de Camargo e outros, aditamentos a Silva Leme.* São Paulo: [Bentivegna], 1948.
————. *A família Monteiro de Barros.* São Paulo: n.p., 1951.
————. *Queirozes: Monteiro de Barros (ramo paulista): apontamentos genealogicos.* São Paulo: n.p., 1937.
Burns, E. Bradford. *A History of Brazil.* 2d ed. New York: Columbia University Press, 1980.
————. *Nationalism in Brazil: A Historical Survey.* New York: Praeger, 1968.
————. *The Poverty of Progress: Latin America in the Nineteenth Century.* Berkeley and Los Angeles: University of California Press, 1980.
————. *The Unwritten Alliance: Rio Branco and Brazilian-American Relations.* New York: Columbia University Press, 1966.
————, ed. *A Documentary History of Brazil.* New York: Knopf, 1966.
————, ed. *Perspectives on Brazilian History.* New York: Columbia University Press, 1967.
Câmara, José Aurélio Saraiva. *Fatos e documentos do Ceará provincial.* Fortaleza, Ceará: Imprensa Universitaria da Universidade do Ceará, 1970.
Cancian, Francesca M., Louis Wolf Goodman, and Peter H. Smith. "Capitalism, Industrialization, and Kinship in Latin America: Major Issues." *Journal of Family History* 3, no. 4 (Winter 1978): 319–36.

———. "Introduction." *Journal of Family History* 3, no. 4 (Winter 1978): 314–17.

Candido, Antônio. "The Brazilian Family." In *Brazil: Portrait of Half a Continent*, edited by T. Lynn Smith and Alexander Marchant. New York: Knopf, 1951.

Candido, Antônio, and J. Aderaldo Castello, eds. *Presença da literatura brasileira: história e antologia*. 3 vols. São Paulo: Difusão Européia do Livro, 1964.

Capri, Roberto. *Album comemorativo: Companhia Vidraria Santa Marina*. São Paulo: n.p., 1919.

Cardoso, Fernando Henrique. "Associated-Dependent Development: Theoretical and Practical Implications." In *Authoritarian Brazil: Origins, Policies, and Future*, edited by Alfred Stepan. New Haven, Conn.: Yale University Press, 1973.

———. "The Industrial Elite." In *Elites in Latin America*, edited by Seymour Martin Lipset and Aldo Solari. New York: Oxford University Press, 1967.

Carlos, Manuel L., and Lois Sellers. "Family, Kinship Structure, and Modernization in Latin America." *Latin American Research Review* 7, no. 2 (Summer 1972): 95–124.

Carneiro, José Fernando. *Psicologia do brasileiro e outros estudos*. Rio de Janeiro: Agir, 1971.

Carone, Edgard. *A primeira república, 1889–1930: texto e contexto*. Corpo e Alma do Brasil, vol. 29. São Paulo: Difusão Européia do Livro, 1969.

———. *A república velha: evolução política*. Corpo e Alma do Brasil, vol. 34. São Paulo: Difusão Européia do Livro, 1971.

———. *A república velha: instituições e classes sociais*. Corpo e Alma do Brasil, vol. 31. São Paulo: Difusão Européia do Livro, 1970.

Catalogue de la bibliothéque Eduardo Prado. São Paulo: Rothschild, 1916.

Catálogo da biblioteca "Paulo Prado" doada em 1944 à Biblioteca Municipal de São Paulo. São Paulo: Departamento de Cultura, 1945.

Chandler, Billy Jaynes. *The Feitosas and the Sertão dos Inhamuns: The History of a Family and a Community in Northeast Brazil, 1700–1930*. Gainesville: University of Florida Press, 1972.

Chateaubriand, Assis. "Sobre Paulo Prado: estrêla guiadora." *Revista do Instituto Histórico e Geográfico Brasileiro* 131 (October–December 1944): 241–47.

Clifford, James L. *From Puzzles to Portraits: Problems of a Literary Biographer*. Chapel Hill: University of North Carolina Press, 1970.

Coelho Netto. "Eduardo Prado como uma visão." *A Manha*, 31 August 1941.

A Comédia (São Paulo Law School). 1881.

O Comércio de São Paulo. 1901.

Companhia Prado Chaves Exportadora, 1887–1947. [São Paulo: n.p., 1947?]

Conrad, Robert. The Destruction of Brazilian Slavery, 1850–1888. Berkeley and Los Angeles: University of California Press, 1972.

O Constitucional (São Paulo Law School). 1881.

Correio Paulistano. 1886, 1889.

Costa, Emília Viotti da. Da senzala à colônia. Corpo e Alma do Brasil, vol. 19. São Paulo: Difusão Européia do Livro, 1966.

_____. "Introdução ao estudo da emancipação política do Brasil." In Brasil em perspectiva. Corpo e Alma do Brasil, no. 23. 2d ed. São Paulo: Difusão Européia do Livro, 1969.

Couty, Louis. Le Brésil en 1884. Rio de Janeiro: Faro e Lino, 1884.

Crosby, Alfred W., Jr. The Columbian Exchange: Biological and Cultural Consequences of 1492. Contributions in American Studies, no. 2. 3d ed. Westport, Conn.: Greenwood Press, 1976.

Cunha, Euclides da. Rebellion in the Backlands (Os sertões). Translated by Samuel Putnam. Chicago: University of Chicago Press, Phoenix Books, 1957.

D'Atri, Alexandre. Entrevista concedida pelo Exmo. Snr. Conselheiro Dr. Antonio da Silva Prado. São Paulo: Typographia Oscar Gouvêa, 1903.

Daunt, Ricardo Gumbleton, ed. Diário da Princesa Isabel: excursão dos Condes d'Eu à província de S. Paulo em 1884. São Paulo: Anhembi, 1957.

Dean, Warren. The Industrialization of São Paulo, 1880–1945. Austin: University of Texas Press, 1969.

_____. Rio Claro: A Brazilian Plantation System, 1820–1920. Stanford, Calif.: Stanford University Press, 1976.

Debes, Célio. Campos Salles: perfil de um estadista. 2 vols. Rio de Janeiro: F. Alves; Brasília: Instituto Nacional do Livro, 1978.

Della Cava, Ralph. "Brazilian Messianism and National Institutions: A Reappraisal of Canudos and Joaseiro." Hispanic American Historical Review 48, no. 3 (August 1968): 402–20.

Diário de São Paulo. 1868.

Dore, Elizabeth W., and John F. Weeks. "Economic Performance and Basic Needs: The Examples of Brazil, Chile, Mexico, Nicaragua, Peru and Venezuela." In Human Rights and Basic Needs in the Americas, edited by Margaret E. Crahan. Washington, D.C.: Georgetown University Press, 1982.

"Dr. Antonio Prado." A Paulicéia 1, no. 3.

"Dr. Antonio Prado." Sao Paulo "Magazine" 1, no. 2 (15 June 1906): 37–45.

"Dr. Martinho Prado." Sao Paulo "Magazine" 1, no. 2 (15 June 1906): 73–74.

Duarte, Nestor. *A ordem privada e a organização política brasileira.* Brasiliana, no. 172. São Paulo: Editôra Nacional, 1939.

Duarte, Paulo, et al. *Fábio Prado.* [São Paulo]: Anhembi, 1964.

Duncan, Julian Smith. *Public and Private Operation of Railways in Brazil.* Faculty of Political Science of Columbia University, Studies in History, Economics, and Public Law, no. 367. New York: Columbia University Press, 1932.

Egas, Eugenio. *Galeria dos presidentes de S. Paulo: periodo monarchico, 1822–1889.* São Paulo: O Estado de São Paulo, 1925.

Ellis, Alfredo. *Raça de gigantes: a civilização no planalto paulista.* São Paulo: Editôra Helios, 1926.

Ellis Júnior, Alfredo. *O café e a paulistânia.* São Paulo: Universidade de São Paulo, 1951.

Engels, Friedrich. *The Origin of the Family, Private Property, and the State in Light of the Researches of Lewis H. Morgan.* 1884. Reprint. New York: International Publishers, 1942.

O Estado de São Paulo, 1–20 November 1895, 1–20 March 1897, 8–9 January 1905.

Expilly, Charles. *Mulheres e costumes do Brasil.* Translated, with preface and notes, by Gastão Penalva. 1863. Reprint. Biblioteca Pedagógica Brasileira, 5th series, vol. 56. São Paulo: Editôra Nacional, 1935.

Fausto, Boris. "A revolução de 1930." In *Brasil em perspectiva,* edited by Carlos Guilherme Mota. Corpo e Almo do Brasil, vol. 23. 2d ed. São Paulo: Difusão Européia do Livro, 1969.

Ferraz, Geraldo. "Figura de romance e inteligencia criadora foi um panfletário e um escritor de escol [Eduardo Prado]." *A Tribuna,* 27 February 1960.

————. "Paulo Prado: centenário: perfil de um homem e de um livro." *Revista do Livro* 12, no. 37 (1969): 141–47.

Ferreira, Tito Lívio. "Eduardo Prado e a expressão humana da sua vida." *Diário Popular,* 27 February 1960.

————. "Eduardo Prado na intimidade familiar de Eça de Queiroz." *Revista do Instituto Histórico e Geográfico de São Paulo* 61 (1965): 35–49.

Figueiredo, Affonso Celso de Assis, visconde de Ouro Prêto (1837–1912). *Contradictas monarchicas.* Rio de Janeiro: Livraria Moderna, 1896.

Figueiredo, Afonso Celso de Assis (1860–1936). *Oito anos de parlamento: poder pessoal de D. Pedro II: reminiscências e notas.* Rev. ed. São Paulo: Melhoramentos, 1928.

Fletcher, James C., and D. P. Kidder. *Brazil and the Brazilians Portrayed in Historical and Descriptive Sketches.* 7th ed., rev. and enlarged. Boston: Little, Brown, 1867.

Fleuiss, Max. [Untitled article on Eduardo Prado.] *A Manhã,* 31 August 1941.

Franco, Afonso Arinos de Melo. *Um estadista da república: Afranio de Melo Franco e seu tempo.* 3 vols. Rio de Janeiro: Olympio, 1955.

Franco, Francisco de Assis Carvalho. *Dicionário de bandeirantes e sertanistas do Brasil: séculos XVI-XVII-XVIII.* São Paulo: Comissão do IV Centenário da Cidade de São Paulo, 1953.

Franco, Jean. *The Modern Culture of Latin America: Society and the Artist.* Harmondsworth, U.K.: Penguin, Pelican Books, 1970.

Freire, Vitor da Silva. "Melhoramentos de S. Paulo." *Revista Politécnica* 5, no. 33 (February–March 1911): 91–145.

Freitas, Leopoldo de. *A Sra. Dona Veridiana Prado: esboço biographico e historico.* São Paulo: Casa Vanorden, 1917.

Freyre, Gilberto. *Casa grande e senzala: formação da família brasileira sob o regime de economia patriarcal.* 4th ed. Coleção Documentos Brasileiros, nos. 36, 36a. Rio de Janeiro: Olympio, 1943.

——. *Ingleses no Brasil: aspectos da influência britânica sobre a vida, a paisagem, e a cultura do Brasil.* Coleção Documentos Brasileiros, no. 58. Rio de Janeiro and São Paulo: Olympio, 1948.

——. *The Mansions and the Shanties.* Translated and edited by Harriet de Onís. New York: Knopf, 1963.

——. *The Masters and the Slaves: A Study in the Development of Brazilian Civilization.* Translated by Samuel Putnam. New York: Knopf, Borzoi Books, 1964.

——. *Ordem e progresso: processo de desintegração das sociedades patriarcal e semipatriarcal no Brasil sob o regime de trabalho livre: aspectos de um quase meio século de transição do trabalho escravo para o trabalho livre: e da Monarquia para a República.* Obras reunidas de Gilberto Freyre, 1st series, Introdução à História da Sociedade Patriarcal no Brasil, no. 3. Rio de Janeiro: Olympio, 1959.

——. *Order and Progress (Ordem e Progresso): Brazil from Monarchy to Republic.* Translated and edited by Rod W. Horton. New York: Knopf, 1970.

——. "The Patriarchal Basis of Brazilian Society." In *Politics of Change in Latin America,* edited by Joseph Maier and Richard Weatherhead. New York: Praeger, 1964.

——. *Sobrados e mucambos: decadência do patriarcado rural e desenvolvimento do urbano.* Introdução à História da Sociedade Patriarcal no Brasil, no. 2. 3d ed. Rio de Janeiro: Olympio, 1961.

Fringer, Katherine. "The Contribution of Capistrano de Abreu to Brazilian Historiography." *Journal of Inter-American Studies and World Affairs* 13, no. 2 (April 1971): 258–78.

Fukui, Lia F. Garcia. "Estudos de família no Brasil: levantamento bibliográfico." In *Introdução ao estudo da sociologia no Brasil,* edited by Maria Isaura Pereira de Queiroz. São Paulo: Instituto de Estudos Brasileiros, 1971.

Furtado, Celso. *The Economic Growth of Brazil: A Survey from Colonial to Modern Times.* Translated by Ricardo W. de Aguiar and Eric Charles Drysdale. Berkeley and Los Angeles: University of California Press, 1965.

A Gazeta, 7 September 1948.

Gazeta de Notícias, 24 May 1890.

Graham, Richard. *Britain and the Onset of Modernization in Brazil, 1850–1914.* Cambridge Latin American Studies, no. 4. Cambridge: Cambridge University Press, 1968.

———. "Os fundamentos da ruptura de relações diplomáticas entre o Brasil e a Grã-Bretanha em 1863: 'A Questão Christie.'" *Revista de História* 24, no. 49 (January–March 1962): 117–38 and 24, no. 50 (April–June 1962): 379–402.

Guimarães, Alberto Prado. "Eduardo Prado: escritor católico e defensor da monarquia." *Engenharia* 18, no. 210 (May 1960): 586–91.

Guimarães, Francisco. *Annuaire du Brésil: economique et financier.* Paris: Annuaire Général du Brésil, 1928.

Hahner, June E. *Civilian-Military Relations in Brazil, 1889–1898.* Columbia: University of South Carolina Press, 1969.

———. "Women and Work in Brazil, 1850–1920: A Preliminary Investigation." In *Essays Concerning the Socioeconomic History of Brazil and Portuguese India,* edited by Dauril Alden and Warren Dean. Gainesville: University Presses of Florida, 1977.

Hall, Michael M. "The Origins of Mass Migration in Brazil, 1871–1914." Ph.D. dissertation, Columbia University, 1969.

Hareven, Tamara K. "Family as Process: The Historical Study of the Family Cycle." *Journal of Social History* 7, no. 3 (Spring 1974): 322–29.

———. "The History of the Family as an Interdisciplinary Field." In *The Family in History: Interdisciplinary Essays,* edited by Theodore K. Rabb and Robert I. Rotberg. New York: Harper and Row, Harper Torchbooks, 1973.

———. "Modernization and Family History: Perspectives on Social Change." *Signs* 2, no. 1 (Autumn 1976): 190–206.

———. "Postscript: The Latin American Essays in the Context of Family History." *Journal of Family History* 3, no. 4 (Winter 1978): 454–57.

Haring, C. H. *Empire in Brazil: A New World Experiment with Monarchy.* New York: Norton, 1968.

Harris, Irving D. *The Promised Seed: A Comparative Study of Eminent First and Later Sons.* New York: Free Press of Glencoe, 1964.

Hilton, Ronald, ed. *Who's Who in Latin America*. Part 6, *Brazil*. 3d ed., rev. and enlarged. Stanford, Calif.: Stanford University Press, 1948.

Hofstadter, Richard. "John C. Calhoun: The Marx of the Master Class." In *The American Political Tradition and the Men Who Made It*, by Richard Hofstadter. New York: Knopf, 1948.

Hoge, Warren. "Machismo Murder Case: Women Bitter in Brazil." *New York Times*, 23 May 1983, p. 5.

Hollanda, Sérgio Buarque de, ed. *História geral da civilização brasileira*. 7 vols. in 2. São Paulo: Difusão Européia do Livro, 1960–72.

Holloway, Thomas H. *The Brazilian Coffee Valorization of 1906: Regional Politics and Economic Dependence*. Madison: Historical Society of Wisconsin, 1975.

————. *Immigrants on the Land: Coffee and Society in São Paulo, 1886–1934*. Chapel Hill: University of North Carolina Press, 1980.

————. "Immigration and Abolition: The Transition from Slave to Free Labor in the São Paulo Coffee Zone." In *Essays Concerning the Socioeconomic History of Brazil and Portuguese India*, edited by Dauril Alden and Warren Dean. Gainesville: University Presses of Florida, 1977.

In memoriam: Martinho Prado Junior, 1843–1943. São Paulo: Elvino Pocai, 1944.

Indice da Revista do Instituto Historico e Geografico Brasileiro: tomos 1 a 90. Rio de Janeiro: Imprensa Nacional, 1927.

"Indice [de] O Estado de São Paulo [A Província de São Paulo], 1875–1876." 2 vols. Typescript.

Instituto Brasileiro de Geografia e Estatística. *Enciclopédia dos municípios brasileiros*. Rio de Janeiro: I.B.G.E., 1957–58.

Jesus, Carolina Maria de. *Child of the Dark*. New York: New American Library, 1962.

Jornal do Brasil, 27 April 1972.

Jornal do Comércio, 10 August 1901.

Jornal de Piracicaba, 1 May 1902.

Kahl, Joseph A. *Modernization, Exploitation and Dependency in Latin America: Germani, Gonzalez Casanova and Cardoso*. New Brunswick, N.J.: Transaction Books, 1976.

Kipling, Rudyard. *Brazilian Sketches*. New York: Doran, 1940.

Kriesberg, Louis. "Entrepreneurs in Latin America and the Role of Culture and Situational Precesses." *International Social Science Journal* 15, no. 4 (1963): 581–96.

Kuznesof, Elizabeth Anne. "Clans, the Militia, and Territorial Government: The Articulation of Kinship with Polity in Eighteenth-

Century São Paulo." In *Social Fabric and Spatial Structure in Colonial Latin America*, edited by David Robinson. Ann Arbor, Mich.: University Microfilms, 1979.

――――. "Household Composition and Headship as Related to Changes in Mode of Production: São Paulo 1765 to 1836." *Comparative Studies in Society and History* 22, no. 1 (January 1980): 78–108.

――――. "The Role of the Female-Headed Household in Brazilian Modernization, São Paulo, 1765–1836." *Journal of Social History* 13, no. 4 (Summer 1980): 589–614.

――――. "The Role of Merchants in the Economic Development of São Paulo, 1765–1850." *Hispanic American Historical Review* 60, no. 2 (November 1980): 571–92.

Ladenburg, Thalman and Co. Offering Statement, $4,000,000 First and Refunding Mortgage Bonds, Paulista Railway Co. April 1922. Sterling Memorial Library, Yale University.

Laërne, C. F. van Delden. *Brazil and Java: Report on Coffee-Culture in America, Asia, and Africa to H. E. the Minister of the Colonies.* London: W. H. Allen, 1885.

Leal, Victor Nunes. *Coronelismo, enxada e voto: o município e o regime representativo no Brasil.* Rio de Janeiro: n.p., 1948.

Leclerc, Max. *Cartas do Brasil.* 1890. Translated, with preface and notes, by Sergio Milliet. Biblioteca Pedagógica Brasileira, 5th series, Brasiliana, no. 215. São Paulo: Editôra Nacional, 1942.

Leite, Aureliano. "Eduardo Prado." *A Gazeta*, 17 August 1959.

――――. "Eduardo Prado: conferência proferida pelo Sr. Aureliano Leite no Instituto Histórico e Geográfico de São Paulo." *A Gazeta*, 22 March 1960.

――――. *Influencia de uma familia paulista do seculo XVI nos destinos do Brasil.* São Paulo: João Bentivegna, 1949.

Leme, Luiz Gonzaga da Silva. *Genealogia paulistana.* 9 vols. São Paulo: Duprat, 1903–5.

Leme, Pedro Taques de Almeida Paes [Pedro Taques]. *Nobilarchia paulistana histórica e genealógica.* 3d ed. Edited by Afonso de E. Taunay. Biblioteca Histórica Paulista, no. 4. 3 vols. São Paulo: Martins, 1953.

Levi, Darrell E. "Brazilian Nationalism: An Introduction." *Canadian Review of Studies in Nationalism, Annual Annotated Bibliography* 3 (1976): 114–23.

――――. "Brazilian Nationalism: Perspectives, Problems, Perplexities." *Canadian Review of Studies in Nationalism, Annual Annotated Bibliography* 6 (1979): 71–92.

————. *A família Prado.* São Paulo: Cultura 70, 1977.

————. "The Modernizing Family in Brazil: The Case of the Prados of São Paulo, 1840–1930." Paper read at the 88th Annual Meeting, American Historical Association, San Francisco, 28–30 December 1973.

————. "The Prado Family, European Culture, and the Rediscovery of Brazil, 1860–1930." In *Proceedings of Conference at Brockport, New York, April 5–7, 1973.* State University of New York at Buffalo, Special Studies Series, no. 43. Buffalo: State University Council on International Studies, 1973.

————. "The Prado Family, European Culture, and the Rediscovery of Brazil, 1860–1930." *Revista de História* 52, no. 104 (October–December 1975): 803–24.

Levine, Robert M. "Brazil's Jews During the Vargas Era and After." *Luso-Brazilian Review* 5, no. 1 (June 1968): 45–58.

Lewin, Linda. "Some Historical Implications of Kinship Organization for Family-based Politics in the Brazilian Northeast." *Comparative Studies in Society and History* 21, no. 2 (April 1979): 262–92.

Lima, Manuel de Oliveira. *Memórias: estas minhas reminiscências.* Documentos Brasileiros, no. 2. Rio de Janeiro: Olympio, 1937.

Love, Joseph L. *São Paulo in the Brazilian Federation, 1889–1937.* Stanford, Calif.: Stanford University Press, 1980.

Marc, Alfred. *Le Brésil: excursion á travers de ses 20 provinces.* Edited by J.-G. D'Argollo-Ferrão. 2 vols. Paris: Jornal Le Brésil, 1890.

Marchant, Anyda. *Viscount Mauá and the Empire of Brazil: A Biography of Irineu Evangelista de Sousa (1813–1889).* Berkeley and Los Angeles: University of California Press, 1965.

Marcílio, Maria-Luiza. *La ville de São Paulo: peuplement et population, 1750–1850, d'apres les registres paroissiaux et les recensements ancients.* Publications de l'Université de Rouen, Faculté des Lettres et Sciences Humaines. Rouen: Université de Rouen, 1968.

Marcus, Howard Allen. "Provincial Government in São Paulo: The Administration of João Teodoro Xavier (1872–1875)." Ph.D. dissertation, Yale University, 1973.

Marques, Cícero. *O último dia de governo do Presidente Washington Luis no Palacio Guanabara.* São Paulo: Impressora Paulista, 1931.

Marques, Manuel Eufrásio de Azevedo. *Apontamentos históricos, geográficos, biográficos, estatísticos e noticiosos da provincia de São Paulo seguidos da cronologia dos acontecimentos mais notáveis desde a fundação da Capitania de São Vicente até o ano de 1876.* Biblioteca Histórica Paulista, no. 1. 2 vols. 1879. Reprint. São Paulo: Martins, 1953.

Martins, José de Souza. *Empresário e emprêsa na biografia do conde Matarazzo*. Monografias do I.C.S., no. 2. Rio de Janeiro: Instituto de Ciências Sociais da Universidade Federal do Rio de Janeiro, 1967.

Martins, Luis. "Eduardo Prado: panfletário." *O Estado de São Paulo,* Suplemento Literário, 31 December 1960.

————. "O patriarca e o bacharel." *Revista do Arquivo Municipal* 83 (May–June 1942): 7–36.

Mattoon, Robert H., Jr. "The Companhia Paulista de Estrados de Ferro, 1868–1900: A Local Railway Enterprise in São Paulo, Brazil." Ph.D. dissertation, Yale University, 1971.

————. "Railroads, Coffee, and the Growth of Big Business in São Paulo, Brazil." *Hispanic American Historical Review* 57, no. 2 (May 1977): 273–95.

Mawe, John. *Travels in the Interior of Brazil, Particularly in the Gold and Diamond Districts of That Country, by Authority of the Prince Regent of Portugal: Including a Voyage to the Rio de la Plata and a Historical Sketch of the Revolution of Buenos Aires.* London: Longman, Hurst, Rees, Orme and Brown, 1912.

Mello, Francisco de Castro Couto. "Memoria sobre a declaração da independencia." *Revista do Instituto Histórico e Geográfico Brasileiro* 41, no. 2 (1878): 333–53.

Melo, Luís Correia de. *Dicionário de autores paulistas.* São Paulo: Commissão do IV Centenário da Cidade de São Paulo, 1954.

Mendes, Fernando. *Estudos de critica.* Rio de Janeiro: n.p., 1880.

Mendonça, Renato. *Um diplomata na côrte de Inglaterra: o barão do Penedo e sua época.* Brasiliana, 5th series, no. 219. São Paulo: Editôra Nacional, 1942.

Menezes, Raimundo. "Curiosidades biograficas: Eduardo Prado." *O Estado de São Paulo,* 11 November 1945.

Metcalf, Alida C. "Marriage, Inheritance, and Family Structure in Eighteenth-Century Brazil: Strategies for Survival in a Changing Society." Paper presented at the American Historical Association meeting, Washington, D.C., 28 December 1982.

"O ministerio familiar." *Revista do Brasil* 1, no. 3 (March 1916): 214.

Monbeig, Pierre. *Pionniers et planteurs de São Paulo.* Cahiers de la Fondation Nationale des Sciences Politiques, no. 28. Paris: Librarie Armand Colin, 1952.

Montello, Josué. "Um pouco de Eduardo Prado." *Diário de São Paulo,* 22 May 1961.

Moog, Clodomiro Viana. *Eça de Queirós e o século XIX.* Obras de Viana Moog, no. 7. 2d ed. Rio de Janeiro: Editôra Delta, 1966.

Moraes, João. "Proclamação da republica em S. Paulo: de 15 a 18 de novembro de 1889." *Revista do Instituto Histórico e Geográfico de São Paulo* 8 (1903): 187–210.

Moraes, Pontes de. "A ilusão americana." *Revista Brasiliense* 11 (May–June 1957): 112–28.

Moraes, Rubens Borba de, and Berrien, William. *Manual bibliográfico de estudos brasileiros.* Rio de Janeiro: Gráfica Editôra Souza, 1949.

Morse, Richard M., ed. *The Bandeirantes: The Historical Role of the Brazilian Pathfinders.* New York: Knopf, 1965.

———. *From Community to Metropolis: A Biography of São Paulo, Brazil.* 2d ed. New York: Octagon Books, 1974.

———. "Crosscurrents in New World History." In *Politics of Change in Latin America,* edited by Joseph Maier and Richard W. Weatherhead. New York: Praeger, 1964.

Motta Filho, Cândido. *A Vida de Eduardo Prado.* Coleção Documentos Brasileiros, no. 129. Rio de Janeiro: Olympio, 1967.

Moura, Paulo Cursino de. *São Paulo de outrora: evocações da metrópole.* 2d ed. São Paulo: Martins, 1943.

Müller, Daniel Pedro. *São Paulo em 1836.* 2d ed. São Paulo: O Estado de São Paulo, 1929.

Nabuco, Carolina. *The Life of Joaquim Nabuco.* Translated and edited by Ronald Hilton. Stanford, Calif.: Stanford University Press, 1950.

Nabuco, Joaquim. *Cartas a amigos.* Collected and annotated by Carolina Nabuco. Obras Completas de Joaquim Nabuco, nos. 13 and 14. 2 vols. São Paulo: Instituto Progresso Editorial, 1949.

———. *Minha formação.* Biblioteca Básica Brasileira, no. 8. [Brasília]: Editôra Universidade de Brasília, 1963.

Nery, F. J. de Sant'Anna. *Le Brésil en 1889.* Paris: Librarie Charles Delagarve, 1889.

Neves, João Alves das. "Eça e Eduardo Prado." *O Estado de São Paulo,* Suplemento Literário, 31 December 1960.

Neves Júnior. "Dr. Antonio Prado." *Kosmos* 2, no. 1 (January 1905).

Nogueira, Emília Costa. "Alguns aspectos da influência francesa em São Paulo na segunda metade do século XIX." *Revista de História* 7, no. 16 (October–December 1953): 317–42.

———. "O movimento republicano em Itú: os fazendeiros do oeste paulista e os prodrómos do movimento republicano (notas prévias)." *Revista de História* 9, no. 20 (October–December 1954): 379–405.

Nogueira, J. L. Almeida. *A academia de São Paulo: tradições e reminiscências: estudantes, estudantões, estudantadas.* 8 vols. São Paulo: Casa Vanorden, 1907–10.

Normano, J. F. *Brazil: A Study in Economic Types*. Chapel Hill: University of North Carolina Press, 1935.

"O que seria aqela coisa." *Veja*, no. 181 (23 February 1972): 3–6.

Ortigão, Ramalho. "Carta a Eduardo Prado." *Revista Nova* 1, no. 1 (15 March 1931): 5–14.

———. "O quadro social da revolução brazileira." *Revista de Portugal* 2 (1890): 79–102.

Owsley, Frank Lawrence. *King Cotton Diplomacy: Foreign Relations of the Confederate States of America*. 2d ed. Revised by Harriet Chappell Owsley. Chicago: University of Chicago Press, [1959].

Pagano, Sebastiano. *Eduardo Prado e sua época*. São Paulo: O Cetro, [1957?].

O Paiz, 1865–66.

Palha, America. "As grandes figuras da nossa história: Eduardo Prado." *Diário Carioca*, 22 October 1944.

Pan American Union. *Index to Latin American Periodical Literature, 1929–1960*. 8 vols. Boston: G. K. Hall, 1962.

———. *Index to Latin American Periodical Literature: First Supplement, 1961–65*. 2 vols. Boston: G. K. Hall, 1968.

Pang, Eul-Soo, and Ron L. Seckinger. "The Mandarins of Imperial Brazil." *Comparative Studies in Society and History* 14, no. 2 (March 1972): 215–44.

Penteado, Jacob. *Belenzinho, 1910: retrato de uma época*. São Paulo: Martins, 1962.

Pereira, Batista. "Eduardo Prado e Julio Mesquita." *Ensaios paulistas*. São Paulo: Anhembi, 1958.

Pereira, Lafayette Rodrigues. *Direitos de familia*. Rio de Janeiro: Garnier, 1869.

Pereira, [Luis] Baptista. *Eduardo Prado: o escriptor, o homem: artigo publicado no "Commercio de São Paulo" a 30 de septembro de 1901*. São Paulo: Salesiana, 1902.

Pestana, Paulo R. "A expansão da lavoura cafeeira em S. Paulo." *Revista do Brasil* 1, no. 2 (February 1916): 110–15, and no. 3 (March 1916): 245–57.

Petrone, Maria Thereza Schorer. *O Barão de Iguape: Um empresário da época da indepêndencia*. Brasiliana, no. 361. São Paulo: Editôra Nacional, 1976.

———. "Um comerciante do ciclo do acucar paulista: Antônio da Silva Prado (1817–1829)." *Revista de História* 36, no. 73 (January–March 1968): 115–38, 37, no. 76 (October–December 1968): 315–43, and 39, no. 79 (July–September 1969): 121–26.

Petrone, Theresa (Maria Thereza Schorer). "Imigração assalariada." In *História geral da civilização brasileira*, edited by Sérgio Buarque de Hollanda. 7 vols. in 2. São Paulo: Difusão Européia do Livro, 1960–72.

Pike, Frederick B. *Spanish America, 1900–1970: Tradition and Social Innovation*. New York: Norton, 1973.

Pinho, Wanderley. *Salões e damas do segundo reinado*. 2d ed. São Paulo: Martins, 1942.

Pinto, Adolfo Augusto. *História da viação pública de S. Paulo*. São Paulo: Casa Vanorden, 1903.

Pinto, Luiz Aguiar da Costa. "Lutas de família no Brasil: era colonial." *Revista do Arquivo Municipal* 87–88 (1942–43): 7–125.

Poppino, Rollie E. *Brazil: The Land and the People*. 2d ed. New York: Oxford University Press, 1973.

Portugal. *Ordenações filipinas: ordenações e leis do Reino de Portugal recopiladas por mandato d'El Rei D. Felipe, o Primeiro*. Edited, with an introduction and notes, by Fernando H. Mendes de Almeida. 3 vols. São Paulo: Saraiva, 1957–66.

_____. *Ordenações do Senhor Rey D. Affonso V.* 5 vols. Coimbra: Real Imprensa da Universidade, 1792.

_____. Arquivo Histórico Ultramarino. *Catálogo de documentos sôbre a história de São Paulo existentes no Arquivo Histórico Ultramarino de Lisboa, elaborado por ordem do Govêrno Português em comemoração ao IV centenário da fundação de São Paulo.* 15 vols. Rio de Janeiro: Departamento de Imprensa Nacional, 1956–59.

Prado, Antônio. "Notas sobre a colonisação em S. Paulo." *Revista do Brasil* 8, no. 99 (March 1924): 195–99.

Prado, Armando. "Discurso." In *O monumento de Diogo Antonio Feijó: sua história, sua execção, festas inauguraes, 1908*, edited by Eugenio Egas et al. São Paulo: Typographia do "Diario Official," 1913.

_____. *Discurso proferido no acto da collação de gráo aos bacharelandos em direito*. São Paulo: Salesiana, 1903.

_____. "A escravidão." *Revista do Brasil* 1, no. 3 (March 1916): 232–51.

_____. "Francisco Adolpho de Varnhagen." *Revista do Brasil* 1, no. 2 (February 1916): 137–59.

Prado, Eduardo. *Annulação das liberdades politicas: commentario ao §4 do art. 90 da Constituição da Republica*. São Paulo: Livraria Civilisação, 1897.

_____. *A bandeira nacional*. São Paulo: Salesiana, 1903.

_____. "O Catholicismo, a Companhia de Jesus, e a colonização do Brasil." In *III centenário do venerável Joseph de Anchieta*. Paris: Aillaud, 1900.

_____. *Collectaneas.* 4 vols. São Paulo: Salesiana, 1904–5.

———. "Destinos políticos do Brasil." *Revista de Portugal* 1 (1889): 467–91.

———. "Discurso de anniversário da fundação do Instituto Histórico de São Paulo." *Revista do Instituto Histórico e Geográfico de São Paulo* 3 (1898): 523–24.

———. "Discurso de posse no Instituto Histórico e Geográphico Brasileiro." *Jornal do Comércio,* 10 August 1901.

———. *Eduardo Prado e a república no Brasil.* Lisbon: Jornal do Comércio, 1894.

———. "Os espanhois no Salto do Avanhandava." *Revista do Instituto Histórico e Geográfico de São Paulo* 4 (1898–99): 243–56.

——— [pseud. Frederico de S.]. *Fastos da dictadura militar no Brazil.* 4th ed. Lisbon: [Revista de Portugal?], 1890.

———. *A illusão americana.* Preface and biographical study by Leopoldo de Freitas. 4th ed., rev. São Paulo: Livraria Magalhães, 1917.

———. "Manoel de Moraes." *Revista Nova* 2, no. 5 (February 1932): 5–23.

——— [pseud. Frederico de S.]. "Practicas e theorias da dictadura republicana no Brazil." *Revista de Portugal* 3 (1890): 74–120.

———. "Primeira dissertação do aluno no. 42 da Faculdade de Direito de S. Paulo, 2a. cadeira do 1o. ano." *Revista da Faculdade de Direito de São Paulo* 31, no. 1 (January–March 1935): 93–98.

——— [pseud. Graccho]. *Salvemos o Brazil.* Rio de Janeiro: n.p., 1899.

———. *Trechos escolhidos.* Edited, with an introduction, by Mário Casasanta. Nossos clássicos, no. 39. Rio de Janeiro: Agir, 1959.

———. *Viagens: America, Oceania e Asia.* São Paulo Salesiana, 1902.

———. *Viagens: A Sicilia, Malta, e o Egypto.* 2d ed. São Paulo: Salesiana, 1902.

Prado, Fábio. *Mensagem do Prefeito Fábio Prado à Camara Municipal de S. Paulo.* São Paulo: Departamento de Cultura, 1936.

Prado, João Fernando de Almeida. "Paulo Prado e a época de sua formação." In *Sociologia e história: 4 precursores brasileiros, 3 filósofos da história.* Federação do Comércio do Estado de São Paulo, Instituto de Sociologia e Política. São Paulo: Editôra Clássico-Científica, 1956.

Prado, Luíz da Silva. Interviews, São Paulo and Fazenda Santa Veridiana, 23 February, 11–14 and 19 March, 11 and 15–18 June, and 7 August 1972.

Prado, Nazareth, comp. *Antonio Prado no imperio e na republica: seus discursos e actos colligidos e apresentados por sua filha.* Rio de Janeiro: F. Briguiet, 1929.

———. "Introdução." In *O meu proprio romance,* by José Pereira da Graça Aranha. [Rio de Janeiro]: Editôra Nacional, 1931.

Prado, Paulo. "O momento." *Revista do Brasil,* March 1923–April 1924.

———. *Paulistica: historia de São Paulo.* 2d ed. Rio de Janeiro: Ariel, 1934.

———. "Poesia pau Brasil." In *Poesias Reunidas*, by Oswald de Andrade. São Paulo: Difusão Européia do Livro, 1966.

———. "Prefacio." In *Joaquim Nabuco: esboço biographico*, by Henrique Coelho. São Paulo: Monteiro Lobato, 1922.

———. *Retrato do Brasil: ensaio sôbre a tristeza brasileira*. Documentos Brasileiros, no. 112. 6th ed. Rio de Janeiro: Olympio, 1962.

Prado, Washington. *História de uma cidade bandeirante*. Mogi-Mirim, São Paulo: Casa Cardona, 1951.

Prado Júnior, Caio. *The Colonial Background of Modern Brazil*. Translated by Suzette Macedo. Berkeley and Los Angeles: University of California Press, 1969.

———. *Evolução política do Brasil*. 2d ed. São Paulo: Brasiliense, 1947.

———. *História econômica do Brasil*. Coleção Grandes Estudos Brasilienses, no. 2. 2d ed. São Paulo: Brasiliense, 1949.

———. Interviews, São Paulo, 18 March and 13 April 1972; personal letters, 4 December 1973 and 22 January 1974.

Prado Júnior, Martinho. *Circular de Martinho Prado Junior, candidato republicano à assembleia geral pelo 90. districto da provincia de São Paulo*. São Paulo: Typographia de "A Provincia de São Paulo," 1884.

Prado [Neto], Martinho. *Pró lavoura*. São Paulo: n.p., 1938.

Primeiro centenário do Conselheiro António da Silva Prado: colectânea de discursos, artigos, comentários e noticiário publicados na imprensa brasileira na passagem do primeiro centenário do Conselheiro António da Silva Prado ocorrido a 25 de fevereiro de 1940. São Paulo: [Revista dos Tribunaes], 1946.

A Província de São Paulo, 1875–76.

A província de São Paulo no Brazil: emigrante, lede este folheto antes de partir. São Paulo: [Sociedade Promotora de Imigração?], 1886.

Queiroz, José Maria de Eça de. "Cartas a Eduardo Prado." *Revista do Livro* 5, no. 18 (June 1960), 101–16.

———. "Cartas inéditas dirigidas a Eduardo Prado." *Revista da Academia Paulista de Letras* 2, no. 7 (12 September 1939): 12–18.

———. *Obras*. 3 vols. Pôrto: Lello e Irmão, [1958].

Queiroz, Maria Isaura Pereira de. *O mandonismo local na vida política brasileira: da colônia à primeira republica: ensaio de sociologia política*. São Paulo: Instituto de Estudos Brasileiros, 1969.

Ramos, Donald. "City and Country: The Family in Minas Gerais, 1804–1838." *Journal of Family History* 3, no. 4 (Winter 1978): 361–75.

———. "Marriage and the Family in Colonial Vila Rica." *Hispanic American Historical Review* 55, no. 2 (May 1975): 200–225.

———. "Vila Rica: Profile of a Colonial Brazilian Urban Center." *Americas* 35, no. 4 (April 1979): 495–526.

Ramos, Graciliano. *Infância (memórias)*. 5th ed. São Paulo: Martins, 1961.

Rebouças, André. *Diário e notas autobiográficas*. Rio de Janeiro: Olympio, 1938.

Rego, José Lins do. "Eduardo Prado." In *A casa e o homem*. Rio de Janeiro: Organização Simoes, 1954.

————. "Eduardo Prado e o bahiano." *Diário de São Paulo*, 8 September 1951.

Rodó, José Enrique. *Ariel*. Edited, with introduction and notes, by Gordon Brotherston. Cambridge: Cambridge University Press, 1967.

Rodrigues, José Honório. "Capistrano de Abreu and Brazilian Historiography." In *Perspectives on Brazilian History*, edited by E. Bradford Burns. New York: Columbia University Press, 1967.

————. *Notícia de vária história*. [Rio de Janeiro]: Livraria São José, 1951.

Rosen, Bernard C. "Socialization and Achievement Motivation in Brazil." *American Sociological Review* 27 (October 1962): 612–24.

Russell-Wood, A. J. R. "Women and Society in Colonial Brazil." *Journal of Latin American Studies* 9, pt. 1 (May 1977): 1–34.

Saint-Hilaire, Augusto de. *Segunda viagem do Rio de Janeiro a Minas Gerais e a São Paulo*. Translated by Affonso de E[scragnolle] Taunay. Bibliotheca Pedagogica Brasileira, Brasiliana, series 5a, 5. 2d ed. São Paulo Editôra Nacional, 1938.

————. *Viagem à provincia de São Paulo e resumo das viagens ao Brasil, Provincia Cisplatina, e missoes do Paraguai*. Translated by Rubens Borba de Moraes. Biblíoteca Histórica Brasileira, no. 2. São Paulo: Martins, 1940.

Sampaio, Ana Cândida Ferraz. Interview, São Paulo, 5 July 1972.

Sant'Anna, Antonio Machado. "Cidadãos do mundo." *A Tarde* (Ribeirão Prêto), 17 November 1952.

Santos, José Maria dos. *Bernardino de Campos e o partido republicano paulista: subsídios para a história da república*. Coleção Documentos Brasileiros, no. 105. Rio de Janeiro: Olympio, 1960.

Santos, José Maria dos. "Martinho Prado Junior." *Folha da Manha*, 17 November 1943.

São Paulo (Cidade). Arquivo Municipal. *Actas da Câmara da Cidade de S. Paulo*. 12 vols. São Paulo: Typographia Piratininga, 1914–18.

————. *Registo Geral da Câmara Municipal de S. Paulo*. 38 vols. São Paulo: Departamento do Arquivo Municipal, 1917–46.

São Paulo (Estado). Departamento do Arquivo do Estado. *Documentos avulsos de interesse para a historia e costumes de São Paulo*. 6 vols. São Paulo: Arquivo do Estado, 1952–55.

————. *Documentos interessantes para a historia e costumes de S. Paulo*. 91 vols. São Paulo: Departamento do Arquivo, 1923–68.

————. *Inventarios e testamentos.* 41 vols. São Paulo: Typographia Piratininga, 1920–66.

————. *Sesmarias.* 4 vols. São Paulo: Typographia Piratininga, 1921–39.

————. Repartição de Estatística e Archivo do Estado. *Annuario estatística, 1900–1916.* 17 vols. São Paulo: Typographia do "Diario Official," 1903–18.

————. Secretaria de Agricultura. *Estatística agricola e zootechnica no anno agricola de 1904–1905.* 5 vols. São Paulo: Carlos Gerke e Rothschild, 1906–10.

————. Secretaria de Agricultura, Industria e Commercio. Directoria de Industria e Commercio. *O café em São Paulo: notas historicas,* by Paulo R. Pestana, Director de Industria e Commercio. São Paulo: Typographia Levi, 1927.

São Paulo (Província). Assembléia. *Discurso proferido na discussão da fixação da força publica em sessão de 28 de fevereiro de 1878 por Martinho Prado Junior, deputado republicano.* 2d ed. São Paulo: Typographia da "Provincia," 1878.

————. *Discurso proferido na discussao da fixação da força publica em sessão de 19 de março de 1879 por Martinho Prado Junior.* São Paulo: Typographia da "Provincia," 1879.

————. *Discurso proferido na sessão de 20 de março de 1879 por Martinho Prado Junior, deputado republicano.* [São Paulo: Typographia da "Provincia," 1879?]

————. Assembléia Legislativa. *Anais,* 1865–66, 1884–85.

————. *Os deputados republicanos na assemblea provincial de São Paulo: sessão de 1888.* São Paulo: Leroy King Bookwalter, 1888.

São Paulo Tramway, Light and Power Co., Ltd. *Annual Report, 1904.* [Toronto: n.p., 1905].

Sartre, Jean-Paul. *Anti-Semite and Jew.* Translated by George J. Becker. New York: Schocken Books, 1948.

Schorske, Carl E. "Politics and Patricide in Freud's *Interpretation of Dreams." American Historical Review* 78, no. 2 (April 1973): 328–47.

Scobie, James R. "Buenos Aires as a Commercial-Bureaucratic City, 1880–1910: Characteristics of a City's Orientation." *American Historical Review* 77, no. 4 (October 1972): 1035–73.

Serva, Maria Pinto. "O centenário de Martinho Prado Junior." *Rotogravura de O Estado de São Paulo,* November 1943.

Shorter, Edward. *The Making of the Modern Family.* New York: Basic Books, 1975.

Silva, Fernando Nascimento, ed. *Rio de Janeiro em seus quatrocentos anos: formação e desenvolvimento da cidade.* Rio de Janeiro: Distribuidora Record, 1965.

Silva, Francisco Eugénio Pacheco e. *A zona paulista: propaganda separatista.* São Paulo: n.p., 1887.

Silveira, Joel. *Grã-finos em São Paulo e outras notícias do Brasil (reportagens).* São Paulo: n.p., 1945.

Simon, S. Fanny. "Anarchism and Anarcho-Syndicalism in South America." *Hispanic American Historical Review* 26, no. 1 (February 1946): 38–59.

Simonsen, Roberto Cochrane. *The Meat and Cattle Industry of Brazil: Its Importance to Anglo-Brazilian Commerce.* London: Industrial Publicity Service, 1919.

Singer, Paul. *Desenvolvimento econômico e evolução urbana: análise da evolução econômica de São Paulo, Blumenau, Pôrto Alegre, Belo Horizonte e Recife.* Biblioteca Universitária, 2d series, Ciências Sociais, no. 22. São Paulo: Universidade de São Paulo, 1968.

Skidmore, Thomas E. *Black into White: Race and Nationality in Brazilian Thought.* New York: Oxford University Press, 1974.

Smith, Raymond T. "Family: Comparative Structure." *International Encyclopedia of the Social Sciences,* 1968, 10:301–13.

Smith, T. Lynn. *Brazil: People and Institutions.* 4th ed., rev. Baton Rouge: Louisiana State University Press, 1972.

"Sociedade e residencias paulistas." *Sao Paulo "Magazine"* 1, no. 2 (15 June 1906): 67–72.

Sodré, Nelson Werneck. *História da imprensa no Brasil.* Retratos do Brasil, no. 51. Rio de Janeiro: Civilização Brasileira, 1966.

Soeiro, Susan A. "The Social and Economic Role of the Convent: Women and Nuns in Colonial Bahia, 1677–1800." *Hispanic American Historical Review* 54, no. 2 (May 1974): 209–32.

Soliday, Gerald L., ed., with Tamara K. Hareven, Richard T. Vann, and Robert Wheaton. *History of the Family and Kinship: A Select International Bibliography.* Millwood, N.Y.: Kraus International Publications, 1980.

Sousa, Otavio Tarquinio de. "Dois amigos em Paris." *Folha de São Paulo,* 29 November 1951.

Sousa, Pedro Luis Pereira de. *Casa Barão de Iguape: recordação e revelação de São Paulo do século XIX.* São Paulo: privately published, 1959.

————. *Meus cinqüenta anos na Companhia Prado Chaves.* São Paulo: n.p., 1950.

Souza, Maria do Carmo Campello de. "O processo político-partidário na primeira república." In *Brasil em perspectiva,* edited by Carlos Guilherme Mota. Corpo e Alma do Brasil, no. 23. 2d ed. São Paulo: Difusão Européia do Livro, 1969.

Spiegel, Henry William. *The Brazilian Economy: Chronic Inflation and Sporadic Industrialization*. Philadelphia: Blakiston, 1949.

Stepan, Alfred C. "The Continuing Problem of Brazilian Integration." In *Latin American History: Select Problems: Identity, Integration, and Nationhood*, edited by Frederick B. Pike. New York: Harcourt, Brace, and World, 1969.

―――. *The Military in Politics: Changing Patterns in Brazil*. Princeton, N.J.: Princeton University Press, 1971.

"Syl." *O Comércio de São Paulo*, 7 September 1901.

Taunay, Affonso de Escragnolle. *História do café no Brasil*. 15 vols. Rio de Janeiro: Departamento Nacional do Café, 1939–43.

―――. *História da cidade de São Paulo no século XVIII*. 2 vols. São Paulo: Imprensa Oficial do Estado, 1934.

―――. *História geral das bandeiras paulistas*. 11 vols. São Paulo: H. L. Canton, 1924–36 (vols. 1–7) and Imprensa Oficial do Estado, 1946–50 (vols. 8–11).

Taylor, William R. *Cavalier and Yankee: The Old South and American National Character*. New York: Harper and Row, 1969.

Thomson, David. *England in the Nineteenth Century*. Pelican History of England, vol. 8. Baltimore: Penguin Books, 1950.

―――. *Europe Since Napoleon*. 2d ed. New York: Knopf, 1964.

Toledo, Lafayette de. "Imprensa paulista." *Revista do Instituto Histórico e Geográfico de São Paulo* 3 (1898): 305–521.

Toplin, Robert Brent. *The Abolition of Slavery in Brazil*. New York: Atheneum, 1972.

"Uma carta de Eça de Queiroz a Eduardo Prado." *Revista da Academia Brasileira de Letras* 47 (January 1935): 110–14.

"Uma carta de Eduardo Prado a Navarro de Andrade, menino." *A Manhã*, 19 January 1947.

Velho Sobrinho, João Francisco. *Dicionário bio-bibliográfico brasileiro*. 2 vols. Rio de Janeiro: Irmãos Pongetti, 1937; Ministério da Educação e Saúde, 1940.

Viana, Hélio. "Rui Barbosa e Eduardo Prado: história de uma amizade." *Revista Brasileira* 3, no. 7 (June 1943): 68–83.

Viana Filho, Luiz. *A Vida do Barão do Rio Branco*. Documentos Brasileiros, no. 106. Rio de Janeiro: Olympio, 1959.

Vianna, José Francisco de Oliveira. *Instituições políticas brasileiras*. 2 vols. Rio de Janeiro: Olympio, 1949.

Wagley, Charles. *An Introduction to Brazil*. Rev. ed. New York: Columbia University Press, 1972.

―――. "Luso-Brazilian Kinship Patterns: The Persistence of a Cultural

Tradition." In *Politics of Change in Latin America,* edited by Joseph
Maier and Richard W. Weatherhead. New York: Praeger, 1964.

Wallerstein, Immanuel. *The Modern World-System: Capitalist Agriculture
and the Origins of the European World-Economy in the Sixteenth
Century.* New York: Academic Press, 1974.

Wardman, Harold William. *Ernest Renan: A Critical Biography.* [London]:
University of London, Athlone Press, 1964.

Willems, Emilio. "The Structure of the Brazilian Family." *Social Forces* 31,
no. 4 (May 1953): 339–45.

Williams, Roger L. *The French Revolution of 1870–1871.* New York: W. W.
Norton, 1969.

"The Women." *Time,* International ed., 12 June 1972, p. 15.

➔ Index ⋐

Note: Luso-Brazilian personal names are alphabetized by *final* name; well-known variations are cross-indexed.

Abreu, João Capistrano de, 130, 134
Albuquerque family, 8
Almeida, Ana Vicência Rodrigues de, 22, 25, 35, 186
Almeida, João Mendes de: political foe of Antônio and Martinico Prado, 96–97; ally of Eduardo Prado, 171
Alves, Antônio de Castro, 40
Alves, Francisco de Paula Rodrigues, 160
Américo Brasiliense. *See* Melo, Américo Brasiliense de Almeida
Andrada family, 27
Andrade, Mário de, 123–24
Aranha, José Pereira da Graça, 240 (n. 34)
Aranha, Luís, 116
Aranha, Maria Prado, 108
Ariel (Rodó), 128
Arinos, Afonso. *See* Franco, Afonso Arinos de Melo
Assis, Joaquim Maria Machado de, 121
Associação Libertadora, 98

Bandeirantes, 17–18
Banking: Prado family in, 39, 69, 83, 141
Bank of Commerce and Industry, 141
Barbosa, Rui, 129, 150, 160; accuses Antônio Prado of nepotism, 78; friendship with Eduardo Prado,

170–71; Antônio Prado ignores campaign trip, 177
Barros, José Prudente de Morais e, 160, 165, 171–72
Barros, Lucas Antônio Monteiro de, 29
Barros, Rodrigo Antônio Monteiro de, 29
Bernabé (Prado slave), 74
Binzer, Ina von, 49
Blaine, James C., 169–70
Brás, Venceslau, 160
Brazil: history, 1–2; independence, 27–28; Empire, 37, 51–52, 88–91; Republic, 159–61
Brazilian Warrant Company, 151
Broca, Paul, 125
Buchner, Ludwig, 125
Bueno, Vicente Ferreira da Silva, 95–96

Campos, Bernardino de, 165
Campos Sales. *See* Sales, Manuel Ferraz de Campos
Canudos rebellion, 172–74
Capitalism: in Prado family, 31, 83, 86–87; family, 140, 157; world market, 157
Capitalist class, 156–58
Carnegie, Andrew, 169–70
Carneiro da Cunha family, 8
Carvalho, José da Costa, 36, 213 (n. 8)

Cavalcanti family, 8
Caxias, duke of, 39
Chaves, Alzira, 112
Chaves, Anézia Prado, 38, 41, 43, 44, 118
Chaves, Anezita Prado, 44
Chaves, Elias Antônio Pacheco e, 108
Chaves, Elias Pacheco e, 43–44
Chaves, Eponina Prado, 44
Chaves, Fernando, 112
Chaves, Lucila Pacheco e, 108
Chaves, Miguel, 112
Childrearing, 39, 49–50. *See also* Parent-child relations
Children: in patriarchal family, 6–8; education of, 8; abandonment of, 11, 19; of masters and slaves, as playmates, 23
Christie affair, 58–59
Civil War of 1893, 128, 168–69, 244 (n. 49)
Coffee, 139–40, 144–46; origins in São Paulo, 67–68; valorization agreements of 1906, 145; during First Republic, 148–53. *See also* Landholdings
Collon, August, 108
O Comércio de São Paulo, 171–72; attacked by republicans, 173
Companhia Registradora de Santos, 151
Comte, Auguste, 125
Conçeicão, João, 143
Constitution of 1824, 88
Constitution of 1891, 164
Constitution of Itú, 96
Coronelismo, 23, 159, 211 (n. 27)
Correia, Antônio, 142
Costa Pinto, Antônio da. *See* Silva, Antônio da Costa Pinto e

Cotegipe, baron of (João Maurício Wanderly), 98
Crespi, Renata, 106
Crespi, Rudolfo, 106, 148

Darwin, Charles, 125
David, Prado slave, 74
Democratic Party, 161, 178–79
Dependency: economic, 87, 181; theory, 188
Derby, Orville, 63, 108, 129
Development, 2, 72, 205 (n. 8); associated-dependent development, 188–89
Dias, Antônio Gonçalves, 219 (n. 32)
Dôres, Maria das, 51
Dreyfus affair, 233 (n. 75)

Eça de Queiroz. *See* Queiroz, José Maria de Eça de
Economic liberalism, 87, 150–51, 156
Economy, 67–68, 138–40; Prado family activities, 21–23, 25–26, 55, 187. *See also* Banking, Industries, Paulista Railway, Prado-Chaves Export Company
Elites: conflict between traditional and capitalist, 71–72; merger of planter and industrial, 106; political, in São Paulo, 160, 241 (n. 62)
Elizabeth, Mademoiselle: Prado family governess, 63
Entrepreneurs: planter versus immigrant, 153–56
European culture: role in Prado family, 187. *See also* Foreign influence; Prado, Antônio (1840–

1929); Prado, Eduardo; Prado, Paulo; Prado, Veridiana

Family, political role of, 164
Family, varieties of, 15. *See also* Patriarchal family, Patriarchalism
Family conflicts: 30–31, 42–43, 110, 121–22, 242 (n. 66); generational, 44–45; marital, 44–45; competing family branches, 50; political, 101
Family history: new, 9–15; in Brazil, 10; in São Paulo, 10, 12–13; in Minas Gerais, 11; in Parnaíba, 13
Family reputations, 8
Fastos da dictadura militar no Brasil, 168–69
Feitosa family, 8
Ferreira, Maria Leme, 22
Firmino (ex-slave, blacksmith of Prados), 108
First Republic: hostile to Prados, 107
Fonseca, Deodoro da, 160, 164–65
Fonseca, Hermes, 160
Fonseca, José Manuel da, 30, 37
Fonseca family, 29
Foreign influence: 42, 65–66, 123; in nineteenth century, 53–54; in São Paulo city, 54; Prados feel shame before foreigners, 60, 237 (n. 44); in São Paulo city, late 1880s, 125; economic, 239 (n. 29)
Forms of address: traditional, 7–8; in Prado family, 50
Franco, Afonso Arinos de Melo, 116
Funerals: in Prado family, 40, 51, 136

Gambetta, Léon, 62
Garrand, padre: tutor of Prado children, 108
Girardin, St. Mar, 57
Glicério, Francisco, 163
Godparenthood (*compadrío*), 5; in Prado family, 36
Graça Aranha. *See* Aranha, José Pereira da Graça
Grandparent-grandchild relations, 41, 109, 111
Greene, Edward, 151

Haeckel, Ernst, 125

Iguape, baron of. *See* Prado, Antônio (1788–1875)
A illusão americana, 119, 128–29; editions, 235 (n. 28); sources, 235 (n. 29)
Immigrants, 149, 154; productivity, 76; Prados' experiences with, 79–83; remuneration, 81–83, 223–24 (n. 45), 224 (nn. 51, 52); brawl with Brazilians, 136
Immigration, 71, 75–83, 152, 222 (nn. 17, 30); Society to Promote Immigration, 76–77. *See also* Prado, Antônio (1840–1929); Prado, Martinico
Imperialism, 131, 133–34
Individualism, 156; in Prado family, 188
Industrialization, 138–39
Industries: Prado family, 144–48
In-law relations, 110–11, 116
Isabela (princess of Brazil), 63
João VI (emperor of Portugal, Brazil, and the Algarves), 27
Joaquim (Botocudo Indian, retainer of Veridiana Prado), 51

Jordão, Antônio Rodrigues de
Almeida, 30–31
Jordão, Elias Fausto Pacheco, 108,
147, 230 (n. 14)
Jordão, Francisco, 97
Jordão, João Elias Pacheco Chaves,
222 (n. 30)
Jordão, José Elias Pacheco: abuse of
slaves and immigrants by, 73
Jordão, Manuel Rodrigues, 28, 30
Jordão, Maria Benedita Pacheco e, 30
Jordão family, 29
Jornal do Comércio, 85–86, 141

Kipling, Rudyard, 124

Lacerda, Gertrudes Galvão de
Moura, 30–31
Landholdings, Prado fazendas:
Campo Alto, 38, 69, 74, 149;
Santa Cruz, 69; Santa Veridiana,
70–71, 79–80; Albertina, 72;
Guatapará, 72, 80, 149, 153, 155;
São Martinho, 72, 149, 155;
Engenho do Arari, 74; Brejão,
108, 149; Loreto, 149
Law of the Free Womb, 89; opposed
by the Prados, 96
Law School, São Paulo, 41–42, 54,
125, 134, 218 (n. 6)
Leo XIII, Pope, 98
Levasseur, Emile, 126
Liberal Alliance, 180
Liberalism: philosophical, 91;
Antônio Prado on, 92; political,
172; role in Prado family, 187.
See also Economic liberalism
Liberal Party, 226 (n. 4); opposed by
Prados, 96
Liberal Revolt of 1842, 30
Lucena, baron of, 164

Machado, João da Silva, 30
Machado de Assis. *See* Assis,
Joaquim Maria Machado de
Marginalization, political: of
Prados, 181–83
Maria I (queen of Portugal), 23
Marriage: in eighteenth-century
São Paulo, 19; in Prado family,
28–30, 35, 37, 43, 47, 105–6,
111; conflicting moral codes
on, 42
Martins, José Francisco de Oliveira,
126
Matarazzo, Francisco, 147; symbol
of immigrant entrepreneur,
153–56
Matarazzo Júnior, Francisco, 155
Matriarchalism, 45
Mauá, viscount of (Irineu
Evangelista de Sousa), 84
Meat-packing industry, 147
Melo, Américo Brasiliense de
Almeida, 97, 165; eulogized by
Eduardo Prado, 243 (n. 22)
Military, 2, 168–69
Miscegenation: in Prado family,
120, 234 (n. 83)
Modern Art Week, 123
Modernization: Latin American
compared to European, 10;
theory, 188
Mogiana railway, 142
Monteiro de Barros family, 29
Morais, Francisca de Siqueira, 21
Morais Leme family, 22
Mourão, Dom Luíz Antônio de
Souza Botelho, 18–19
Müller, Daniel Pedro, 37, 213 (n. 13)
Multinational corporations, 156,
241 (n. 60)
municipalismo, 161

Nabuco, Joaquim, 132, 172; Prados
seek help of, on abolition, 97–98
Nationalism, 123–24, 157, 167,
182; Paulo Prado and, 130–37;
economic, 151–52, 175
Nery, Joseph Frederick Sant'Anna,
126
Nunes Paes family, 210 (n. 22)

Oliveira, Alberto de, 111
Oliveira Lima family, 210 (n. 22)
Ortigão, Ramalho, 126; impressions
of Veridiana Prado, 63–64
Ouchy Agreement, 152, 241 (n. 53)
Ouro Prêto, viscount of (Afônso
Celso de Assis Figueiredo), 162

Pacheco, Antônio, 51
Pacheco family, 29
Paraguayan War, 42–43
Parent-child relations, 46, 48, 55,
63, 109, 187, 217 (n. 52)
Parentela, 5
Parnaíba (town), 21, 22
Partido Libertador, 179
Patriarchal family: in Brazil, 5–9;
influence of, 8; as minority type,
12
Patriarchalism: nineteenth-century
decline, 13; in São Paulo, 20; in
nineteenth century, 33; erosion
of, in Prado family, 43–44; during
First Republic, 104
Patrocínio José do, 121
Paulista Railway, 84–85, 142–44;
1906 strike, 136; Prado relatives
on board of directors, 144. *See
also* Prado, Antônio (1840–1929)
Paulista Republican Party, 161;
criticized by Antônio Prado, 180
Paulistas: character, 19, 113, 134

Paulistica: historia de São Paulo,
133–34
Pedro I (emperor of Brazil), 27
Pedro II (emperor of Brazil), 39, 48,
50–51, 57, 89, 92, 165; Prados'
reaction to his death, 107
Peixoto, Floriano, 160, 164
Pena, Afônso, 160
Penedo, baron of (Francisco Inácio
de Carvalho Moreira), 85
Penteado, Antônio Alvares Leite,
106, 148
Pereira Barreto family, 71
Pereira Mendes family, 29
Pereira de Queiros family, 22
Pessoa, Epitácio, 160
Pinto, Antônio Pereira, 213
Pinto Júnior, Antônio Pereira, 35,
45
Poder pátrio, 6
Politics: family basis of, 95–98;
Prados', role in, during late
Empire, 101–3; during First
Republic, 159–61; Prados as
mayors, 161, 182; impact of, on
Prado family, 187
Poverty, 1, 184; Prado family and,
58, 59, 64, 71–72, 166, 170,
189–91
Prado, Albertina Morais Pinto,
43–44, 48–49
Prado, Ana Blandina, 35, 41, 63,
118, 121, 220 (n. 46); birth, 38;
marriage, 45
Prado, Ana Joaquina, 22
Prado, Anézia, 38, 41, 43, 44, 118
Prado, Antônio da Silva do (d. 1737),
17, 21
Prado, Antônio (d. 1793), 22, 35
Prado, Antônio (baron of Iguape,
1788–1875), 25–32, 37, 45, 141,

Prado, Antônio (*continued*)
188, 227 (n. 15); as tax collector, 26; political activities of, 27–28, 39, 91; marital diplomacy, 28–30; role in family, 32; personality, 40; economic activities, 68–69

Prado, Antônio (1840–1929), 35, 45, 47–49, 74, 85, 91, 106, 111, 112, 113, 134, 149, 182, 188, 189; birth, 38; youth, 41; European sojourn, 42, 54–60; as father, 48–49; on Brazilian politics, 57, 91–93; on "civilized" and "backward" nations, 59–60; as coffee fazendeiro, 68–69; role in abolition and immigration, 77–79; awarded contract to restore theater, 84; promotes extensions of Paulista Railway, 84–85; political offices of, 90; and politics during Second Empire, 95–98; "connected" political style of, 99; dislike of early First Republic, 107; personality of, 115–17; establishes Bank of Commerce and Industry, 141; and Paulista Railway's controversy with Piracicaba, 142–43; as economic "Jacobin," 143; establishes tannery, glassworks, and meat-packing plant, 146–47; criticized for exporting meat, 147; and coffee crisis, 150; at center of economic conflicts, 151; as economic nationalist, 151; relations with foreign companies, 151–52; criticizes government's "servile" financial policy, 152, 175; abortive immigration effort, 152; as symbol of planter-entrepreneur, 153–56; declines

immigration post, 162–63; politics of, in 1889–1890, 162–64; as mayor of São Paulo, 175–77; politics of, in 1899–1929, 175–80; and Paulista Railway strike, 177, 246 (n. 79); rancor for Washington Luís, 178; founder of Democratic Party, 178–79; supports "popular action," 180; promotes cotton as small-farm alternative, 218 (n. 16); on European women, 219 (n. 20); on Germany, 219 (n. 21); in Chamber of Deputies, 228 (n. 36); on shameful treatment of war draftees, 237 (n. 44); forces son out of business, 240 (n. 47)

Prado, Armando, 120; writings on Brazilian historical figures, 120; criticizes Western imperialism, 131

Prado, Caio (b. 1872), 49–50, 148

Prado, Caio (Antônio Caio, 1853–1889), 38–39, 49, 90–91, 114, 118; letters on family, 43–44; as president of Alagoas and Ceará, 93–94; family influences presidential appointment of, 97; satirizes Martinico Prado's republicanism, 101

Prado, Carolina, 46–47, 51, 111

Prado, Cássio, 148

Prado, Cícero, 148

Prado, Eduardo, 38–39, 91, 108, 111, 113, 114, 132, 182, 188, 189, 191; relationship with mother, 46–47, 215–16 (n. 42); European financial interests of, 85–86; view of Brazilian politics in 1888, 94; approaches Nabuco on abolition, 98; attacks Martinico Prado's republicanism, 101;

marriage to Carolina Prado, 111;
anti-Semitism of, 119, 233
(nn. 75, 76); personality of, 113,
118–20, 233 (n. 69); and foreign
influence in Brazil, 124–30;
world travels of, 125–26; on the
United States, 126, 128–29,
167–70; in Paris, 126–27; spirit
divided between Europe and
Brazil, 127; critical of Brazil, 127;
and relationship of people to
their native land, 127–28; on
destructive effects of European
culture, 130; historical studies
by, 130; economic activities in
Europe, 141–42; negotiates
purchase of Rio Claro Railway,
142; as coffee planter, 149–50;
monarchist reaction to First
Republic, 166–74; first exile, 170;
anti-government newspaper
articles of, 171–72; second exile,
174; attempts to exploit civilian-
military differences, 174; warns
against imitation of foreign
politics, 227 (n. 27); library of,
235 (n. 26); hides news of Brazil
from English butler, 237 (n. 44);
accuses Fonsecas of nepotism,
246 (n. 70). See also *Fastos da
dictadura militar no Brasil* and *A
illusão americana*
Prado, Eglantina Penteado, 110
Prado, Eleutério (d. 1849), 22–23,
27, 35
Prado, Eleutério (1836–1905),
120–21
Prado, Fábio, 106, 114, 148, 182
Prado, Felippa do, 21
Prado, Francisco, 27, 30
Prado, Joaquim (b. 1700s), 23, 30, 69
Prado, Joaquim (b. 1885/86), 121

Prado, Lavínia, 49, 111
Prado, Luíz, 48, 108, 110, 113, 116,
144, 152
Prado, Maria Catarina, 35, 44,
109–10, 113, 116; personality of,
48; at court, 48
Prado, Maria Marcolina, 29
Prado, Martinho (d. 1770), 21, 22
Prado, Martinho (1811–1891), 31,
38, 72, 74, 84, 112, 149, 155;
youth of, 37; as coffee pioneer,
69–70; as money-lender, 69–70
Prado, Martinico (Martinho Prado
Júnior, 1843–1906), 43–44,
48–49, 74–75, 91, 108, 111, 112,
114, 134, 136, 149, 162, 182, 188,
191; birth of, 38; rebellious youth
of, 41, 42, 61; uses pen name of
French Communard, 61;
attitudes toward Europe, 61–62;
political ideas of, 61–62; as coffee
pioneer, 71–72; favors easing of
interprovincial slave trade ban,
75–76; promotes immigration,
76–77; alleged abuse of
immigrants by, 80–81;
Republican politician, 90;
satirizes Pedro II's speeches,
94–95; defends brother from
political attack, 95–96; views on
slavery, 97–98, 237 (n. 44);
"disconnected" political style,
99–101; admires Martin Luther,
117; personality of, 117–18; and
early First Republic, 164–66; on
profitability of free labor, 223
(n. 35); repugnance for João
Mendes de Almeida, 228 (n. 37)
Prado, Nazareth, 107, 113, 116, 186,
236 (n. 43); modern wedding of,
110
Prado, Paulo, 64, 113, 114, 120,

Prado, Paulo (*continued*)
130–37, 182, 188, 230 (n. 18);
youth of, 108–9; young
adulthood of, 131; as organizer of
Jornal do Brasil, 131; on relations
of Europe and Brazil, 132;
promotes Modern Art Week, 132;
on politics in 1920s, 132–33,
177–78; on Brazil's deformed
reality, 133; on the United States,
135; member of federal coffee
board, 146; director of
Companhia Registradora de
Santos, 151; and coffee crisis,
152–53; call for "insurrection,"
178. See also *Paulistica: historia
de São Paulo* and *Retrato do
Brasil*
Prado, Paulo Caio, 135, 230 (n. 18)
Prado, Plínio, 49–50, 108, 149
Prado, Raimundo, 23, 210 (n. 22)
Prado, Veridiana, 28, 97, 113, 114,
174, 186, 188, 189; youth of,
37–38; birth of children, 38;
separation from husband, 45;
palatial residence of, 45;
character of, 47, 51; portrait of,
62–63; first trip to Europe, 63;
salon of, 63–64; traditional
habits of, 65; as grandparent, 111;
as "revolutionary mother,"
215–16 (n. 42)
Prado Chaves, Anézia, 38, 41, 43,
44, 118
Prado-Chaves Export Company,
109, 144–46, 153, 155; sells land
to small farmers, 146
Prado Júnior, Antônio, 182; youth
of, 110; as mayor of Rio de
Janeiro, 178, 246–47 (n. 88)
Prado Júnior, Caio, 114, 182–83,
190–91

Prado Neto, Martinho: 50, 148,
156; and multinational
corporations, 241 (n. 60)
Prado family: overview, 2–5;
eighteenth-century origins, 31;
separate from do Prado and
Almeida Prado families, 31;
tradition of protest in, 182, 187;
structure of, 185–86; dynamics
of, 186–87; intellectual tradition
of, 191
Prado parentela, 16, 34, 104–7;
different "personalities" of
component branches, 113
Prado-surname extended family, 16,
28, 35, 104–7
Prestes, Luís Carlos: sends
condolences on death of Antônio
Prado, 247 (n. 96)
Proudhon, Pierre-Joseph, 57
Prudente de Morais. *See* Barros, José
Prudente de Morais e

Queiros Teles family, 22
Queiroz, José Maria de Eça de, 125,
126, 131; sees Brazilian Empire as
colony, 127

Race: in Prado family, 120–21;
Eduardo Prado's views on,
120–21, 130. *See also*
Miscegenation, Slavery
Railroads, 84–85, 142–44
Reclus, Elisée, 126
Religion: in Prado family, 46–47,
58, 119–20, 171, 215 (n. 41), 228
(n. 37)
Renan, Ernest, 58, 219 (n. 14)
Republican Party, 89; in São Paulo
during Empire, 96
Retrato do Brasil, 134–36
Revolution of 1930, 135, 190

Rio Branco, baron of (José Maria de Silva Paranhos Júnior), 126, 129, 130, 132, 164
Rio Claro Railway, 142
Rodrigues, José Carlos, 85, 132
Rodrigues Alves. *See* Alves, Francisco de Paula Rodrigues
Romantic love, 43
Rossel, Louis-Nathaniel, 219 (n. 36)
Rothschild family, 85, 141–42
Rudge, Maria Sophia, 47
Ruling, Mademoiselle (Prado governess), 108

Sales, Manuel Ferraz de Campos, 160, 162, 165, 172–73
Sampaio, Teodoro, 63, 121, 128
Santa Marina Glassworks, 147
Santos, Francisco Alves dos, 228 (n. 38)
Santos, José Alves dos, 96
Santos, marquise of, 37
São Paulo (captaincy), 17–20; John Mawe's impressions in 1808, 23; Saint-Hilaire's impressions in 1819, 24–25
São Paulo (city): mid-nineteenth century, 54; changes during First Republic, 124; in the 1880s, 124–25; politics in, 226–27 (n. 15)
São Paulo (province): separatism, 227 (n. 22)
São Paulo (province/state), 184–85
São Paulo (state), 1; economy during First Republic, 138–40; politics during First Republic, 160–66, 171–74, 242 (n. 2)
Sibling relations, 40, 61, 76, 115, 117; during civil war of 1893, 111
Siciliano, Alexandre, 147

Skepticism: as theme of Prados' politics, 91–95
Silva, Antônio da Costa Pinto e, 48, 95–96, 213 (n. 5); on customs separating Brazil from Europe, 131
Silva, Oduvaldo Pacheco e, 110
Silva, Rodrigo Augusto da, 97
Slavery, 21, 89–90; in Prado family, 23; Prados' attitudes toward, 73; Paulistas' attitude toward, 73
Slave trade, 26
Sousa, Everardo Vallim Pereira de: psychological portrait of Antônio Prado, 116
Sousa, Washington Luís Pereira de, 160, 161
Sousa Leão family, 8
Spencer, Herbert, 125

Tannery: Cortume Agua Branca, 146
Teles, Antônio Queiros, 77, 83
Teresa Cristina (empress of Brazil), 48
Theodor Wille Company, 151
Thiers, Louis Adolphe, 62
Tibério (Prado slave), 75
Tibiriçá, Jorge, 161
Tiradentes (Joaquim José da Silva Xavier), 101, 229 (n. 57)

Urban-rural integration: in Prado family, 31–32, 86

Values: Prado family, 37, 39, 48, 109–10, 114, 181–82. *See also* Individualism, Liberalism, Race, Religion, Skepticism
Vargas, Getúlio, 135, 161, 190; praises coffee policies of Antônio Prado, 180

Vaz, Antônia Emília de Moura, 30
Vaz, Maria Cândida de Moura
   (baroness of Iguape), 28, 41
Veridiana Prado and Sons, 149

Wanderley family, 8
War of the Emboabas, 18
Washington Luís. *See* Sousa,
   Washington Luís Pereira de
Women: submission of, 6–7;
   influence of, 7; in São Paulo, 11,
   14; history of, in Brazil, 13–14;
   nuns in Destêrro convent, 14; in
1850–1920 era, 14; forced into
prostitution, 19, 25; surplus of, in
São Paulo, 20; during early
nineteenth century, 23; as
"slaves," 24; in the Paulista elite,
25, 50; in nineteenth century, 33,
62; education of, 37; in Prado
family, 186; described as
"ornaments," 231 (n. 28). *See also*
Almeida, Ana Vicência Rodrigues
de; Prado, Ana Blandina; Prado,
Maria Catarina; Prado, Nazareth;
Prado, Veridiana